REPRESENTATIVE PLAYS BY JOHN GALSWORTHY

REPRESENTATIVE PLAYS

BY

JOHN GALSWORTHY

With an Introduction by

GEORGE P. BAKER

Professor of the History and Technique of the Drama and
Director of the University Theatre, Yale University
Formerly Professor of Dramatic Literature in Harvard University

CHARLES SCRIBNER'S SONS
NEW YORK   CHICAGO   BOSTON

COPYRIGHT, 1909, 1910, 1912, 1915, 1922, 1924, BY
CHARLES SCRIBNER'S SONS

Printed in the United States of America

The plays in this book are fully protected by the International Copyright Act and the professional and amateur stage rights are reserved by the author.

B

INTRODUCTION

"L'art pour l'art," ("art for art's sake"),—three utterly meaningless words Dumas fils declared them half a century ago, when he was fighting in play, feuilleton and preface for the ideas of love, marriage and divorce which his plays presented and defended.

Not "art for art's sake," not "man for art's sake," but "art for man's sake" he insisted should be the slogan for any thoughtful dramatist closely observing his time and seeking painstakingly to depict some of his problems. Differ from Dumas fils as Mr. Galsworthy undoubtedly does in subjects and artistic methods, nevertheless it is "art for man's sake" which is the essence of his work. He has himself said that "he is not conscious of any desire to solve problems in his plays, or to effect direct reforms. His only ambition in drama is to present truth as he sees it and, gripping with it his readers or his audience, to produce in them a sort of mental ferment whereby vision may be enlarged, imagination livened, and understanding promoted."* Clearly Mr. Galsworthy believes what many a co-worker in the drama has come to believe in the past twenty years, that the province of the dramatist is not to preach definite reforms, but to arrest attention and stimulate thinking on the conditions depicted.

Born at Coombe, Surrey, in 1867, passing his childhood in a cultivated home, educated at Oxford, taking at New College an Honor degree in Law, he would seem destined

* Works. Manaton edition. Vol. XVIII. p. XIV.

v

for one of the careers accepted in England for a gentleman's son. Like many of his period, however, the world over, in his leisurely days he became deeply interested in his fellow-men—the seeming chance inequalities of class, the striking injustices of modern life. Everywhere these days of Mr. Galsworthy's early manhood were days of restless doubt and questioning—with, in the drama, Ibsen as the great protagonist. What the young Galsworthy felt with his generation, he has phrased recently: "There is a true saying, 'Whatever is, is right.' And if all men from the world's beginning had said that, the world would never have begun at all. Not even the protoplasmic jelly could have commenced its journey; there would have been no motive force to make it start."* Thinking thus, he longed more and more to join the Great Adventurers, not those who discover new lands or chart hitherto uncharted seas, but the Adventurers who fare forth in the ship, Independent Thinking, over the supposedly well-charted Sea of Human Experience. And sometimes they return to the lands of Smug Acceptance with discoveries more exciting, more disturbing, than those of any voyager in Arctic or Antarctic. In and out of the universities men and women were waking to a new social consciousness, to a stronger sense of the responsibility of one class for another, of the individual for his fellows. In the colleges and universities thinking youth was restlessly seeking new causes beyond the issues which had deeply stirred their fathers, to set their own souls aflame. Little wonder, then, that though called to the bar at Lincoln's Inn (1890) young Galsworthy was unsatisfied by the law. Soon he turned to travel, watching men and manners for nearly two years in Canada, British Columbia, Australia, the Fiji Islands and South Africa. He began writing and in 1899 published

*Preface to *The Island Pharisees*. Manaton edition.

INTRODUCTION

Jocelyn, a novel, not adjudged by him worthy of reprinting in the Manaton edition. In the next ten years he published ten volumes of fiction, winning wide-spread attention—particularly by *The Man of Property, The Country House* and *Fraternity*. In 1906 his play *The Silver Box* was produced in London; in 1907, *Joy;* in 1909, *Strife;* in 1910, *Justice*. This group of plays at once established Mr. Galsworthy's reputation as one of the foremost English dramatists of the day.

Not his the ordinary experience of the dramatist: years of writing in accepted ways, either of classic standards or purely popular forms of the moment; passage through one artistic mood, such as romanticism, to another; years of failure or of slowly developing success. From the start, as a dramatist, Mr. Galsworthy knew what he wanted to treat. He was very fortunate in coming forward when all the newer work on the Continent, when the pioneer efforts in England of Henry Arthur Jones and Sir Arthur Pinero, had gone far to establish the right of a dramatist to choose his subject at will and to be equally free in treatment of it. He has said of his total writing to the present day that it seems to divide into three periods: from 1901-1910, in which time the critical in his work was stronger than the emotional; 1910-1918, when the emotional dominated the critical; and from 1918-1923, when it has been, in his own phrase, very much a "dead heat." Doubtless that dominance of the critical in the first period came from the wide reading he was doing and the rapid development therefrom of critical standards for his own fiction—whether novel or drama. "Let me pay," Mr. Galsworthy wrote recently, "a passing tribute to the three great dead writers to whom I owe, beyond all others, inspiration and training—the Russians—Turgenev and Tolstoi; and the Frenchman—De Maupassant. The poetic art of Turgenev's novels is unequalled so far by any other novelist. Its singular balance and elusive strength; its economy, ease and utter lack of pose or self-consciousness; its creative reality and essential wisdom, philosophic breadth and tolerance, combine to give it an unique position in the world of fiction. Turgenev was a perfect master of form, atmosphere and concise character-drawing. Though Turgenev always inspired me more than the Frenchman, I learned more from De Maupassant. Without question, in the essentials of style, De Maupassant is the prince of teachers. The vigor of his vision, and thought, the economy and clarity of the expression in which he clothes them, have not yet been surpassed. No writer so disgusts one with turgidity, shallow expression and formless egoism. Disciplined to his finger-nails and fastidious though he was, he yet contrived to reach and display the very depths of human feeling. His sardonic nature, loathing prejudice and stupidity, had in it a vein of deep and indignant pity, a burning curiosity, piercing vision, and a sensitiveness seldom equalled. Tolstoi, at his best, is as great—perhaps even greater than the other two—but from Tolstoi a writer learns his craft as much but no more than he learns it from life itself. Tolstoi's work is spread and edgeless, and its priceless and inspiring quality is due not to its form or style, but to its deep insight, the unflinching truth of its expression, his range and the breadth of his character-drawing."*

These, then, have been his ideals in fiction for twenty years: moved by deep indignant pity, to paint with unflinching truth those subjects in the life around him which an eager curiosity, piercing vision and rare sensitiveness have made plain to him. All this he has wanted to treat, hating turgidity, shallow expressionism, formless egoism,

*Preface to *Beyond,* Manaton Edition.

INTRODUCTION ix

with economy, ease and lack of self-consciousness. Wisdom, philosophic breadth resting on tolerance he has sought. Poetic art, form exactly fitted to the task he has in each case set himself, he has desired. Later, as his plays, especially those in this volume, are reviewed with passing comment, we shall see that he reached his artistic goals—especially in his plays—very early in his career.

As has been said, practically all of Mr. Galsworthy's work—novels or plays—rests on questioning Society as Society accepts itself. "The Institutions of this country, like the Institutions of all other countries, are but half-truths; they are the working, daily clothing of the nation; no more the body's permanent dress than is a baby's frock. Slowly but surely they wear out, or are outgrown; and in their fashion they are always thirty years at least behind the fashions of those spirits who are concerned with what shall take their place. The conditions which dictate our education, the distribution of our property, our marriage laws, amusements, worship, prisons, and all other things, change imperceptibly from hour to hour; the moulds containing them, being inelastic, do not change, but hold on to the point of bursting, and then are hastily, often clumsily, enlarged. The ninety desiring peace and comfort for their spirit, the ninety of the well-marked beds, will have it that the fashions need not change, that mortality is fixed, that all is ordered and immutable, that every one will always marry, play, and worship in the way that they themselves are marrying, playing, worshipping. They have no speculation, and they hate with a deep hatred those who speculate with thought. They were not made for taking risks. They are the dough, and they dislike that yeasty stuff of life which comes and works about in them. The Yeasty Stuff—the other ten—chafed by all things that are, desirous ever of new forms and moulds, hate in

INTRODUCTION

their turn the comfortable ninety. Each party has invented for the other the hardest names that it can think of: Philistines, Bourgeois, Mrs. Grundy—Rebels, Anarchists, and Ne'er-do-wells. So we go on! And so, as each of us is born to go his journey, he finds himself in time ranged on one side or on the other, and joins the choruses of name-slingers.

"But now and then—ah! very seldom—we find ourselves so near that thing which has no breadth, the middle line, that we can watch them both, and smile to see the fun." This is the position Mr. Galsworthy has striven for and won.

Observing his fellowmen, Mr. Galsworthy has wished through sympathy, understanding and a pity that is not sentimental but judical, to write of them with truth. This, "to the human consciousness at least, is but that vitally just relation of part to whole which is the very condition of life itself. The task of the imaginative writer is the presentation of a vision which to the eye and ear and mind has the implicit proportions of truth." He is no believer in "impersonal elucidations of the truths of Nature." There are "no such things as the truths of Nature apart from the individual vision of the artist. Seer and things seen, inextricably involved one with the other, form the texture of any masterpiece; and I, at least, demand therefrom a distinct impression of temperament. Such subtle mingling of seer with thing seen is the outcome only of long and intricate brooding, a process not too favored by modern life, yet without which we achieve little but a fluent chaos of clever, insignificant impressions, a kind of glorified journalism holding much the same relation to the deeply impregnated work of Turgenev, Hardy and Conrad, as a film bears to a play." Any treatment Mr. Galsworthy may give to truth as he finds it in the turmoil of life around

INTRODUCTION

him he wishes should have flavor. "I confess to have always looked for a certain flavor in the writings of others, and craved it for my own, believing that all true vision is so coloured by the temperament of the seer, as to have not only the just proportions but the essential novelty of a living thing—for, after all, no two living things are alike. A work of fiction should carry the hall-mark of its author as surely as a Goya, a Daumier, a Velasquez, and a Mathew Maris should be the unmistakable creations of those masters. This is not to speak of tricks and manners which lend themselves to that facile elf, the caricaturist, but of a certain individual way of thinking and feeling."*

Consistently for more than twenty years, Mr. Galsworthy has sought to attain in both his novels and his plays these standards, whether borrowed from his masters or created from his own thinking. In his first play, *The Silver Box,* it is the inequality of two men before the law, where one is poor and friendless, the other rich and aided by a family with power, which rouses his "indignant pity." Inequality, injustice, is at the core of this play. In *Strife,* which first brought its author wide reputation as a dramatist, it is not the rights or wrongs of the struggle between Labor and Capital represented which is of significance. Rather it is the utter futility of the struggle even when carried on by two extremists, who, like Anthony and Roberts, do only what they honestly believe to be right. The bitter irony of the last lines of the play has done much to make it famous:

HARNESS: A woman dead; and the two best men both broken!

TENCH: *(Staring at him—suddenly excited)* D'you know, sir—these terms, they're the *very same* we drew up

*Preface to *Villa Rubein,* Manaton Edition.

together, you and I, and put to both sides before the fight began? All this—all this—and—and what for?

HARNESS: (*In a slow, grim voice*) That's where the fun comes in!

(*Underwood, without turning from the door, makes a gesture of assent.*)

The curtain falls.

Dogged, unimaginative, unwilling to search for truth and to face it squarely, courageously when found, people go on bringing misery to themselves and their fellows. Of course *Justice*, when first produced, was declared a problem play, a *drame à thèse*. It is easy to think this from the terrible pantomime of Falder in his cell and these words of his:

"What I mean, sir, is that if we'd been treated differently the first time, and put under somebody that could look after us a bit, and not put in prison, not a quarter of us would have got there."

But it is not the one particular injustice, imprisonment, of which Mr. Galsworthy is writing but of "man's inhumanity to man" which still, as in Dr. Johnson's day, "makes countless thousands mourn." At the end of *Justice* everybody of the group we watch is willing to help Falder, but with human nature as weak, and human law as indiscriminating as it is, thinking more of punishing by rule than of helping or training the individual, tragedy is sure.

And all the bitter irony in the tragedies he treats Mr. Galsworthy feels intensely. Yet, if as he views life's injustices he sees terrible irony in the futilities with which Society tries to counter the blows of Fate, irony has for him some of the illuminating quality that Aristotle gave to pity and terror in tragedy. With John Galsworthy irony saves us from letting honest sentiment lapse into the excess that is sentimentality. Watching the pity, the injustice, the futility of life when we view it clear-eyed, to what shall we turn—sentimentality or despair? Neither if we have a sense of the ironies of life. As Ferrand says in *The Pigeon:* "There is nothing that gives more courage than to see the irony of things." Poor bewildered Mrs. Megan, just rescued from drowning herself, might have the protective philosophy of Ferrand could she see clearly, as he does, that "not a soul in the world wants her alive—and now she's prosecuted for trying to be where everyone wishes her." She would have something to make her fight on if she could feel as Ferrand does: "If I were rich, should I not be simply veree original, 'ighly respected, with soul above commerce travelling to see the world? And that young girl, would she not be 'that charming ladee,' 'veree chic,' you know." There is much of Mr. Galsworthy's own philosophy of life in *The Pigeon*.

Naturally, no dramatist may observe the injustices of life and pass by the confusions, contradictions and tragedies caused by the passion too easily called Love. *The Eldest Son,* 1912; *The Fugitive,* 1913; and *A Bit o' Love,* 1915; are Mr. Galsworthy's earlier treatments of this subject. Broadly, they are contemporaneous with his studies of the same subject in the novels *The Dark Flower* and *Beyond.* In the plays, travelling anew the ground already beaten flat by countless other dramatists who could treat no other topic, he has worked less notably than in his individual and very thoughtful presentations of similar material in *The Dark Flower* and *Beyond.* For his best results in this subject he needs the chance the novel offers to carry us with him by illuminating analysis and suggestive comment, by the slow presentation of a character detail by detail, scene after scene, rather than by the telegraphic dots and dashes of the most compact of artistic forms—the drama. *A Bit o' Love* has been selected from this group as most characteristic, as more than the others combining "seer with thing seen," as holding more of the "poetic art" Mr. Galsworthy admires in Turgenev. Full of deep feeling, delicate characterization, it has its own atmosphere. Profoundly painful as it is, no wonder that amusement seekers have not greatly cared for it, but for what it accomplishes when dealing with time-worn subjects, background and to a great extent, people, it is a notably fine play.

He returns to his more personal material in *The Mob*. Again he takes up the cause of the one in a hundred, the adventurer in human conduct, who sees with the eyes of the future, not with that of the benumbed or befogged present. Whether wholly convincing or not—and it caused much debate—*The Mob* will remain noteworthy, because in 1914 it so clearly foreshadowed the tragedies in 1914-1918 of pacificists and war-objectors. It was a veritable handwriting on the wall.

After *The Mob*, save for *A Bit o' Love*, in 1915, and *The Foundations*, in 1917, there is silence as a playwright till 1920. Yet these five years were rich in novels that added materially to their author's fame: especially *Beyond*, *Five Tales*, *Saint's Progress*, and *In Chancery*. In 1920 came a reawakening of dramatic expression. In quick succession appeared *The Skin Game*, and *A Family Man*, 1922; *Loyalties*, and *Windows*, 1923. The first of these plays, and *The Foundations*, 1917, grew out of the War: neither could have existed except as a consequence of it. *The Foundations* contains admirable characterization and much humor, but the intended satire which is its essence missed the desired effect because the general public did not understand its significance, or in what mood exactly the play should be taken. As a mere story, and as satire, it lacked the great essential—clarity. *The Skin Game* created much discussion. Passage after passage, such as "Mother re-

INTRODUCTION

minds one of England according to herself—always right whatever she does," convinced some that the play was a careful allegory of the War. It stands as that indeed, in so far as it is the dramatization of a duel *à outrance*, with all the throwing overboard of standards and gentility which such a duel entails. *A Family Man* studies Builder, an obstinate nature, settled in his point of view, determined to have his own way, who learns the truth in his brother's admonition: "Let's boss our own natures before we boss those of other people." For persons who have found the purpose of *Windows* uncertain, Mr. Galsworthy has stated it: "If we cleaned our windows better and looked things straight in the face, we should not be disconcerted; for instance, when the fourteen points don't function, because we never should have hazarded the fourteen points. We all admit that we must have ideals, but the play objects to our saying die because human nature, like Faith, is forever hiding away from them." *Loyalties,* Mr. Galsworthy's greatest recent success, treats incidentally the clash of classes or social groups already treated in *Strife* and *The Skin Game;* but its main purpose is to throw up into relief the incessant clash of differing loyalties, which makes the path of right action so difficult. First, last, and always, it is the right relation of the part (as observed in play and novel) to the whole of life, truth, at which Mr. Galsworthy aims.

Rarely does a dramatist formulate for us the principles underlying his practice. Rather he prefers to give his time and thought to the new problem each fresh dramatic effort is. From the outset, however, Mr. Galsworthy seems to have been deeply interested in the technique of fictional expression. His careful study of Turgenev, Tolstoi and De Maupassant proves this. So, too, does his article *Some Platitudes Concerning the Drama,* first published in 1909.

It is surprising that after the experience of writing only three plays he could go so directly to the core of his subject and reveal what he finds in phrase so final. Already, for students of dramatic technique, the essay has taken its proper place, side by side with Congreve's *Essay on Humor in Comedy* and George Meredith's classic *Essay on Comedy*. Reading this article of Mr. Galsworthy's, one sees that for him the play and the novel are basically much the same. He anticipates, in 1909, in writing of his plays, much that he re-phrases in 1922-1923 as to his short stories and novels. To his mind, "drama must have a spire of meaning." Mere entertainment of the idly unthinking has no interest for him. "In writing a play there are, philosophically speaking, three courses open to the serious dramatist. The first is to set definitely before the public that which it wishes to have set before it; the views and codes of life by which the public lives, and in which it believes. This way is the most common, successful and popular. The second course is to set definitely before the public the views and codes of life by which the dramatist himself lives, those theories in which he himself believes—the more effectively if they are the opposite of what the public wishes to have placed before it—presenting them so that the audience may swallow them like a powder in a spoonful of jam. There is a third course: to set before the public no cut and dried codes, but the phenomena of life and character, selected and combined, *but not distorted,* by the dramatist's outlook, set down without fear, favor or prejudice, leaving the public to draw such poor moral as nature may afford. This third method," obviously enough Mr. Galsworthy's, "requires a certain detachment; it requires a sympathy with, a love of, and a curiosity as to, things for their own sake; it requires a far view, together with patient industry for no immediately practical result."

INTRODUCTION

Any careful examination of Galsworthy's plays will reveal that these needed qualities are his. Granted, however, this detachment, this judicial attitude of seeking truth without favorites in persons or ideas, whence—we ask —came the stories, later to be moulded by the technical skill of Mr. Galsworthy into the plots of his plays? "A good plot is that sure edifice which slowly rises out of the interplay of circumstance on temperament and temperament on circumstance, within the enclosing atmosphere of an idea. The perfect dramatist rounds up his characters and facts within the ring fence of a dominant idea which fulfills the craving of his spirit,—having got them there he suffers them to live their own lies. The dramatist who depends his characters to his plot, instead of his plot to his characters, ought himself to be depended." In characterization, Mr. Galsworthy has added memorable figure after memorable figure to our drama. Roberts, Anthony, Falder, DeLevis, and Ferrand, the down and out philosopher who is quite worthy to stand before Gorki's Satine in *The Lower Depths*. The women of the plays are perhaps less unusual than the men, but all have an equal truth to life, an equally understanding interpretation. Certainly in all the plays of this volume, the plots grow from the characters. Mr. Galsworthy runs no chance that, because of these plays, he will be "depended" by some critical hand. Developing his dramatic theories, he adds: "Take care of character: action and dialogue will take care of themselves. True dramatic action is what characters do, at once contrary as it were to expectation, and yet because they have already done other things. No dramatist should let his audience know what is coming, but neither should he suffer his characters to act without making his audience feel that these actions are in harmony with temperament and rise from previous known actions, together with the tempera-

INTRODUCTION

ments and previous known actions of the other characters." It is these ideas which have made the characters of John Galsworthy from the beginning of his play-writing, alive, convincing, as creative of discussion as are real people, making friends and enemies.

In turn, "good dialogue is character marshalled so as continually to stimulate interest and excitement." It "requires not only a knowledge of what interests or excites, but such a feeling for character itself as brings misery to the dramatist's heart when his creatures speak as they should not speak—ashes to his mouth when they say things for the sake of saying them—disgust when they are 'smart.' The art of writing good dialogue is an austere art, denying itself all license, grudging every sentence devoted to the mere machinery of the play, suppressing all jokes and epigrams severed from character, relying for fun and pathos on the fun and tears of life." Mr. Galsworthy, in his recent preface to the first volume of his plays, returns to these ideas on dialogue. "It might be said that I create characters who have feelings they cannot express. I think this comes from the sort of subject and the range of character which I temperamentally select and still more from the severely naturalistic medium to which I am predisposed. The English man or woman of today—and my characters are practically all Englishmen and women of today—do not express themselves glowingly, they have almost a genius for under-expression and even on the stage seem to resent being made to 'slop-over.'" Feeling this, Mr. Galsworthy naturally fully recognizes the value of pantomime without speech. Recall Falder in his cell. Mr. Galsworthy has chosen as, perhaps, the best moment in any of his plays, that when, Anthony and Roberts, knowing that they have failed, face each other: *"Anthony rises with an effort. He turns to Roberts, who looks at him. They stand several seconds, gazing at each other fixedly. Anthony lifts his hand, as to salute, but lets it fall. The expression of Robert's face changes from hostility to wonder. They bend their heads in token of respect. Anthony turns and slowly walks toward the curtained door. Suddenly he sways as if about to fall, recovers himself, and is assisted out. Roberts remains motionless for several seconds, staring intently after Anthony, then goes into the hall.*" There is the same quality in a stage direction in *The Pigeon*: "*Mrs. Megan turns slowly and slips away.*" Fully sensing the seeming hopelessness of her life, as Ferrand has summed it up to Wellwyn, silently the girl slips out to drown herself. When Mr. Galsworthy has such exacting standards of dialogue and keeps to them, no wonder that Mr. Lewisohn has said: "Whoever wishes to attain to style in dramatic dialogue, exact but always restrained, natural but never redundant, must give his days and nights to the volumes of Galsworthy."

For drama as for the novel, Mr. Galsworthy demands "flavor, the thin, poignant spirit which hovers up out of a drama, and is as much differentiating essence of it as is nicotine of tobacco or caffeine of coffee—the spirit of the dramatist projected into his work in a state of volatility, so that no one can exactly lay hands on it here, there or anywhere—the one thing at which the dramatist cannot work, for it is outside his consciousness." Is there not a personal touch, an individual spirit in all that John Galsworthy writes? Hard to trace exactly to its sources it certainly is. Yet it is so unmistakable that were anyone who knows Galsworthy's plays well to read an unsigned typed manuscript of his, its author must be recognized at once.

The medium he chooses for his plays is naturalism. The

aim of the dramatist employing it is obviously "to create such an illusion of actual life passing on the stage as to compel the spectator for the moment to lose all sense of artifice, to think, talk and move with the people he sees thinking, talking and moving in front of him." The service of such naturalistic drama will be "the swaying and focusing of men's feelings and thoughts in the various departments of national life. It will be like a steady lamp, held up from time to time, in whose light things will be seen for a space clearly and in due proportion, freed from the mists of prejudice and partisanship."

Evidently the necessary attitude of the dramatist is "not that of the impulsive writer, driven by enthusiasm to push his pen ahead as fast as he can." He must be impartial as the scientist. He must have "an almost passionate love of discipline, a white-heat of self-respect, a desire to make the truest, finest thing in his power, an eye that does not flinch. Such qualities alone will bring a drama the self-less character which soaks it with inevitability and convinces its audience."

John Galsworthy has written then, with ideals definite, high, exacting. For more than twenty years he has been refining his work, re-writing, perfecting his skill. Today he asks—yet asking admits it may be a counsel of perfection—that his readers "accept the plane chosen by the artist, and, having accepted, should criticise the work for being or for not being what it is meant to be, without embittering blame or praise by imputing disappointment at the absence of other planes, however temperamentally preferred." Surely we must admit willingly that his are the qualities he admired in his masters: a "deep indignant pity, piercing vision, and a sensitiveness seldom equalled, disgust for turgidity and shallow expressionism, economy, ease, lack of self-consciousness, and elusive strength."

INTRODUCTION

Mr. Galsworthy is in the fullness of his powers as novelist and dramatist. What he has done names him the master realist of English drama today. What the future holds for him as he continues his judicial, unflinching, yet sympathetic and understanding studies of individuals clashing with individuals, ideas with ideas, in this profoundly disturbed social life which is England today, his thousands of admirers eagerly await. What he has written, what he will write, is dramatized social history. More than any other English dramatist John Galsworthy is the historian of this turbulent, confused time when "social-consciousness" has given way to a fierce if somewhat bewildered and bewildering struggle of the individual for as complete self-expression as possible.

GEORGE P. BAKER.

CONTENTS

	PAGE
INTRODUCTION	v
THE SILVER BOX	1
STRIFE	73
JUSTICE	161
THE PIGEON	249
A BIT O'LOVE	319
LOYALTIES	387

THE SILVER BOX
A COMEDY IN THREE ACTS

PERSONS OF THE PLAY

JOHN BARTHWICK, M. P., *a wealthy Liberal*
MRS. BARTHWICK, *his wife*
JACK BARTHWICK, *their son*
ROPER, *their solicitor*
MRS. JONES, *their charwoman*.
MARLOW, *their manservant*
WHEELER, *their maidservant*
JONES, *the stranger within their gates.*
MRS. SEDDON, *a landlady*
SNOW, *a detective*
A POLICE MAGISTRATE
AN UNKNOWN LADY, *from beyond*.
TWO LITTLE GIRLS, *homeless*
LIVENS, *their father*
A RELIEVING OFFICER
A MAGISTRATE'S CLERK
AN USHER
POLICEMEN, CLERKS, AND OTHERS

TIME: The present. The action of the first two Acts takes place on Easter Tuesday; the action of the third on Easter Wednesday week.

ACT I., SCENE I. Rockingham Gate. John Barthwick's dining-room.
 SCENE II. The same.
 SCENE III. The same.

ACT II., SCENE I. The Jones's lodgings, Merthyr Street.
 SCENE II. John Barthwick's dining-room.

ACT III. A London police court.

ACT I

SCENE I

The curtain rises on the BARTHWICK'S *dining-room, large, modern, and well furnished; the window curtains drawn. Electric light is burning. On the large round dining-table is set out a tray with whisky, a syphon, and a silver cigarette box. It is past midnight.*

A fumbling is heard outside the door. It is opened suddenly; JACK BARTHWICK *seems to fall into the room. He stands holding by the doorknob, staring before him, with a beatific smile. He is in evening dress and opera hat, and carries in his hand a sky-blue velvet lady's reticule. His boyish face is freshly coloured and clean-shaven. An overcoat is hanging on his arm.*

JACK. Hello! I've got home all ri——[*Defiantly.*] Who says I sh'd never 've opened th' door without 'sistance. [*He staggers in, fumbling with the reticule. A lady's handkerchief and purse of crimson silk fall out.*] Serve her joll' well right—everything droppin' out. Th' cat. I've scored her off—I've got her bag. [*He swings the reticule.*] Serves her joll' well right. [*He takes a cigarette out of the silver box and puts it in his mouth.*] Never gave tha' fellow anything! [*He hunts through all his pockets and pulls a shilling out; it drops and rolls away. He looks for it.*] Beastly shilling! [*He looks again.*] Base ingratitude!

Absolutely nothing. [*He laughs.*] Mus' tell him I've got absolutely nothing.

> [*He lurches through the door and down a corridor, and presently returns, followed by* JONES, *who is advanced in liquor.* JONES, *about thirty years of age, has hollow cheeks, black circles around his eyes, and rusty clothes. He looks as though he might be unemployed, and enters in a hang-dog manner.*]

JACK. Sh! sh! sh! Don't you make a noise, whatever you do. Shu' the door, an' have a drink. [*Very solemnly.*] You helped me to open the door—I've got nothin' for you. This is my house. My father's name's Barthwick; he's Member of Parliament—Liberal Member of Parliament: I've told you that before. Have a drink! [*He pours out whisky and drinks it up.*] I'm not drunk—— [*Subsiding on a sofa.*] Tha's all right. Wha's your name? My name's Barthwick, so's my father's; *I'm* a Liberal too—wha're you?

JONES. [*In a thick, sardonic voice.*] I'm a bloomin' Conserv*ative*. My name's Jones! My wife works 'ere; she's the char; she works 'ere.

JACK. Jones? [*He laughs.*] There's 'nother Jones at College with me. I'm not a Socialist myself; I'm a Liberal—there's ve-lill difference, because of the principles of the Lib—Liberal Party. We're all equal before the law—tha's rot, tha's silly. [*Laughs.*] Wha' was I about to say? Give me some whisky.

> [JONES *gives him the whisky he desires, together with a squirt of syphon.*]

Wha' I was goin' tell you was—I've had a row with her. [*He waves the reticule.*] Have a drink, Jones—sh'd never have got in without you—tha's why I'm giving you a drink. Don' care who knows I've scored her off. Th' cat. [*He*

THE SILVER BOX

throws his feet up on the sofa.] Don' you make a noise, whatever you do. You pour out a drink—you make yourself good long, long drink—you take cigarette—you take everything you like. Sh'd never have got in without you. [*Closing his eyes.*] You're a Tory—you're a Tory Socialist. I'm Liberal myself—have a drink—I'm an excel'nt chap.

> [*His head drops back. He, smiling, falls asleep, and* JONES *stands looking at him; then, snatching up* JACK's *glass, he drinks it off. He picks the reticule from off* JACK's *shirt-front, holds it to the light, and smells at it.*]

JONES. Been on the tiles and brought 'ome some of yer cat's fur. [*He stuffs it into* JACK's *breast pocket.*]

JACK. [*Murmuring.*] I've scored you off! You cat!

> [JONES *looks around him furtively; he pours out whisky and drinks it. From the silver box he takes a cigarette, puffs at it, and drinks more whisky. There is no sobriety left in him.*]

JONES. Fat lot o' things they've got 'ere! [*He sees the crimson purse lying on the floor.*] More cat's fur. Puss, puss! [*He fingers it, drops it on the tray, and looks at* JACK.] Calf! Fat calf! [*He sees his own presentment in a mirror. Lifting his hands, with fingers spread, he stares at it; then looks again at* JACK, *clenching his fist as if to batter in his sleeping, smiling face. Suddenly he tilts the rest of the whisky into the glass and drinks it. With cunning glee he takes the silver box and purse and pockets them.*] I'll score *you* off too, that's wot I'll do!

> [*He gives a little snarling laugh and lurches to the door. His shoulder rubs against the switch; the light goes out. There is a sound as of a closing outer door.*]

The curtain falls.

THE SILVER BOX

The curtain rises again at once.

SCENE II

In the BARTHWICK's *dining-room.* JACK *is still asleep; the morning light is coming through the curtains. The time is half-past eight.* WHEELER, *brisk person, enters with a dust-pan, and* MRS. JONES *more slowly with a scuttle.*

WHEELER. [*Drawing the curtains.*] That precious husband of yours was round for you after you'd gone yesterday, Mrs. Jones. Wanted your money for drink, I suppose. He hangs about the corner here half the time. I saw him outside the "Goat and Bells" when I went to the post last night. If I were you I wouldn't live with him. I wouldn't live with a man that raised his hand to me. I wouldn't put up with it. Why don't you take your children and leave him? If you put up with 'im it'll only make him worse. I never can see why, because a man's married you, he should knock you about.

MRS. JONES. [*Slim, dark-eyed, and dark-haired; oval-faced, and with a smooth, soft, even voice; her manner patient, her way of talking quite impersonal; she wears a blue linen dress, and boots with holes.*] It was nearly two last night before he come home, and he wasn't himself. He made me get up, and he knocked me about; he didn't seem to know *what* he was saying or doing. Of course I *would* leave him, but I'm really afraid of what he'd do to me. He's such a violent man when he's not himself.

WHEELER. Why don't you get him locked up? You'll never have any peace until you get him locked up. If I were you I'd go to the police court to-morrow. That's what I would do.

MRS. JONES. Of course I ought to go, because he does

THE SILVER BOX

treat me so badly when he's not himself. But you see, Bettina, he has a very hard time—he's been out of work two months, and it preys upon his mind. When he's in work he behaves himself much better. It's when he's out of work that he's so violent.

WHEELER. Well, if you won't take any steps you'll never get rid of him.

MRS. JONES. Of course it's very wearing to me; I don't get my sleep at nights. And it's not as if I were getting help from him, because I have to do for the children and all of us. And he throws such dreadful things up at me, talks of my having men to follow me about. Such a thing never happens; no man ever speaks to me. And of course it's just the other way. It's what he does that's wrong and makes me so unhappy. And then he's always threatenin' to cut my throat if I leave him. It's all the drink, and things preying on his mind; he's not a bad man really. Sometimes he'll speak quite kind to me, but I've stood so much from him, I don't feel it in me to speak kind back, but just keep myself to myself. And he's all right with the children too, except when he's not himself.

WHEELER. You mean when he's drunk, the beauty.

MRS. JONES. Yes. [*Without change of voice.*] There's the young gentleman asleep on the sofa.

[*They both look silently at Jack.*

MRS. JONES. [*At last, in her soft voice.*] He doesn't look quite himself.

WHEELER. He's a young limb, that's what he is. It's my belief he was tipsy last night, like your husband. It's another kind of bein' out of work that sets *him* to drink. I'll go and tell Marlow. This is his job.

[*She goes.*
[*Mrs. Jones, upon her knees, begins a gentle sweeping.*]

8   THE SILVER BOX

JACK. [*Waking.*] Who's there? What is it?

MRS. JONES. It's me, sir, Mrs. Jones.

JACK. [*Sitting up and looking round.*] Where is it—what—time is it?

MRS. JONES. It's getting on for nine o'clock, sir.

JACK. For nine! Why—what! [*Rising, and loosening his tongue; putting hand to his head, and staring hard at* MRS. JONES.] Look here, you, Mrs.—Mrs. Jones—don't you say you caught me asleep here.

MRS. JONES. No, sir, of course I won't sir.

JACK. It's quite an accident; I don't know how it happened. I must have forgotten to go to bed. It's a queer thing. I've got a most beastly headache. Mind you don't say anything, Mrs. Jones.

> [*Goes out and passes* MARLOW *in the doorway.*
> MARLOW *is young and quiet; he is clean-shaven, and his hair is brushed high from his forehead in a coxcomb. Incidentally a butler, he is first a man. He looks at* MRS. JONES, *and smiles a private smile.*]

MARLOW. Not the first time, and won't be the last. Looked a bit dicky, eh, Mrs. Jones?

MRS. JONES. He didn't look quite himself. Of course I didn't take notice.

MARLOW. You're used to them. How's your old man?

MRS. JONES. [*Softly as throughout.*] Well, he was very bad last night; he didn't seem to know what he was about. He was very late, and he was most abusive. But now, of course, he's asleep.

MARLOW. That's his way of finding a job, eh?

MRS. JONES. As a rule, Mr. Marlow, he goes out early every morning looking for work, and sometimes he comes in fit to drop—and of course I can't say he doesn't try to get

THE SILVER BOX

it, because he does. Trade's very bad. [*She stands quite still, her pan and brush before her, at the beginning and the end of long vistas of experience, traversing them with her impersonal eye.*] But he's not a good husband to me—last night he hit me, and he was so dreadfully abusive.

MARLOW. Bank 'oliday, eh! He's too fond of the "Goat and Bells," that's what's the matter with him. I see him at the corner late every night. He hangs about.

MRS. JONES. He gets to feeling very low walking about all day after work, and being refused so often, and then when he gets a drop in him it goes to his head. But he shouldn't treat his wife as he treats me. Sometimes I've had to go and walk about at night, when he wouldn't let me stay in the room; but he's sorry for it afterwards. And he hangs about after me, he waits for me in the street; and I don't think he ought to, because I've always been a good wife to him. And I tell him Mrs. Barthwick wouldn't like him coming about the place. But that only makes him angry, and he says dreadful things about the gentry. Of course it was through me that he first lost his place, through his not treating me right; and that's made him bitter against the gentry. He had a very good place as groom in the country; but it made such a stir, because of course he didn't treat me right.

MARLOW. Got the sack?

MRS. JONES. Yes; his employer said he couldn't keep him, because there was a great deal of talk; and he said it was such a bad example. But it's very important for me to keep my work here; I have the three children, and I don't want him to come about after me in the streets, and make a disturbance as he sometimes does.

MARLOW. [*Holding up the empty decanter.*] Not a drain! Next time he hits you get a witness and go down to the court——

Mrs. Jones. Yes, I think I've made up my mind. I think I ought to.

Marlow. That's right. Where's the ciga——?

> [*He searches for the silver box; he looks at* Mrs. Jones, *who is sweeping on her hands and knees; he checks himself and stands reflecting. From the tray he picks two half-smoked cigarettes, and reads the name on them.*]

Nestor—where the deuce——?

> [*With a meditative air he looks again at* Mrs. Jones, *and, taking up* Jack's *overcoat, he searches in the pockets.* Wheeler, *with a tray of breakfast things, comes in.*]

Marlow. [*Aside to* Wheeler.] Have you seen the cigarette-box?

Wheeler. No.

Marlow. Well, it's gone. I put it on the tray last night. And he's been smoking. [*Showing her the ends of cigarettes.*] It's not in these pockets. He can't have taken it upstairs this morning! Have a good look in his room when he comes down. Who's been in here?

Wheeler. Only me and Mrs. Jones.

Mrs. Jones. I've finished here; shall I do the drawing-room now?

Wheeler. [*Looking at her doubtfully.*] Have you seen——Better do the boudwower first.

> [Mrs. Jones *goes out with pan and brush.* Marlow *and* Wheeler *look each other in the face.*]

Marlow. It'll turn up.

Wheeler. [*Hesitating.*] You don't think *she*—— [*Nodding at the door.*]

Marlow. [*Stoutly.*] I don't—I never believes anything of anybody.

Wheeler. But the master'll have to be told.

THE SILVER BOX

MARLOW. You wait a bit, and see if it don't turn up. Suspicion's no business of ours. I set my mind against it.

The curtain falls.

The curtain rises again at once.

SCENE III

BARTHWICK *and* MRS. BARTHWICK *are seated at the breakfast table. He is a man between fifty and sixty; quietly important, with a bald forehead, and pince-nez, and the "Times" in his hand. She is a lady of nearly fifty, well dressed, with greyish hair, good features, and a decided manner. They face each other.*

BARTHWICK. [*From behind his paper.*] The Labour man has got in at the by-election for Barnside, my dear.

MRS. BARTHWICK. Another Labour? I can't think what on earth the country is about.

BARTHWICK. I predicted it. It's not a matter of vast importance.

MRS. BARTHWICK. Not? How can you take it so calmly, John? To me it's simply outrageous. And there you sit, you Liberals, and pretend to encourage these people!

BARTHWICK. [*Frowning.*] The representation of all parties is necessary for any proper reform, for any proper social policy.

MRS. BARTHWICK. I've no patience with your talk of reform—all that nonsense about social policy. We know perfectly well what it is they want; they want things for themselves. Those Socialists and Labour men are an absolutely selfish set of people. They have no sense of patriotism, like the upper classes; *they simply want what we've got*.

BARTHWICK. Want what we've got! [*He stares into space.*] My dear, what are you talking about? [*With a contortion.*] I'm no alarmist.

MRS. BARTHWICK. Cream? Quite uneducated men! Wait until they begin to tax our investments. I'm convinced that when they once get a chance they will tax everything—they've no feeling for the country. You Liberals and Conservatives, you're all alike; you don't see an inch before your noses. You've no imagination, not a scrap of imagination between you. You ought to join hands and nip it in the bud.

BARTHWICK. You're talking nonsense! How is it possible for Liberals and Conservatives to join hands, as you call it? That shows how absurd it is for women—Why, the very essence of a Liberal is to trust in the people!

MRS. BARTHWICK. Now, John, eat your breakfast. As if there were any real difference between you and the Conservatives. All the upper classes have the same interests to protect, and the same principles. [*Calmly.*] Oh! you're sitting upon a volcano, John.

BARTHWICK. What!

MRS. BARTHWICK. I read a letter in the paper yesterday. I forget the man's name, but it made the whole thing perfectly clear. You don't look things in the face.

BARTHWICK. Indeed! [*Heavily.*] I am a Liberal! Drop the subject, please!

MRS. BARTHWICK. Toast? I quite agree with what this man says: Education is simply ruining the lower classes. It unsettles them, and that's the worst thing for us all. I see an enormous difference in the manner of servants.

BARTHWICK. [*With suspicious emphasis.*] I welcome any change that will lead to something better. [*He opens a*

THE SILVER BOX

letter.] H'm! This is that affair of Master Jack's again. "High Street, Oxford. Sir, We have received Mr. John Barthwick, Senior's, draft for forty pounds!" Oh! the letter's to him! "We now enclose the cheque you cashed with us, which, as we stated in our previous letter, was not met on presentation at your bank. We are, Sir, yours obediently, Moss and Sons, Tailors." H'm! [*Staring at the cheque.*] A pretty business altogether! The boy might have been prosecuted.

MRS. BARTHWICK. Come, John, you know Jack didn't mean anything; he only thought he was overdrawing. I still think his bank ought to have cashed that cheque. They must know your position.

BARTHWICK. [*Replacing in the envelope the letter and the cheque.*] Much good that would have done him in a court of law. [*He stops as* JACK *comes in, fastening his waistcoat and staunching a razor cut upon his chin.*]

JACK. [*Sitting down between them, and speaking with an artificial joviality.*] Sorry I'm late. [*He looks lugubriously at the dishes.*] Tea, please, mother. Any letters for me? [BARTHWICK *hands the letter to him.*] But look here, I say, this has been opened! I do wish you wouldn't——

BARTHWICK. [*Touching the envelope.*] I suppose I'm entitled to this name.

JACK. [*Sulkily.*] Well, I can't help having your name, father! [*He reads the letter, and mutters.*] Brutes!

BARTHWICK. [*Eyeing him.*] You don't deserve to be so well out of that.

JACK. Haven't you ragged me enough, dad?

MRS. BARTHWICK. Yes, John, let Jack have his breakfast.

BARTHWICK. If you hadn't had me to come to, where would you have been? It's the merest accident—suppose you had been the son of a poor man or a clerk. Obtaining money with a cheque you knew your bank could not meet. It might have ruined you for life. I can't see what's to become of you if these are your principles. I never did anything of the sort myself.

JACK. I expect you always had lots of money. If you've got plenty of money, of course——

BARTHWICK. On the contrary, I had not your advantages. My father kept me very short of money.

JACK. How much had you, dad?

BARTHWICK. It's not material. The question is, do you feel the gravity of what you did?

JACK. I don't know about the gravity. Of course, I'm very sorry if you think it was wrong. Haven't I said so! I should never have done it at all if I hadn't been so jolly hard up.

BARTHWICK. How much of that forty pounds have you got left, Jack?

JACK. [*Hesitating.*] I don't know—not much.

BARTHWICK. How much?

JACK. [*Desperately.*] I haven't got any.

BARTHWICK. What?

JACK. I know I've got the most beastly headache.

[*He leans his head on his hand.*]

MRS. BARTHWICK. Headache? My dear boy! Can't you eat any breakfast?

JACK. [*Drawing in his breath.*] Too jolly bad!

MRS. BARTHWICK. I'm so sorry. Come with me, dear; I'll give you something that will take it away at once.

[*They leave the room; and* BARTHWICK, *tearing up the letter, goes to the fireplace and puts the pieces in the fire. While he is doing this* MARLOW *comes in, and looking round him, is about quietly to withdraw.*]

BARTHWICK. What's that? What d' you want?

THE SILVER BOX

MARLOW. I was looking for Mr. John, sir.

BARTHWICK. What d' you want Mr. John for?

MARLOW. [*With hesitation.*] I thought I should find him here, sir.

BARTHWICK. [*Suspiciously.*] Yes, but what do you want him for?

MARLOW. [*Offhandedly.*] There's a lady called—asked to speak to him for a minute, sir.

BARTHWICK. A lady, at this time in the morning. What sort of a lady?

MARLOW. [*Without expression in his voice.*] I can't tell, sir; no particular sort. She might be after charity. She might be a Sister of Mercy, I should think, sir.

BARTHWICK. Is she dressed like one?

MARLOW. No, sir, she's in plain clothes, sir.

BARTHWICK. Didn't she say what she wanted?

MARLOW. No, sir.

BARTHWICK. Where did you leave her?

MARLOW. In the hall, sir.

BARTHWICK. In the hall? How do you know she's not a thief—not got designs on the house?

MARLOW. No, sir, I don't fancy so, sir.

BARTHWICK. Well, show her in here; I'll see her myself.

> [MARLOW *goes out with a private gesture of dismay. He soon returns, ushering in a young pale lady with dark eyes and pretty figure, in a modish, black, but rather shabby dress, a black and white trimmed hat with a bunch of Parma violets wrongly placed, and fuzzy-spotted veil. At the sight of* MR. BARTHWICK *she exhibits every sign of nervousness.* MARLOW *goes out.*]

UNKNOWN LADY. Oh! but—I beg pardon—there's some mistake—I—— [*She turns to fly.*]

BARTHWICK. Whom did you want to see, madam?

UNKNOWN. [*Stopping and looking back.*] It was Mr. *John* Barthwick I wanted to see.

BARTHWICK. I am John Barthwick, madam. What can I have the pleasure of doing for you?

UNKNOWN. Oh! I—I don't—— [*She drops her eyes.* BARTHWICK *scrutinizes her, and purses his lips.*]

BARTHWICK. It was my son, perhaps, you wished to see?

UNKNOWN. [*Quickly.*] Yes, of course, it's your son.

BARTHWICK. May I ask whom I have the pleasure of speaking to?

UNKNOWN. [*Appeal and hardiness upon her face.*] My name is—oh! it doesn't matter—I don't want to make any fuss. I just want to see your son for a minute. [*Boldly.*] In fact, I *must* see him.

BARTHWICK. [*Controlling his uneasiness.*] My son is not very well. If necessary, no doubt I could attend to the matter; be so kind as to let me know——

UNKNOWN. Oh! but I *must* see him—I've come on purpose—[*She bursts out nervously.*] I don't want to make any fuss, but the fact is, last—last night your son took away—he took away my—— [*She stops.*]

BARTHWICK. [*Severely.*] Yes, madam, what?

UNKNOWN. He took away my—my reticule.

BARTHWICK. Your reti——?

UNKNOWN. I don't care about the reticule; it's not *that* I want—I'm sure I don't want to make any fuss—[*her face is quivering*]—but—but—all my money was in it!

BARTHWICK. In what—in what?

UNKNOWN. In my purse, in the reticule. It was a crimson silk purse. Really, I wouldn't have come—I don't want to make any fuss. But I must get my money back—mustn't I?

BARTHWICK. Do you tell me that my son——?

THE SILVER BOX

UNKNOWN. Oh! well, you see, he wasn't quite—I mean he was—— [*She smiles mesmerically*.

BARTHWICK. I beg your pardon.

UNKNOWN. [*Stamping her foot*.] Oh! don't you see—tipsy! We had a quarrel.

BARTHWICK. [*Scandalized*.] How? Where?

UNKNOWN. [*Defiantly*.] At my place. We'd had supper at the —— and your son——

BARTHWICK. [*Pressing the bell*.] May I ask how you knew this house? Did he give you his name and address?

UNKNOWN. [*Glancing sidelong*.] I got it out of his overcoat.

BARTHWICK. [*Sardonically*.] Oh! you got it out of his overcoat. And may I ask if my son will know you by daylight?

UNKNOWN. Know me? I should jolly—I mean, of course he will! [MARLOW *comes in*.

BARTHWICK. Ask Mr. John to come down.

[MARLOW *goes out, and* BARTHWICK *walks uneasily about*.]

And how long have you enjoyed his acquaintanceship?

UNKNOWN. Only since—only since Good Friday.

BARTHWICK. I am at a loss—I repeat I am at a loss——

[*He glances at this unknown lady, who stands with eyes cast down, twisting her hands. And suddenly Jack appears. He stops on seeing who is here, and the unknown lady hysterically giggles. There is a silence*.]

BARTHWICK. [*Portentously*.] This young—er—lady says that last night—I think you said last night, madam—you took away——

UNKNOWN. [*Impulsively*.] My reticule, and all my money was in a crimson silk purse.

THE SILVER BOX

JACK. Reticule. [*Looking round for any chance to get away.*] I don't know anything about it.

BARTHWICK. [*Sharply.*] Come, do you deny seeing this young lady last night?

JACK. Deny? No, of course. [*Whispering.*] Why did you give me away like this? What on earth did you come here for?

UNKNOWN. [*Tearfully.*] I'm sure I didn't want to—it's not likely, is it? You snatched it out of my hand—you know you did—and the purse had all my money in it. I didn't follow you last night because I didn't want to make a fuss and it was so late, and you were so——

BARTHWICK. Come, sir, don't turn your back on me—explain!

JACK. [*Desperately.*] I don't remember anything about it. [*In a low voice to his friend.*] Why on earth couldn't you have written?

UNKNOWN. [*Sullenly.*] I want it now; I must have it—I've got to pay my rent to-day. [*She looks at* BARTHWICK.] They're only too glad to jump on people who are not—not *well off*.

JACK. I don't remember anything about it, really. I don't remember anything about last night at all. [*He puts his hand up to his head.*] It's all—cloudy, and I've got such a beastly headache.

UNKNOWN. But you *took* it; you know you did. You said you'd score me off.

JACK. Well, then, it must be here. I remember now—I remember something. Why did I take the beastly thing?

BARTHWICK. Yes, why did you take the beastly——

[*He turns abruptly to the window.*

UNKNOWN. [*With her mesmeric smile.*] You weren't quite——were you?

THE SILVER BOX 19

JACK. [*Smiling pallidly.*] I'm *awfully* sorry. If there's anything I can do——

BARTHWICK. Do? You can restore this property, I suppose.

JACK. I'll go and have a look, but I really don't think I've got it.

> [*He goes out hurriedly. And* BARTHWICK, *placing a chair, motions to the visitor to sit, then, with pursed lips, he stands and eyes her fixedly. She sits, and steals a look at him; then turns away, and, drawing up her veil, stealthily wipes her eyes. And Jack comes back.*]

JACK. [*Ruefully holding out the empty reticule.*] Is that the thing? I've looked all over—I can't find the purse anywhere. Are you sure it was there?

UNKNOWN. [*Tearfully.*] Sure? Of course I'm sure. A crimson silk purse. It was all the money I had.

JACK. I really am awfully sorry—my head's so jolly bad. I've asked the butler, but he hasn't seen it.

UNKNOWN. I *must* have my money——

JACK. Oh! Of course—that'll be all right; I'll see that that's all right. How much?

UNKNOWN. [*Sullenly.*] Seven pounds—twelve—it's all I've got in the world.

JACK. That'll be all right; I'll—send you a—cheque.

UNKNOWN. [*Eagerly.*] No; now, please. Give me what was in my purse; I've got to pay my rent this morning. They won't give me another day; I'm a fortnight behind already.

JACK. [*Blankly.*] I'm awfully sorry; I really haven't a penny in my pocket.

> [*He glances stealthily at* BARTHWICK.

UNKNOWN. [*Excitedly.*] Come I say you must—it's

my money, and you took it. I'm not going away without it. They'll turn me out of my place.

JACK. [*Clasping his head.*] But I can't give you what I haven't got. Don't I tell you I haven't a beastly cent?

UNKNOWN. [*Tearing at her handkerchief.*] Oh! do give it to me! [*She puts her hands together in appeal; then, with sudden fierceness.*] If you don't I'll summons you. It's stealing, that's what it is!

BARTHWICK. [*Uneasily.*] One moment, please. As a matter of—er—principle, I shall settle this claim. [*He produces money.*] Here is eight pounds; the extra will cover the value of the purse and your cab fares. I need make no comment—no thanks are necessary.

> [*Touching the bell, he holds the door ajar in silence. The unknown lady stores the money in her reticule, she looks from* JACK *to* BARTHWICK, *and her face is quivering faintly with a smile. She hides it with her hand, and steals away. Behind her* BARTHWICK *shuts the door.*]

BARTHWICK. [*With solemnity.*] H'm! This is a nice thing to happen!

JACK. [*Impersonally.*] What awful luck!

BARTHWICK. So this is the way that forty pounds has gone! One thing after another! Once more I should like to know where you'd have been if it hadn't been for me! You don't seem to have any principles. You—you're one of those who are a nuisance to society; you—you're dangerous! What your mother would say I don't know. Your conduct, as far as I can see, is absolutely unjustifiable. It's —it's criminal. Why, a poor man who behaved as you've done . . . d' you think he'd have any mercy shown him? What you want is a good lesson. You and your sort are—[*he speaks with feeling*]—a nuisance to the community. Don't ask me to help you next time. You're not fit to be helped.

JACK. [*Turning upon his sire, with unexpected fierceness.*] All right, I won't then, and see how you like it. You wouldn't have helped me this time, I know, if you hadn't been scared the thing would get into the papers. Where are the cigarettes?

BARTHWICK. [*Regarding him uneasily.*] Well—I'll say no more about it. [*He rings the bell.*] I'll pass it over for this once, but—— [MARLOW *comes in.*] You can clear away.

[*He hides his face behind the "Times."*

JACK. [*Brightening.*] I say, Marlow, where are the cigarettes?

MARLOW. I put the box out with the whisky last night, sir, but this morning I can't find it anywhere.

JACK. Did you look in my room?

MARLOW. Yes, sir; I've looked all over the house. I found two Nestor ends in the tray this morning, so you must have been smokin' last night, sir. [*Hesitating.*] I'm really afraid some one's purloined the box.

JACK. [*Uneasily.*] Stolen it!

BARTHWICK. What's that? The cigarette-box! Is anything else missing?

MARLOW. No, sir; I've been through the plate.

BARTHWICK. Was the house all right this morning? None of the windows open?

MARLOW. No, sir. [*Quietly to* JACK.] You left your latch-key in the door last night, sir.

[*He hands it back, unseen by* BARTHWICK.

JACK. Tst!

BARTHWICK. Who's been in the room this morning?

MARLOW. Me and Wheeler, and Mrs. Jones is all, sir, as far as I know.

BARTHWICK. Have you asked Mrs. Barthwick? [*To* JACK.] Go and ask your mother if she's had it; ask her to look and see if she's missed anything else.

[JACK *goes upon this mission.*
Nothing is more disquieting than losing things like this.

MARLOW. No, sir.

BARTHWICK. Have you any suspicions?

MARLOW. No, sir.

BARTHWICK. This Mrs. Jones—how long has she been working here?

MARLOW. Only this last month, sir.

BARTHWICK. What sort of person?

MARLOW. I don't know much about her, sir; seems a very quiet, respectable woman.

BARTHWICK. Who did the room this morning?

MARLOW. Wheeler and Mrs. Jones, sir.

BARTHWICK. [*With his forefinger upraised.*] Now, was this Mrs. Jones in the room alone at any time?

MARLOW. [*Expressionless.*] Yes, sir.

BARTHWICK. How do you know that?

MARLOW. [*Reluctantly.*] I found her here, sir.

BARTHWICK. And has Wheeler been in the room alone?

MARLOW. No, sir, she's not, sir. I should say, sir, that Mrs. Jones seems a very honest——

BARTHWICK. [*Holding up his hand.*] I want to know this: Has this Mrs. Jones been here the whole morning?

MARLOW. Yes, sir—no, sir—she stepped over to the greengrocer's for cook.

BARTHWICK. H'm! Is she in the house now?

MARLOW. Yes, sir.

BARTHWICK. Very good. I shall make a point of clearing this up. On principle I shall make a point of fixing the responsibility; it goes to the foundations of security. In all your interests——

THE SILVER BOX

MARLOW. Yes, sir.

BARTHWICK. What sort of circumstances is this Mrs. Jones in? Is her husband in work?

MARLOW. I believe not, sir.

BARTHWICK. Very well. Say nothing about it to any one. Tell Wheeler not to speak of it, and ask Mrs. Jones to step up here.

MARLOW. Very good, sir.

> [MARLOW *goes out, his face concerned; and* BARTHWICK *stays, his face judicial and a little pleased, as befits a man conducting an inquiry.* MRS. BARTHWICK *and her son come in.*]

BARTHWICK. Well, my dear, you've not seen it, I suppose?

MRS. BARTHWICK. No. But what an extraordinary thing, John! Marlow, of course, is out of the question. I'm certain none of the maids——as for cook!

BARTHWICK. Oh, cook!

MRS. BARTHWICK. Of course! It's perfectly detestable to me to suspect anybody.

BARTHWICK. It is not a question of one's feelings. It's a question of justice. On principle——

MRS. BARTHWICK. I shouldn't be a bit surprised if the charwoman knew something about it. It was Laura who recommended her.

BARTHWICK. [*Judicially.*] I am going to have Mrs. Jones up. Leave it to me; and—er—remember that nobody is guilty until they're proven so. I shall be careful. I have no intention of frightening her; I shall give her every chance. I hear she's in poor circumstances. If we are not able to do much for them we are bound to have the greatest sympathy with the poor. [MRS. JONES *comes in.* [*Pleasantly.*] Oh! good morning, Mrs. Jones.

MRS. JONES. [*Soft, and even, unemphatic.*] Good morning, sir! Good morning, ma'am!

BARTHWICK. About your husband—he's not in work, I hear?

MRS. JONES. No, sir; of course, he's not in work just now.

BARTHWICK. Then I suppose he's earning nothing.

MRS. JONES. No, sir, he's not earning anything just now, sir.

BARTHWICK. And how many children have you?

MRS. JONES. Three children; but of course they don't eat very much sir. [*A little silence.*

BARTHWICK. And how old is the eldest?

MRS. JONES. Nine years old, sir.

BARTHWICK. Do they go to school?

MRS. JONES. Yes, sir, they all three go to school every day.

BARTHWICK. [*Severely.*] And what about their food when you're out at work?

MRS. JONES. Well, sir, I have to give them their dinner to take with them. Of course I'm not always able to give them anything; sometimes I have to send them without; but my husband is very good about the children when he's in work. But when he's not in work of course he's a very difficult man.

BARTHWICK. He drinks, I suppose?

MRS. JONES. Yes, sir. Of course I can't say he doesn't drink, because he does.

BARTHWICK. And I suppose he takes all your money?

MRS. JONES. No, sir, he's very good about my money, except when he's not himself, and then, of course, he treats me very badly.

BARTHWICK. Now what is he—your husband?

MRS. JONES. By profession, sir, of course he's a groom.

THE SILVER BOX

BARTHWICK. A groom! How came he to lose his place?

MRS. JONES. He lost his place a long time ago, sir, and he's never had a very long job since; and now, of course, the motor-cars are against him.

BARTHWICK. When were you married to him, Mrs. Jones?

MRS. JONES. Eight years ago, sir—that was in—

MRS. BARTHWICK. [*Sharply.*] Eight? You said the eldest child was nine.

MRS. JONES. Yes, ma'am; of course that was why he lost his place. He didn't treat me rightly, and of course his employer said he couldn't keep him because of the example.

BARTHWICK. You mean he—ahem——

MRS. JONES. Yes, sir; and of course after he lost his place he married me.

MRS. BARTHWICK. You actually mean to say you—you were——

BARTHWICK. My dear——

MRS. BARTHWICK. [*Indignantly.*] How disgraceful!

BARTHWICK. [*Hurriedly.*] And where are you living now, Mrs. Jones?

MRS. JONES. We've not got a home, sir. Of course we've been obliged to put away most of our things.

BARTHWICK. Put your things away! You mean to—to—er—to pawn them?

MRS. JONES. Yes, sir, to put them away. We're living in Merthyr Street—that is close by here, sir—at No. 34. We just have the one room.

BARTHWICK. And what do you pay a week?

MRS. JONES. We pay six shillings a week, sir, for a furnished room.

BARTHWICK. And I suppose you're behind in the rent?

MRS. JONES. Yes, sir, we're a little behind in the rent.

BARTHWICK. But *you're* in good work, aren't you?

MRS. JONES. Well, sir, I have a day in Stamford Place Thursdays. And Mondays and Wednesdays and Fridays I come here. But to-day, of course, is a half-day, because of yesterday's Bank Holiday.

BARTHWICK. I see; four days a week, and you get half a crown a day, is that it?

MRS. JONES. Yes, sir, and my dinner; but sometimes it's only half a day, and that's eighteenpence.

BARTHWICK. And when your husband earns anything he spends it in drink, I suppose?

MRS. JONES. Sometimes he does, sir, and sometimes he gives it to me for the children. Of course he would work if he could get it, sir, but it seems there are a great many people out of work.

BARTHWICK. Ah! Yes. We—er—won't go into that. [*Sympathetically.*] And how about your work here? Do you find it hard?

MRS. JONES. Oh! no, sir, not very hard, sir; except of course, when I don't get my sleep at night.

BARTHWICK. Ah! And you help do all the rooms? And sometimes, I suppose, you go out for cook?

MRS. JONES. Yes, sir.

BARTHWICK. And you've been out this morning?

MRS. JONES. Yes, sir, of course I had to go to the greengrocer's.

BARTHWICK. Exactly. So your husband earns nothing? And he's a bad character.

MRS. JONES. No, sir, I don't say that, sir. I think there's a great deal of good in him; though he does treat me very bad sometimes. And of course I don't like to leave him, but I think I ought to, because really I hardly know how to stay with him. He often raises his hand to me. Not long ago he gave me a blow here [*touches her*

THE SILVER BOX

breast] and I can feel it now. So I think I ought to leave him, don't *you,* sir?

BARTHWICK. Ah! I can't help you there. It's a very serious thing to leave your husband. Very serious thing.

MRS. JONES. Yes, sir, of course I'm afraid of what he might do to me if I were to leave him; he can be so very violent.

BARTHWICK. H'm! Well, that I can't pretend to say anything about. It's the bad principle I'm speaking of——

MRS. JONES. Yes, sir; I know nobody can help me. I know I must decide for myself, and of course I know that he has a very hard life. And he's fond of the children, and it's very hard for him to see them going without food.

BARTHWICK. [*Hastily.*] Well—er—thank you, I just wanted to hear about you. I don't think I need detain you any longer, Mrs.—Jones.

MRS. JONES. No, sir, thank you, sir.

BARTHWICK. Good morning, then.

MRS. JONES. Good morning, sir; good morning, ma'am.

BARTHWICK. [*Exchanging glances with his wife.*] By the way, Mrs. Jones—I think it is only fair to tell you, a silver cigarette-box—er—is missing.

MRS. JONES. [*Looking from one face to the other.*] I am very sorry, sir.

BARTHWICK. Yes; you have not seen it, I suppose?

MRS. JONES. [*Realising that suspicion is upon her; with an uneasy movement.*] Where was it, sir; if you please, sir?

BARTHWICK. [*Evasively.*] Where did Marlow say? Er —in this room, yes, in *this* room.

MRS. JONES. No, sir, I haven't seen it—of course if I'd seen it I should have noticed it.

THE SILVER BOX

BARTHWICK. [*Giving her a rapid glance.*] You—you are sure of that?

MRS. JONES. [*Impassively.*] Yes, sir. [*With a slow nodding of her head.*] I have not seen it, and of course I *don't* know where it is.

[*She turns and goes quietly out.*]

BARTHWICK. H'm!

[*The three* BARTHWICKS *avoid each other's glances.*]

The curtain falls.

ACT II

SCENE I

The JONES's *lodgings, Merthyr Street, at half-past two o'clock.*

The bare room, with tattered oilcloth and damp, distempered walls, has an air of tidy wretchedness. On the bed lies JONES, *half-dressed; his coat is thrown across his feet, and muddy boots are lying on the floor close by. He is asleep. The door is opened and* MRS. JONES *comes in, dressed in a pinched black jacket and old black sailor hat; she carries a parcel wrapped up in the "Times." She puts her parcel down, unwraps an apron, half a loaf, two onions, three potatoes, and a tiny piece of bacon. Taking a teapot from the cupboard, she rinses it, shakes into it some powdered tea out of a screw of paper, puts it on the hearth, and sitting in a wooden chair quietly begins to cry.*

JONES. [*Stirring and yawning.*] That you? What's the time?

THE SILVER BOX

MRS. JONES. [*Drying her eyes, and in her usual voice.*] Half-past two.

JONES. What you back so soon for?

MRS. JONES. I only had the half day to-day, Jem.

JONES. [*On his back, and in a drowsy voice.*] Got anything for dinner?

MRS. JONES. Mrs. Barthwick's cook gave me a little bit of bacon. I'm going to make a stew. [*She prepares for cooking.*] There's fourteen shillings owing for rent, James, and of course I've only got two and fourpence. They'll be coming for it to-day.

JONES. [*Turning towards her on his elbow.*] Let 'em come and find my surprise packet. I've had enough o' this tryin' for work. Why should I go round and round after a job like a bloomin' squirrel in a cage. "Give us a job, sir"—"Take a man on"—"Got a wife and three children." Sick of it I am! I'd sooner lie here and rot. "Jones, you come and join the demonstration; come and 'old a flag, and listen to the ruddy orators, and go 'ome as empty as you came." There's some that seems to like *that*—the sheep! When I go seekin' for a job now, and see the brutes lookin' me up an' down, it's like a thousand serpents in me. I'm not arskin' for any treat. A man wants to sweat hisself silly and not allowed—that's a rum start, ain't it? A man wants to sweat his soul out to keep the breath in him and ain't allowed—that's justice—that's freedom and all the rest of it! [*He turns his face towards the wall.*] You're so milky mild; you don't know what goes on inside o' me. I'm done with the silly game. If they want me, let 'em come for me!

[MRS. JONES *stops cooking and stands unmoving at the table.*]

I've tried and done with it, I tell you. I've never been afraid of what's before *me*. You mark my words—if you think they've broke my spirit, you're mistook. I'll lie and rot sooner than arsk 'em again. What makes you stand like that—you long-sufferin', Gawd-forsaken image—that's why I can't keep my hands off you. So now you know. Work! You can work, but you haven't the spirit of a louse!

MRS. JONES. [*Quietly.*] You talk more wild sometimes when you're yourself, James, than when you're not. If you don't get work, how are we to go on? They won't let us stay here; they're looking to their money to-day, I know.

JONES. I see this Barthwick o' yours every day goin' down to Pawlyment snug and comfortable to talk his silly soul out; an' I see that young calf, his son, swellin' it about, and goin' on the razzle-dazzle. Wot 'ave they done that makes 'em any better than wot I am? They never did a day's work in their lives. I see 'em day after day——

MRS. JONES. And I wish you wouldn't come after me like that, and hang about the house. You don't seem able to keep away at all, and whatever you do it for I can't think, because of course they notice it.

JONES. I suppose I may go where I like. Where *may* I go? The other day I went to a place in the Edgware Road. "Gov'nor," I says to the boss, "take me on," I says. "I 'aven't done a stroke o' work not these two months; it takes the heart out of a man," I says; "I'm one to work; I'm not afraid of anything you can give me!" "My good man," 'e says, "I've had thirty of you here this morning. I took the first two," he says, "and that's all I want." "Thank you, then rot the world!" I says. "Blasphemin'," he says, "is not the way to get a job. Out you go, my lad!" [*He laughs sardonically.*] Don't you raise your voice because you're starvin'; don't yer even think of it; take it lyin' down! Take it like a sensible man, carn't you? And a little way down the street a lady says to me: [*Pinching his*

THE SILVER BOX

voice.] "D' you want to earn a few pence, my man?" and gives me her dog to 'old outside a shop—fat as a butler 'e was—tons o' meat had gone to the makin' of *him*. It did 'er good, it did, made 'er feel 'erself that *charitable,* but I see 'er lookin' at the copper standin' alongside o' me, for fear I should make off with 'er bloomin' fat dog. [*He sits on the edge of the bed and puts a boot on. Then looking up.*] What's in that head o' yours? [*Almost pathetically.*] Carn't you speak for once?

> [*There is a knock, and* MRS. SEDDON, *the landlady, appears, an anxious, harassed, shabby woman in working clothes.*]

MRS. SEDDON. I thought I 'eard you come in, Mrs. Jones. I've spoke to my 'usband, but he says he really can't afford to wait another day.

JONES. [*With scowling jocularity.*] Never you mind what your 'usband says, you go your own way like a proper independent woman. Here, Jenny, chuck her that.

> [*Producing a sovereign from his trousers pocket, he throws it to his wife, who catches it in her apron with a gasp.* JONES *resumes the lacing of his boots.*]

MRS. JONES. [*Rubbing the sovereign stealthily.*] I'm very sorry we're so late with it, and of course it's fourteen shillings, so if you've got six that will be right.

> [MRS. SEDDON *takes the sovereign and fumbles for the change.*]

JONES. [*With his eyes fixed on his boots.*] Bit of a surprise for yer, ain't it?

MRS. SEDDON. Thank you, and I'm sure I'm very much obliged. [*She does indeed appear surprised.*] I'll bring you the change.

JONES. [*Mockingly.*] Don't mention it.

MRS. SEDDON. Thank you, and I'm sure I'm very much obliged.   [*She slides away.*

[MRS. JONES *gazes at* JONES *who is still lacing up his boots.*]

JONES. I've had a bit of luck. [*Pulling out the crimson purse and some loose coins.*] Picked up a purse—seven pound and more.

MRS. JONES. Oh, James!

JONES. Oh, James! What about Oh, James! I picked it up I tell you. This is lost property, this is!

MRS. JONES. But isn't there a name in it, or something?

JONES. Name? No, there ain't no name. This don't belong to such as 'ave visitin' cards. This belongs to a perfec' lidy. Tike an' smell it. [*He pitches her the purse, which she puts gently to her nose.*] Now, you tell me what I ought to have done. You tell me that. You can always tell me what I ought to ha' done, can't yer?

MRS. JONES. [*Laying down the purse.*] I can't say what you ought to have done, James. Of course the money wasn't yours; you've taken somebody else's money.

JONES. Finding's keeping. I'll take it as wages for the time I've gone about the streets asking for what's my rights. I'll take it for what's *overdue*, d'ye hear? [*With strange triumph.*] I've got money in my pocket, my girl.

[MRS. JONES *goes on again with the preparation of the meal*, JONES *looking at her furtively.*]

Money in my pocket! And I'm not goin' to waste it. With this 'ere money I'm goin' to Canada. I'll let you have a pound. [*A silence.*] You've often talked of leavin' me. You've often told me I treat you badly—well I 'ope you'll be glad when I'm gone.

MRS. JONES. [*Impassively.*] You *have* treated me very badly, James, and of course I can't prevent your going; but I can't tell whether I shall be glad when you're gone.

THE SILVER BOX

JONES. It'll change my luck. I've 'ad nothing but bad luck since I first took up with you. [*More softly.*] And you've 'ad no bloomin' picnic.

MRS. JONES. Of course it would have been better for us if we had never met. We weren't meant for each other. But you're set against me, that's what you are, and you *have* been for a long time. And you treat me so badly, James, going after that Rosie and all. You don't ever seem to think of the children that I've had to bring into the world, and of all the trouble I've had to keep them, and what'll become of them when you're gone.

JONES. [*Crossing the room gloomily.*] If you think I want to leave the little beggars you're bloomin' well mistaken.

MRS. JONES. Of course I know you're fond of them.

JONES. [*Fingering the purse, half angrily.*] Well, then, you stow it, old girl. The kids'll get along better with you than when I'm here. If I'd ha' known as much as I do now, I'd never ha' had one o' them. What's the use o' bringin' 'em into a state o' things like this? It's a crime, that's what it is; but you find it out too late; that's what's the matter with this 'ere world.

[*He puts the purse back in his pocket.*

MRS. JONES. Of course it would have been better for them, poor little things; but they're your own children, and I wonder at you talkin' like that. I should miss them dreadfully if I was to lose them.

JONES. [*Sullenly.*] An' you ain't the only one. If I make money out there——[*Looking up, he sees her shaking out his coat—in a changed voice.*] Leave that coat alone!

[*The silver box drops from the pocket, scattering the cigarettes upon the bed. Taking up the box she stares at it; he rushes at her and snatches the box away.*]

THE SILVER BOX

Mrs. Jones. [*Cowering back against the bed.*] Oh, Jem! oh, Jem!

Jones. [*Dropping the box on to the table.*] You mind what you're sayin'! When I go out I'll take and chuck it in the water along with that there purse. I 'ad it when I was in liquor, and for what you do when you're in liquor you're not responsible—and that's Gawd's truth as you ought to know. I don't want the thing—I won't have it. I took it out o' spite. I'm no thief, I tell you; and don't you call me one, or it'll be the worse for you.

Mrs. Jones. [*Twisting her apron strings.*] It's Mr. Barthwick's! You've taken away my reputation. Oh, Jem, whatever made you?

Jones. What d' you mean?

Mrs. Jones. It's been missed; they think it's me. Oh! whatever made you do it, Jem?

Jones. I tell you I was in liquor. I don't want it; what's the good of it to me? If I were to pawn it they'd only nab me. I'm no thief. I'm no worse than wot that young Barthwick is; he brought 'ome that purse that I picked up—a lady's purse—'ad it off 'er in a row, kept sayin' 'e'd scored 'er off. Well, I scored 'im off. Tight as an owl 'e was! And d' you think anything'll happen to him?

Mrs. Jones. [*As though speaking to herself.*] Oh, Jem! it's the bread out of our mouths!

Jones. Is it then? I'll make it hot for 'em yet. What about that purse? What about young Barthwick?

[Mrs. Jones *comes forward to the table and tries to take the box;* Jones *prevents her.*]

What do you want with that? You drop it, I say!

Mrs. Jones. I'll take it back and tell them all about it.
   [*She attempts to wrest the box from him.*

Jones. Ah, would yer?

   [*He drops the box, and rushes on her with a*

THE SILVER BOX 35

snarl. She slips back past the bed. He follows; a chair is overturned. The door is opened; SNOW *comes in, a detective in plain clothes and bowler hat, with clipped moustaches.* JONES *drops his arms,* MRS. JONES *stands by the window gasping;* SNOW, *advancing swiftly to the table, puts his hand on the silver box.*]

SNOW. Doin' a bit o' skylarkin'? Fancy this is what I'm after. J. B., the very same. [*He gets back to the door, scrutinising the crest and cypher on the box. To* MRS. JONES.] I'm a police officer. Are you Mrs. Jones?

MRS. JONES. Yes, sir.

SNOW. My instructions are to take you on a charge of stealing this box from J. Barthwick, Esquire, M. P., of 6, Rockingham Gate. Anything you say may be used against you. Well, Missis?

MRS. JONES. [*In her quiet voice, still out of breath, her hand upon her breast.*] Of course I did *not* take it, sir. I never have taken anything that didn't belong to me; and of course I know nothing about it.

SNOW. You were at the house this morning; you did the room in which the box was left; you were alone in the room. I find the box 'ere. You say you didn't take it?

MRS. JONES. Yes, sir, of course I say I did not take it, because I did *not*.

SNOW. Then how does the box come to be here?

MRS. JONES. I would rather not say anything about it.

SNOW. Is this your husband?

MRS. JONES. Yes, sir, this is my husband, sir.

SNOW. Do you wish to say anything before I take her?

[JONES *remains silent, with his head bent down.*]

Well then, Missis. I'll just trouble you to come along with me quietly.

MRS. JONES. [*Twisting her hands.*] Of course I wouldn't

say I hadn't taken it if I had—and I *didn't* take it, indeed I didn't. Of course I know appearances are against me, and I can't tell you what really happened. But my children are at school, and they'll be coming home—and I don't know what they'll do without me!

Snow. Your 'usband'll see to them, don't you worry.
                [*He takes the woman gently by the arm.*

Jones. You drop it—she's all right! [*Sullenly.*] I took the thing myself.

Snow. [*Eyeing him.*] There, there, it does you credit. Come along, Missis.

Jones. [*Passionately.*] Drop it, I say, you blooming teck. She's my wife; she's a respectable woman. Take her if you dare!

Snow. Now, now. What's the good of this? Keep a civil tongue, and it'll be the better for all of us.

    [*He puts his whistle in his mouth and draws the woman to the door.*]

Jones. [*With a rush.*] Drop her, and put up your 'ands, or I'll soon make yer. You leave her alone, will yer! Don't I tell yer, I took the thing myself!

Snow. [*Blowing his whistle.*] Drop your hands, or I'll take you too. Ah, would you?

    [Jones, *closing, deals him a blow. A Policeman in uniform appears; there is a short struggle and* Jones *is overpowered.* Mrs. Jones *raises her hands and drops her face on them.*]

The curtain falls.

SCENE II

The Barthwick's *dining-room the same evening. The* Barthwick's *are seated at dessert.*

THE SILVER BOX

MRS. BARTHWICK. John! [*A silence broken by the cracking of nuts.*] John!

BARTHWICK. I wish you'd speak about the nuts—they're uneatable. [*He puts one in his mouth.*

MRS. BARTHWICK. It's not the season for them. I called on the Holyroods.

[BARTHWICK *fills his glass with port.*

JACK. Crackers, please, Dad.

[BARTHWICK *passes the crackers. His demeanour is reflective.*]

MRS. BARTHWICK. Lady Holyrood has got very stout. I've noticed it coming for a long time.

BARTHWICK. [*Gloomily.*] Stout? [*He takes up the crackers—with transparent airiness.*] The Holyroods had some trouble with their servants, didn't they?

JACK. Crackers, please, Dad.

BARTHWICK. [*Passing the crackers.*] It got into the papers. The cook, wasn't it?

MRS. BARTHWICK. No, the lady's maid. I was talking it over with Lady Holyrood. The girl used to have her young man to see her.

BARTHWICK. [*Uneasily.*] I'm not sure they were wise——

MRS. BARTHWICK. My dear John, what are you talking about? How could there be any alternative? Think of the effect on the other servants!

BARTHWICK. Of course in principle—I wasn't thinking of that.

JACK. [*Maliciously.*] Crackers, please, Dad.

BARTHWICK *is compelled to pass the crackers.*

MRS. BARTHWICK. Lady Holyrood told me: "I had her up," she said; "I said to her, 'You'll leave my house at once; I think your conduct disgraceful. I can't tell, I don't know, and I don't wish to know, what you were doing.

I send you away on principle; you need not come to me for a character.' And the girl said: 'If you don't give me my notice, my lady, I want a month's wages. I'm perfectly respectable. I've done nothing.' "—Done nothing!

BARTHWICK. H'm!

MRS. BARTHWICK. Servants have too much license. They hang together so terribly you never can tell what they're really thinking; it's as if they were all in a conspiracy to keep you in the dark. Even with Marlow, you feel that he never lets you know what's really in his mind. I hate that secretiveness; it destroys all confidence. I feel sometimes I should like to shake him.

JACK. Marlow's a most decent chap. It's simply beastly every one knowing your affairs.

BARTHWICK. The less you say about that the better!

MRS. BARTHWICK. It goes all through the lower classes. You can *not* tell when they are speaking the truth. To-day when I was shopping after leaving the Holyroods, one of these unemployed came up and spoke to me. I suppose I only had twenty yards or so to walk to the carriage, but he seemed to spring up in the street.

BARTHWICK. Ah! You must be very careful whom you speak to in these days.

MRS. BARTHWICK. I didn't answer him, of course. But I could see at once that he wasn't telling the truth.

BARTHWICK. [*Cracking a nut.*] There's one very good rule—look at their eyes.

JACK. Crackers, please, Dad.

BARTHWICK. [*Passing the crackers.*] If their eyes are straightforward I sometimes give them sixpence. It's against my principles, but it's most difficult to refuse. If you see that they're desperate, and dull, and shifty-looking, as so many of them are, it's certain to mean drink, or crime, or something unsatisfactory.

THE SILVER BOX

Mrs. Barthwick. This man had dreadful eyes. He looked as if he could commit a murder. "I've 'ad nothing to eat to-day," he said. Just like that.

Barthwick. What was William about? He ought to have been waiting.

Jack. [*Raising his wine-glass to his nose.*] Is this the '63, Dad?

[Barthwick, *holding his wine-glass to his eye, lowers it and passes it before his nose.*]

Mrs. Barthwick. I hate people that can't speak the truth. [*Father and son exchange a look behind their port.*] It's just as easy to speak the truth as not. *I've* always found it easy enough. It makes it impossible to tell what is genuine; one feels as if one were continually being taken in.

Barthwick. [*Sententiously.*] The lower classes are their own enemies. If they would only trust us, they would get on so much better.

Mrs. Barthwick. But even then it's so often their own fault. Look at that Mrs. Jones this morning.

Barthwick. I only want to do what's right in that matter. I had occasion to see Roper this afternoon. I mentioned it to him. He's coming in this evening. It all depends on what the detective says. I've had my doubts. I've been thinking it over.

Mrs. Barthwick. The woman impressed me most unfavourably. She seemed to have no shame. That affair she was talking about—she and the man when they were young, so immoral! And before you and Jack! I could have put her out of the room!

Barthwick. Oh! I don't want to excuse them, but in looking at these matters one must consider——

Mrs. Barthwick. Perhaps you'll say the man's employer was wrong in dismissing him?

THE SILVER BOX

BARTHWICK. Of course not. It's not there that I feel doubt. What I ask myself is——

JACK. Port, please, Dad.

BARTHWICK. [*Circulating the decanter in religious imitation of the rising and setting of the sun.*] I ask myself whether we are sufficiently careful in making inquiries about people before we engage them, especially as regards moral conduct.

JACK. Pass the port, please, Mother!

MRS. BARTHWICK. [*Passing it.*] My dear boy, aren't you drinking too much?

[JACK *fills his glass.*

MARLOW. [*Entering.*] Detective Snow to see you, sir.

BARTHWICK. [*Uneasily.*] Ah! say I'll be with him in a minute.

MRS. BARTHWICK. [*Without turning.*] Let him come in here, Marlow.

[SNOW *enters in an overcoat, his bowler hat in hand.*]

BARTHWICK. [*Half-rising.*] Oh! Good-evening!

SNOW. Good evening, sir; good evening, ma'am. I've called around to report what I've done, rather late, I'm afraid—another case took me away. [*He takes the silver box out of his pocket, causing a sensation in the* BARTHWICK *family.*] This is the identical article, I believe.

BARTHWICK. Certainly, certainly.

SNOW. Havin' your crest and cypher, as you described to me, sir, I'd no hesitation in the matter.

BARTHWICK. Excellent. Will you have a glass of [*he glances at the waning port*]—er—sherry—[*pours out sherry.*] Jack, just give Mr. Snow this.

[JACK *rises and gives the glass to* SNOW; *then, lolling in his chair, regards him indolently.*]

SNOW. [*Drinking off wine and putting down the glass.*]

After seeing you I went round to this woman's lodgings, sir. It's a low neighborhood, and I thought it as well to place a constable below—and not without 'e was wanted, as things turned out.

BARTHWICK. Indeed!

SNOW. Yes, sir, I 'ad some trouble. I asked her to account for the presence of the article. She could give me no answer, except to deny the theft; so I took her into custody; then her husband came for me, so I was obliged to take him, too, for assault. He was very violent on the way to the station—very violent—threatened you and your son, and altogether he was a handful, I can tell you.

MRS. BARTHWICK. What a ruffian he must be!

SNOW. Yes, ma'am, a rough customer.

JACK. [*Sipping his wine, bemused.*] Punch the beggar's head.

SNOW. Given to drink, as I understand, sir.

MRS. BARTHWICK. It's to be hoped he will get a severe punishment.

SNOW. The odd thing is, sir, that he persists in sayin' he took the box himself.

BARTHWICK. Took the box himself! [*He smiles.*] What does he think to gain by that?

SNOW. He says the young gentleman was intoxicated last night—[JACK *stops the cracking of a nut, and looks at* SNOW. BARTHWICK, *losing his smile, has put his wine-glass down; there is a silence*—SNOW, *looking from face to face, remarks*]—took him into the house and gave him whisky; and under the influence of an empty stomach the man says he took the box.

MRS. BARTHWICK. The impudent wretch!

BARTHWICK. D' you mean that he—er—intends to put this forward tomorrow——

SNOW. That'll be his line, sir; but whether he's endeavouring to shield his wife, or whether [*he looks at* JACK] there's something in it, will be for the magistrate to say.

MRS. BARTHWICK. [*Haughtily.*] Something in what? I don't understand you. As if my son would bring a man like that into the house!

BARTHWICK. [*From the fireplace, with an effort to be calm.*] My son can speak for himself, no doubt.—Well, Jack, what do you say?

MRS. BARTHWICK. [*Sharply.*] What does he say? Why, of course, he says the whole story's stuff!

JACK. [*Embarrassed.*] Well, of course, I—of course, I don't know anything about it.

MRS. BARTHWICK. I should think not, indeed! [*To Snow.*] The man is an audacious ruffian!

BARTHWICK. [*Suppressing jumps.*] But in view of my son's saying there's nothing in this—this fable—will it be necessary to proceed against the man under the circumstances?

SNOW. We shall have to charge him with the assault, sir. It would be as well for your son to come down to the Court. There'll be a remand, no doubt. The queer thing is there was quite a sum of money found on him, and a crimson silk purse. [BARTHWICK *starts;* JACK *rises and sits down again.*] I suppose the lady hasn't missed her purse?

BARTHWICK. [*Hastily.*] Oh, no! Oh! No!

JACK. No.

MRS. BARTHWICK. [*Dreamily.*] No! [*To Snow.*] I've been inquiring of the servants. This man *does* hang about the house. I shall feel much safer if he gets a good long sentence; I do think we ought to be protected against such ruffians.

BARTHWICK. Yes, yes, of course, on principle—but in this case we have a number of things to think of. [*To*

Snow.] I suppose, as you say, the man *must* be charged, eh?

Snow. No question about that, sir.

Barthwick. [*Staring gloomily at* Jack.] This prosecution goes very much against the grain with me. I have great sympathy with the poor. In my position I'm bound to recognise the distress there is amongst them. The condition of the people leaves much to be desired. D' you follow me? I wish I could see my way to drop it.

Mrs. Barthwick. [*Sharply.*] John! it's simply not fair to other people. It's putting property at the mercy of any one who likes to take it.

Barthwick. [*Trying to make signs to her aside.*] I'm not defending him, not at all. I'm trying to look at the matter broadly.

Mrs. Barthwick. Nonsense, John, there's a time for everything.

Snow. [*Rather sardonically.*] I might point out, sir, that to withdraw the charge of stealing would not make much difference, because the facts must come out [*he looks significantly at* Jack] in reference to the assault; and as I said that charge will have to go forward.

Barthwick. [*Hastily.*] Yes, ah! exactly! It's entirely on the woman's account—entirely a matter of my own private feelings.

Snow. If I were you, sir, I should let things take their course. It's not likely there'll be much difficulty. These things are very quick settled.

Barthwick. [*Doubtfully.*] You think so—you think so?

Jack. [*Rousing himself.*] I say, what shall I have to swear to?

Snow. That's best known to yourself, sir. [*Retreating to the door.*] Better employ a solicitor, sir, in case anything should arise. We shall have the butler prove the loss of the article. You'll excuse me going, I'm rather pressed to-night. The case may come on any time after eleven. Good evening, sir; good evening, ma'am. I shall have to produce the box in court tomorrow, so if you'll excuse me, sir, I may as well take it with me.

[*He takes the silver box and leaves them with a little bow.*]

[BARTHWICK *makes a move to follow him, then dashing his hands beneath his coat-tails, speaks with desperation.*]

BARTHWICK. I do wish you'd leave me to manage things myself. You *will* put your nose into matters you know nothing of. A pretty mess you've made of this!

MRS. BARTHWICK. [*Coldly.*] I don't in the least know what you're talking about. If you can't stand up for your rights, I can. I've no patience with your principles, it's such nonsense.

BARTHWICK. Principles! Good Heavens! What have principles to do with it, for goodness sake? Don't you know that Jack was drunk last night!

JACK. Dad!

MRS. BARTHWICK. [*In horror, rising.*] Jack!

JACK. Look here, Mother—I had supper. Everybody does. I mean to say—you know what I mean—it's absurd to call it being drunk. At Oxford everybody gets a bit "on" sometimes——

MRS. BARTHWICK. Well, I think it's most dreadful! If that is really what you do at Oxford——

JACK. [*Angrily.*] Well, why did you send me there? One must do as other fellows do. It's such nonsense, I mean, to call it being drunk. Of course I'm awfully sorry. I've had such a beastly headache all day.

BARTHWICK. Tcha! If you'd only had the common decency to remember what happened when you came in.

THE SILVER BOX

Then we should know what truth there was in what this fellow says—as it is, it's all the most confounded darkness.

JACK. [*Staring as though at half-formed visions.*] I just get a—and then—it's gone——

MRS. BARTHWICK. Oh, Jack! do you mean to say you were so tipsy you can't even remember——

JACK. Look here, Mother! Of course I remember I came—I must have come——

BARTHWICK. [*Unguardedly, and walking up and down.*] Tcha!—and that infernal purse! Good Heavens! It'll get into the papers. Who on earth could have foreseen a thing like this? Better to have lost a dozen cigarette-boxes, and said nothing about it. [*To his wife.*] It's all your doing. I told you so from the first. I wish to goodness Roper would come!

MRS. BARTHWICK. [*Sharply.*] I don't know what you're talking about, John.

BARTHWICK. [*Turning on her.*] No, you—you—you don't know anything! [*Sharply.*] Where the devil is Roper? If he can see a way out of this he's a better man than I take him for. I defy *any* one to see a way out of it. *I* can't.

JACK. Look here, don't excite Dad—I can simply say I was too beastly tired, and don't remember anything except that I came in and [*in a dying voice*] went to bed the same as usual.

BARTHWICK. Went to bed? Who knows where you went —I've lost all confidence. For all I know you slept on the floor.

JACK. [*Indignantly.*] I didn't, I slept on the——

BARTHWICK. [*Sitting on the sofa.*] Who cares where you slept; what does it matter if he mentions the—the— a perfect disgrace?

Mrs. Barthwick. *What?* [*A silence.*] I *insist* on knowing.

Jack. Oh! nothing——

Mrs. Barthwick. Nothing? What do you mean by nothing, Jack? There's your father in such a state about it——

Jack. It's only my purse.

Mrs. Barthwick. Your purse! You know perfectly well you haven't got one.

Jack. Well, it was somebody else's—it was all a joke—I didn't want the beastly thing——

Mrs. Barthwick. Do you mean that you had another person's purse, and that this man took it too?

Barthwick. Tcha! Of course he took it too! A man like that Jones will make the most of it. It'll get into the papers.

Mrs. Barthwick. I don't understand. What on earth is all the fuss about? [*Bending over* Jack, *and softly.*] Jack, now tell me, dear! Don't be afraid. What is it? Come!

Jack. Oh, don't, Mother!

Mrs. Barthwick. But don't what, dear?

Jack. It was pure sport. I don't know how I got the thing. Of course I'd had a bit of a row—I didn't know what I was doing—I was—I was—well, you know—I suppose I must have pulled the bag out of her hand.

Mrs. Barthwick. Out of her hand? Whose hand? What bag—whose bag?

Jack. Oh! I don't know—*her* bag—it belonged to—[*in a desperate and rising voice*] a woman.

Mrs. Barthwick. A woman? *Oh! Jack! No!*

Jack. [*Jumping up.*] You *would* have it. I didn't want to tell you. It's not my fault.

[*The door opens and* Marlow *ushers in a man*

THE SILVER BOX

of middle age, inclined to corpulence, in evening dress.. He has a ruddy, thin moustache, and dark, quick-moving little eyes. His eyebrows are Chinese.]

MARLOW. Mr. Roper, sir. [*He leaves the room.*

ROPER. [*With a quick look around.*] How do you do? [*But neither* JACK *nor* MRS. BARTHWICK *make a sign.*

BARTHWICK. [*Hurrying.*] Thank goodness you've come, Roper. You remember what I told you this afternoon; we've just had the detective here.

ROPER. Got the box?

BARTHWICK. Yes, yes, but look here—it wasn't the charwoman at all; her drunken loafer of a husband took the things—he says that fellow there [*he waves his hand at* JACK, *who with his shoulder raised, seems trying to ward off a blow*] let him into the house last night. Can you imagine such a thing?

[*Roper laughs.*

BARTHWICK. [*With excited emphasis.*] It's no laughing matter, Roper. I told you about that business of Jack's too—don't you see—the brute took both the things—took that infernal purse. It'll get into the papers.

ROPER. [*Raising his eyebrows.*] H'm! The purse! Depravity in high life! What does your son say?

BARTHWICK. He remembers nothing. D——n! Did you ever see such a mess? It'll get into the papers.

MRS. BARTHWICK. [*With her hand across her eyes.*] Oh! it's not that——

[BARTHWICK *and* ROPER *turn and look at her.*]

BARTHWICK. It's the idea of that woman—she's just heard——

[ROPER *nods. And* MRS. BARTHWICK, *setting her lips, gives a slow look at* JACK, *and sits down at the table.*]

What on earth's to be done, Roper? A ruffian like this Jones will make all the capital he can out of that purse.

MRS. BARTHWICK. I don't believe that Jack took that purse.

BARTHWICK. What—when the woman came here for it this morning?

MRS. BARTHWICK. Here? She had the impudence? Why wasn't I told?

> [*She looks round from face to face—no one answers her, there is a pause.*]

BARTHWICK. [*Suddenly.*] What's to be done, Roper?

ROPER. [*Quietly to* JACK.] I suppose you didn't leave your latch-key in the door?

JACK. [*Sullenly.*] Yes, I did.

BARTHWICK. Good heavens! What next?

MRS. BARTHWICK. I'm certain you never let that man into the house, Jack, it's a wild invention. I'm sure there's not a word of truth in it, Mr. Roper.

ROPER. [*Very suddenly.*] Where did you sleep last night?

JACK. [*Promptly.*] On the sofa, there—[*hesitating*] that is—I——

BARTHWICK. On the sofa? D' you mean to say you didn't go to bed?

JACK. [*Sullenly.*] No.

BARTHWICK. If you don't remember anything, how can you remember that?

JACK. Because I woke up there in the morning.

MRS. BARTHWICK. Oh, Jack!

BARTHWICK. Good Gracious!

JACK. And Mrs. Jones saw me. I wish you wouldn't bait me so.

ROPER. Do you remember giving any one a drink?

JACK. By Jove, I do seem to remember a fellow with—

THE SILVER BOX

a fellow with——[*He looks at Roper.*] I say, d' you want me——?

ROPER. [*Quick as lightning.*] With a dirty face?

JACK. [*With illumination.*] I do—I distinctly remember his——

> [BARTHWICK *moves abruptly;* MRS. BARTHWICK *looks at* ROPER *angrily, and touches her son's arm.*]

MRS. BARTHWICK. You don't remember, it's ridiculous! I don't believe the man was ever here at all.

BARTHWICK. You must speak the truth; if it *is* the truth. But if you *do* remember such a dirty business, I shall wash my hands of you altogether.

JACK. [*Glaring at them.*] Well, what the devil——

MRS. BARTHWICK. Jack!

JACK. Well, Mother, I—I—don't know what you *do* want.

MRS. BARTHWICK. We want you to speak the truth and say you never let this low man into the house.

BARTHWICK. Of course if you think that you really gave this man whisky in that disgraceful way, and let him see what you'd been doing, and were in such a disgusting condition that you don't remember a word of it——

ROPER. [*Quick.*] I've no memory myself—never had.

BARTHWICK. [*Desperately.*] I don't know what you're to say.

ROPER. [*To* JACK.] Say nothing at all! Don't put yourself in a false position. The man stole the things or the woman stole the things, you had nothing to do with it. You were asleep on the sofa.

MRS. BARTHWICK. Your leaving the latch-key in the door was quite bad enough, there's no need to mention anything else. [*Touching his forehead softly.*] My dear, how hot your head is!

JACK. But I want to know what I'm to do. [*Passionately.*] I won't be badgered like this.

[MRS. BARTHWICK *recoils from him.*

ROPER. [*Very quickly.*] You forget all about it. You were asleep.

JACK. Must I go down to the Court to-morrow?

ROPER. [*Shaking his head.*] No.

BARTHWICK. [*In a relieved voice.*] Is that so?

ROPER. Yes.

BARTHWICK. But *you'll* go, Roper.

ROPER. Yes.

JACK. [*With wan cheerfulness.*] Thanks, awfully! So long as I don't have to go. [*Putting his hand up to his head.*] I think if you'll excuse me—I've had a most beastly day. [*He looks from his father to his mother.*]

MRS. BARTHWICK. [*Turning quickly.*] Good-night, my boy.

JACK. Good-night, Mother.

[*He goes out.* MRS. BARTHWICK *heaves a sigh. There is a silence.*]

BARTHWICK. He gets off too easily. But for my money that woman would have prosecuted him.

ROPER. You find money useful.

BARTHWICK. I've my doubts whether we ought to hide the truth——

ROPER. There'll be a remand.

BARTHWICK. What! D' you mean he'll have to *appear* on the remand.

ROPER. Yes.

BARTHWICK. H'm, I thought you'd be able to—— Look here, Roper, you *must* keep that purse out of the papers. [*Roper fixes his little eyes on him and nods.*]

MRS. BARTHWICK. Mr. Roper, don't you think the magistrate ought to be told what sort of people these Joneses are; I mean about their immorality before they were married. I don't know if John told you.

ROPER. Afraid it's not material.

MRS. BARTHWICK. Not material?

ROPER. Purely private life! May have happened to the magistrate.

BARTHWICK. [*With a movement as if to shift a burden.*] Then you'll take the thing into your hands?

ROPER. If the gods are kind. [*He holds his hand out.*]

BARTHWICK. [*Shaking it dubiously.*] Kind—eh? What? You going?

ROPER. Yes. I've another case, something like yours—most unexpected.

> [*He bows to* MRS. BARTHWICK, *and goes out, followed by* BARTHWICK, *talking to the last.* MRS. BARTHWICK *at the table bursts into smothered sobs.* BARTHWICK *returns.*]

BARTHWICK. [*To himself.*] There'll be a scandal!

MRS. BARTHWICK. [*Disguising her grief at once.*] I simply can't imagine what Roper means by making a joke of a thing like that!

BARTHWICK. [*Staring strangely.*] You! You can't imagine anything! You've no more imagination than a fly!

MRS. BARTHWICK. [*Angrily.*] You dare to tell me that I have no imagination.

BARTHWICK. [*Flustered.*] I—I'm upset. From beginning to end, the whole thing has been utterly against my principles.

MRS. BARTHWICK. *Rubbish!* You haven't any! Your principles are nothing in the world but sheer—fright!

BARTHWICK. [*Walking to the window.*] I've never been frightened in my life. You heard what Roper said. It's enough to upset one when a thing like this happens. Everything one says and does seems to turn in one's mouth—it's—it's uncanny. It's not the sort of thing I've been accustomed to. [*As though stifling, he throws the windows open. The faint sobbing of a child comes in.*] What's that?

[*They listen.*

MRS. BARTHWICK. [*Sharply.*] I can't stand that crying. I must send Marlow to stop it. My nerves are all on edge.

[*She rings the bell.*

BARTHWICK. I'll shut the window; you'll hear nothing.

[*He shuts the window. There is silence.*

MRS. BARTHWICK. [*Sharply.*] That's no good! It's on my nerves. Nothing upsets me like a child's crying. [*Marlow comes in.*] What's that noise of crying, Marlow? It sounds like a child.

BARTHWICK. It is a child. I can see it against the railings.

MARLOW. [*Opening the window, and looking out—quietly.*] It's Mrs. Jones's little boy, ma'am; he came here after his mother.

MRS. BARTHWICK. [*Moving quickly to the window.*] Poor little chap! John, we oughtn't to go on with this!

BARTHWICK. [*Sitting heavily in a chair.*] Ah! but it's out of our hands!

[MRS. BARTHWICK *turns her back to the window. There is an expression of distress on her face. She stands motionless, compressing her lips. The crying begins again.* BARTHWICK *covers his ears with his hands, and* MARLOW *shuts the window. The crying ceases.*]

The curtain falls.

THE SILVER BOX 53

ACT III

Eight days have passed, and the scene is a London Police Court at one o'clock. A canopied seat of Justice is surmounted by the lion and unicorn. Before the fire a worn-looking MAGISTRATE *is warming his coat-tails, and staring at two little girls in faded blue and orange rags, who are placed before the dock. Close to the witness-box is a* RELIEVING OFFICER *in an overcoat, and a short brown beard. Beside the little girls stands a bald* POLICE CONSTABLE. *On the front bench are sitting* BARTHWICK *and* ROPER, *and behind them* JACK. *In the railed enclosure are seedy-looking men and women. Some prosperous constables sit or stand about.*

MAGISTRATE. [*In his paternal and ferocious voice, hissing his s's.*] Now let us dispose of these young ladies.

USHER. Theresa Livens, Maud Livens.

> [*The bald* CONSTABLE *indicates the little girls, who remain silent, disillusioned, inattentive.*]

Relieving Officer!

> [*The* RELIEVING OFFICER *steps into the witness-box.*]

USHER. The evidence you give to the Court shall be the truth, the whole truth, and nothing but the truth, so help you God! Kiss the book!

> [*The book is kissed.*

RELIEVING OFFICER. [*In a monotone, pausing slightly at each sentence end, that his evidence may be incribed.*] About ten o'clock this morning, your Worship, I found these two little girls in Blue Street, Pulham, crying outside a public-house. Asked where their home was, they said they had no home. Mother had gone away. Asked about their father. Their father had no work. Asked where they slept last night. At their aunt's. I've made inquiries, your Worship. The wife has broken up the home and gone on the streets. The husband is out of work and living in common lodging-houses. The husband's sister has eight children of her own, and says she can't afford to keep these little girls any longer.

MAGISTRATE. [*Returning to his seat beneath the canopy of Justice.*] Now, let me see. You say the mother is on the streets; what evidence have you of that?

RELIEVING OFFICER. I have the husband here, your Worship.

MAGISTRATE. Very well; then let us see him.

> [*There are cries of* "LIVENS." *The* MAGISTRATE *leans forward, and stares with hard compassion at the little girls.* LIVENS *comes in. He is quiet, with grizzled hair, and a muffler for a collar. He stands beside the witness-box.*]

And you are their father? Now, why don't you keep your little girls at home. How is it you leave them to wander about the streets like this?

LIVENS. I've got no home, your Worship. I'm living from 'and to mouth. I've got no work; and nothin' to keep them on.

MAGISTRATE. How is that?

LIVENS. [*Ashamedly.*] My wife, she broke my 'ome up, and pawned the things.

MAGISTRATE. But what made you let her?

LIVENS. Your Worship, I'd no chance to stop 'er; she did it when I was out lookin' for work.

MAGISTRATE. Did you ill-treat her?

LIVENS. [*Emphatically.*] I never raised my 'and to her in my life, your Worship.

MAGISTRATE. Then what was it—did she drink?

LIVENS. Yes, your Worship.

MAGISTRATE. Was she loose in her behaviour?

THE SILVER BOX

LIVENS. [*In a low voice.*] Yes, your Worship.

MAGISTRATE. And where is she now?

LIVENS. I don't know, your Worship. She went off with a man, and after that I——

MAGISTRATE. Yes, yes. Who knows anything of her? [*To the bald* CONSTABLE.] Is she known here?

RELIEVING OFFICER. Not in this district, your Worship; but I have ascertained that she is well known——

MAGISTRATE. Yes—yes; we'll stop at that. Now [*To the Father*] you say that she has broken up your home, and left these little girls. What provision can you make for them? You look a strong man.

LIVENS. So I am, your Worship. I'm willin' enough to work, but for the life of me I can't get anything to do.

MAGISTRATE. But have you tried?

LIVENS. I've tried everything, your Worship—I've tried my 'ardest.

MAGISTRATE. Well, well—— [*There is a silence.*

RELIEVING OFFICER. If your Worship thinks it's a case, my people are willing to take them.

MAGISTRATE. Yes, yes, I know; but I've no evidence that this man is not the proper guardian for his children.

[*He rises and goes back to the fire.*

RELIEVING OFFICER. The mother, your Worship, is able to get access to them.

MAGISTRATE. Yes, yes; the mother, of course, is an improper person to have anything to do with them. [*To the Father.*] Well, now what do you say?

LIVENS. Your Worship, I can only say that if I could get work I should be only too willing to provide for them. But what can I do, your Worship? Here I am obliged to live from 'and to mouth in these 'ere common lodging-houses. I'm a strong man—I'm willing to work—I'm half as alive again as some of 'em—but you see, your Worship, my 'air's turned a bit, owing to the fever—[*Touches his hair*]—and that's against me; and I don't seem to get a chance anyhow.

MAGISTRATE. Yes—yes. [*Slowly.*] Well, I think it's a case. [*Staring his hardest at the little girls.*] Now, are you willing that these little girls should be sent to a home?

LIVENS. Yes, your Worship, I should be very willing.

MAGISTRATE. Well, I'll remand them for a week. Bring them again to-day week; if I see no reason against it then, I'll make an order.

RELIEVING OFFICER. To-day week, your Worship.

[*The bald* CONSTABLE *takes the little girls out by the shoulders. The father follows them. The* MAGISTRATE, *returning to his seat, bends over and talks to his* CLERK *inaudibly.*]

BARTHWICK. [*Speaking behind his hand.*] A painful case, Roper; very distressing state of things.

ROPER. Hundreds like this in the Police Courts.

BARTHWICK. Most distressing! The more I see of it, the more important this question of the condition of the people seems to become. I shall certainly make a point of taking up the cudgels in the House. I shall move——

[*The* MAGISTRATE *ceases talking to his* CLERK.

CLERK. Remands!

[BARTHWICK *stops abruptly. There is a stir and* MRS. JONES *comes in by the public door;* JONES, *ushered by policemen, comes from the prisoner's door. They file into the dock.*]

CLERK. James Jones, Jane Jones.
USHER. Jane Jones!
BARTHWICK. [*In a whisper.*] The purse—the purse

THE SILVER BOX

must be kept out of it, Roper. Whatever happens you must keep that out of the papers.

[ROPER *nods*.

BALD CONSTABLE. Hush!

[MRS. JONES, *dressed in her thin, black, wispy dress, and black straw hat, stands motionless with hands crossed on the front rail of the dock.* JONES *leans against the back rail of the dock, and keeps half turning, glancing defiantly about him. He is haggard and unshaven.*]

CLERK. [*Consulting with his papers.*] This is the case remanded from last Wednesday, sir. Theft of a silver cigarette-box and assault on the police; the two charges were taken together. Jane Jones! James Jones!

MAGISTRATE. [*Staring.*] Yes, yes; I remember.

CLERK. Jane Jones.

MRS. JONES. Yes, sir.

CLERK. Do you admit stealing a silver cigarette-box valued at five pounds, ten shillings, from the house of John Barthwick, M.P., between the hours of 11 P.M. on Easter Monday and 8.45 A.M. on Easter Tuesday last? Yes, or no?

MRS. JONES. [*In a low voice.*] No, sir, I do not, sir.

CLERK. James Jones? Do you admit stealing a silver cigarette-box valued at five pounds, ten shillings, from the house of John Barthwick, M.P., between the hours of 11 P. M. on Easter Monday and 8.45 A. M. on Easter Tuesday last. And further making an assault on the police when in the execution of their duty at 3 P.M. on Easter Tuesday? Yes, or no?

JONES. [*Sullenly.*] Yes, but I've got a lot to say about it.

MAGISTRATE. [*To the* CLERK.] Yes—yes. But how comes it that these two people are charged with the same offence? Are they husband and wife?

CLERK. Yes, sir. You remember you ordered a remand for further evidence as to the story of the male prisoner.

MAGISTRATE. Have they been in custody since?

CLERK. You released the woman on her own recognisances, sir.

MAGISTRATE. Yes, yes, this is the case of the silver box; I remember now. Well?

CLERK. Thomas Marlow.

[*The cry of "THOMAS MARLOW" is repeated. MARLOW comes in, and steps into the witness-box.*]

USHER. The evidence you give to the court shall be the truth, the whole truth, and nothing but the truth, so help you God. Kiss the book.

[*The book is kissed. The silver box is handed up, and placed on the rail.*]

CLERK. [*Reading from his papers.*] Your name is Thomas Marlow? Are you butler to John Barthwick, M.P., of 6, Rockingham Gate?

MARLOW. Yes, sir.

CLERK. Is that the box?

MARLOW. Yes, sir.

CLERK. And did you miss the same at 8.45 on the following morning, on going to remove the tray?

MARLOW. Yes, sir.

CLERK. Is the female prisoner known to you?

[MARLOW *nods.*

Is she the charwoman employed at 6, Rockingham Gate?

[*Again* MARLOW *nods.*

Did you at the time of your missing the box find her in the room alone?

MARLOW. Yes, sir.

CLERK. Did you afterwards communicate the loss to your employer, and did he send you to the police station?

THE SILVER BOX

MARLOW. Yes, sir.

CLERK [*To* MRS. JONES.] Have you anything to ask him?

MRS. JONES. No, sir, nothing, thank you, sir.

CLERK. [*To* JONES.] James Jones, have you anything to ask this witness?

JONES. I don't know 'im.

MAGISTRATE. Are you sure you put the box in the place you say at the time you say?

MARLOW. Yes, your Worship.

MAGISTRATE. Very well; then now let us have the officer.

[MARLOW *leaves the box, and* SNOW *goes into it.*

USHER. The evidence you give to the court shall be the truth, the whole truth, and nothing but the truth, so help you God. [*The book is kissed.*

CLERK. [*Reading from his papers.*] Your name is Robert Snow? You are a detective in the X. B. division of the Metropolitan police force? According to instructions received did you on Easter Tuesday last proceed to the prisoner's lodgings at 34, Merthyr Street, St. Soames's? And did you on entering see the box produced, lying on the table?

SNOW. Yes, sir.

CLERK. Is that the box?

SNOW. [*Fingering the box.*] Yes, sir.

CLERK. And did you thereupon take possession of it, and charge the female prisoner with theft of the box from 6, Rockingham Gate? And did she deny the same?

SNOW. Yes, sir.

CLERK. Did you take her into custody?

SNOW. Yes, sir.

MAGISTRATE. What was her behaviour?

SNOW. Perfectly quiet, your Worship. She persisted in the denial. That's all.

MAGISTRATE. Do you know her?

SNOW. No, your Worship.

MAGISTRATE. Is she known here?

BALD CONSTABLE. No, your Worship, they're neither of them known, we've nothing against them at all.

CLERK. [*To* MRS. JONES.] Have you anything to ask the officer?

MRS. JONES. No, sir, thank you, I've nothing to ask him.

MAGISTRATE. Very well then—go on.

CLERK. [*Reading from his papers.*] And while you were taking the female prisoner did the male prisoner interpose, and endeavour to hinder you in the execution of your duty, and did he strike you a blow?

SNOW. Yes, sir.

CLERK. And did he say, "You let her go, I took the box myself"?

SNOW. He did.

CLERK. And did you blow your whistle and obtain the assistance of another constable, and take him into custody?

SNOW. I did.

CLERK. Was he violent on the way to the station, and did he use bad language, and did he several times repeat that he had taken the box himself?

[SNOW *nods.*

Did you thereupon ask him in what manner he had stolen the box? And did you understand him to say he had entered the house at the invitation of young Mr. Barthwick

[BARTHWICK, *turning in his seat, frowns at* ROPER.]

after midnight on Easter Monday, and partaken of whisky, and that under the influence of the whisky he had taken the box?

SNOW. I did, sir.

THE SILVER BOX

CLERK. And was his demeanour throughout very violent?

SNOW. It *was* very violent.

JONES. [*Breaking in.*] Violent—of course it was! You put your 'ands on my wife when I kept tellin' you I took the thing myself.

MAGISTRATE. [*Hissing, with protruded neck.*] Now—you will have your chance of saying what you want to say presently. Have you anything to ask the officer?

JONES. [*Sullenly.*] No.

MAGISTRATE. Very well then. Now let us hear what the female prisoner has to say first.

MRS. JONES. Well, your Worship, of course I can only say what I've said all along, that I didn't take the box.

MAGISTRATE. Yes, but did you know that it was taken?

MRS. JONES. No, your Worship. And, of course, to what my husband says, your Worship, I can't speak of my own knowledge. Of course, I know that he came home very late on the Monday night. It was past one o'clock when he came in, and he was not himself at all.

MAGISTRATE. Had he been drinking?

MRS. JONES. Yes, your Worship.

MAGISTRATE. And was he drunk?

MRS. JONES. Yes, your Worship, he was almost quite drunk.

MAGISTRATE. And did he say anything to you?

MRS. JONES. No, your Worship, only to call me names. And of course in the morning when I got up and went to work he was asleep. And I don't know anything more about it until I came home again. Except that Mr. Barthwick—that's my employer, your Worship—told me the box was missing.

MAGISTRATE. Yes, yes.

MRS. JONES. But of course when I was shaking out my

husband's coat the cigarette-box fell out and all the cigarettes were scattered on the bed.

MAGISTRATE. You say all the cigarettes were scattered on the bed? [*To* SNOW.] Did you see the cigarettes scattered on the bed?

SNOW. No, your Worship, I did not.

MAGISTRATE. You see he says he didn't see them.

JONES. Well, they were there for all that.

SNOW. I can't say, your Worship, that I had the opportunity of going round the room; I had all my work cut out with the male prisoner.

MAGISTRATE. [*To* MRS. JONES.] Well, what more have you to say?

MRS. JONES. Of course when I saw the box, your Worship, I was dreadfully upset, and I couldn't think why he had done such a thing; when the officer came we were having words about it, because it is ruin to me, your Worship, in my profession, and I have three little children dependent on me.

MAGISTRATE. [*Protruding his neck.*] Yes—yes—but what did he say to you?

MRS. JONES. I asked him whatever came over him to do such a thing—and he said it was the drink. He said he had had too much to drink, and something came over him. And of course, your Worship, he had had very little to eat all day, and the drink does go to the head when you have not had enough to eat. Your Worship may not know, but it is the truth. And I would like to say that all through his married life, I have never known him to do such a thing before, though we have passed through great hardships and [*speaking with soft emphasis*] I am quite sure he would not have done it if he had been himself at the time.

MAGISTRATE. Yes, yes. But don't you know that that is no excuse?

THE SILVER BOX

Mrs. Jones. Yes, your Worship. I know that it is no excuse.

[*The* Magistrate *leans over and parleys with his* Clerk.]

Jack. [*Leaning over from his seat behind.*] I say, Dad——

Barthwick. Tsst! [*Sheltering his mouth he speaks to* Roper.] Roper, you had better get up now and say that considering the circumstances and the poverty of the prisoners, we have no wish to proceed any further, and if the magistrate would deal with the case as one of disorder only on the part of——

Bald Constable. Hssshh!

[Roper *shakes his head.*

Magistrate. Now, supposing what you say and what your husband says is true, what I have to consider is—how did he obtain access to this house, and were you in any way a party to his obtaining access? You are the charwoman employed at the house?

Mrs. Jones. Yes, your Worship, and of course if I had let him into the house it would have been very wrong of me; and I have never done such a thing in any of the houses where I have been employed.

Magistrate. Well—so you say. Now let us hear what story the male prisoner makes of it.

Jones. [*Who leans with his arms on the dock behind, speaks in a slow, sullen voice.*] Wot I say is wot my wife says. I've never been 'ad up in a police court before, an' I can prove I took it when in liquor. I told her, and she can tell you the same, that I was goin' to throw the thing into the water sooner then 'ave it on my mind.

Magistrate. But how did you get into the *house?*

Jones. I was passin'. I was goin' 'ome from the "Goat and Bells."

MAGISTRATE. The "Goat and Bells,"—what is that? A public-house?

JONES. Yes, at the corner. It was Bank 'oliday, an' I'd a drop to drink. I see this young Mr. Barthwick tryin' to find the keyhole on the wrong side of the door.

MAGISTRATE. Well?

JONES. [*Slowly and with many pauses.*] Well—I 'elped 'im to find it—drunk as a lord 'e was. He goes on, an' comes back again, and says, I've got nothin' for you, 'e says, but come in an' 'ave a drink. So I went in just as you might 'ave done yourself. We 'ad a drink o' whisky just as you might have 'ad, 'nd young Mr. Barthwick says to me, "Take a drink 'nd a smoke. Take anything you like, 'e says." And then he went to sleep on the sofa. I 'ad some more whisky—an' I 'ad a smoke—and I 'ad some more whisky—an' I carn't tell yer what 'appened after that.

MAGISTRATE. Do you mean to say that you were so drunk that you can remember nothing?

JACK. [*Softly to his father.*] I say, that's exactly what——

BARTHWICK. Tssh!

JONES. That's what I do mean.

MAGISTRATE. And yet you say you stole the box?

JONES. I never stole the box. I took it.

MAGISTRATE. [*Hissing with protruded neck.*] You did not steal it—you took it. Did it belong to you—what is that but stealing?

JONES. I took it.

MAGISTRATE. You took it—you took it away from their house and you took it to your house——

JONES. [*Sullenly breaking in.*] I ain't got a house.

MAGISTRATE. Very well, let us hear what this young man Mr.—Mr. Barthwick—has to say to your story.

[SNOW *leaves the witness-box. The* BALD CON-

THE SILVER BOX

STABLE *beckons* JACK, *who, clutching his hat, goes into the witness-box.* ROPER *moves to the table set apart for his profession.*]

SWEARING CLERK. The evidence you give to the court shall be the truth, the whole truth, and nothing but the truth, so help you God. Kiss the book.

[*The book is kissed.*

ROPER. [*Examining.*] What is your name?

JACK. [*In a low voice.*] John Barthwick, Junior.

[*The* CLERK *writes it down.*

ROPER. Where do you live?

JACK. At 6, Rockingham Gate.

[*All his answers are recorded by the Clerk.*

ROPER. You are the son of the owner?

JACK. [*In a very low voice.*] Yes.

ROPER. Speak up, please. Do you know the prisoners?

JACK. [*Looking at the* JONESES, *in a low voice.*] I've seen Mrs. Jones. I—[*in a loud voice*] don't know the man.

JONES. Well, I know you!

BALD CONSTABLE. Hssh!

ROPER. Now, did you come in late on the night of Easter Monday?

JACK. Yes.

ROPER. And did you by mistake leave your latch-key in the door?

JACK. Yes.

MAGISTRATE. Oh! You left your latch-key in the door?

ROPER. And is that all you can remember about your coming in?

JACK. [*In a loud voice.*] Yes, it is.

MAGISTRATE. Now, you have heard the male prisoner's story, what do you say to that?

JACK. [*Turning to the* MAGISTRATE, *speaks suddenly in a confident, straightforward voice.*] The fact of the matter is, sir, that I'd been out to the theatre that night, and had supper afterwards, and I came in late.

MAGISTRATE. Do you remember this man being outside when you came in?

JACK. No, sir. [*He hesitates.*] I don't think I do.

MAGISTRATE. [*Somewhat puzzled.*] Well, did he help you to open the door, as he says? Did *any* one help you to open the door?

JACK. No, sir—I don't think so, sir—I don't know.

MAGISTRATE. You don't know? But you must know. It isn't a usual thing for you to have the door opened for you, is it?

JACK. [*With a shamefaced smile.*] No.

MAGISTRATE. Very well, then——

JACK. [*Desperately.*] The fact of the matter is, sir, I'm afraid I'd had too much champagne that night.

MAGISTRATE. [*Smiling.*] Oh! you'd had too much champagne?

JONES. May I ask the gentleman a question?

MAGISTRATE. Yes—yes—you may ask him what questions you like.

JONES. Don't you remember you said you was a Liberal, same as your father, and you asked me wot I was?

JACK. [*With his hand against his brow.*] I seem to remember——

JONES. And I said to you, "I'm a bloomin' Conservative," I said; an' you said to me, "You look more like one of these 'ere Socialists. Take wotever you like," you said.

JACK. [*With sudden resolution.*] No, I don't. I don't remember anything of the sort.

JONES. Well, I do, an' my word's as good as yours. I've never been had up in a police court before. Look 'ere, don't you remember you had a sky-blue bag in your 'and——

[BARTHWICK *jumps.*

THE SILVER BOX

ROPER. I submit to your Worship that these questions are hardly to the point, the prisoner having admitted that he himself does not remember anything. [*There is a smile on the face of Justice.*] It is a case of the blind leading the blind.

JONES. [*Violently.*] I've done no more than wot he 'as. I'm a poor man; I've got no money an' no friends—he's a toff—he can do wot I can't.

MAGISTRATE. Now, now! All this won't help you—you must be quiet. You say you took this box? Now, what made you take it? Were you pressed for money?

JONES. I'm always pressed for money.

MAGISTRATE. Was that the reason you took it?

JONES. No.

MAGISTRATE. [*To* SNOW.] Was anything found on him?

SNOW. Yes, your Worship. There was six pounds twelve shillin's found on him, and this purse.

[*The red silk purse is handed to the* MAGISTRATE. BARTHWICK *rises in his seat, but hastily sits down again.*]

MAGISTRATE. [*Staring at the purse.*] Yes, yes—let me see—— [*There is a silence.*] No, no, I've nothing before me as to the purse. How did you come by all that money?

JONES. [*After a long pause, suddenly.*] I declines to say.

MAGISTRATE. But if you had all that money, what made you take this box?

JONES. I took it out of spite.

MAGISTRATE. [*Hissing, with protruded neck.*] You took it out of spite? Well now, that's something! But do you imagine you can go about the town taking things out of spite?

JONES. If you had my life, if you'd been out of work——

MAGISTRATE. Yes, yes; I know—because you're out of work you think it's an excuse for everything.

JONES. [*Pointing at* JACK.] You ask 'im wot made 'im take the——

ROPER. [*Quietly.*] Does your Worship require this witness in the box any longer?

MAGISTRATE. [*Ironically.*] I think not; he is hardly profitable.

> [JACK *leaves the witness-box, and hanging his head, resumes his seat.*]

JONES. You ask 'im wot made 'im take the lady's——

> [*But the* BALD CONSTABLE *catches him by the sleeve.*]

BALD CONSTABLE. Sssh!

MAGISTRATE. [*Emphatically.*] Now listen to me. I've nothing to do with what he may or may not have taken. Why did you resist the police in the execution of their duty?

JONES. It warn't their duty to take my wife, a respectable woman, that 'adn't done nothing.

MAGISTRATE. But I say it was. What made you strike the officer a blow?

JONES. Any man would a struck 'im a blow. I'd strike 'im again, I would.

MAGISTRATE. You are not making your case any better by violence. How do you suppose we could get on if everybody behaved like you?

JONES. [*Leaning forward, earnestly.*] Well, wot about 'er; who's to make up to 'er for this? Who's to give 'er back 'er good name?

MRS. JONES. Your Worship, it's the children that's preying on his mind, because of course I've lost my work. And I've had to find another room owing to the scandal.

THE SILVER BOX

MAGISTRATE. Yes, yes, I know—but if he hadn't acted like this nobody would have suffered.

JONES. [*Glaring round at* JACK.] I've done no worse than wot 'e 'as. Wot I want to know is wot's goin' to be done to 'im.

[*The* BALD CONSTABLE *again says* "*Hssh!*"]

ROPER. Mr. Barthwick wishes it known, your Worship, that considering the poverty of the prisoners he does not press the charge as to the box. Perhaps your Worship would deal with the case as one of disorder.

JONES. I don't want it smothered up, I want it all dealt with fair—I want my rights——

MAGISTRATE. [*Rapping his desk.*] Now you have said all you have to say, and you will be quiet.

[*There is a silence; the* MAGISTRATE *bends over and parleys with his* CLERK.]

Yes, I think I may discharge the woman. [*In a kindly voice he addresses* MRS. JONES, *who stands unmoving with her hands crossed on the rail.*] It is very unfortunate for you that this man has behaved as he has. It is not the consequences to him but the consequences to you. You have been brought here twice, you have lost your work—[*He glares at* JONES]—and this is what always happens. Now you may go away, and I am very sorry it was necessary to bring you here at all.

MRS. JONES. [*Softly.*] Thank you very much, your Worship.

[*She leaves the dock, and looking back at* JONES, *twists her fingers and is still.*]

MAGISTRATE. Yes, yes, but I can't pass it over. Go away, there's a good woman.

[MRS. JONES *stands back. The* MAGISTRATE *leans his head on his hand: then raising it he speaks to* JONES.]

Now, listen to me. Do you wisn the case to be settled here, or do you wish it to go before a jury?

JONES. [*Muttering.*] I don't want no jury.

MAGISTRATE. Very well then, I will deal with it here. [*After a pause.*] You have pleaded guilty to stealing this box——

JONES. Not to stealin'——

BALD CONSTABLE. Hssshh!

MAGISTRATE. And to assaulting the police——

JONES. Any man as was a man——

MAGISTRATE. Your conduct here has been most improper. You give the excuse that you were drunk when you stole the box. I tell you that is no excuse. If you choose to get drunk and break the law afterwards you must take the consequences. And let me tell you that men like you, who get drunk and give way to your spite or whatever it is that's in you, are—are—*a nuisance to the community.*

JACK. [*Leaning from his seat.*] Dad, that's what you said to me!

BARTHWICK. Tsst!

[*There is a silence, while the* MAGISTRATE *consults his* CLERK; JONES *leans forward waiting.*]

MAGISTRATE. This is your first offence, and I am going to give you a light sentence. [*Speaking sharply, but without expression.*] One month with hard labour.

[*He bends, and parleys with his* CLERK. *The* BALD CONSTABLE *and another help* JONES *from the dock.*]

JONES. [*Stopping and twisting round.*] Call this justice? What about 'im? 'E got drunk! 'E took the purse —'e took the purse but [*in a muffled shout*] it's '*is money got 'im off—Justice!*

[*The prisoner's door is shut on* JONES, *and from*

THE SILVER BOX

the seedy-looking men and women comes a hoarse and whispering groan.]

MAGISTRATE. We will now adjourn for lunch! [*He rises from his seat.*]

[*The Court is in a stir.* ROPER *gets up and speaks to the reporter.* JACK, *throwing up his head, walks with a swagger to the corridor;* BARTHWICK *follows.*]

MRS. JONES. [*Turning to him with a humble gesture.*] Oh! sir!——

[BARTHWICK *hesitates, then yielding to his nerves, he makes a shame-faced gesture of refusal, and hurries out of court.* MRS. JONES *stands looking after him.*]

The curtain falls.

STRIFE

A DRAMA IN THREE ACTS

PERSONS OF THE PLAY

JOHN ANTHONY, *Chairman of the Trenartha Tin Plate Works*
EDGAR ANTHONY, *his son,*
FREDERIC H. WILDER,
WILLIAM SCANTLEBURY, } *Directors of the same*
OLIVER WANKLIN,
HENRY TENCH, *Secretary of the same*
FRANCIS UNDERWOOD, C. E., *Manager of the same*
SIMON HARNESS, *a Trades Union official*
DAVID ROBERTS,
JAMES GREEN,
JOHN BULGIN, } *the workmen's committee*
HENRY THOMAS,
GEORGE ROUS,
HENRY ROUS,
LEWIS,
JAGO,
EVANS, } *workmen at the Trenartha Tin Plate Works*
A BLACKSMITH,
DAVIES,
A RED-HAIRED YOUTH
BROWN,
FROST, *valet to John Anthony*
ENID UNDERWOOD, *wife of Francis Underwood, daughter of John Anthony*
ANNIE ROBERTS, *wife of David Roberts*
MADGE THOMAS, *daughter of Henry Thomas*
MRS. ROUS, *mother of George and Henry Rous*
MRS. BULGIN, *wife of John Bulgin*
MRS. YEO, *wife of a workman*
A PARLOURMAID *to the Underwoods*
JAN, *Madge's brother, a boy of ten*
A CROWD OF MEN ON STRIKE

The action takes place on February 7th between the hours of noon and six in the afternoon, close to the Trenartha Tin Plate Works, on the borders of England and Wales, where a strike has been in progress throughout the winter.

ACT I. *The dining-room of the Manager's house.*
ACT II., SCENE I. *The kitchen of the Roberts' cottage near the works.*
 SCENE II. *A space outside the works.*
ACT III. *The drawing-room of the Manager's house.*

ACT I

It is noon. In the Underwood's dining-room a bright fire is burning. On one side of the fireplace are double-doors leading to the drawing-room, on the other side a door leading to the hall. In the centre of the room a long dining-table without a cloth is set out as a Board table. At the head of it, in the Chairman's seat, sits JOHN ANTHONY, *an old man, big, clean-shaven, and high-coloured, with thick white hair, and thick dark eyebrows. His movements are rather slow and feeble, but his eyes are very much alive. There is a glass of water by his side. On his right sits his son* EDGAR, *an earnest-looking man of thirty, reading a newspaper. Next him* WANKLIN, *a man with jutting eyebrows, and silver-streaked light hair, is bending over transfer papers.* TENCH, *the Secretary, a short and rather humble, nervous man, with side whiskers, stands helping him. On* WANKLIN'S *right sits* UNDERWOOD, *the Manager, a quiet man, with a long, stiff jaw, and steady eyes. Back to the fire is* SCANTLEBURY, *a very large, pale, sleepy man, with grey hair, rather bald. Between him and the Chairman are two empty chairs.*

WILDER. [*Who is lean, cadaverous, and complaining, with drooping grey moustaches, stands before the fire.*] I say, this fire's the devil! Can I have a screen, Tench?

SCANTLEBURY. A screen, ah!

TENCH. Certainly, Mr. Wilder. [*He looks at* UNDERwood.] That is—perhaps the Manager—perhaps Mr. Underwood——

SCANTLEBURY. These fireplaces of yours, Underwood——

UNDERWOOD. [*Roused from studying some papers.*] A screen? Rather! I'm sorry. [*He goes to the door with a little smile.*] We're not accustomed to complaints of too much fire down here just now.

> [*He speaks as though he holds a pipe between his teeth, slowly, ironically.*]

WILDER. [*In an injured voice.*] You mean the men. H'm! [UNDERWOOD *goes out.*

SCANTLEBURY. Poor devils!

WILDER. It's their own fault, Scantlebury.

EDGAR. [*Holding out his paper.*] There's great distress among them, according to the *Trenartha News*.

WILDER. Oh, that rag! · Give it to Wanklin. Suit his Radical views. They call us monsters, I suppose. The editor of that rubbish ought to be shot.

EDGAR. [*Reading.*] "If the Board of worthy gentlemen who control the Trenartha Tin Plate Works from their arm-chairs in London would condescend to come and see for themselves the conditions prevailing amongst their workpeople during this strike——"

WILDER. Well, we *have* come.

EDGAR. [*Continuing.*] "We cannot believe that even their leg-of-mutton hearts would remain untouched."

> [WANKLIN *takes the paper from him.*

WILDER. Ruffian! I remember that fellow when he hadn't a penny to his name; little snivel of a chap that's made his way by blackguarding everybody who takes a different view to himself.

> [ANTHONY *says something that is not heard.*

WILDER. What does your father say?

EDGAR. He says "The kettle and the pot."

WILDER. H'm!

[*He sits down next to* SCANTLEBURY.

SCANTLEBURY. [*Blowing out his cheeks.*] I shall boil if I don't get that screen.

[UNDERWOOD *and* ENID *enter with a screen, which they place before the fire.* ENID *is tall; she has a small, decided face, and is twenty-eight years old.*]

ENID. Put it closer, Frank. Will that do, Mr. Wilder? It's the highest we've got.

WILDER. Thanks, capitally.

SCANTLEBURY. [*Turning, with a sigh of pleasure.*] Ah! Merci, Madame!

ENID. Is there anything else you want, Father? [ANTHONY *shakes his head.*] Edgar—anything?

EDGAR. You might give me a "J" nib, old girl.

ENID. There are some down there by Mr. Scantlebury.

SCANTLEBURY. [*Handing a little box of nibs.*] Ah! your brother uses "J's." What does the manager use? [*With expansive politeness.*] What does your husband use, Mrs. Underwood?

UNDERWOOD. A quill!

SCANTLEBURY. The homely product of the goose.

[*He holds out quills.*

UNDERWOOD. [*Drily.*] Thanks, if you can spare me one. [*He takes a quill.*] What about lunch, Enid?

ENID. [*Stopping at the double-doors and looking back.*] We're going to have lunch here, in the drawing-room, so you needn't hurry with your meeting.

[WANKLIN *and* WILDER *bow, and she goes out.*

SCANTLEBURY. [*Rousing himself, suddenly.*] Ah! Lunch! That hotel—— Dreadful! Did you try the whitebait last night? Fried fat!

WILDER. Past twelve! Aren't you going to read the minutes, Tench?

TENCH. [*Looking for the* CHAIRMAN'S *assent, reads in a rapid and monotonous voice.*] "At a Board Meeting held the 31st of January at the Company's Offices, 512, Cannon Street, E. C. Present—Mr. Anthony in the chair, Messrs. F. H. Wilder, William Scantlebury, Oliver Wanklin, and Edgar Anthony. Read letters from the Manager dated January 20th, 23d, 25th, 28th, relative to the strike at the Company's Works. Read letters to the Manager of January 21st, 24th, 26th, 29th. Read letter from Mr. Simon Harness, of the Central Union, asking for an interview with the Board. Read letters from the Men's Committee, signed David Roberts, James Green, John Bulgin, Henry Thomas, George Rous, desiring conference with the Board; and it was resolved that a special Board Meeting be called for February 7th at the house of the Manager, for the purpose of discussing the situation with Mr. Simon Harness and the Men's Committee on the spot. Passed twelve transfers, signed and sealed nine certificates and one balance certificate."

[*He pushes the book over to the* CHAIRMAN.

ANTHONY. [*With a heavy sigh.*] If it's your pleasure, sign the same.

[*He signs, moving the pen with difficulty.*

WANKLIN. What's the Union's game, Tench? They haven't made up their split with the men. What does Harness want this interview for?

TENCH. Hoping we shall come to a compromise, I think, sir; he's having a meeting with the men this afternoon.

WILDER. Harness! Ah! He's one of those cold-blooded, cool-headed chaps. I distrust them. I don't know that we didn't make a mistake to come down. What time'll the men be here?

STRIFE

UNDERWOOD. Any time now.

WILDER. Well, if we're not ready, they'll have to wait—won't do them any harm to cool their heels a bit.

SCANTLEBURY. [*Slowly.*] Poor devils! It's snowing. *What* weather!

UNDERWOOD. [*With meaning slowness.*] This house'll be the warmest place they've been in this winter.

WILDER. Well, I hope we're going to settle this business in time for me to catch the 6.30. I've got to take my wife to Spain to-morrow. [*Chattily.*] My old father had a strike at his works in '69; just such a February as this. They wanted to shoot him.

WANKLIN. What! In the close season?

WILDER. By George, there was no close season for employers then! He used to go down to his office with a pistol in his pocket.

SCANTLEBURY. [*Faintly alarmed.*] Not seriously?

WILDER. [*With finality.*] Ended in his shootin' one of 'em in the legs.

SCANTLEBURY. [*Unavoidably feeling his thigh.*] No? Which?

ANTHONY. [*Lifting the agenda paper.*] To consider the policy of the Board in relation to the strike.

[*There is a silence.*

WILDER. It's this infernal three-cornered duel—the Union, the men, and ourselves.

WANKLIN. We needn't consider the Union.

WILDER. It's my experience that you've always got to consider the Union, confound them! If the Union were going to withdraw their support from the men, as they've done, why did they ever allow them to strike at all?

EDGAR. We've had that over a dozen times.

WILDER. Well, I've never understood it! It's beyond me. They talk of the engineers' and furnacemen's demands being excessive—so they are—but that's not enough to make the Union withdraw their support. What's behind it?

UNDERWOOD. Fear of strikes at Harper's and Tinewell's.

WILDER. [*With triumph.*] Afraid of other strikes—now, that's a reason! Why couldn't we have been told that before?

UNDERWOOD. You were.

TENCH. You were absent from the Board that day, sir.

SCANTLEBURY. The men must have seen they had no chance when the Union gave them up. It's madness.

UNDERWOOD. It's Roberts!

WILDER. Just our luck, the men finding a fanatical firebrand like Roberts for leader. [*A pause.*

WANKLIN. [*Looking at* ANTHONY.] Well?

WILDER. [*Breaking in fussily.*] It's a regular mess. I don't like the position we're in; I don't like it; I've said so for a long time. [*Looking at* WANKLIN.] When Wanklin and I came down here before Christmas it looked as if the men must collapse. You thought so too, Underwood.

UNDERWOOD. Yes.

WILDER. Well, they haven't! Here we are, going from bad to worse—losing our customers—shares going down!

SCANTLEBURY. [*Shaking his head.*] M'm! M'm!

WANKLIN. What loss have we made by this strike, Tench?

TENCH. Over fifty thousand, sir!

SCANTLEBURY. [*Pained.*] You don't say!

WILDER. We shall never get it back.

TENCH. No, sir.

WILDER. Who'd have supposed the men were going to stick out like this—nobody suggested that.

[*Looking angrily at* TENCH.

SCANTLEBURY. [*Shaking his head.*] I've never liked a fight—never shall.

STRIFE

ANTHONY. No surrender! [*All look at him.*

WILDER. Who wants to surrender? [ANTHONY *looks at him.*] I—I want to act reasonably. When the men sent Roberts up to the Board in December—then was the time. We ought to have humoured him; instead of that the Chairman—[*Dropping his eyes before* ANTHONY'S]—er—we snapped his head off. We could have got them in then by a little tact.

ANTHONY. No compromise!

WILDER. There we are! This strike's been going on now since October, and as far as I can see it may last another six months. Pretty mess we shall be in by then. The only comfort is, the men'll be in a worse!

EDGAR. [*To Underwood.*] What sort of state are they really in, Frank?

UNDERWOOD. [*Without expression.*] Damnable!

WILDER. Well, who on earth would have thought they'd have held on like this without support!

UNDERWOOD. Those who know them.

WILDER. I defy any one to know them! And what about tin? Price going up daily. When we do get started we shall have to work off our contracts at the top of the market.

WANKLIN. What do you say to that, Chairman?

ANTHONY. Can't be helped!

WILDER. Shan't pay a dividend till goodness knows when!

SCANTLEBURY. [*With emphasis.*] We ought to think of the shareholders. [*Turning heavily.*] Chairman, I say we ought to think of the shareholders. [ANTHONY *mutters.*

SCANTLEBURY. What's that?

TENCH. The Chairman says he *is* thinking of you, sir.

SCANTLEBURY. [*Sinking back into torpor.*] Cynic!

WILDER. It's past a joke. *I* don't want to go without

a dividend for years if the Chairman does. We can't go on playing ducks and drakes with the Company's prosperity.

EDGAR. [*Rather ashamedly.*] I think we ought to consider the men.

[*All but* ANTHONY *fidget in their seats.*]

SCANTLEBURY. [*With a sigh.*] We mustn't think of our private feelings, young man. That'll never do.

EDGAR. [*Ironically.*] I'm not thinking of our feelings. I'm thinking of the men's.

WILDER. As to that—we're men of business.

WANKLIN. That *is* the little trouble.

EDGAR. There's no necessity for pushing things so far in the face of all this suffering—it's—it's cruel.

[*No one speaks, as though* EDGAR *had uncovered something whose existence no man prizing his self-respect could afford to recognize.*]

WANKLIN. [*With an ironical smile.*] I'm afraid we mustn't base our policy on luxuries like sentiment.

EDGAR. I detest this state of things.

ANTHONY. We didn't seek the quarrel.

EDGAR. I know that sir, but surely we've gone far enough.

ANTHONY. No. [*All look at one another.*]

WANKLIN. Luxuries apart, Chairman, we must look out what we're doing.

ANTHONY. Give way to the men once and there'll be no end to it.

WANKLIN. I quite agree, but——

[ANTHONY *shakes his head.*]

You make it a question of bedrock principle?

[ANTHONY *nods.*]

Luxuries again, Chairman! The shares are below par.

WILDER. Yes, and they'll drop to a half when we pass the next dividend.

SCANTLEBURY. [*With alarm.*] Come, come! Not so bad as that.

WILDER. [*Grimly.*] You'll see! [*Craning forward to catch* ANTHONY's *speech.*] I didn't catch——

TENCH. [*Hesitating.*] The Chairman says, sir, "Fais que—que—devra——"

EDGAR. [*Sharply.*] My father says: "Do what we ought—and let things rip."

WILDER. Tcha!

SCANTLEBURY. [*Throwing up his hands.*] The Chairman's a Stoic—I always said the Chairman was a Stoic.

WILDER. Much good that'll do us.

WANKLIN. [*Suavely.*] Seriously, Chairman, are you going to let the ship sink under you, for the sake of—a principle?

ANTHONY. She won't sink.

SCANTLEBURY. [*With alarm.*] Not while I'm on the Board I hope.

ANTHONY. [*With a twinkle.*] Better rat, Scantlebury.

SCANTLEBURY. What a man!

ANTHONY. I've always fought them; I've never been beaten yet.

WANKLIN. We're with you in theory, Chairman. But we're not all made of cast-iron.

ANTHONY. We're only to hold on.

WILDER. [*Rising and going to the fire.*] And go to the devil as fast as we can!

ANTHONY. Better go to the devil than give in!

WILDER. [*Fretfully.*] That may suit you, sir, but it doesn't suit me, or any one else I should think.

[ANTHONY *looks him in the face—a silence.*

EDGAR. I don't see how we can get over it that to go on like this means starvation to the men's wives and families.

[WILDER *turns abruptly to the fire, and* SCANTLEBURY *puts out a hand to push the idea away.*]

WANKLIN. I'm afraid again that sounds a little sentimental.

EDGAR. Men of business are excused from decency, you think?

WILDER. Nobody's more sorry for the men than I am, but if they [*lashing himself*] choose to be such a pig-headed lot, it's nothing to do with us; we've quite enough on *our* hands to think of ourselves and the shareholders.

EDGAR. [*Irritably.*] It won't kill the shareholders to miss a dividend or two; I don't see that *that's* reason enough for knuckling under.

SCANTLEBURY. [*With grave discomfort.*] You talk very lightly of your dividends, young man; I don't know where we are.

WILDER. There's only one sound way of looking at it. We can't go on ruining *ourselves* with this strike.

ANTHONY. No caving in!

SCANTLEBURY. [*With a gesture of despair.*] Look at him!

[ANTHONY *is leaning back in his chair. They do look at him.*]

WILDER. [*Returning to his seat.*] Well, all I can say is, if that's the Chairman's view, I don't know what we've come down here for.

ANTHONY. To tell the men that we've got nothing for them— [*Grimly.*] They won't believe it till they hear it spoken in plain English.

WILDER. H'm! Shouldn't be a bit surprised if that brute Roberts hadn't got us down here with the very same idea. I hate a man with a grievance.

EDGAR. [*Resentfully.*] We didn't pay him enough for his discovery. I always said that at the time.

STRIFE

WILDER. We paid him five hundred and a bonus of two hundred three years later. If that's not enough! What does he want, for goodness' sake?

TENCH. [*Complainingly.*] Company made a hundred thousand out of his brains, and paid him seven hundred—that's the way he goes on, sir.

WILDER. The man's a rank agitator! Look here, I hate the Unions. But now we've got Harness here let's get him to settle the whole thing.

ANTHONY. No! [*Again they look at him.*

UNDERWOOD. Roberts won't let the men assent to that.

SCANTLEBURY. Fanatic! Fanatic!

WILDER. [*Looking at* ANTHONY.] And not the only one! [FROST *enters from the hall.*

FROST. [*To* ANTHONY.] Mr. Harness from the Union, waiting, sir. The men are here too, sir.

[ANTHONY *nods.* UNDERWOOD *goes to the door, returning with* HARNESS, *a pale, clean-shaven man with hollow cheeks, quick eyes, and lantern jaw—*FROST *has retired.*]

UNDERWOOD. [*Pointing to* TENCH's *chair.*] Sit there next to the Chairman, Harness, won't you?

[*At* HARNESS's *appearance, the Board have drawn together, as it were, and turned a little to him, like cattle at a dog.*]

HARNESS. [*With a sharp look around, and a bow.*] Thanks! [*He sits—his accent is slightly nasal.*] Well, gentlemen, we're going to do business at last, I hope.

WILDER. Depends on what you *call* business, Harness. Why don't you make the men come in?

HARNESS. [*Sardonically.*] The men are far more in the right than you are. The question with us is whether we shan't begin to support them again.

[*He ignores them all, except* ANTHONY, *to whom he turns in speaking.*]

ANTHONY. Support them if you like; we'll put in free labour and have done with it.

HARNESS. That won't do, Mr. Anthony. You can't get free labour, and you know it.

ANTHONY. We shall see that.

HARNESS. I'm quite frank with you. We were forced to withhold our support from your men because some of their demands are in excess of current rates. I expect to make them withdraw those demands to-day: if they do, take it straight from me, gentlemen, we shall back them again at once. Now, I want to see something fixed upon before I go back to-night. Can't we have done with this old-fashioned tug-of-war business? What good's it doing you? Why don't you recognise once for all that these people are men like yourselves, and want what's good for them just as you want what's good for you— [*Bitterly.*] Your motor-cars, and champagne, and eight-course dinners.

ANTHONY. If the men will come in, we'll do something for them.

HARNESS. [*Ironically.*] Is that your opinion too, sir— and yours—and yours? [*The Directors do not answer.*] Well, all I can say is: It's a kind of high and mighty aristocratic tone I thought we'd grown out of—seems I was mistaken.

ANTHONY. It's the tone the men use. Remains to be seen which can hold out longest—they without us, or we without them.

HARNESS. As business men, I wonder you're not ashamed of this waste of force, gentlemen. You know what it'll all end in.

ANTHONY. What?

HARNESS. Compromise—it always does.

SCANTLEBURY. Can't you persuade the men that their interests are the same as ours?

HARNESS. [*Turning, ironically.*] I could persuade them of that, sir, if they were.

WILDER. Come, Harness, you're a clever man, you don't believe all the Socialistic claptrap that's talked nowadays. There's no real difference between their interests and ours.

HARNESS. There's just one very simple question I'd like to put to you. Will you pay your men one penny more than they force you to pay them?

[WILDER *is silent.*

WANKLIN. [*Chiming in.*] I humbly thought that not to pay more than was necessary was the A B C of commerce.

HARNESS. [*With irony.*] Yes, that seems to be the A B C of commerce, sir; and the A B C of commerce is between your interests and the men's.

SCANTLEBURY. [*Whispering.*] We ought to arrange something.

HARNESS. [*Drily.*] Am I to understand then, gentlemen, that your Board is going to make no concessions?

[WANKLIN *and* WILDER *bend forward as if to speak, but stop.*]

ANTHONY. [*Nodding.*] None.

[WANKLIN *and* WILDER *again bend forward, and* SCANTLEBURY *gives an unexpected grunt.*]

HARNESS. You were about to say something, I believe?

[*But* SCANTLEBURY *says nothing.*

EDGAR. [*Looking up suddenly.*] We're sorry for the state of the men.

HARNESS. [*Icily.*] The men have no use for your pity, sir. What they want is justice.

ANTHONY. Then let *them* be just.

HARNESS. For that word "just" read "humble," Mr.

Anthony. Why should they be humble? Barring the accident of money, aren't they as good men as you?

ANTHONY. Cant!

HARNESS. Well, I've been five years in America. It colours a man's notions.

SCANTLEBURY. [*Suddenly, as though avenging his uncompleted grunt.*] Let's have the men in and hear what they've got to say!

[ANTHONY *nods, and* UNDERWOOD *goes out by the single door.*]

HARNESS. [*Drily.*] As I'm to have an interview with them this afternoon, gentlemen, I'll ask you to postpone your final decision till that's over.

[*Again* ANTHONY *nods, and taking up his glass drinks.*]

[UNDERWOOD *comes in again, followed by* ROBERTS, GREEN, BULGIN, THOMAS, ROUS. *They file in, hat in hand, and stand silent in a row.* ROBERTS *is lean, of middle height, with a slight stoop. He has a little rat-gnawn, brown-grey beard, moustaches, high cheek-bones, hollow cheeks, small fiery eyes. He wears an old and grease-stained blue serge suit, and carries an old bowler hat. He stands nearest the Chairman.* GREEN, *next to him, has a clean, worn face, with a small grey goatee beard and drooping moustaches, iron spectacles, and mild, straightforward eyes. He wears an overcoat, green with age, and a linen collar. Next to him is* BULGIN, *a tall, strong man, with a dark moustache, and fighting jaw, wearing a red muffler, who keeps changing his cap from one hand to the other. Next to him is* THOMAS, *an old man with a grey moustache, full beard, and weatherbeaten, bony face, whose overcoat discloses a lean, plucky-looking neck. On his right, ROUS, the youngest of the five, looks like a soldier; he has a glitter in his eyes.*]

UNDERWOOD. [*Pointing.*] There are some chairs there against the wall, Roberts; won't you draw them up and sit down?

ROBERTS. Thank you, Mr. Underwood—we'll stand—in the presence of the Board. [*He speaks in a biting and staccato voice, rolling his r's, pronouncing his a's like an Italian a, and his consonants short and crisp.*] How are you, Mr. Harness? Didn't expect t' have the pleasure of seeing you till this afternoon.

HARNESS. [*Steadily.*] We shall meet again then, Roberts.

ROBERTS. Glad to hear that; we shall have some news for you to take to your people.

ANTHONY. What do the men want?

ROBERTS. [*Acidly.*] Beg pardon, I don't quite catch the Chairman's remark.

TENCH. [*From behind the Chairman's chair.*] The Chairman wishes to know what the men have to say.

ROBERTS. It's what the Board has to say we've come to hear. It's for the Board to speak first.

ANTHONY. The Board has nothing to say.

ROBERTS. [*Looking along the line of men.*] In that case we're wasting the Directors' time. We'll be taking our feet off this pretty carpet.

[*He turns, the men move slowly, as though hypnotically influenced.*]

WANKLIN. [*Suavely.*] Come, Roberts, you didn't give us this long cold journey for the pleasure of saying that.

THOMAS. [*A pure Welshman.*] No, sir, an' what I say iss——

ROBERTS. [*Bitingly.*] Go on, Henry Thomas, go on. You're better able to speak to the—Directors than me.

[THOMAS *is silent.*

TENCH. The Chairman means, Roberts, that it was the men who asked for the conference, the Board wish to hear what they have to say.

ROBERTS. Gad! If I was to begin to tell ye all they have to say, I wouldn't be finished today. And there'd be some that'd wish they'd never left their London palaces.

HARNESS. What's your proposition, man? Be reasonable.

ROBERTS. You want reason, Mr. Harness? Take a look round this afternoon before the meeting. [*He looks at the men; no sound escapes them.*] You'll see some very pretty scenery.

HARNESS. All right my friend; you won't put me off.

ROBERTS. [*To the men.*] We shan't put Mr. Harness off. Have some champagne with your lunch, Mr. Harness; you'll want it, sir.

HARNESS. Come, get to business, man!

THOMAS. What we're asking, look you, is just simple justice.

ROBERTS. [*Venomously.*] Justice from London? What are you talking about, Henry Thomas? Have you gone silly? [THOMAS *is silent.*] We know very well what we are—discontented dogs—never satisfied. What did the Chairman tell me up in London? That I didn't know what I was talking about. I was a foolish, uneducated man, that knew nothing of the wants of the men I spoke for.

EDGAR. Do please keep to the point.

ANTHONY. [*Holding up his hand.*] There can only be one master, Roberts.

ROBERTS. Then, be Gad, it'll be us.

[*There is a silence;* ANTHONY *and* ROBERTS *stare at one another.*]

STRIFE

UNDERWOOD. If you've nothing to say to the Directors, Roberts, perhaps you'll let Green or Thomas speak for the men.

[GREEN *and* THOMAS *look anxiously at* ROBERTS, *at each other, and the other men.*]

GREEN. [*An Englishman.*] If I'd been listened to, gentlemen——

THOMAS. What I'fe got to say iss what we'fe all got to say——

ROBERTS. Speak for yourself, Henry Thomas.

SCANTLEBURY. [*With a gesture of deep spiritual discomfort.*] Let the poor men call their souls their own!

ROBERTS. Aye, they shall keep their souls, for it's not much body that you've left them, Mr. [*with biting emphasis, as though the word were an offence*] Scantlebury! [*To the men.*] Well, will you speak, or shall I speak for you?

ROUS. [*Suddenly.*] Speak out, Roberts, or leave it to others.

ROBERTS. [*Ironically.*] Thank you, George Rous. [*Addressing himself to* ANTHONY.] The Chairman and Board of Directors have honoured us by leaving London and coming all this way to hear what we've got to say; it would not be polite to keep them any longer waiting.

WILDER. Well, thank God for that!

ROBERTS. Ye will not dare to thank Him when I have done, Mr. Wilder, for all your piety. May be your God up in London has no time to listen to the working man. I'm told He is a wealthy God; but if he listens to what I tell Him, He will know more than ever He learned in Kensington.

HARNESS. Come, Roberts, you have your own God. Respect the God of other men.

ROBERTS. That's right, sir. We have another God down here; I doubt He is rather different to Mr. Wilder's. Ask

Henry Thomas; he will tell you whether his God and Mr. Wilder's are the same.

> [THOMAS *lifts his hand, and cranes his head as though to prophesy.*]

WANKLIN. For goodness' sake, let's keep to the point, Roberts.

ROBERTS. I rather think it is the point, Mr. Wanklin. If you can get the God of Capital to walk through the streets of Labour, and pay attention to what he sees, you're a brighter man than I take you for, for all that you're a Radical.

ANTHONY. Attend to me, Roberts! [*Roberts is silent.*] You are here to speak for the men, as I am here to speak for the Board.

> [*He looks slowly round.*]
>
> [WILDER, WANKLIN, *and* SCANTLEBURY *make movements of uneasiness, and* EDGAR *gazes at the floor. A faint smile comes on* HARNESS'S *face.*]

Now then, what is it?

ROBERTS. Right, sir!

> [*Throughout all that follows, he and* ANTHONY *look fixedly upon each other. Men and Directors show in their various ways suppressed uneasiness, as though listening to words that they themselves would not have spoken.*]

The men can't afford to travel up to London; and they don't trust you to believe what they say in black and white. They know what the post is [*he darts a look at* UNDERWOOD *and* TENCH], and what Directors' meetings are: "Refer it to the manager—let the manager advise us on the men's condition. Can we squeeze them a little more?"

UNDERWOOD. [*In a low voice.*] Don't hit below the belt, Roberts!

STRIFE

ROBERTS. Is it below the belt, Mr. Underwood? The men know. When I came up to London, I told you the position straight. An' what came of it? I was told I didn't know what I was talkin' about. I can't afford to travel up to London to be told that again.

ANTHONY. What have you to say for the men?

ROBERTS. I have this to say—and first as to their condition. Ye shall 'ave no need to go and ask your manager. Ye can't squeeze them any more. Every man of us is well-nigh starving. [*A surprised murmur rises from the men.* ROBERTS *looks round.*] Ye wonder why I tell ye that? Every man of us is going short. We can't be no worse off than we've been these weeks past. Ye needn't think that by waiting ye'll drive us to come in. We'll die first, the whole lot of us. The men have sent for ye to know, once and for all, whether ye are going to grant them their demands. I see the sheet of paper in the Secretary's hand. [TENCH *moves nervously.*] That's it, I think, Mr. Tench. It's not very large.

TENCH. [*Nodding.*] Yes.

ROBERTS. There's not one sentence of writing on that paper that we can do without.

[*A movement amongst the men.* ROBERTS *turns on them sharply.*]

Isn't that so?

[*The men assent reluctantly.* ANTHONY *takes from* TENCH *the paper and peruses it.*]

Not one single sentence. All those demands are fair. We have not asked anything that we are not entitled to ask. What I said up in London, I say again now: there is not anything on that piece of paper that a just man should not ask, and a just man give. [*A pause.*

ANTHONY. There is not one single demand on this paper that we will grant.

[*In the stir that follows on these words,* ROBERTS *watches the Directors and* ANTHONY *the men.* WILDER *gets up abruptly and goes over to the fire.*]

ROBERTS. D' ye mean that?

ANTHONY. I do.

[WILDER *at the fire makes an emphatic movement of disgust.*]

ROBERTS. [*Noting it, with dry intensity.*] Ye best know whether the condition of the Company is any better than the condition of the men. [*Scanning the Directors' faces.*] Ye best know whether you can afford your tyranny—but this I tell ye: if ye think the men will give way the least part of an inch, ye're making the worst mistake ye ever made. [*He fixes his eyes on* SCANTLEBURY.] Ye think because the Union is not supporting us—more shame to it!—that we'll be coming on our knees to you one fine morning. Ye think because the men have got their wives an' families to think of—that it's just a question of a week or two——

ANTHONY. It would be better if you did not speculate so much on what we think.

ROBERTS. Aye! It's not much profit to us! I will say this for you, Mr. Anthony—ye know your own mind! [*Staring at* ANTHONY.] I can reckon on ye!

ANTHONY. [*Ironically.*] I am obliged to you!

ROBERTS. And I know mine. I tell ye this: The men will send their wives and families where the country will have to keep them; an' they will starve sooner than give way. I advise ye, Mr. Anthony, to prepare yourself for the worst that can happen to your Company. We are not so ignorant as you might suppose. We know the way the cat is jumping. Your position is not all that it might be—not exactly!

STRIFE

ANTHONY. Be good enough to allow us to judge of our position for ourselves. Go back, and reconsider your own.

ROBERTS. [*Stepping forward.*] Mr. Anthony, you are not a young man now; from the time I remember anything ye have been an enemy to every man that has come into your works. I don't say that ye're a mean man, or a cruel man, but ye've grudged them the say of any word in their own fate. Ye've fought them down four times. I've heard ye say ye love a fight—mark my words—ye're fighting the last fight ye'll ever fight——

[TENCH *touches* ROBERTS' *sleeve.*

UNDERWOOD. Roberts! Roberts!

ROBERTS. Roberts! Roberts! I mustn't speak my mind to the Chairman, but the chairman may speak his mind to me!

WILDER. What are things coming to?

ANTHONY. [*With a grim smile at* WILDER.] Go on, Roberts; say what you like!

ROBERTS. [*After a pause.*] I have no more to say.

ANTHONY. The meeting stands adjourned to five o'clock.

WANKLIN. [*In a low voice to* UNDERWOOD.] We shall never settle anything like this.

ROBERTS. [*Bitingly.*] We thank the Chairman and Board of Directors for their gracious hearing.

[*He moves towards the door; the men cluster together stupefied; then* ROUS, *throwing up his head, passes* ROBERTS *and goes out. The others follow.*]

ROBERTS. [*With his hand on the door—maliciously.*] Good day, gentlemen! [*He goes out.*

HARNESS. [*Ironically.*] I congratulate you on the conciliatory spirit that's been displayed. With your permission, gentlemen, I'll be with you again at half-past five. Good morning!

[*He bows slightly, rests his eyes on* ANTHONY, *who returns his stare unmoved, and, followed by* UNDERWOOD, *goes out. There is a moment of uneasy silence.* UNDERWOOD *reappears in the doorway.*]

WILDER. [*With emphatic disgust.*] Well!

[*The double-doors are opened.*

ENID. [*Standing in the doorway.*] Lunch is ready.

[EDGAR, *getting up abruptly, walks out past his sister.*]

WILDER. Coming to lunch, Scantlebury?

SCANTLEBURY. [*Rising heavily.*] I suppose so, I suppose so. It's the only thing we can do.

[*They go out through the double-doors.*

WANKLIN. [*In a low voice.*] Do you really mean to fight to a finish, Chairman? [ANTHONY *nods.*

WANKLIN. Take care! The essence of things is to know when to stop.

[ANTHONY *does not answer.*

WANKLIN. [*Very gravely.*] This way disaster lies. The ancient Trojans were fools to your father, Mrs. Underwood.

[*He goes out through the double-doors.*

ENID. I want to speak to father, Frank.

[UNDERWOOD *follows* WANKLIN *out.* TENCH, *passing round the table, is restoring order to the scattered pens and papers.*]

ENID. Aren't you coming, Dad?

[ANTHONY *shakes his head.* ENID *looks meaningly at* TENCH.]

ENID. Won't you go and have some lunch, Mr. Tench?

TENCH. [*With papers in his hand.*] Thank you, ma'am, thank you! [*He goes slowly, looking back.*

ENID. [*Shutting the doors.*] I do hope it's settled, Father!

STRIFE

ANTHONY. No!

ENID. [*Very disappointed.*] Oh! Haven't you done anything? [ANTHONY *shakes his head.*

ENID. Frank says they all want to come to a compromise, really, except that man Roberts.

ANTHONY. *I* don't.

ENID. It's such a horrid position for us. If you were the wife of the manager, and lived down here, and saw it all. You can't realise, Dad!

ANTHONY. Indeed?

ENID. We see *all* the distress. You remember my maid Annie, who married Roberts? [*Anthony nods.*] It's so wretched, her heart's weak; since the strike began, she hasn't even been getting proper food. I know it for a fact, Father.

ANTHONY. Give her what she wants, poor woman!

ENID. Roberts won't let her take anything from *us*.

ANTHONY. [*Staring before him.*] I can't be answerable for the men's obstinacy.

ENID. They're all suffering. Father! Do stop it, for my sake!

ANTHONY. [*With a keen look at her.*] You don't understand, my dear.

ENID. If I were on the Board, I'd do something.

ANTHONY. What would you do?

ENID. It's because you can't bear to give way. It's so——

ANTHONY. Well?

ENID. So unnecessary.

ANTHONY. What do *you* know about necessity? Read your novels, play your music, talk your talk, but don't try and tell *me* what's at the bottom of a struggle like this.

ENID. I live down here, and see it.

ANTHONY. What d' you imagine stands between you and your class and these men that you're so sorry for?

ENID. [*Coldly.*] I don't know what you mean, Father.

ANTHONY. In a few years you and your children would be down in the condition they're in, but for those who have the eyes to see things as they are and the backbone to stand up for themselves.

ENID. You don't know the state the men are in.

ANTHONY. I know it well enough.

ENID. You don't, Father; if you did, you wouldn't——

ANTHONY. It's you who don't know the simple facts of the position. What sort of mercy do you suppose you'd get if no one stood between you and the continual demands of labour? This sort of mercy— [*He puts his hand up to his throat and squeezes it.*] First would go your sentiments, my dear; then your culture, and your comforts would be going all the time!

ENID. I don't believe in barriers between classes.

ANTHONY. You—don't—believe—in—barriers—between the classes?

ENID. [*Coldly.*] And I don't know what that has to do with this question.

ANTHONY. It will take a generation or two for you to understand.

ENID. It's only you and Roberts, Father, and you know it! [ANTHONY *thrusts out his lower lip.*] It'll ruin the Company.

ANTHONY. Allow me to judge of that.

ENID. [*Resentfully.*] I won't stand by and let poor Annie Roberts suffer like this! And think of the children, Father! I warn you.

ANTHONY. [*With a grim smile.*] What do you propose to do?

ENID. That's my affair.

[ANTHONY *only looks at her.*

ENID. [*In a changed voice, stroking his sleeve.*] Father, you *know* you oughtn't to have this strain on you—you know what Dr. Fisher said!

ANTHONY. No old man can afford to listen to old women.

ENID. But you *have* done enough, even if it really is such a matter of principle with you.

ANTHONY. You think so?

ENID. Don't Dad! [*Her face works.*] You—you might think of *us!*

ANTHONY. I am.

ENID. It'll break you down.

ANTHONY. [*Slowly.*] My dear, I am not going to funk; on that you may rely.

[*Re-enter* TENCH *with papers; he glances at them, then plucking up courage.*]

TENCH. Beg pardon, Madam, I think I'd rather see these papers were disposed of before I get my lunch.

[ENID, *after an impatient glance at him, looks at her father, turns suddenly, and goes into the drawing-room.*]

TENCH. [*Holding the papers and a pen to* ANTHONY, *very nervously.*] Would you sign these for me, please, sir?

[ANTHONY *takes the pen and signs.*

TENCH. [*Standing with a sheet of blotting-paper behind* EDGAR's *chair, begins speaking nervously.*] I owe my position to you, sir.

ANTHONY. Well?

TENCH. I'm obliged to see everything that's going on, sir; I—I depend upon the Company entirely. If anything were to happen to it, it'd be disastrous for me. [ANTHONY *nods.*] And, of course, my wife's just had another; and so it makes me doubly anxious just now. And the rates are really terrible down our way.

ANTHONY. [*With grim amusement.*] Not more terrible than they are up mine.

TENCH. No, sir? [*Very nervously.*] I know the Company means a great deal to you, sir.

ANTHONY. It does; I founded it.

TENCH. Yes, sir. If the strike goes on it'll be very serious. I think the Directors are beginning to realise that, sir.

ANTHONY. [*Ironically.*] Indeed?

TENCH. I know you hold very strong views, sir, and it's always your habit to look things in the face; but I don't think the Directors—like it, sir, now they—they see it.

ANTHONY. [*Grimly.*] Nor you, it seems.

TENCH. [*With a ghost of a smile.*] No, sir; of course I've got my children, and my wife's delicate; in my position I *have* to think of these things. [ANTHONY *nods.*] It wasn't *that* I was going to say, sir, if you'll excuse me [*hesitates*]——

ANTHONY. Out with it, then!

TENCH. I know—from my own father, sir, that when you get on in life you do feel things dreadfully——

ANTHONY. [*Almost paternally.*] Come, out with it, Tench!

TENCH. I don't like to say it, sir.

ANTHONY. [*Stonily.*] You must.

TENCH. [*After a pause, desperately bolting it out.*] I think the Directors are going to throw you over, sir.

ANTHONY. [*Sits in silence.*] Ring the bell!

[TENCH *nervously rings the bell and stands by the fire.*]

TENCH. Excuse me for saying such a thing. I was *only* thinking of you, sir.

STRIFE   101

> [FROST *enters from the hall, he comes to the foot of the table, and looks at* ANTHONY; TENCH *covers his nervousness by arranging papers.*]

ANTHONY. Bring me a whisky and soda.

FROST. Anything to eat, sir?

> [ANTHONY *shakes his head.* FROST *goes to the sideboard, and prepares the drink.*]

TENCH. [*in a low voice, almost supplicating.*] If you *could* see your way, sir, it would be a great relief to my mind, it would indeed. [*He looks up at* ANTHONY, *who has not moved.*] It does make me so very anxious. I haven't slept properly for weeks, sir, and that's a fact.

> [ANTHONY *looks in his face, then slowly shakes his head.*]

TENCH. [*Disheartened.*] No, sir? [*He goes on arranging papers.* FROST *places the whisky and soda and a salver and puts it down by* ANTHONY'S *right hand. He stands away, looking gravely at* ANTHONY.]

FROST. *Nothing* I can get you, sir?

> [ANTHONY *shakes his head.*]

You're aware, sir, of what the doctor said, sir?

ANTHONY. I am.

> [*A pause.* FROST *suddenly moves closer to him, and speaks in a low voice.*]

FROST. This strike, sir; puttin' all this strain on you. Excuse me, sir, is it—is it worth it, sir?

> [ANTHONY *mutters some words that are inaudible.*]

Very good, sir!

> [*He turns and goes out into the hall.* TENCH *makes two attempts to speak; but meeting his Chairman's gaze he drops his eyes, and, turning dismally, he too goes out.* ANTHONY *is left alone. He grips the glass, tilts it, and*

*drinks deeply; then sets it down with a deep
and rumbling sigh, and leans back in his chair.*]

The curtain falls.

ACT II

SCENE I

*It is half-past three. In the kitchen of Roberts's cottage
a meagre little fire is burning. The room is clean and
tidy, very barely furnished, with a brick floor and
white-washed walls, much stained with smoke. There
is a kettle on the fire. A door opposite the fireplace
opens inward from a snowy street. On the wooden
table are a cup and saucer, a teapot, knife, and plate
of bread and cheese. Close to the fireplace in an old
arm-chair, wrapped in a rug, sits* MRS. ROBERTS, *a
thin and dark-haired woman about thirty-five, with
patient eyes. Her hair is not done up, but tied back
with a piece of ribbon. By the fire, too, is* MRS. YEO;
*a red-haired, broad-faced person. Sitting near the
table is* MRS. ROUS, *an old lady, ashen-white, with
silver hair; by the door, standing, as if about to go,
is* MRS. BULGIN, *a little pale, pinched-up woman. In
a chair, with her elbows resting on the table, and her
face resting in her hands, sits* MADGE THOMAS, *a good-
looking girl, of twenty-two, with high cheek-bones,
deep-set eyes, and dark untidy hair. She is listening
to the talk, but she neither speaks nor moves.*

MRS. YEO. So he give me a sixpence, and that's the first
bit o' money *I* seen this week. There an't much 'eat to

STRIFE

this fire. Come and warm yerself, Mrs. Rous, you're lookin' as white as the snow, you are.

MRS. ROUS. [*Shivering—placidly.*] Ah! but the winter my old man was took was the proper winter. Seventy-nine that was, when none of you was hardly born—not Madge Thomas, nor Sue Bulgin. [*Looking at them in turn.*] Annie Roberts, 'ow old were you, dear?

MRS. ROBERTS. Seven, Mrs. Rous.

MRS. ROUS. Seven—well, ther'! A tiny little thing!

MRS. YEO. [*Aggressively.*] Well, I was ten myself, I remembers it.

MRS. ROUS. [*Placidly.*] The Company hadn't been started three years. Father was workin' on the acid, that's 'ow he got 'is pisoned leg. I kep' sayin' to 'im, "Father, you've got a pisoned leg." "Well," 'e says, "Mother, pison or no pison, I can't afford to go a-layin' up." An' two days after, he was on 'is back, and never got up again. It was Providence! There wasn't none o' these Compensation Acts then.

MRS. YEO. Ye hadn't no strike that winter. [*With grim humour.*] This winter's 'ard enough for me. Mrs. Roberts, you don't want no 'arder winter, do you? Wouldn't seem natural to 'ave a dinner, would it, Mrs. Bulgin?

MRS. BULGIN. We've had no bread and tea last four days.

MRS. YEO. You got that Friday's laundry job?

MRS. BULGIN. [*Dispiritedly.*] They said they'd give it me, but when I went last Friday, they were full up. I got to go again next week.

MRS. YEO. Ah! There's too many after that. I send Yeo out on the ice to put on the gentry's skates an' pick up what 'e can. Stops 'im from broodin' about the 'ouse.

MRS. BULGIN. [*In a desolate, matter-of-fact voice.*] Leavin' out the men—it's bad enough with the children. I keep 'em in bed, they don't get so hungry when they're not running about; but they're that restless in bed they worry your life out.

MRS. YEO. You're lucky they're all so small. It's the goin' to school that makes 'em 'ungry. Don't Bulgin give you *any*thin'?

MRS. BULGIN [*Shakes her head, then, as though by afterthought.*] Would if he could, I s'pose.

MRS. YEO. [*Sardonically.*] What! 'Aven't 'e got no shares in the Company?

MRS. ROUS. [*Rising with tremulous cheerfulness.*] Well, good-bye, Annie Roberts, I'm going along home.

MRS. ROBERTS. Stay an' have a cup of tea, Mrs. Rous?

MRS. ROUS. [*With the faintest smile.*] Roberts'll want 'is tea when he comes in. I'll just go an' get to bed; it's warmer there than anywhere.

[*She moves very shakily towards the door.*

MRS. YEO. [*Rising and giving her an arm.*] Come on, Mother, take my arm; we're all goin' the same way.

MRS. ROUS. [*Taking the arm.*] Thank you, my dearies! [*They go out, followed by* MRS. BULGIN.

MADGE. [*Moving for the first time.*] There, Annie, you see that! I told George Rous, "Don't think to have my company till you've made an end of all this trouble. You ought to be ashamed," I said, "with your own mother looking like a ghost, and not a stick to put on the fire. So long as you're able to fill your pipes, you'll let us starve." "I'll take my oath, Madge," he said, "I've not had smoke nor drink these three weeks!" "Well, then, why do you go on with it?" "I can't go back on Roberts!" . . . That's it! Roberts, always Roberts! They'd all drop it but for him. When *he* talks it's the devil that comes into them.

[*A silence.* MRS. ROBERTS *makes a movement of pain.*] Ah! *You* don't want him beaten! He's your man. With

STRIFE 105

everybody like their own shadows! [*She makes a gesture towards* MRS. ROBERTS.] If Rous wants me he must give up Roberts. If *he* gave him up—they all would. They're only waiting for a lead. Father's against him—they're all against him in their hearts.

MRS. ROBERTS. You won't beat Roberts! [*They look silently at each other.*]

MADGE. Won't I? The cowards—when their own mothers and their own children don't know where to turn.

MRS. ROBERTS. Madge!

MADGE. [*Looking searchingly at* MRS. ROBERTS.] I wonder he can look *you* in the face. [*She squats before the fire, with her hands out to the flame.*] Harness is here again. They'll have to make up their minds to-day.

MRS. ROBERTS. [*In a soft, slow voice, with a slight West-country burr.*] Roberts will never give up the furnacemen and engineers. 'T wouldn't be right.

MADGE. You can't deceive me. It's just his pride.

> [*A tapping at the door is heard, the women turn as* ENID *enters. She wears a round fur cap, and a jacket of squirrel's fur. She closes the door behind her.*]

ENID. Can I come in, Annie?

MRS. ROBERTS. [*Flinching.*] Miss Enid! Give Mrs. Underwood a chair, Madge!

> [MADGE *gives* ENID *the chair she has been sitting on.*]

ENID. Thank you!

ENID. Are you any better?

MRS. ROBERTS. Yes, M'm; thank you, M'm.

ENID. [*Looking at the sullen* MADGE *as though requesting her departure.*] Why did you send back the jelly? I call that really wicked of you!

MRS. ROBERTS. Thank you, M'm, I'd no need for it.

ENID. Of course! It was Roberts's doing, wasn't it? How can he let all this suffering go on amongst you?

MADGE. [*Suddenly.*] What suffering?

ENID. [*Surprised.*] I beg your pardon!

MADGE. Who said there was suffering?

MRS. ROBERTS. Madge!

MADGE. [*Throwing her shawl over her head.*] Please to let us keep ourselves to ourselves. We don't want you coming here and spying on us.

ENID. [*Confronting her, but without rising.*] I didn't speak to *you*.

MADGE. [*In a low, fierce voice.*] Keep your kind feelings to yourself. You think you can come amongst us, but you're mistaken. Go back and tell the Manager that.

ENID. [*Stonily.*] This is not your house.

MADGE. [*Turning to the door.*] No, it is not my house; keep clear of my house, Mrs. Underwood.

[*She goes out. ENID taps her fingers on the table.*

MRS. ROBERTS. Please to forgive Madge Thomas, M'm; she's a bit upset today. [*A pause.*

ENID. [*Looking at her.*] Oh, I think they're so *stupid*, all of them.

MRS. ROBERTS. [*With a faint smile.*] Yes, M'm.

ENID. Is Roberts out?

MRS. ROBERTS. Yes, M'm.

ENID. It is *his doing*, that they don't come to an agreement. Now isn't it, Annie?

MRS. ROBERTS. [*Softly, with her eyes on ENID, and moving the fingers of one hand continually on her breast.*] They do say that your father, M'm——

ENID. My father's getting an old man, and you know what old men are.

MRS. ROBERTS. I am sorry, M'm.

STRIFE 107

ENID. [*More softly.*] I don't expect *you* to feel sorry, Annie. I know it's his fault as well as Roberts's.

MRS. ROBERTS. I'm sorry for any one that gets old, M'm; it's dreadful to get old, and Mr. Anthony was such a fine old man I always used to think.

ENID. [*Impulsively.*] He always liked you, don't you remember? Look here, Annie, what can I do? I do so want to know. You don't get what you ought to have. [*Going to the fire, she takes the kettle off, and looks for coals.*] And you're so naughty sending back the soup and things!

MRS. ROBERTS. [*With a faint smile.*] Yes, M'm?

ENID. [*Resentfully.*] Why, you haven't even got coals?

MRS. ROBERTS. If you please, M'm, to put the kettle on again; Roberts won't have long for his tea when he comes in. He's got to meet the men at four.

ENID. [*Putting the kettle on.*] That means he'll lash them into a fury again. Can't you stop his going, Annie? [MRS. ROBERTS *smiles ironically.*] Have you tried? [*A silence.*] Does he know how ill you are?

MRS. ROBERTS. It's only my weak 'eart, M'm.

ENID. You used to be so well when you were with us.

MRS. ROBERTS. [*Stiffening.*] Roberts is always good to me.

ENID. But you ought to have everything you want, and you have nothing!

MRS. ROBERTS. [*Appealingly.*] They tell me I don't look like a dyin' woman?

ENID. Of course you don't; if you could only have proper— Will you see my doctor if I send him to you? I'm sure he'd do you good.

MRS. ROBERTS. [*With faint questioning.*] Yes, M'm.

ENID. Madge Thomas oughtn't to come here; she only excites you. As if I didn't know what suffering there is amongst the men! I do feel for them dreadfully, but you know they *have* gone too far.

Mrs. Roberts. [*Continually moving her fingers.*] They say there's no other way to get better wages, M'm.

Enid. [*Earnestly.*] But, Annie, that's why the Union won't help them. My husband's very sympathetic with the men, but he says they're not underpaid.

Mrs. Roberts. No, M'm?

Enid. They never think how the Company could go on if we paid the wages they want.

Mrs. Roberts. [*With an effort.*] But the dividends having been so big, M'm.

Enid. [*Taken aback.*] You all seem to think the shareholders are rich men, but they're not—most of them are really no better off than working men. [Mrs. Roberts *smiles.*] They have to keep up appearances.

Mrs. Roberts. Yes, M'm?

Enid. You don't have to pay rates and taxes, and a hundred other things that they do. If the men didn't spend such a lot in drink and betting they'd be quite well off!

Mrs. Roberts. They say, workin' so hard, they must have some pleasure.

Enid. But surely not low pleasure like that.

Mrs. Roberts. [*A little resentfully.*] Roberts never touches a drop; and he's never had a bet in his life.

Enid. Oh! but he's not a com—— I mean he's an engineer—a superior man.

Mrs. Roberts. Yes, M'm. Roberts says they've no chance of other pleasures.

Enid. [*Musing.*] Of course, I know it's hard.

Mrs. Roberts. [*With a spice of malice.*] And they say gentlefolk's just as bad.

STRIFE

ENID. [*With a smile.*] I go as far as most people, Annie, but you know, yourself, that's nonsense.

MRS. ROBERTS. [*With painful effort.*] A lot 'o the men never go near the Public; but even they don't save but very little, and that goes if there's illness.

ENID. But they've got their clubs, haven't they?

MRS. ROBERTS. The clubs only give up to eighteen shillin's a week, M'm, and it's not much amongst a family. Roberts says workin' folk have always lived from hand to mouth. Sixpence to-day is worth more than a shillin' to-morrow, that's what they say.

ENID. But that's the spirit of gambling.

MRS. ROBERTS. [*With a sort of excitement.*] Roberts says a working man's life is all a gamble, from the time 'e's born to the time 'e dies.

[ENID *leans forward, interested.* MRS. ROBERTS *goes on with a growing excitement that culminates in the personal feeling of the last words.*]

He says, M'm, that when a working man's baby is born, it's a toss-up from breath to breath whether it ever draws another, and so on all 'is life; an' when he comes to be old, it's the workhouse or the grave. He says that without a man is very near, and pinches and stints 'imself and 'is children to save, there can't be neither surplus nor security. That's why he wouldn't have no children. [*She sinks back*], not though I *wanted* them.

ENID. Yes, yes, I know!

MRS. ROBERTS. No, you don't, M'm. You've got your children, and you'll never need to trouble for them.

ENID. [*Gently.*] You oughtn't to be talking so much, Annie. [*Then, in spite of herself.*] But Roberts was paid a lot of money, wasn't he, for discovering that process?

MRS. ROBERTS. [*On the defensive.*] All Roberts's savin's have gone. He's always looked forward to this strike. He says he's no right to a farthing when the others are suffering. 'Tisn't so with all o' them! Some don't seem to care no more than that—so long as they get their own.

ENID. I don't see how they can be expected to when they're suffering like this. [*In a changed voice.*] But Roberts ought to think of *you!* It's all terrible! The kettle's boiling. Shall I make the tea? [*She takes the teapot and, seeing tea there, pours water into it.*] Won't you have a cup?

MRS. ROBERTS. No, thank you, M'm. [*She is listening, as though for footsteps.*] I'd sooner you didn't see Roberts, M'm, he gets so wild.

ENID. Oh! but I must, Annie; I'll be quite calm, I promise.

MRS. ROBERTS. It's life an' death to him, M'm.

ENID. [*Very gently.*] I'll get him to talk to me outside, we won't excite you.

MRS. ROBERTS. [*Faintly.*] No, M'm.

[*She gives a violent start.* ROBERTS *has come in, unseen.*]

ROBERTS. [*Removing his hat—with subtle mockery.*] Beg pardon for coming in; you're engaged with a lady, I see.

ENID. Can I speak to you, Mr. Roberts?

ROBERTS. Whom have I the pleasure of addressing, Ma'am?

ENID. But surely you know me! I'm Mrs. Underwood.

ROBERTS. [*With a bow of malice.*] The daughter of our Chairman.

ENID. [*Earnestly.*] I've come on purpose to speak to you; will you come outside a minute?

[*She looks at* MRS. ROBERTS.

STRIFE

ROBERTS. [*Hanging up his hat.*] I have nothing to say, Ma'am.

ENID. But I *must* speak to you, please.

[*She moves towards the door.*

ROBERTS. [*With sudden venom.*] I have not the time to listen!

MRS. ROBERTS. David!

ENID. Mr. Roberts, *please!*

ROBERTS. [*Taking off his overcoat.*] I am sorry to disoblige a lady—Mr. Anthony's daughter.

ENID. [*Wavering, then with sudden decision.*] Mr. Roberts, I know you've another meeting of the men.

[ROBERTS *bows.*

I came to appeal to you. Please, please, try to come to some compromise; give way a little, if it's only for your own sakes!

ROBERTS. [*Speaking to himself.*] The daughter of Mr. Anthony begs me to give way a little, if it's only for our own sakes!

ENID. For everybody's sake; for your wife's sake.

ROBERTS. For my wife's sake, for everybody's sake— for the sake of Mr. Anthony.

ENID. Why are you so bitter against my father? He has never done anything to you.

ROBERTS. Has he not?

ENID. He can't help his views, any more than you can help yours.

ROBERTS. I really didn't know that I had a right to views!

ENID. He's an old man, and you——

[*Seeing his eyes fixed on her, she stops.*

ROBERTS. [*Without raising his voice.*] If I saw Mr. Anthony going to die, and I could save him by lifting my hand, I would not lift the little finger of it.

ENID. You—you— [*She stops again, biting her lips.*
ROBERTS. I would not, and that's flat!

ENID. [*Coldly.*] You don't mean what you say, and you know it!

ROBERTS. I mean every word of it.

ENID. But why?

ROBERTS. [*With a flash.*] Mr. Anthony stands for tyranny! That's why!

ENID. Nonsense!

[MRS. ROBERTS *makes a movement as if to rise, but sinks back in her chair.*]

ENID. [*With an impetuous movement.*] Annie!

ROBERTS. Please not to touch my wife!

ENID. [*Recoiling with a sort of horror.*] I believe—you are mad.

ROBERTS. The house of a madman then is not the fit place for a lady.

ENID. I'm not afraid of you.

ROBERTS. [*Bowing.*] I would not expect the daughter of Mr. Anthony to be afraid. Mr. Anthony is not a coward like the rest of them.

ENID. [*Suddenly.*] I suppose you think it brave, then, to go on with the struggle.

ROBERTS. Does Mr. Anthony think it brave to fight against women and children? Mr. Anthony is a rich man, I believe; does he think it brave to fight against those who haven't a penny? Does he think it brave to set children crying with hunger, an' women shivering with cold?

ENID. [*Putting up her hand, as though warding off a blow.*] My father is acting on his principles, and you know it!

ROBERTS. And so am I!

ENID. You hate us; and you can't bear to be beaten!

STRIFE

ROBERTS. Neither can Mr. Anthony, for all that he may say.

ENID. At any rate you might have pity on your wife.

> [MRS. ROBERTS *who has her hand pressed to her breast, takes it away, and tries to calm her breathing.*]

ROBERTS. Madam, I have no more to say.

> [*He takes up the loaf. There is a knock at the door, and* UNDERWOOD *comes in. He stands looking at them,* ENID *turns to him, then seems undecided.*]

UNDERWOOD. Enid!

ROBERTS. [*Ironically.*] Ye were not needing to come for your wife, Mr. Underwood. We are not rowdies.

UNDERWOOD. I know that, Roberts. I hope Mrs. Roberts is better.

> [ROBERTS *turns away without answering.*]

Come, Enid!

ENID. I make one more appeal to you, Mr. Roberts, for the sake of your wife.

ROBERTS. [*With polite malice.*] If I might advise ye, Ma'am—make it for the sake of your husband and your father.

> [ENID, *suppressing a retort, goes out.* UNDERWOOD *opens the door for her and follows.* ROBERTS, *going to the fire, holds out his hands to the dying glow.*]

ROBERTS. How goes it, my girl? Feeling better, are you?

> [MRS. ROBERTS *smiles faintly. He brings his overcoat and wraps it round her.*]

[*Looking at his watch.*] Ten minutes to four! [*As though inspired.*] I've seen their faces, there's no fight in them, except for that one old robber.

Mrs. Roberts. Won't you stop and eat, David? You've 'ad nothing all day!

Roberts. [*Putting his hand to his throat.*] Can't swallow till those old sharks are out o' the town. [*He walks up and down.*] I shall have a bother with the men—there's no heart in them, the cowards. Blind as bats, they are—can't see a day before their noses.

Mrs. Roberts. It's the women, David.

Roberts. Ah! So they say! They can remember the women when their own bellies speak! The women never stop them from the drink; but from a little suffering to themselves in a sacred cause, the women stop them fast enough.

Mrs. Roberts. But think o' the children, David.

Roberts. Ah! If they will go breeding themselves for slaves, without a thought o' the future o' them they breed—

Mrs. Roberts. [*Gasping.*] That's enough, David; don't begin to talk of that—I won't—I can't——

Roberts. [*Staring at her.*] Now, now, my girl!

Mrs. Roberts. [*Breathlessly.*] No, no, David—I won't!

Roberts. There, there! Come, come! That's right! [*Bitterly.*] Not one penny will they put by for a day like this. Not they! Hand to mouth—Gad!—I know them! They've broke my heart. There was no holdin' them at the start, but now the pinch 'as come.

Mrs. Roberts. How can you expect it, David? They're not made of iron.

Roberts. Expect it? Wouldn't I expect what I would do meself? Wouldn't I starve an' rot rather than give in? What one man can do, another can.

Mrs. Roberts. And the women?

Roberts. This is not women's work.

STRIFE 115

Mrs. Roberts. [*With a flash of malice.*] No, the women may die for all you care. That's their work.

Roberts. [*Averting his eyes.*] Who talks of dying? No one will die till we have beaten these——

> [*He meets her eyes again, and again turns his away. Excitedly.*]

This is what I've been waiting for all these months. To get the old robbers down, and send them home again without a farthin's worth o' change. I've seen their faces, I tell you, in the valley of the shadow of defeat.

> [*He goes to the peg and takes down his hat.*

Mrs. Roberts. [*Following with her eyes—softly.*] Take your overcoat, David; it must be bitter cold.

Roberts. [*Coming up to her—his eyes are furtive.*] No, no! There, there, stay quiet and warm. I won't be long, my girl.

Mrs. Roberts. [*With soft bitterness.*] You'd better take it.

> [*She lifts the coat. But* Roberts *puts it back, and wraps it round her. He tries to meet her eyes, but cannot.* Mrs. Roberts *stays huddled in the coat, her eyes, that follow him about, are half malicious, half yearning. He looks at his watch again, and turns to go. In the doorway he meets* Jan Thomas, *a boy of ten in clothes too big for him, carrying a penny whistle.*]

Roberts. Hallo, boy!

> [*He goes. Jan stops within a yard of* Mrs. Roberts, *and stares at her without a word.*]

Mrs. Roberts. Well, Jan!

Jan. Father's coming; sister Madge is coming.

> [*He sits at the table, and fidgets with his whistle;*

>   *he blows three vague notes; then imitates a cuckoo.*]
>
>   [*There is a tap on the door. Old* THOMAS *comes in.*]

THOMAS. A very coot tay to you, Ma'am. It is petter that you are.

MRS. ROBERTS. Thank you, Mr. Thomas.

THOMAS. [*Nervously.*] Roberts in?

MRS. ROBERTS. Just gone on to the meeting, Mr. Thomas.

THOMAS. [*With relief, becoming talkative.*] This is fery unfortunate, look you! I came to tell him that we must make terms with London. It is a fery great pity he is gone to the meeting. He will be kicking against the pricks, I am thinking.

MRS. ROBERTS. [*Half rising.*] He'll never give in, Mr. Thomas.

THOMAS. You must not be fretting, that is very pat for you. Look you, there iss hartly any mans for supporting him now, but the engineers and George Rous. [*Solemnly.*] This strike is no longer coing with Chapel, look you! I have listened carefully, an' I have talked with her. [JAN *blows.*] Sst! I don't care what th' others say, I say that *Chapel means us* to be stopping the trouble, that is what I make of her; and it is my opinion that this is the fery best thing for all of us. If it wasn't my opinion, I ton't say—but it is my opinion, look you.

MRS. ROBERTS. [*Trying to suppress her excitement.*] I don't know what'll come to Roberts, if you give in.

THOMAS. It is no disgrace whateffer! All that a mortal man coult do he hass tone. It iss against Human Nature he hass gone; fery natural—any man may do that; but Chapel has spoken and he must not go against her. [JAN *imitates the cuckoo.*] Ton't make that squeaking! [*Going*

STRIFE

to the door.] Here iss my daughter come to sit with you. A fery goot day, Ma'am—no fretting—rememper!

[MADGE *comes in and stands at the open door, watching the street.*]

MADGE. You'll be late, Father; they're beginning. [*She catches him by the sleeve.*] For the love of God, stand up to him, Father—this time!

THOMAS. [*Detaching his sleeve with dignity.*] Leave me to do what's proper, girl!

[*He goes out.* MADGE, *in the centre of the open doorway, slowly moves in, as though before the approach of some one.*]

ROUS. [*Appearing in the doorway.*] Madge!

[MADGE *stands with her back to* MRS. ROBERTS, *staring at him with her head up and her hands behind her.*]

ROUS. [*Who has a fierce distracted look.*] Madge! I'm going to the meeting.

[MADGE, *without moving, smiles contemptuously.*] D'ye hear me? [*They speak in quick low voices.*

MADGE. I hear! Go, and kill your own mother, if you must.

[ROUS *seizes her by both her arms. She stands rigid, with her head bent back. He releases her, and he too stands motionless.*]

ROUS. I swore to stand by Roberts. I swore that! Ye want me to go back on what I've sworn.

MADGE. [*With slow soft mockery.*] You are a pretty lover!

ROUS. Madge!

MADGE. [*Smiling.*] I've heard that lovers do what their girls ask them—[JAN *sounds the cuckoo's notes.*]— but that's not true, it seems!

ROUS. You'd make a blackleg of me!

MADGE. [*With her eyes half-closed.*] Do it for me!

ROUS. [*Dashing his hand across his brow.*] Damn! I can't!

MADGE. [*Swiftly.*] Do it for me!

ROUS. [*Through his teeth.*] Don't play the wanton with me!

MADGE. [*With a movement of her hand towards* JAN— *quick and low.*] I would be *that* for the children's sake!

ROUS. [*In a fierce whisper.*] Madge! Oh, Madge!

MADGE. [*With soft mockery.*] But *you* can't break your word for me!

ROUS. [*With a choke.*] Then, Begod, I can!

[*He turns and rushes off.*

[MADGE *stands, with a faint smile on her face, looking after him. She turns to* MRS. ROBERTS.]

MADGE. I have done for Roberts!

MRS. ROBERTS. [*Scornfully.*] Done for my man, with that——!

[*She sinks back.*

MADGE. [*Running to her, and feeling her hands.*] You're as cold as a stone! You want a drop of brandy. Jan, run to the "Lion"; say, I sent you for Mrs. Roberts.

MRS. ROBERTS. [*With a feeble movement.*] I'll just sit quiet, Madge. Give Jan—his—tea.

MADGE. [*Giving* JAN *a slice of bread.*] There, ye little rascal. Hold your piping. [*Going to the fire, she kneels.*] It's going out.

MRS. ROBERTS. [*With a faint smile.*] 'Tis all the same!

[JAN *begins to blow his whistle.*

MADGE. Tsht! Tsht!—you—— [JAN *stops.*

MRS. ROBERTS. [*Smiling.*] Let 'im play, Madge.

MADGE. [*On her knees at the fire, listening.*] Waiting an' waiting. I've no patience with it; waiting an' wait-

STRIFE

ing—that's what a woman has to do! Can you hear them at it—I can!

> [JAN *begins again to play his whistle;* MADGE *gets up; half tenderly she ruffles his hair; then, sitting, leans her elbows on the table, and her chin on her hands. Behind her, on* MRS. ROBERT'S *face the smile has changed to horrified surprise. She makes a sudden movement, sitting forward, pressing her hands against her breast. Then slowly she sinks back; slowly her face loses the look of pain, the smile returns. She fixes her eyes again on* JAN, *and moves her lips and finger to the tune.*]

The curtain falls.

SCENE II

It is past four. In a grey, failing light, an open muddy space is crowded with workmen. Beyond, divided from it by a barbed-wire fence, is the raised towing-path of a canal, on which is moored a barge. In the distance are marshes and snow-covered hills. The "Works" high wall runs from the canal across the open space, and in the angle of this wall is a rude platform of barrels and boards. On it, HARNESS *is standing.* ROBERTS, *a little apart from the crowd, leans his back against the wall. On the raised towing-path two bargemen lounge and smoke indifferently.*

HARNESS. [*Holding out his hand.*] Well, I've spoken to you straight. If I speak till to-morrow I can't say more.

JAGO. [*A dark, sallow, Spanish-looking man with a short, thin beard.*] Mister, want to ask you! Can they get blacklegs?

BULGIN. [*Menacing.*] Let 'em try.

[*There are savage murmurs from the crowd.*]

BROWN. [*A round-faced man.*] Where could they get 'em then?

EVANS. [*A small, restless, harassed man, with a fighting face.*] There's always blacklegs; it's the nature of 'em. There's always men that'll save their own skins.

[*Another savage murmur. There is a movement, and old* THOMAS, *joining the crowd, takes his stand in front.*]

HARNESS. [*Holding up his hand.*] They can't get them. But that won't help you. Now men, be reasonable. Your demands would have brought on us the burden of a dozen strikes at a time when we were not prepared for them. The Unions live by Justice, not to one, but all. Any fair man will tell you—you were ill-advised! I don't say you go too far for that which you're entitled to, but you're going too far for the moment; you've dug a pit for yourselves. Are you to stay there, or are you to climb out? Come!

LEWIS. [*A clean-cut Welshman with a dark moustache.*] You've hit it, Mister! Which is it to be?

[*Another movement in the crowd, and* ROUS, *coming quickly, takes his stand next* THOMAS.]

HARNESS. Cut your demands to the right pattern, and we'll see you through; refuse, and don't expect me to waste my time coming down here again. I'm not the sort that speaks at random, as you ought to know by this time. If you're the sound men I take you for—no matter who advises you against it—[*he fixes his eyes on* ROBERTS] you'll make up your minds to come in, and trust to us to get your terms. Which is it to be? Hands together, and victory—or—the starvation you've got now?

[*A prolonged murmur from the crowd.*

STRIFE

JAGO. [*Sullenly.*] Talk about what you know.

HARNESS. [*Lifting his voice above the murmur.*] Know? [*With cold passion.*] All that you've been through, my friend, I've been through—I was through it when I was no bigger than [*pointing to a youth*] that shaver there; the Unions then weren't what they are now. What's made them strong? It's hands together that's made them strong. I've been through it all, I tell you, the brand's on my soul yet. I know what you've suffered—there's nothing you can tell me that I don't know; but the whole is greater than the part, and you are only the part. Stand by us, and we will stand by you.

> [*Quartering them with his eyes, he waits. The murmuring swells; the men form little groups.*
> GREEN, BULGIN, *and* LEWIS *talk together.*]

LEWIS. Speaks very sensible, the Union chap.

GREEN. [*Quietly.*] Ah! if I'd been *listened* to, you'd 'ave 'eard sense these two months past.

> [*The bargemen are seen laughing.*

LEWIS. [*Pointing.*] Look at those two blanks over the fence there!

BULGIN. [*With gloomy violence.*] They'd best stop their cackle, or I'll break their jaws.

JAGO. [*Suddenly.*] You say the furnacemen's paid enough?

HARNESS. I did not say they were paid enough; I said they were paid as much as the furnacemen in similar works elsewhere.

EVANS. That's a lie! [*Hubbub.*] What about Harper's?

HARNESS. [*With cold irony.*] You may look at home for lies, my man. Harper's shifts are longer, the pay works out the same.

HENRY ROUS. [*A dark edition of his brother George.*] Will ye support us in double pay overtime Saturdays?

HARNESS. Yes, we will.

JAGO. What have ye done with our subscriptions?

HARNESS. [*Coldly.*] I have told you what we *will* do with them.

EVANS. Ah! *will*, it's always will! Ye'd have our mates desert us. [*Hubbub.*

BULGIN. [*Shouting.*] Hold your row!

[EVANS *looks round angrily.*

HARNESS. [*Lifting his voice.*] Those who know their right hands from their lefts know that the Unions are neither thieves nor traitors. I've said my say. Figure it out, my lads; when you want me you know where I shall be.

> [*He jumps down, the crowd gives way, he passes through them, and goes away. A* BARGEMAN *looks after him jerking his pipe with a derisive gesture. The men close up in groups, and many looks are cast at* ROBERTS, *who stands alone against the wall.*]

EVANS. He wants you to turn blacklegs, that's what he wants. He wants ye to go back on us. Sooner than turn blackleg—I'd starve, I would.

BULGIN. Who's talkin' o' blacklegs—mind what you're saying, will you?

BLACKSMITH. [*A youth with yellow hair and huge arms.*] What about the women?

EVANS. They can stand what we can stand, I suppose, can't they?

BLACKSMITH. Ye've no wife?

EVANS. An' don't want one.

THOMAS. [*Raising his voice.*] Aye! Give us the power to come to terms with London, lads.

DAVIES. [*A dark, slow-fly, gloomy man.*] Go up the platform, if you got anything to say, go up an' say it.

STRIFE

[*There are cries of "Thomas!" He is pushed towards the platform; he ascends it with difficulty, and bares his head, waiting for silence. A hush.*]

RED-HAIRED YOUTH. [*Suddenly.*] Coot old Thomas!

[*A hoarse laugh; the bargemen exchange remarks; a hush again, and* THOMAS *begins speaking.*]

THOMAS. We are all in the tepth together, and it iss Nature that has put us there.

HENRY ROUS. It's London put us there!

EVANS. It's the Union.

THOMAS. It iss not Lonton; nor it iss not the Union—it iss Nature. It iss no disgrace whateffer to a potty to give in to Nature. For this Nature iss a fery pig thing; it is pigger than what a man is. There iss more years to my hett than to the hett of any one here. It is fery pat, look you, this coing against Nature. It is pat to make other potties suffer, when there is nothing to pe cot py it.

[*A laugh.* THOMAS *angrily goes on.*]

What are ye laughing at? It is pat, I say! We are fighting for principle; there is no potty that shall say I am not a peliever in principle. Putt when Nature says "No further," then it is no coot snapping your fingers in her face.

[*A laugh from* ROBERTS, *and murmurs of approval.*]

This Nature must pe humort. It is a man's pisiness to be pure, honest, just, and merciful. That's what Chapel tells you. [*To* ROBERTS, *angrily.*] And, look you, David Roberts, Chapel tells you ye can do that without coing against Nature.

JAGO. What about the Union?

THOMAS. I ton't trust the Union; they haf treated us

like tirt. "Do what we tell you," said they. I haf peen captain of the furnacemen twenty years, and I say to the Union—[*excitedly*]—"Can you tell me then, as well as I can tell you, what iss the right wages for the work that these men do?" For fife and twenty years I haf paid my moneys to the Union and—[*with great excitement*]—for nothings! What iss that but roguery, for all that this Mr. Harness says! [*Murmurs.*

EVANS. Hear, hear.

HENRY ROUS. Get on with you! Cut on with it then!

THOMAS. Look you, if a man toes not trust me, am I coing to trust him?

JAGO. That's right.

THOMAS. Let them alone for rogues, and act for ourselves. [*Murmurs.*

BLACKSMITH. That's what we been doin', haven't we?

THOMAS. [*With increased excitement.*] I wass brought up to do for meself. I wass brought up to go without a thing, if I hat not moneys to puy it. There iss too much, look you, of doing things with other people's moneys. We haf fought fair, and if we haf peen beaten, it iss no fault of ours. Gif us the power to make terms with London for ourself; if we ton't succeed, I say it iss petter to take our peating like men, than to tie like togs, or hang on to others' coat-tails to make them do our pisiness for us!

EVANS. [*Muttering.*] Who wants to?

THOMAS. [*Craning.*] What's that? If I stand up to a potty, and he knocks me town, I am not to go hollering to other potties to help me; I am to stand up again; and if he knocks me town properly, I am to stay there, isn't that right? [*Laughter.*

JAGO. No Union!

HENRY ROUS. Union! [*Others take up the shout.*

STRIFE

Evans. Blacklegs!

[Bulgin *and the* Blacksmith *shake their fists at* Evans.]

Thomas. [*With a gesture.*] I am an olt man, look you.

[*A sudden silence, then murmurs again.*

Lewis. Olt fool, with his "No Union!"

Bulgin. Them furnace chaps! For twopence I'd smash the faces o' the lot of them.

Green. If I'd a been listened to at the first——

Thomas. [*Wiping his brow.*] I'm comin' now to what I was coing to say——

Davies. [*Muttering.*] An' time too!

Thomas. [*Solemnly.*] Chapel says: Ton't carry on this strife! Put an end to it!

Jago. That's a lie! Chapel says go on!

Thomas. [*Scornfully.*] Inteet! I haf ears to my head.

Red-Haired Youth. Ah! long ones! [*A laugh.*

Jago. Your ears have misbeled you then.

Thomas. [*Excitedly.*] Ye cannot be right if I am, ye cannot haf it both ways.

Red-Haired Youth. Chapel can though!

[*"The Shaver" laughs; there are murmurs from the crowd.*]

Thomas. [*Fixing his eyes on "The Shaver."*] Ah! ye're coing the roat to tamnation. An' so I say to all of you. If ye co against Chapel I will not pe with you, nor will any other Got-fearing man.

[*He steps down from the platform.* Jago *makes his way towards it. There are cries of "Don't let 'im go up!"*]

Jago. Don't let him go up? That's free speech, that is. [*He goes up.*] I ain't got much to say to you. Look at the matter plain; ye've come the road this far, and now you want to chuck the journey. We've all been in one boat; and now you want to pull in two. We engineers have stood by you; ye're ready now, are ye, to give us the go-by? If we'd a-known that before, we'd not a-started out with you so early one bright morning! That's all I've got to say. Old man Thomas a'n't got his Bible Lesson right. If you give up to London, or to Harness, now, it's givin' us the chuck—to save your skins—you won't get over that, my boys; it's a dirty thing to do.

> [*He gets down; during his little speech, which is ironically spoken, there is a restless discomfort in the crowd.* ROUS, *stepping forward, jumps on the platform. He has an air of fierce distraction. Sullen murmurs of disapproval from the crowd.*]

ROUS. [*Speaking with great excitement.*] I'm no blanky orator, mates, but wot I say is drove from me. What I say is yuman nature. Can a man set an' see 'is mother starve? Can 'e now?

ROBERTS. [*Starting forward.*] Rous!

ROUS. [*Staring at him fiercely.*] Slim 'Arness said fair! I've changed my mind!

ROBERTS. Ah! Turned your coat you mean!

> [*The crowd manifests a great surprise.*

LEWIS. [*Apostrophising* ROUS.] Hallo! What's turned him round?

ROUS. [*Speaking with intense excitement.*] 'E said fair. "Stand by us," 'e said, "and we'll stand by you." That's where we've been makin' our mistake this long time past; and who's to blame for 't? [*He points at* ROBERTS.] That man there! "No," 'e said, "fight the robbers," 'e said, "squeeze the breath out o' them!" But it's not the breath out o' them that's being squeezed; it's the breath out of *us* and *ours,* and that's the book of truth. I'm no orator, mates, it's the flesh and blood in me that's

STRIFE

speakin', it's the heart o' me. [*With a menacing, yet half-ashamed movement towards* ROBERTS.] He'll speak to you again, mark my words, but don't ye listen. [*The crowd groans.*] It's hell fire that's on the man's tongue. [ROBERTS *is seen laughing.*] Slim 'Arness is right. What are we without the Union—handful o' parched leaves—a puff o' smoke. I'm no orator, but I say: Chuck it up! Chuck it up! Sooner than go on starving the women and the children.

> [*The murmurs of acquiescence almost drown the murmurs of dissent.*]

EVANS. What's turned *you* to blacklegging?

ROUS. [*With a furious look.*] Sim 'Arness knows what he's talking about. Give us power to come to terms with London; I'm no orator, but I say—have done wi' this black misery!

> [*He gives his muffler a twist, jerks his head back, and jumps off the platform. The crowd applauds and surges forward. Amid cries of* "That's enough!" "Up Union!" "Up Harness!" ROBERTS *quietly ascends the platform. There is a moment of silence.*]

BLACKSMITH. We don't want to hear you. Shut it!

HENRY ROUS. Get down!

> [*Amid such cries they surge towards the platform.*]

EVANS. [*Fiercely.*] Let' im speak! Roberts! Roberts!

BULGIN. [*Muttering.*] He'd better look out that I don't crack his skull.

> [ROBERTS *faces the crowd, probing them with his eyes till they gradually become silent. He begins speaking. One of the bargemen rises and stands.*]

ROBERTS. You don't want to hear me, then? You'll

listen to Rous and to that old man, but not to me. You'll listen to Sim Harness of the Union that's treated you *so fair;* maybe you'll listen to those men from London? Ah! you groan! What for? You love their feet on your necks, don't you? [*Then as* BULGIN *elbows his way towards the platform, with calm pathos.*] You'd like to break my jaw, John Bulgin. Let me speak, then do your smashing, if it gives you pleasure. [BULGIN *stands motionless and sullen.*] Am I a liar, a coward, a traitor? If only I were, ye'd listen to me, I'm sure. [*The murmurings cease, and there is now dead silence.*] Is there a man of you here that has less to gain by striking? Is there a man of you that had more to lose? Is there a man of you that has given up *eight hundred* pounds since this trouble here began? Come now, is there? How much has Thomas given up—ten pounds or five, or what? You listened to him, and what had he to say? "None can pretend," he said, "that I'm not a believer in principle—[*with biting irony*]—but when Nature says: 'No further, 't es going agenst Nature.'" *I* tell you if a man cannot say to Nature: "Budge me from this if you can!" [*with a sort of exaltation*]—his principles are but his belly. "Oh, but," Thomas says, "a man can be pure and honest, just and merciful, and take off his hat to Nature!" *I* tell you Nature's neither pure nor honest, just nor merciful. You chaps that live over the hill, an' go home dead beat in the dark on a snowy night—don't ye fight your way every inch of it? Do ye go lyin' down an' trustin' to the tender mercies of this merciful Nature? Try it and you'll soon know with what ye've got to deal. 'T es only by that— [*he strikes a blow with his clenched fist*]—in Nature's face that a man can be a man. "Give in," says Thomas, "go down on your knees; throw up your foolish fight, an' perhaps," he said, "perhaps your enemy will chuck you down a crust."

Jago. Never!

Evans. Curse them!

Thomas. I nefer said that.

Roberts. [*Bitingly.*] If ye did not say it, man, ye meant it. An' what did ye say about Chapel? "Chapel's against it," ye said. "She's against it!" Well, if Chapel and Nature go hand in hand, it's the first I've ever heard of it. That young man there—[*pointing to* Rous]—said I 'ad 'ell fire on my tongue. If I had I would use it all to scorch and wither this talking of surrender. Surrendering's the work of cowards and traitors.

Henry Rous. [*As* George Rous *moves forward.*] Go for him, George—don't stand his lip!

Roberts. [*Flinging out his finger.*] Stop there, George Rous, it's no time this to settle personal matters. [Rous *stops.*] But there was one other spoke to you—Mr. Simon Harness. We have not much to thank Mr. Harness and the Union for. They said to us "Desert your mates, or we'll desert you." An' they did desert us.

Evans. They did.

Roberts. Mr. Simon Harness is a clever man, but he has come too late. [*With intense conviction.*] For all that Mr. Simon Harness says, for all that Thomas, Rous, for all that any man present here can say—*We've won the fight!*

[*The crowd sags nearer, looking eagerly up. With withering scorn.*]

You've felt the pinch o't in your bellies. You've forgotten what that fight 'as been; many times I have told you; I will tell you now this once again. The fight o' the country's body and blood against a blood-sucker. The fight of those that spend themselves with every blow they strike and every breath they draw, against a thing that fattens on them, and grows and grows by the law of *merciful* Nature. That thing is Capital! A thing that buys the sweat o' men's brows, and the tortures o' their brains, at its own price. *Don't* I know that? Wasn't the work o' *my* brains bought for seven hundred pounds, and hasn't one hundred thousand pounds been gained them by that seven hundred without the stirring of a finger. It is a thing that will take as much and give you as little as it can. That's *Capital!* A thing that will say—"I'm very sorry for you, poor fellows—you have a cruel time of it, I know," but will not give one sixpence of its dividends to help you have a better time. That's Capital! Tell me, for all their talk, is there one of them that will consent to another penny on the Income Tax to help the poor? That's Capital! A white-faced, stony-hearted monster! Ye have got it on its knees; are ye to give up at the last minute to save your miserable bodies pain? When I went this morning to those old men from London, I looked into their very 'earts. One of them was sitting there—Mr. Scantlebury, a mass of flesh nourished on us: sittin' there for all the world like the shareholders in this Company, that sit not moving tongue nor finger, takin' dividends—a great dumb ox that can only be roused when its food is threatened. I looked into his eyes and I saw *he was afraid*—afraid for himself and his dividends, afraid for his fees, afraid of the very shareholders he stands for; and all but one of them's afraid—like children that go into a wood at night, and start at every rustle of the leaves. I ask you, men—[*he pauses, holding out his hand till there is utter silence*]—give me a free hand to tell them: "Go back to London. The men have nothing for you!" [*A murmuring.*] Give me that, an' I swear to you, within a week you shall have from London all you want.

STRIFE

EVANS, JAGO, *and* OTHERS. A free hand! Give him a free hand! Bravo—bravo!

ROBERTS. 'Tis not for this little moment of time we're fighting [*the murmuring dies*], not for ourselves, our own little bodies, and their wants, 'tis for all those that come after throughout all time. [*With intense sadness.*] Oh! men—for the love o' them, don't roll up another stone upon their heads, don't help to blacken the sky, an' let the bitter sea in over them. They're welcome to the worst that can happen to me, to the worst that can happen to us all, aren't they—aren't they? If we can shake [*passionately*] that white-faced monster with the bloody lips, that has sucked the life out of ourselves, our wives, and children, since the world began. [*Dropping the note of passion, but with utmost weight and intensity.*] If we have not the hearts of men to stand up against it breast to breast, and eye to eye, and force it backward till it cry for mercy, it will go on sucking life; and we shall stay forever what we are [*in almost a whisper*], less than the very dogs.

> [*An utter stillness, and* ROBERTS *stands rocking his body slightly, with his eyes burning the faces of the crowd.*]

EVANS and JAGO. [*Suddenly.*] Roberts! [*The shout is taken up.*]

> [*There is a slight movement in the crowd, and* MADGE *passing below the towing-path, stops by the platform, looking up at* ROBERTS. *A sudden doubting silence.*]

ROBERTS. "Nature," says that old man, "give in to Nature." I tell you, strike your blow in Nature's face— an' let it do its worst!

> [*He catches sight of Madge, his brows contract, he looks away.*]

132 STRIFE

MADGE. [*In a low voice—close to the platform.*] Your wife's dying!

> [ROBERTS *glares at her as if torn from some pinnacle of exaltation.*]

ROBERTS. [*Trying to stammer on.*] I say to you—answer them—answer them——

> [*He is drowned by the murmur in the crowd.*

THOMAS. [*Stepping forward.*] Ton't you hear her, then?

ROBERTS. What is it? [*A dead silence.*

THOMAS. Your wife, man!

> [ROBERTS *hesitates, then with a gesture, he leaps down, and goes away below the towing-path, the men making way for him. The standing bargeman opens and prepares to light a lantern. Daylight is fast failing.*]

MADGE. He needn't have hurried! Annie Roberts is dead. [*Then in the silence, passionately.* You pack of blinded hounds! How many more women are you going to let to die?

> [*The crowd shrinks back from her, and breaks up in groups, with a confused, uneasy movement.* MADGE *goes quickly away below the towing-path. There is a hush as they look after her.*]

LEWIS. There's a spitfire, for ye!

BULGIN. [*Growling.*] I'll smash 'er jaw.

GREEN. If I'd a-been listened to, that poor woman—

THOMAS. It's a judgment on him for coing against Chapel. I tolt him how 't would be!

EVANS. All the more reason for sticking by 'im. [*A cheer.*] Are you goin' to desert him now 'e 's down? Are you going to chuck him over, now e' 's lost 'is wife?

STRIFE

[*The crowd is murmuring and cheering all at once.*]

Rous. [*Stepping in front of platform.*] Lost his wife! Aye! Can't ye see? Look at home, look at your own wives! What's to save them? Ye'll have the same in all your houses before long!

Lewis. Aye, aye!

Henry Rous. Right! George, right!

[*There are murmurs of assent.*

Rous. It's not us that's blind, it's Roberts. How long will ye put up with 'im!

Henry Rous, Bulgin, Davies. Give 'im the chuck!

[*The cry is taken up.*

Evans. [*Fiercely.*] Kick a man that's down? Down?

Henry Rous. Stop his jaw there!

[Evans *throws up his arm at a threat from* Bulgin. *The bargeman, who has lighted the lantern, holds it high above his head.*]

Rous. [*Springing on to the platform.*] What brought him down then, but 'is own black obstinacy? Are ye goin' to follow a man that can't see better than that where he's goin'?

Evans. He's lost 'is wife.

Rous. An' who's fault's that but his own. 'Ave done with 'im, I say, before he's killed your own wives and mothers.

Davies. Down 'im!

Henry Rous. He's finished!

Brown. We've had enough of 'im!

Blacksmith. Too much!

[*The crowd takes up these cries, excepting only* Evans, Jago, *and* Green, *who is seen to argue mildly with the* Blacksmith.]

Rous. [*Above the hubbub.*] We'll make terms with the Union, lads. [*Cheers.*

Evans. [*Fiercely.*] Ye blacklegs!

Bulgin. [*Savagely—squaring up to him.*] Who are ye callin' blacklegs, Rat?

> [Evans *throws up his fists, parries the blow, and returns it. They fight. The bargemen are seen holding up the lantern and enjoying the sight. Old* Thomas *steps forward and holds out his hands.*]

Thomas. Shame on your strife!

> [*The* Blacksmith, Brown, Lewis, *and the* Red-haired Youth *pull* Evans *and* Bulgin *apart. The stage is almost dark.*]

The curtain falls.

ACT III

It is five o'clock. In the Underwood's *drawing-room, which is artistically furnished,* Enid *is sitting on the sofa working at a baby's frock.* Edgar, *by a little spindle-legged table in the centre of the room, is fingering a china-box. His eyes are fixed on the double-doors that lead into the dining-room.*

Edgar. [*Putting down the china-box, and glancing at his watch.*] Just on five, they're all in there waiting, except Frank. Where's he?

Enid. He's had to go down to Gasgoyne's about a contract. Will you want him?

Edgar. He can't help us. This is a director's job. [*Motioning towards a single door half hidden by a curtain.*] Father in his room?

STRIFE

ENID. Yes.

EDGAR. I wish he'd stay there, Enid.

[ENID *looks up at him.*

This is a beastly business, old girl?

[*He takes up the little box again and turns it over and over.*]

ENID. I went to the Roberts's this afternoon, Ted.

EDGAR. That wasn't very wise.

ENID. He's simply killing his wife.

EDGAR. We are you mean.

ENID. [*Suddenly.*] Roberts *ought* to give way!

EDGAR. There's a lot to be said on the men's side.

ENID. I don't feel half so sympathetic with them as I did before I went. They just set up class feeling against you. Poor Annie was looking dreadfully bad—fire going out, and nothing fit for her to eat.

[EDGAR *walks to and fro.*

But she would stand up for Roberts. When you see all this wretchedness going on and feel you can do nothing, you have to shut your eyes to the whole thing.

EDGAR. If you can.

ENID. When I went I was all on their side, but as soon as I got there I began to feel quite different at once. People talk about sympathy with the working classes, they don't know what it means to try and put it into practice. It seems hopeless.

EDGAR. Ah! well.

ENID. It's dreadful going on with the men in this state. I do hope the Dad will make concessions.

EDGAR. He won't. [*Gloomily.*] It's a sort of religion with him. Curse it! I know what's coming! He'll be voted down.

ENID. They wouldn't dare!

EDGAR. They will—they're in a funk.

ENID. [*Indignantly.*] He'd never stand it!

EDGAR. [*With a shrug.*] My dear girl, if you're beaten in a vote, you've got to stand it.

ENID. Oh! [*She gets up in alarm.*] But would he resign?

EDGAR. Of course! It goes to the roots of his beliefs.

ENID. But he's so *wrapped up in this company,* Ted! There'd be nothing left for him! It'd be dreadful!

[EDGAR *shrugs his shoulders.*
Oh, Ted, he's so old now! You mustn't let them!

EDGAR. [*Hiding his feelings in an outburst.*] My sympathies in this strike are all on the side of the men.

ENID. He's been Chairman for more than thirty years! He made the whole thing! And think of the bad times they've had; it's always been he who pulled them through. Oh, Ted, you must——

EDGAR. What is it you want? You said just now you hoped he'd make concessions. Now you want me to back him in not making them. This isn't a game, Enid!

ENID. [*Hotly.*] It isn't a game to *me* that the Dad's in danger of losing all he cares about in life. If he won't give way, and he's beaten, it'll simply break him down!

EDGAR. Didn't you say it was dreadful going on with the men in this state?

ENID. But you can't see, Ted. Father'll never get over it! You must stop them somehow. The others are afraid of him. If you back him up——

EDGAR. [*Putting his hand to his head.*] Against my convictions—against yours! The moment it begins to pinch one personally——

ENID. It isn't personal, it's the Dad!

EDGAR. Your family or yourself, and over goes the show!

STRIFE

ENID. [*Resentfully.*] If you don't take it seriously, I do.

EDGAR. I am as fond of him as you are; that's nothing to do with it.

ENID. We can't tell about the men; it's all guesswork. But we know the Dad might have a stroke any day. D'you mean to say that he isn't more to you than——

EDGAR. Of course he is.

ENID. I don't understand you then.

EDGAR. H'm!

ENID. If it were for oneself it would be different, but for our own Father! You don't seem to realize.

EDGAR. I realize perfectly.

ENID. It's your first duty to save him.

EDGAR. I wonder.

ENID. [*Imploring.*] Oh, Ted! It's the only interest he's got left; it'll be like a death-blow to him!

EDGAR. [*Restraining his emotion.*] I know.

ENID. Promise!

EDGAR. I'll do what I can.

[*He turns to the double-doors.*]
[*The curtained door is opened, and* ANTHONY *appears.* EDGAR *opens the double-doors, and passes through.*]
[SCANTLEBURY'S *voice is faintly heard:* "*Past five; we shall never get through—have to eat another dinner at that hotel!*" *The doors are shut.* ANTHONY *walks forward.*]

ANTHONY. You've been seeing Roberts, I hear.

ENID. Yes.

ANTHONY. Do you know what trying to bridge such a gulf as this is like?

[ENID *puts her work on the little table, and faces him.*]

Filling a sieve with sand!

ENID. Don't!

ANTHONY. You think with your gloved hands you can cure the trouble of the century. [*He passes on.*

ENID. Father! [ANTHONY *stops at the double-doors.*] I'm only thinking of you!

ANTHONY. [*More softly.*] I can take care of myself, my dear.

ENID. Have you thought what'll happen if you're beaten —[*she points*]—in there?

ANTHONY. I don't mean to be.

ENID. Oh! Father, don't give them a chance. You're not well; need you go to the meeting at all?

ANTHONY. [*With a grim smile.*] Cut and run?

ENID. But they'll out-vote you!

ANTHONY. [*Putting his hand on the doors.*] We shall see!

ENID. I beg you, Dad!

[ANTHONY *looks at her softly.*

Won't you?

[ANTHONY *shakes his head. He opens the doors. A buzz of voices comes in.*]

SCANTLEBURY. Can one get dinner on that 6.30 train up?

TENCH. No, sir, I believe not, sir.

WILDER. Well, I shall speak out; I've had enough of this.

EDGAR. [*Sharply.*] What?

[*It ceases instantly.* ANTHONY *passes through, closing the doors behind him.* ENID *springs to them with a gesture of dismay. She puts her hand on the knob, and begins turning it; then goes to the fireplace, and taps her foot on the*

fender. Suddenly she rings the bell. FROST
comes in by the door that leads into the hall.]

FROST. Yes, M'm?

ENID. When the men come, Frost, please show them in here; the hall's cold.

FROST. I could put them in the pantry, M'm.

ENID. No. I don't want to—to offend them; they're so touchy.

FROST. Yes, M'm. [*Pause.*] Excuse me, Mr. Anthony's 'ad nothing to eat all day.

ENID. I know, Frost.

FROST. Nothin' but two whiskies and sodas, M'm.

ENID. Oh! you oughtn't to have let him have those.

FROST. [*Gravely.*] Mr. Anthony is a little difficult, M'm. It's not as if he were a younger man, an' knew what was good for 'im; he will have his own way.

ENID. I suppose we all want that.

FROST. Yes, M'm. [*Quietly.*] Excuse me speakin' about the strike. I'm sure if the other gentlemen were to give up to Mr. Anthony, and quietly let the men 'ave what they want, afterwards, that'd be the best way. I find that very useful with him at times, M'm.

[ENID *shakes her head.*
If he's crossed, it makes him violent [*with an air of discovery*], and I've noticed in my own case, when I'm violent I'm always sorry for it afterwards.

ENID. [*With a smile.*] Are *you* ever violent, Frost?

FROST. Yes, M'm; oh! sometimes very violent.

ENID. I've never seen you.

FROST. [*Impersonally.*] No, M'm; that is so.

[ENID *fidgets towards the back of the door.*
[*With feeling.*] Bein' with Mr. Anthony, as you know, M'm, ever since I was fifteen, it worries me to see him crossed like this at his age. I've taken the liberty to speak

to Mr. Wanklin [*dropping his voice*]—seems to be the most sensible of the gentlemen—but 'e said to me: "That's all very well, Frost, but this strike's a very serious thing," 'e said. "Serious for all parties, no doubt," I said, "but yumour 'im, sir," I said, "yumour 'im. It's like this, if a man comes to a stone wall, 'e doesn't drive 'is 'ead against it, 'e gets over it." "Yes," 'e said, "you'd better tell your master that." [FROST *looks at his nails.*] That's where it is, M'm. I said to Mr. Anthony this morning: "Is it worth it, sir?" "Damn it," he said to me, "Frost! Mind your own business, or take a month's notice!" Beg pardon, M'm, for using such a word.

ENID. [*Moving to the double-doors, and listening.*] Do you know that man Roberts, Frost?

FROST. Yes, M'm; that's to say, not to speak to. But to *look* at 'im you can tell what *he's* like.

ENID. [*Stopping.*] Yes?

FROST. He's not one of these 'ere ordinary 'armless Socialists. 'E's violent; got a fire inside 'im. What I call "personal." A man may 'ave what opinions 'e likes, so long as 'e's not personal; when 'e's that 'e's *not* safe.

ENID. I think that's what my father feels about Roberts.

FROST. No doubt, M'm, Mr. Anthony has a feeling against him.

> [ENID *glances at him sharply, but finding him in perfect earnest, stands biting her lips, and looking at the double-doors.*]

It's a regular right down struggle between the two. I've no patience with this Roberts, from what I 'ear he's just an ordinary workin' man like the rest of 'em. If he did invent a thing he's no worse off than 'undreds of others. My brother invented a new kind o' dumb-waiter—nobody gave *him* anything for it, an' there it is, bein' used all over

STRIFE

the place. [ENID *moves closer to the double-doors.* There's a kind o' man that never forgives the world, because 'e wasn't born a gentleman. What I say is—no man that's a gentleman looks down on another because e' 'appens to be a class or two above 'im, no more than if 'e 'appens to be a class or two below.

ENID. [*With slight impatience.*] Yes, I know, Frost, of course. Will you please go in and ask if they'll have some tea; say I sent you.

FROST. Yes, M'm.

> [*He opens the doors gently and goes in. There is a momentary sound of earnest, rather angry talk.*]

WILDER. I don't agree with you.

WANKLIN. We've had this over a dozen times.

EDGAR. [*Impatiently.*] Well, what's the proposition?

SCANTLEBURY. Yes, what does your father say? Tea? Not for me, not for me!

WANKLIN. What I understand the Chairman to say is this——

> [FROST *re-enters closing the door behind him.*]

ENID. [*Moving from the door.*] Won't they have any tea, Frost?

> [*She goes to the little table, and remains motionless, looking at the baby's frock.*]
> [*A parlourmaid enters from the hall.*

PARLOURMAID. A Miss Thomas, M'm.

ENID. [*Raising her head.*] Thomas? What Miss Thomas—d' you mean a——?

PARLOURMAID. Yes, M'm.

ENID. [*Blankly.*] Oh! Where is she?

PARLOURMAID. In the porch.

ENID. I don't want—— [*She hesitates.*]

FROST. Shall I dispose of her, M'm?

142 STRIFE

ENID. I'll come out. No, show her in here, Ellen.

[*The* PARLOURMAID *and* FROST *go out.* ENID *pursing her lips, sits at the little table, taking up the baby's frock. The* PARLOURMAID *ushers in* MADGE THOMAS *and goes out;* MADGE *stands by the door.*]

ENID. Come in. What is it? What have you come for, please?

MADGE. Brought a message from Mrs. Roberts.

ENID. A message? Yes.

MADGE. She asks you to look after her mother.

ENID. I don't understand.

MADGE. [*Sullenly.*] That's the message.

ENID. But—what—why?

MADGE. Annie Roberts is dead.

[*There is a silence.*]

ENID. [*Horrified.*] But it's only a little more than an hour since I saw her.

MADGE. Of cold and hunger.

ENID. [*Rising.*] Oh! that's not true! the poor thing's heart— What makes you look at me like that? I tried to help her.

MADGE. [*With suppressed savagery.*] I thought you'd like to know.

ENID. [*Passionately.*] It's so unjust! Can't you see that I want to help you all?

MADGE. I never harmed any one that hadn't harmed me first.

ENID. [*Coldly.*] What harm have I done you? Why do you speak to me like that?

MADGE. [*With the bitterest intensity.*] You come out of your comfort to spy on us! A week of hunger, that's what *you* want!

ENID. [*Standing her ground.*] Don't talk nonsense!

STRIFE

MADGE. I saw her die; her hands were blue with the cold.

ENID. [*With a movement of grief.*] Oh! why wouldn't she let me help her? It's such senseless pride!

MADGE. Pride's better than nothing to keep your body warm.

ENID. [*Passionately.*] I won't talk to you! How can you tell what I feel? It's not my fault that I was born better off than you.

MADGE. We don't want your money.

ENID. You don't understand, and you don't want to; please to go away!

MADGE. [*Balefully.*] You've killed her, for all your soft words, you and your father——

ENID. [*With rage and emotion.*] That's wicked! My father is suffering himself through this wretched strike.

MADGE. [*With sombre triumph.*] Then tell him Mrs. Roberts is dead! That'll make him better.

ENID. Go away!

MADGE. When a person hurts us we get it back on them.

> [*She makes a sudden and swift movement towards* ENID, *fixing her eyes on the child's frock lying across the little table.* ENID *snatches the frock up, as though it were the child itself. They stand a yard apart, crossing glances.*]

MADGE. [*Pointing to the frock with a little smile.*] Ah! You felt *that!* Lucky it's her mother—not her children—you've to look after, isn't it? *She* won't trouble you long!

ENID. Go away!

MADGE. I've given you the message.

> [*She turns and goes out into the hall.* ENID, *motionless till she has gone, sinks down at the table, bending her head over the frock, which*

she is still clutching to her. The double-doors are opened, and ANTHONY *comes slowly in; he passes his daughter, and lowers himself into an arm-chair. He is very flushed.*]

ENID. [*Hiding her emotion—anxiously.*] What is it, Dad? [ANTHONY *makes a gesture, but does not speak.*] Who was it?

[ANTHONY *does not answer.* ENID *going to the double-doors meets* EDGAR *coming in. They speak together in low tones.*] What is it, Ted?

EDGAR. That fellow Wilder! Taken to personalities! He was downright insulting.

ENID. What did he say?

EDGAR. Said, Father was too old and feeble to know what he was doing! The Dad's worth six of him!

ENID. Of course he is. [*They look at* ANTHONY.

[*The doors open wider,* WANKLIN *appears with* SCANTLEBURY.]

SCANTLEBURY. [*Sotto voce.*] I don't like the look of this!

WANKLIN. [*Going forward.*] Come, Chairman! Wilder sends you his apologies. A man can't do more.

[WILDER, *followed by* TENCH, *comes in, and goes to* ANTHONY.]

WILDER. [*Glumly.*] I withdraw my words, sir. I'm sorry. [ANTHONY *nods to him.*

ENID. You haven't come to a decision, Mr. Wanklin?

[WANKLIN *shakes his head.*

WANKLIN. We're all here, Chairman; what do you say? Shall we get on with the business, or shall we go back to the other room?

SCANTLEBURY. Yes, yes; let's get on. We must settle something.

[*He turns from a small chair, and settles himself*

suddenly in the largest chair with a sigh of comfort.]

[WILDER *and* WANKLIN *also sit; and* TENCH, *drawing up a straight-backed chair close to his Chairman, sits on the edge of it with the minute-book and a stylographic pen.*]

ENID. [*Whispering.*] I want to speak to you a minute, Ted. [*They go out through the double-doors.*

WANKLIN. Really, Chairman, it's no use soothing ourselves with a sense of false security. If this strike's not brought to an end before the General Meeting, the shareholders will certainly haul us over the coals.

SCANTLEBURY. [*Stirring.*] What—what's that?

WANKLIN. I know it for a fact.

ANTHONY. Let them!

WILDER. And get turned out?

WANKLIN. [*To* ANTHONY.] I don't mind martyrdom for a policy in which I believe, but I object to being burnt for some one else's principles.

SCANTLEBURY. Very reasonable—you must see that, Chairman.

ANTHONY. We owe it to other employers to stand firm.

WANKLIN. There's a limit to that.

ANTHONY. You were all full of fight at the start.

SCANTLEBURY. [*With a sort of groan.*] We thought the men would give in, but they—haven't!

ANTHONY. They will!

WILDER. [*Rising and pacing up and down.*] I can't have my reputation as a man of business destroyed for the satisfaction of starving the men out. [*Almost in tears.*] I can't have it! How can we meet the shareholders with things in the state they are?

SCANTLEBURY. Hear, hear—hear, hear!

WILDER. [*Lashing himself.*] If any one expects me to

say to them I've lost you fifty thousand pounds and sooner than put my pride in my pocket I'll lose you another. [*Glancing at Anthony.*] It's—it's unnatural! *I don't want to go against you, sir*——

WANKLIN. [*Persuasively.*] Come Chairman, we're *not* free agents. We're part of a machine. Our only business is to see the Company earns as much profit as it safely can. If you blame me for want of principle: I say that we're Trustees. Reason tells us we shall never get back in the saving of wages what we shall lose if we continue this struggle—really, Chairman, we *must* bring it to an end, on the best terms we can make.

ANTHONY. No.

[*There is a pause of general dismay.*]

WILDER. It's a deadlock then. [*Letting his hands drop with a sort of despair.*] Now I shall never get off to Spain!

WANKLIN. [*Retaining a trace of irony.*] You hear the consequences of your victory, Chairman?

WILDER. [*With a burst of feeling.*] My wife's *ill*!

SCANTLEBURY. Dear, dear! You don't say so.

WILDER. If I don't get her out of this cold, I won't answer for the consequences.

[*Through the double-doors* EDGAR *comes in looking very grave.*]

EDGAR. [*To his father.*] Have you heard this, sir? Mrs. Roberts is dead!

[*Every one stares at him, as if trying to gauge the importance of this news.*]

Enid saw her this afternoon, she had no coals, or food, or anything. It's enough!

[*There is a silence, every one avoiding the other's eyes, except* ANTHONY, *who stares hard at his son.*]

STRIFE

SCANTLEBURY. You don't suggest that we could have helped the poor thing?

WILDER. [*Flustered.*] The woman was in bad health. Nobody can say there's any responsibility on us. At least—not on me.

EDGAR. [*Hotly.*] I say that we *are* responsible.

ANTHONY. War is war!

EDGAR. Not on women!

WANKLIN. It not infrequently happens that women are the greatest sufferers.

EDGAR. If we knew that, all the more responsibility rests on us.

ANTHONY. This is no matter for amateurs.

EDGAR. Call me what you like, sir. It's sickened me. We had no right to carry things to such a length.

WILDER. I don't like this business a bit—that Radical rag will twist it to their own ends; see if they don't! They'll get up some cock and bull story about the poor woman's dying from starvation. I wash my hands of it.

EDGAR. You can't. None of us can.

SCANTLEBURY. [*Striking his fist on the arm of his chair.*] But I protest against this——

EDGAR. Protest as you like, Mr. Scantlebury, it won't alter facts.

ANTHONY. That's enough.

EDGAR. [*Facing him angrily.*] No, sir. I tell you exactly what I think. If we pretend the men are not suffering, it's humbug; and if they're suffering, we know enough of human nature to know the women are suffering more, and as to the children—well—it's damnable!

[SCANTLEBURY *rises from his chair.*

I don't say that we meant to be cruel, I don't say anything of the sort; but I do say it's criminal to shut our eyes to the facts. We employ these men, and we can't get

148 STRIFE

out of it. I don't care so much about the men, but I'd sooner resign my position on the Board than go on starving women in this way.

> [*All except* ANTHONY *are now upon their feet,* ANTHONY *sits grasping the arms of his chair and staring at his son.*]

SCANTLEBURY. I don't—I don't like the way you're putting it, young sir.

WANKLIN. You're rather overshooting the mark.

WILDER. I should think so indeed!

EDGAR. [*Losing control.*] It's no use blinking things! If *you* want to have the death of women on your hands— *I* don't!

SCANTLEBURY. Now, now, young man!

WILDER. On *our* hands? Not on *mine,* I won't have it!

EDGAR. We are five members of this Board; if we were four against it, why did we let it drift till it came to this? You know perfectly well why—because we hoped we should starve the men out. Well, all we've done is to starve one woman out!

SCANTLEBURY. [*Almost hysterically.*] I protest, I protest! I'm a humane man—we're all humane men!

EDGAR. [*Scornfully.*] There's nothing wrong with our *humanity*. It's our imaginations, Mr. Scantlebury.

WILDER. Nonsense! My imagination's as good as yours.

EDGAR. If so, it isn't good enough.

WILDER. I foresaw this!

EDGAR. Then why didn't you put your foot down!

WILDER. Much good that would have done.

> [*He looks at* ANTHONY.

EDGAR. If you, and I, and each one of us here who say that our imaginations are so good——

SCANTLEBURY. [*Flurried.*] I never said so.

EDGAR. [*Paying no attention.*] —had put our feet down,

STRIFE

the thing would have been ended long ago, and this poor woman's life wouldn't have been crushed out of her like this. For all we can tell there may be a dozen other starving women.

SCANTLEBURY. For God's sake, sir, don't use that word at a—at a Board meeting; it's—it's monstrous.

EDGAR. I *will* use it, Mr. Scantlebury.

SCANTLEBURY. Then I shall not listen to you. I shall not listen! It's painful to me.

[*He covers his ears.*

WANKLIN. None of us are opposed to a settlement, except your Father.

EDGAR. I'm certain that if the shareholders knew——

WANKLIN. I don't think you'll find their imaginations are any better than ours. Because a woman happens to have a weak heart——

EDGAR. A struggle like this finds out the weak spots in everybody. Any child knows that. If it hadn't been for this cut-throat policy, she needn't have died like this; and there wouldn't be all this misery that any one who isn't a fool can see is going on.

[*Throughout the foregoing* ANTHONY *has eyed his son; he now moves as though to rise, but stops as* EDGAR *speaks again.*]

I don't defend the men, or myself, or anybody.

WANKLIN. You may have to! A coroner's jury of disinterested sympathisers may say some very nasty things. We mustn't lose sight of our position.

SCANTLEBURY. [*Without uncovering his ears.*] Coroner's jury! No, no, it's not a case for that!

EDGAR. I've had enough of cowardice.

WANKLIN. Cowardice is an unpleasant word, Mr. Edgar Anthony. It will look very like cowardice if we suddenly concede the men's demands when a thing like this happens; we must be careful!

WILDER. Of course we must. We've no knowledge of this matter, except a rumour. The proper course is to put the whole thing into the hands of Harness to settle for us; that's natural, that's what we *should* have come to any way.

SCANTLEBURY. [*With dignity.*] Exactly! [*Turning to* EDGAR.] And as to you, young sir, I can't sufficiently express my—my distaste for the way you've treated the whole matter. You ought to withdraw! Talking of starvation, talking of cowardice! Considering what our views are! Except your own father—we're all agreed the only policy is—is one of goodwill—it's most irregular, it's most improper, and all I can say is it's—it's given me pain——

[*He places his hand over his heart.*]

EDGAR. [*Stubbornly.*] I withdraw nothing.

[*He is about to say more when* SCANTLEBURY *once more covers up his ears.* TENCH *suddenly makes a demonstration with the minute-book. A sense of having been engaged in the unusual comes over all of them, and one by one they resume their seats.* EDGAR *alone remains on his feet.*]

WILDER. [*With an air of trying to wipe something out.*] I pay no attention to what young Mr. Anthony has said. Coroner's jury! The idea's preposterous. I—I move this amendment to the Chairman's Motion: That the dispute be placed at once in the hands of Mr. Simon Harness for settlement, on the lines indicated by him this morning. Any one second that? [TENCH *writes in his book.*

WANKLIN. I do.

WILDER. Very well, then; I ask the Chairman to put it to the Board.

ANTHONY. [*With a great sigh—slowly.*] We have been made the subject of an attack. [*Looking round at* WILDER

STRIFE

and SCANTLEBURY *with ironical contempt.*] I take it on *my* shoulders. I am seventy-six years old. I have been Chairman of this Company since its inception two-and-thirty years ago. I have seen it pass through good and evil report. My connection with it began in the year that this young man was born.

> [EDGAR *bows his head.* ANTHONY, *gripping his chair, goes on.*]

I have had to do with "men" for fifty years; I've always stood up to them; I have never been beaten yet. I have fought the men of this Company four times, and four times I have beaten them. It has been said that I am not the man I was. [*He looks at Wilder.*] However that may be, I am man enough to stand to my guns.

> [*His voice grows stronger. The double-doors are opened.* ENID *slips in, followed by* UNDERWOOD, *who restrains her.*]

The men have been treated justly, they have had fair wages, we have always been ready to listen to complaints. It has been said that times have changed; if they have, I have not changed with them. Neither will I. It has been said that masters and men are equal! Cant! There can only be one master in a house! Where two men meet the better man will rule. It has been said that Capital and Labour have the same interests. Cant! Their interests are as wide asunder as the poles. It has been said that the Board is only part of a machine. Cant! We *are* the machine; its brains and sinews; it is for us to lead and to determine what is to be done, and to do it without fear or favour. Fear of the men! Fear of the shareholders! Fear of our own shadows! Before I am like that, I hope to die.

> [*He pauses, and meeting his son's eyes, goes on.*]

There is only one way of treating "men"—with *the iron*

hand. This half and half business, the half and half manners of this generation, has brought all this upon us. Sentiment and softness, and what this young man, no doubt, would call his social policy. You can't eat cake and have it! This middle-class sentiment, or socialism, or whatever it may be, is rotten. Masters are masters, men are men! Yield one demand, and they will make it six. They are [*he smiles grimly*] like Oliver Twist, asking for more. If I were in *their* place I should be the same. But I am not in their place. Mark my words: one fine morning, when you have given way here, and given way there—you will find you have parted with the ground beneath your feet, and are deep in the bog of bankruptcy; and with you, floundering in that bog, will be the very men you have given way to. I have been accused of being a domineering tyrant, thinking only of my pride—I am thinking of the future of this country, threatened with the black waters of confusion, threatened with mob government, threatened with what I cannot see. If by any conduct of mine I help to bring this on us, I shall be ashamed to look my fellows in the face.

> [ANTHONY *stares before him, at what he cannot see, and there is perfect stillness.* FROST *comes in from the hall, and all but* ANTHONY *look round at him uneasily.*]

FROST. [*To his master.*] The men are here, sir.

> [ANTHONY *makes a gesture of dismissal.*]

Shall I bring them in, sir?

ANTHONY. Wait!

> [FROST *goes out,* ANTHONY *turns to face his son.*]

I come to the attack that has been made upon me.

> [EDGAR, *with a gesture of deprecation, remains motionless with his head a little bowed.*]

A woman has died. I am told that her blood is on my

hands; I am told that on my hands is the starvation and the suffering of other women and of children.

EDGAR. I said "on *our* hands," sir.

ANTHONY. It is the same. [*His voice grows stronger and stronger, his feeling is more and more manifest.*] I am not aware that if my adversary suffer in a fair fight not sought by me, it is *my* fault. If I fall under *his* feet—as fall I may—I shall not complain. That will be *my* lookout—and this is—his. I cannot separate, as I would, these men from their women and children. A fair fight is a fair fight! Let them learn to think before they pick a quarrel!

EDGAR. [*In a low voice.*] But is it a fair fight, Father? Look at them, and look at us! They've only this one weapon!

ANTHONY. [*Grimly.*] And you're weak-kneed enough to teach them how to use it! It seems the fashion nowadays for men to take their enemy's side. I have not learnt that art. Is it my fault that they quarreled with their Union too?

EDGAR. There is such a thing as Mercy.

ANTHONY. And Justice comes before it.

EDGAR. What seems just to one man, sir, is injustice to another.

ANTHONY. [*With suppressed passion.*] You accuse me of injustice—of what amounts to inhumanity—of cruelty—

[EDGAR *makes a gesture of horror — a general frightened movement.*]

WANKLIN. Come, come, Chairman.

ANTHONY. [*In a grim voice.*] These are the words of my own son. They are the words of a generation that I don't understand; the words of a soft breed.

[*A general murmur. With a violent effort* ANTHONY *recovers his control.*]

EDGAR. [*Quietly.*] I said it of *myself*, too, Father.

[*A long look is exchanged between them, and* ANTHONY *puts out his hand with a gesture as if to sweep the personalities away; then places it against his brow, swaying as though from giddiness. There is a movement towards him. He moves them back.*]

ANTHONY. Before I put this amendment to the Board, I have one more word to say. [*He looks from face to face.*] If it is carried, it means that we shall fail in what we set ourselves to do. It means that we shall fail in the duty that we owe to all Capital. It means that we shall fail in the duty that we owe ourselves. It means that we shall be open to constant attack to which we as constantly shall have to yield. Be under no misapprehension—run this time, and you will never make a stand again! You will have to fly like curs before the whips of your own men. If that is the lot you wish for, you will vote for this amendment.

[*He looks again, from face to face, finally resting his gaze on* EDGAR; *all sit with their eyes on the ground.* ANTHONY *makes a gesture, and* TENCH *hands him the book. He reads.*]

"Moved by Mr. Wilder, and seconded by Mr. Wanklin: 'That the men's demands be placed at once in the hands of Mr. Simon Harness for settlement on the lines indicated by him this morning.'" [*With sudden vigor.*] Those in favour: Signify the same in the usual way!

[*For a minute no one moves; then hastily, just as* ANTHONY *is about to speak,* WILDER'S *hand and* WANKLIN'S *are held up, then* SCANTLEBURY'S, *and last* EDGAR'S *who does not lift his head.*]

Contrary? [ANTHONY *lifts his own hand.*
[*In a clear voice.*] The amendment is carried. I resign my position on this Board.

[ENID *gasps, and there is dead silence.* ANTHONY

STRIFE

sits motionless, his head slowly drooping; suddenly he heaves as though the whole of his life had risen up within him.]

Fifty years! You have disgraced me, gentlemen. Bring in the men!

[*He sits motionless, staring before him. The Board draws hurriedly together, and forms a group.* TENCH *in a frightened manner speaks into the hall.* UNDERWOOD *almost forces* ENID *from the room.*]

WILDER. [*Hurriedly.*] What's to be said to them? Why isn't Harness here? Ought we to see the men before he comes? I don't——

TENCH. Will you come in, please?

[*Enter* THOMAS, GREEN, BULGIN, *and* ROUS, *who file up in a row past the little table.* TENCH *sits down and writes. All eyes are fixed on* ANTHONY, *who makes no sign.*]

WANKLIN. [*Stepping up to the little table, with nervous cordiality.*] Well, Thomas, how's it to be? What's the result of your meeting?

ROUS. Sim Harness has our answer. He'll tell you what it is. We're waiting for him. He'll speak for us.

WANKLIN. Is that so, Thomas?

THOMAS. [*Sullenly.*] Yes. Roberts will not be coming, his wife is dead.

SCANTLEBURY. Yes, yes! Poor woman! Yes! Yes!

FROST. [*Entering from the hall.*] Mr. Harness, sir!

[*As* HARNESS *enters he retires.*

[HARNESS *has a piece of paper in his hand, he bows to the Directors, nods towards the men, and takes his stand behind the little table in the very centre of the room.*]

HARNESS. Good evening, gentlemen.

[TENCH, *with the paper he has been writing, joins him, they speak together in low tones.*]

WILDER. We've been waiting for you, Harness. Hope we shall come to some——

FROST. [*Entering from the hall.*] Roberts!

[*He goes.*

[ROBERTS *comes hastily in, and stands staring at* ANTHONY. *His face is drawn and old.*]

ROBERTS. Mr. Anthony, I am afraid I am a little late, I would have been here in time but for something that— has happened. [*To the men.*] Has anything been said?

THOMAS. No! But, man, what made ye come?

ROBERTS. Ye told us this morning, gentlemen, to go away and consider our position. We have reconsidered it; we are here to bring you the men's answer. [*To* ANTHONY.] Go ye back to London. We have nothing for you. By no jot or tittle do we abate our demands, nor will we until the whole of those demands are yielded.

[ANTHONY *looks at him but does not speak. There is a movement amongst the men as though they were bewildered.*]

HARNESS. Roberts!

ROBERTS. [*Glancing fiercely at him, and back to* ANTHONY.] Is that clear enough for ye? Is it short enough and to the point? Ye made a mistake to think that we would come to heel. Ye may break the body, but ye cannot break the spirit. Get back to London, the men have nothing for ye.

[*Pausing uneasily he takes a step towards the unmoving* ANTHONY.]

EDGAR. We're all sorry for you, Roberts, but——

ROBERTS. Keep your sorrow, young man. Let your father speak!

STRIFE

HARNESS. [*With the sheet of paper in his hand, speaking from behind the little table.*] Roberts!

ROBERTS. [*To* ANTHONY, *with passionate intensity.*] Why don't ye answer?

HARNESS. Roberts!

ROBERTS. [*Turning sharply.*] What is it?

HARNESS. [*Gravely.*] You're talking without the book; things have travelled past you.

> [*He makes a sign to* TENCH, *who beckons the Directors. They quickly sign his copy of the terms.*]

Look at this, man! [*Holding up his sheet of paper.*] "Demands conceded, *with the exception of those relating to the engineers and furnacemen. Double wages for Saturday's overtime. Night-shifts as they are.*" These terms have been agreed. The men go back to work again to-morrow. The strike is at an end.

ROBERTS. [*Reading the paper, and turning on the men. They shrink from him, all but* ROUS, *who stands his ground. With deadly stillness.*] Ye have gone back on me? I stood by ye to the death; ye waited for *that* to throw me over!

> [*The men answer, all speaking together.*

ROUS. It's a lie!

THOMAS. Ye were past endurance, man.

GREEN. If ye'd listen to me——

BULGIN. [*Under his breath.*] Hold your jaw!

ROBERTS. Ye waited for *that!*

HARNESS. [*Taking the Directors' copy of the terms, and handing his own to* TENCH.] That's enough, men. You had better go.

> [*The men shuffle slowly, awkwardly away.*

WILDER. [*In a low, nervous voice.*] There's nothing to

stay for now, I suppose. [*He follows to the door.*] I shall have a try for that train! Coming, Scantlebury?

SCANTLEBURY. [*Following with* WANKLIN.] Yes, yes; wait for me. [*He stops as* ROBERTS *speaks.*

ROBERTS. [*To* ANTHONY.] But ye have not signed them terms! They can't make terms without their Chairman! Ye would never sign them terms!

[ANTHONY *looks at him without speaking.*
Don't tell me ye have! for the love o' God! [*With passionate appeal.*] I reckoned on ye!

HARNESS. [*Holding out the Directors' copy of the terms.*] *The Board* has signed!

[ROBERTS *looks dully at the signatures—dashes the paper from him, and covers up his eyes.*]

SCANTLEBURY. [*Behind his hand to* TENCH.] Look after the Chairman! He's not well; he's not well—he had no lunch. If there's any fund started for the women and children put me down for—for twenty pounds.

[*He goes out into the hall, in cumbrous haste; and* WANKLIN, *who has been staring at* ROBERTS *and* ANTHONY *with twitchings on his face, follows.* EDGAR *remains seated on the sofa, looking at the ground;* TENCH, *returning to the bureau, writes in his minute-book.* HARNESS *stands by the little table, gravely watching* ROBERTS.]

ROBERTS. Then you're no longer Chairman of this Company! [*Breaking into half-mad laughter.*] Ah! ha—ah, ha, ha! They've thrown ye over—thrown over their Chairman: Ah—ha—ha! [*With a sudden dreadful calm.*] So they've done us both down, Mr. Anthony?

[ENID, *hurrying through the double-doors, comes quickly to her father.*]

ANTHONY. Both broken men, my friend Roberts!

STRIFE

HARNESS. [*Coming down and laying his hands on* ROBERTS's *sleeve.*] For shame, Roberts! Go home quietly, man; go home!

ROBERTS. [*Tearing his arm away.*] Home? [*Shrinking together—in a whisper.*] Home!

ENID. [*Quietly to her father.*] Come away, dear! Come to your room!

> [ANTHONY *rises with an effort. He turns to* ROBERTS *who looks at him. They stand several seconds, gazing at each other fixedly;* ANTHONY *lifts his hand, as though to salute, but lets it fall. The expression of* ROBERTS's *face changes from hostility to wonder. They bend their heads in token of respect.* ANTHONY *turns, and slowly walks towards the curtained door. Suddenly he sways as though about to fall, recovers himself, and is assisted out by* EDGAR *and* ENID; UNDERWOOD *follows, but stops at the door.* ROBERTS *remains motionless for several seconds, staring intently after* ANTHONY, *then goes out into the hall.*]

TENCH. [*Approaching* HARNESS.] It's a great weight off my mind, Mr. Harness! But what a painful scene, sir!
[*He wipes his brow.*

> [HARNESS, *pale and resolute, regards with a grim half-smile the quavering* TENCH.]

It's all been so violent! What did he mean by: "Done us both down?" If he has lost his wife, poor fellow, he oughtn't to have spoken to the Chairman like that!

HARNESS. A woman dead; and the two best men both broken!

TENCH. [*Staring at him—suddenly excited.*] D'you know, sir—these terms, they're the *very same* we drew up together, you and I, and put to both sides before the fight began? All this—all this—and—and what for?

HARNESS. [*In a slow grim voice.*] That's where the fun comes in!

[UNDERWOOD *without turning from the door makes a gesture of assent.*]

The curtain falls.

JUSTICE

A TRAGEDY IN FOUR ACTS

PERSONS OF THE PLAY

JAMES HOW
WALTER HOW, *his son* } *solicitors*
ROBERT COKESON, *their managing clerk*
WILLIAM FALDER, *their junior clerk*
SWEEDLE, *their office-boy*
WISTER, *a detective*
COWLEY, *a cashier*
MR. JUSTICE FLOYD, *a judge*
HAROLD CLEAVER, *an old advocate*
HECTOR FROME, *a young advocate*
CAPTAIN DANSON, V. C., *a prison governor*
THE REV. HUGH MILLER, *a prison chaplain*
EDWARD CLEMENTS, *a prison doctor*
WOODER, *a chief warder*
MOANEY
CLIFTON } *convicts*
O'CLEARY
RUTH HONEYWILL, *a woman*
A NUMBER OF BARRISTERS, SOLICITORS, SPECTATORS, USHERS, REPORTERS, JURYMEN, WARDERS, AND PRISONERS

TIME: The present.

ACT I. *The office of James and Walter How. Morning. July*

ACT II. *Assizes. Afternoon. October.*

ACT III. *A prison. December.*
    SCENE I. *The Governor's office.*
    SCENE II. *A corridor.*
    SCENE III. *A cell.*

ACT IV. *The office of James and Walter How. Morning. March, two years later.*

ACT I

*The scene is the managing clerk's room, at the offices of
JAMES and WALTER HOW, on a July morning. The
room is old-fashioned, furnished with well-worn
mahogany and leather, and lined with tin boxes and
estate plans. It has three doors. Two of them are
close together in the centre of a wall. One of these
two doors leads to the outer office, which is only divided
from the managing clerk's room by a partition of wood
and clear glass; and when the door into this outer
office is opened there can be seen the wide outer door
leading out on to the stone stairway of the building.
The other of these two centre doors leads to the junior
clerk's room. The third door is that leading to the
partners' room.*

*The managing clerk, COKESON, is sitting at his table adding
up figures in a pass-book, and murmuring their numbers to himself. He is a man of sixty, wearing
spectacles; rather short, with a bald head, and an
honest, pug-dog face. He is dressed in a well-worn
black frock-coat and pepper-and-salt trousers.*

COKESON. And five's twelve, and three—fifteen, nineteen, twenty-three, thirty-two, forty-one—and carry four.
[*He ticks the page, and goes on murmuring.*] Five, seven,
twelve, seventeen, twenty-four and nine, thirty-three, thirteen and carry one.

[*He again makes a tick. The outer office door is*

opened, and SWEEDLE, *the office-boy, appears, closing the door behind him. He is a pale youth of sixteen, with spiky hair.*]

COKESON. [*With grumpy expectation.*] And carry one.

SWEEDLE. There's a party wants to see Falder, Mr. Cokeson.

COKESON. Five, nine, sixteen, twenty-one, twenty-nine—and carry two. Send him to Morris's. What name?

SWEEDLE. Honeywill.

COKESON. What's his business?

SWEEDLE. It's a woman.

COKESON. A lady?

SWEEDLE. No, a person.

COKESON. Ask her in. Take this pass-book to Mr. James. [*He closes the pass-book.*

SWEEDLE. [*Reopening the door.*] Will you come in, please?

[RUTH HONEYWILL *comes in. She is a tall woman, twenty-six years old, unpretentiously dressed, with black hair and eyes, and an ivory-white, clear-cut face. She stands very still, having a natural dignity of pose and gesture.* SWEEDLE *goes out into the partners' room with the pass-book.*

COKESON. [*Looking around at* RUTH.] The young man's out. [*Suspiciously.*] State your business, please.

RUTH. [*Who speaks in a matter-of-fact voice, and with a slight West-Country accent.*] It's a personal matter, sir.

COKESON. We don't allow private callers here. Will you leave a message?

RUTH. I'd rather see him, please.

[*She narrows her dark eyes and gives him a honeyed look.*]

COKESON. [*Expanding.*] It's all against the rules.

JUSTICE

Suppose I had *my* friends here to see me! It'd never do!

RUTH. No, sir.

COKESON. [*A little taken aback.*] Exactly! And here you are wanting to see a *junior* clerk!

RUTH. Yes, sir; I must see him.

COKESON. [*Turning full round to her with a sort of outraged interest.*] But this is a lawyer's office. Go to his private address.

RUTH. He's not there.

COKESON. [*Uneasy.*] Are you related to the party?

RUTH. No, sir.

COKESON. [*In real embarrassment.*] I don't know what to say. It's no affair of the office.

RUTH. But what am I to do?

COKESON. Dear me! I can't tell you that.

[SWEEDLE *comes back. He crosses to the outer office and passes through into it, with a quizzical look at* COKESON, *carefully leaving the door an inch or two open.*]

COKESON. [*Fortified by this look.*] This won't do, you know, this won't do at all. Suppose one of the partners came in!

[*An incoherent knocking and chuckling is heard from the outer door of the outer office.*]

SWEEDLE. [*Putting his head in.*] There's some children outside here.

RUTH. They're mine, please.

SWEEDLE. Shall I hold them in check?

RUTH. They're quite small, sir. [*She takes a step towards* COKESON.]

COKESON. You must'nt take up his time in office hours; we're a clerk short as it is.

RUTH. It's a matter of life and death.

COKESON. [*Again outraged.*] Life and death!

SWEEDLE. Here *is* Falder.

> [FALDER *has entered through the outer office. He is a pale, good-looking young man, with quick, rather scared eyes. He moves towards the door of the clerk's office, and stands there irresolute.*]

COKESON. Well, I'll give you a minute. It's not regular.

> [*Taking up a bundle of papers, he goes out into the partners' room.*]

RUTH. [*In a low, hurried voice.*] He's on the drink again, Will. He tried to cut my throat last night. I came out with the children before he was awake. I went round to you——

FALDER. I've changed my digs.

RUTH. Is it all ready for to-night?

FALDER. I've got the tickets. Meet me 11.45 at the booking office. For God's sake don't forget we're man and wife! [*Looking at her with tragic intensity.*] Ruth!

RUTH. You're not afraid of going, are you?

FALDER. Have you got your things, and the children's?

RUTH. Had to leave them, for fear of waking Honeywill, all but one bag. I can't go near home again.

FALDER. [*Wincing.*] All that money gone for nothing. How much *must* you have?

RUTH. Six pounds—I could do with that, I think.

FALDER. Don't give away where we're going. [*As if to himself.*] When I get out there I mean to forget it all.

RUTH. If you're sorry, say so. I'd sooner he killed me than take you against your will.

FALDER. [*With a queer smile.*] We've *got* to go. I don't care; I'll have *you*.

RUTH. You've just to say; it's not too late.

FALDER. It *is* too late. Here's seven pounds. Booking office—11.45 to-night. If you weren't what you are to me, Ruth——!

JUSTICE

RUTH. Kiss me!

> [*They cling together passionately, then fly apart just as* COKESON *re-enters the room.* RUTH *turns and goes out through the outer office.* COKESON *advances deliberately to his chair and seats himself.*]

COKESON. This isn't right, Falder.

FALDER. It shan't occur again, sir.

COKESON. It's an improper use of these premises.

FALDER. Yes, sir.

COKESON. You quite understand—the party was in some distress; and, having children with her, I allowed my feelings—— [*He opens a drawer and produces from it a tract.*] Just take this! "Purity in the Home." It's a well-written thing.

FALDER. [*Taking it, with a peculiar expression.*] Thank you, sir.

COKESON. And look here, Falder, before Mr. Walter comes, have you finished up that cataloguing Davis had in hand before he left?

FALDER. I shall have done with it to-morrow, sir—for good.

COKESON. It's over a week since Davis went. Now it won't do, Falder. You're neglecting your work for private life. I shan't mention about the party having called, but——

FALDER. [*Passing into his room.*] Thank you, sir.

> [COKESON *stares at the door through which* FALDER *has gone out; then shakes his head, and is just settling down to write, when* WALTER How *comes in through the outer office. He is a rather refined-looking man of thirty-five, with a pleasant, almost apologetic voice.*]

WALTER. Good-morning, Cokeson.

COKESON. Morning, Mr. Walter.

WALTER. My father here?

COKESON. [*Always with a certain patronage as to a young man who might be doing better.*] Mr. James has been here since eleven o'clock.

WALTER. I've been in to see the pictures, at the Guildhall.

COKESON. [*Looking at him as though this were exactly what was to be expected.*] Have you now—ye-es. This lease of Boulter's—am I to send it to counsel?

WALTER. What does my father say?

COKESON. 'Aven't bothered him.

WALTER. Well, we can't be too careful.

COKESON. It's such a little thing—hardly worth the fees. I thought you'd do it yourself.

WALTER. Send it, please. I don't want the responsibility.

COKESON. [*With an indescribable air of compassion.*] Just as you like. This "right-of-way" case—we've got 'em on the deeds.

WALTER. I know; but the intention was obviously to exclude that bit of common ground.

COKESON. We needn't worry about that. We're the *right* side of the law.

WALTER. I don't like it.

COKESON. [*With an indulgent smile.*] We shan't want to set ourselves up against the law. Your father wouldn't waste his time doing that.

[*As he speaks* JAMES HOW *comes in from the partners' room. He is a shortish man, with white side-whiskers, plentiful grey hair, shrewd eyes, and gold pince-nez.*]

JAMES. Morning, Walter.

JUSTICE

WALTER. How are you, father?

COKESON. [*Looking down his nose at the papers in his hand as though deprecating their size.*] I'll just take Boulter's lease in to young Falder to draft the instructions.

[*He goes out into* FALDER's *room.*

WALTER. About that right-of-way case?

JAMES. Oh, well, we must go forward there. I thought you told me yesterday the firm's balance was over four hundred.

WALTER. So it is.

JAMES. [*Holding out the pass-book to his son.*] Three—five—one, no recent cheques. Just get me out the cheque-book.

[WALTER *goes to a cupboard, unlocks a drawer, and produces a cheque-book.*]

JAMES. Tick the pounds in the counterfoils. Five, fifty-four, seven, five, twenty-eight, twenty, ninety, eleven, fifty-two, seventy-one. Tally?

WALTER. [*Nodding.*] I can't understand. Made sure it was over four hundred.

JAMES. Give me the cheque-book. [*He takes the cheque-book and cons the counterfoils.*] What's this ninety?

WALTER. Who drew it?

JAMES. You.

WALTER. [*Taking the cheque-book.*] July 7th? That's the day I went down to look over the Trenton Estate—last Friday week; I came back on the Tuesday, you remember. But look here, father, it was *nine* I drew a cheque for. Five guineas to Smithers and my expenses. It just covered all but half a crown.

JAMES. [*Gravely.*] Let's look at that ninety cheque. [*He sorts the cheque out from the bundle in the pocket of the pass-book.*] Seems all right. There's no nine here. This is bad. Who cashed that nine-pound cheque?

WALTER. [*Puzzled and pained.*] Let's see! I was finishing Mrs. Reddy's will—only just had time; yes—I gave it to Cokeson.

JAMES. Look at that t y: that yours?

WALTER. [*After consideration.*] My y's curl back a little; this doesn't.

JAMES. [*As* COKESON *re-enters from* FALDER's *room.*] We must ask him. Just come here and carry your mind back a bit, Cokeson. D'you remember cashing a cheque for Mr. Walter last Friday week—the day he went to Trenton?

COKESON. Ye-es. Nine pounds.

JAMES. Look at this. [*Handing him the cheque.*

COKESON. No! Nine pounds. My lunch was just coming in; and of course I *like* it hot; I gave the cheque to Davis to run round to the bank. He brought it back, all gold—you remember, Mr. Walter, you wanted some silver to pay your cab. [*With a certain contemptuous compassion.*] Here, let *me* see. You've got the wrong cheque.

[*He takes cheque-book and pass-book from* WALTER.]

WALTER. Afraid not.

COKESON. [*Having seen for himself.*] It's funny.

JAMES. You gave it to Davis, and Davis sailed for Australia on Monday. Looks black, Cokeson.

COKESON. [*Puzzled and upset.*] Why this'd be a felony! No, no! there's some mistake.

JAMES. I hope so.

COKESON. There's never been anything of that sort in the office the twenty-nine years I've been here.

JAMES. [*Looking at cheque and counterfoil.*] This is a very clever bit of work; a warning to you not to leave space after your figures, Walter.

WALTER. [*Vexed.*] Yes, I know—I was in such a tearing hurry that afternoon.

COKESON. [*Suddenly.*] This has upset me.

JAMES. The counterfoil altered too—very deliberate piece of swindling. What was Davis's ship?

WALTER. *City of Rangoon.*

JAMES. We ought to wire and have him arrested at Naples; he can't be there yet.

COKESON. His poor young wife. I liked the young man. Dear, oh dear! In this office!

WALTER. Shall I go to the bank and ask the cashier?

JAMES. [*Grimly.*] Bring him round here. And ring up Scotland Yard.

WALTER. Really?

[*He goes out through the outer office.* JAMES *paces the room. He stops and looks at* COKESON, *who is disconsolately rubbing the knees of his trousers.*]

JAMES. Well, Cokeson! There's something in character, isn't there?

COKESON. [*Looking at him over his spectacles.*] I don't quite take you, sir.

JAMES. Your story would sound d——d thin to any one who didn't know you.

COKESON. Ye-es! [*He laughs. Then with sudden gravity.*] I'm sorry for that young man. I feel it as if it was my own son, Mr. James.

JAMES. A nasty business!

COKESON. It unsettles you. All goes on regular, and then a thing like this happens. Shan't relish my lunch to-day.

JAMES. As bad as that, Cokeson?

COKESON. It makes you think. [*Confidentially.*] He must have had temptation.

JAMES. Not so fast. We haven't convicted him yet.

COKESON. I'd sooner have lost a month's salary than had this happen. [*He broods.*

JAMES. I hope that fellow will hurry up.

COKESON. [*Keeping things pleasant for the cashier.*] It isn't fifty yards, Mr. James. He won't be a minute.

JAMES. The idea of dishonesty about this office—it hits me hard, Cokeson.

[*He goes towards the door of the partners' robm.*

SWEEDLE. [*Entering quietly, to* COKESON *in a low voice.*] She's popped up again, sir—something she forgot to say to Falder.

COKESON. [*Roused from his abstraction.*] Eh? Impossible. Send her away!

JAMES. What's that?

COKESON. Nothing, Mr. James. A private matter. Here, I'll come myself. [*He goes into the outer office as* JAMES *passes into the partners' room.*] Now, you really mustn't—we can't have anybody just now.

RUTH. Not for a minute, sir?

COKESON. Reely! Reely! I can't have it. If you want him, wait about; he'll be going out for his lunch directly.

RUTH. Yes, sir.

[WALTER, *entering with the cashier, passes* RUTH *as she leaves the outer office.*]

COKESON. [*To the cashier, who resembles a sedentary dragoon.*] Good-morning. [*To* WALTER.] Your father's in there

[WALTER *crosses and goes into the partners' room.*]

COKESON. It's a nahsty, unpleasant little matter, Mr. Cowley. I'm quite ashamed to have to trouble you.

COWLEY. I remember the cheque quite well. [*As if it were a liver.*] Seemed in perfect order.

JUSTICE

COKESON. Sit down, won't you? I'm not a sensitive man, but a thing like this about the place—it's not nice. I like people to be open and jolly together.

COWLEY. Quite so.

COKESON. [*Buttonholing him, and glancing towards the partners' room.*] Of course he's a young man. I've told him about it before now—leaving space after his figures, but he *will* do it.

COWLEY. I should remember the person's face—quite a youth.

COKESON. I don't think we shall be able to show him to you, as a matter of fact.

[JAMES *and* WALTER *have come back from the partners' room.*]

JAMES. Good-morning, Mr. Cowley. You've seen my son and myself, you've seen Mr. Cokeson, and you've seen Sweedle, my office-boy. It was none of us, I take it.

[*The cashier shakes his head with a smile.*

JAMES. Be so good as to sit there. Cokeson, engage Mr. Cowley in conversation, will you?

[*He goes towards* FALDER'S *room.*

COKESON. Just a word, Mr. James.

JAMES. Well?

COKESON. You don't want to upset the young man in there, do you? He's a nervous young feller.

JAMES. This must be thoroughly cleared up, Cokeson, for the sake of Falder's name, to say nothing of yours.

COKESON. [*With some dignity.*] That'll look after itself, sir. He's been upset once this morning; I don't want him startled again.

JAMES. It's a matter of form; but I can't stand upon niceness over a thing like this—too serious. Just talk to Mr. Cowley.

[*He opens the door of* FALDER'S *room.*

JAMES. Bring in the papers in Boulter's lease, will you, Falder?

COKESON. [*Bursting into voice.*] Do you keep dogs?

> [*The cashier, with his eyes fixed on the door, does not answer.*]

COKESON. You haven't such a thing as a bulldog pup you could spare me, I suppose?

> [*At the look on the cashier's face his jaw drops, and he turns to see* FALDER *standing in the doorway, with his eyes fixed on* COWLEY, *like the eyes of a rabbit fastened on a snake.*]

FALDER. [*Advancing with the papers.*] Here they are, sir!

JAMES. [*Taking them.*] Thank you.

FALDER. Do you want me, sir?

JAMES. No, thanks!

> [FALDER *turns and goes back into his own room. As he shuts the door* JAMES *gives the cashier an interrogative look, and the cashier nods.*]

JAMES. Sure? This isn't as we suspected.

COWLEY. Quite. He knew me. I suppose he can't slip out of that room?

COKESON. [*Gloomily.*] There's only the window—a whole floor and a basement.

> [*The door of* FALDER'S *room is quietly opened, and* FALDER, *with his hat in his hand, moves towards the door of the outer office.*]

JAMES. [*Quietly.*] Where are you going, Falder?

FALDER. To have my lunch, sir.

JAMES. Wait a few minutes, would you? I want to speak to you about this lease.

FALDER. Yes, sir.   [*He goes back into his room.*

COWLEY. If I'm wanted, I can swear that's the young man who cashed the cheque. It was the last cheque I

JUSTICE

handled that morning before my lunch. These are the numbers of the notes he had. [*He puts a slip of paper on the table; then, brushing his hat round.*] Good-morning!

JAMES. Good-morning, Mr. Cowley!

COWLEY. [*To* COKESON.] Good-morning.

COKESON. [*With stupefaction.*] Good-morning.

> [*The cashier goes out through the outer office.* COKESON *sits down in his chair, as though it were the only place left in the morass of his feelings.*]

WALTER. What are you going to do?

JAMES. Have him in. Give me the cheque and the counterfoil.

COKESON. I don't understand. I thought young Davis——

JAMES. We shall see.

WALTER. One moment, father: have you thought it out?

JAMES. Call him in!

COKESON. [*Rising with difficulty and opening* FALDER's *door; hoarsely.*] Step in here a minute.

> [FALDER *comes in.*

FALDER. [*Impassively.*] Yes, sir?

JAMES. [*Turning to him suddenly with the cheque held out.*] You know this cheque, Falder?

FALDER. No, sir.

JAMES. Look at it. You cashed it last Friday week.

FALDER. Oh! yes, sir; that one—Davis gave it me.

JAMES. I know. And you gave Davis the cash?

FALDER. Yes, sir.

JAMES. When Davis gave you the cheque was it exactly like this?

FALDER. Yes, I think so, sir.

JAMES. You know that Mr. Walter drew that cheque for *nine* pounds?

FALDER. No, sir—ninety.

JAMES. Nine, Falder.

FALDER. [*Faintly.*] I don't understand, sir.

JAMES. The suggestion, of course, is that the cheque was altered; whether by you or Davis is the question.

FALDER. I—I——

COKESON. Take your time, take your time.

FALDER. [*Regaining his impassivity.*] Not by me, sir.

JAMES. The cheque was handed to Cokeson by Mr. Walter at one o'clock; we know that because Mr. Cokeson's lunch had just arrived.

COKESON. I couldn't leave it.

JAMES. Exactly; he therefore gave the cheque to Davis. It was cashed by you at 1.15. We know that because the cashier recollects it for the last cheque he handled before *his* lunch.

FALDER. Yes, sir, Davis gave it to me because some friends were giving him a farewell luncheon.

JAMES. [*Puzzled.*] You accuse Davis, then?

FALDER. I don't know, sir—it's very funny.

[*Walter, who has come close to his father, says something to him in a low voice.*]

JAMES. Davis was not here again after that Saturday, was he?

COKESON. [*Anxious to be of assistance to the young man, and seeing faint signs of their all being jolly once more.*] No, he sailed on the Monday.

JAMES. Was he, Falder?

FALDER. [*Very faintly.*] No, sir.

JAMES. Very well, then, how do you account for the fact that this nought was added to the nine in the counterfoil on or after *Tuesday?*

JUSTICE

COKESON. [*Surprised.*] How's that?

[FALDER *gives a sort of lurch; he tries to pull himself together, but he has gone all to pieces.*]

JAMES. [*Very grimly.*] Out, I'm afraid, Cokeson. The cheque-book remained in Mr. Walter's pocket till he came back from Trenton on Tuesday morning. In the face of this, Falder, do you still deny that you altered both cheque and counterfoil?

FALDER. No, sir—no, Mr. How. I did it, sir; I did it.

COKESON. [*Succumbing to his feelings.*] Dear, dear! what a thing to do!

FALDER. I wanted the money so badly, sir. I didn't know what I was doing.

COKESON. However such a thing could have come into your head!

FALDER. [*Grasping at the words.*] I can't think, sir, really! It was just a minute of madness.

JAMES. A long minute, Falder. [*Tapping the counterfoil.*] Four days at least.

FALDER. Sir, I swear I didn't know what I'd done till afterwards, and then I hadn't the pluck. Oh! sir, look over it! I'll pay the money back—I will, I promise.

JAMES. Go into your room.

[FALDER, *with a swift imploring look, goes back into his room. There is silence.*]

JAMES. About as bad a case as there could be.

COKESON. To break the law like that—in here!

WALTER. What's to be done?

JAMES. Nothing for it. Prosecute.

WALTER. It's his first offence.

JAMES. [*Shaking his head.*] I've grave doubts of that. Too neat a piece of swindling altogether.

COKESON. I shouldn't be surprised if he was tempted.

JAMES. Life's one long temptation, Cokeson.

COKESON. Ye-es, but I'm speaking of the flesh and the devil, Mr. James. There was a woman come to see him this morning.

WALTER. The woman we passed as we came in just now. Is it his wife?

COKESON. No, no relation. [*Restraining what in jollier circumstances would have been a wink.*] A married person, though.

WALTER. How do you know?

COKESON. Brought her children. [*Scandalised.*] There they were outside the office.

JAMES. A real bad egg.

WALTER. I should like to give him a chance.

JAMES. I can't forgive him for the sneaky way he went to work—counting on our suspecting young Davis if the matter came to light. It was the merest accident the cheque-book stayed in your pocket.

WALTER. It *must* have been the temptation of a moment. He hadn't time.

JAMES. A man doesn't succumb like that in a moment, if he's a clean mind and habits. He's rotten; got the eyes of a man who can't keep his hands off when there's money about.

WALTER. [*Drily.*] We hadn't noticed that before.

JAMES. [*Brushing the remark aside.*] I've seen lots of those fellows in my time. No doing anything with them except to keep 'em out of harm's way. They've got a blind spot.

WALTER. It's penal servitude.

COKESON. They're *nahsty* places—prisons.

JAMES. [*Hesitating.*] I don't see how it's possible to spare him. Out of the question to keep him in this office—honesty's the *sine qua non*.

COKESON. [*Hypnotised.*] Of course it *is*.

JUSTICE 179

JAMES. Equally out of the question to send him out amongst people who've no knowledge of his character. One must think of society.

WALTER. But to brand him like this?

JAMES. If it had been a straightforward case I'd give him another chance. It's far from that. He has dissolute habits.

COKESON. I didn't say that—extenuating circumstances.

JAMES. Same thing. He's gone to work in the most cold-blooded way to defraud his employers, and cast the blame on an innocent man. If that's not a case for the law to take its course, I don't know what is.

WALTER. For the sake of his future, though.

JAMES. [*Sarcastically.*] According to you, no one would ever prosecute.

WALTER. [*Nettled.*] I hate the idea of it.

COKESON. That's *rather ex parte,* Mr. Walter! We must have protection.

JAMES. This is degenerating into talk.

[*He moves towards the partners' room.*]

WALTER. Put yourself in his place, father.

JAMES. You ask too much of me.

WALTER. We can't possibly tell the pressure there was on him.

JAMES. You may depend on it, my boy, if a man is going to do this sort of thing he'll do it, pressure or no pressure; if he isn't nothing'll make him.

WALTER. He'll never do it again.

COKESON. [*Fatuously.*] S'pose I were to have a talk with him. We don't want to be hard on the young man.

JAMES. That'll do, Cokeson. I've made up my mind.

[*He passes into the partners' room.*]

COKESON. [*After a doubtful moment.*] We must excuse

your father. I don't want to go against your father; if he thinks it right.

WALTER. Confound it, Cokeson! why don't you back me up? You know you feel——

COKESON. [*On his dignity.*] I really can't say what I feel.

WALTER. We shall regret it.

COKESON. He must have known what he was doing.

WALTER. [*Bitterly.*] "The quality of mercy is not strained."

COKESON. [*Looking at him askance.*] Come, come, Mr. Walter. We must try and see it sensible.

SWEEDLE. [*Entering with a tray.*] Your lunch, sir.

COKESON. Put it down!

[*While SWEEDLE is putting it down on COKESON's table, the detective, WISTER, enters the outer office, and, finding no one there, comes to the inner doorway. He is a square, medium-sized man, clean-shaved, in a serviceable blue serge suit and strong boots.*]

WISTER. [*To WALTER.*] From Scotland Yard, sir. Detective-Sergeant Wister.

WALTER. [*Askance.*] Very well! I'll speak to my father.

[*He goes into the partners' room. JAMES enters.*

JAMES. Morning! [*In answer to an appealing gesture from Cokeson.*] I'm sorry; I'd stop short of this if I felt I could. Open that door. [*Sweedle, wondering and scared, opens it.*] Come here, Mr. Falder.

[*As FALDER comes shrinkingly out, the detective, in obedience to a sign from JAMES, slips his hand out and grasps his arm.*]

FALDER. [*Recoiling.*] Oh! no,—oh! no!

WISTER. Come, come, there's a good lad.

JAMES. I charge him with felony.

FALDER. Oh, sir! There's some one—I did it for her. Let me be till to-morrow.

> [JAMES *motions with his hand. At that sign of hardness,* FALDER *becomes rigid. Then, turning, he goes out quietly in the detective's grip.* JAMES *follows, stiff and erect.* SWEEDLE, *rushing to the door with open mouth, pursues them through the outer office into the corridor. When they have all disappeared* COKESON *spins completely round and makes a rush for the outer office.*]

COKESON. [*Hoarsely.*] Here! Here! What are we doing?
> [*There is silence. He takes out his handkerchief and mops the sweat from his face. Going back blindly to his table, sits down, and stares blankly at his lunch.*]

The curtain falls.

ACT II

A Court of Justice, on a foggy October afternoon—crowded with barristers, solicitors, reporters, ushers, and jurymen. Sitting in the large, solid dock is FALDER, *with a warder on either side of him, placed there for his safe custody, but seemingly indifferent to and unconscious of his presence.* FALDER *is sitting exactly opposite to the* JUDGE, *who, raised above the clamour of the court, also seems unconscious of and indifferent to everything.* HAROLD CLEAVER, *the counsel for the Crown, is a dried, yellowish man, of more than middle age, in a wig worn almost to the colour of his face.* HECTOR FROME, *the counsel for the defence, is a young, tall man, clean-shaved, in a very white wig. Among the spectators, having already given their evidence, are* JAMES *and* WALTER HOW, *and* COWLEY, *the cashier.* WISTER, *the detective, is just leaving the witness-box.*

CLEAVER. That is the case for the Crown, me lud!
  [*Gathering his robes together, he sits down.*
FROME. [*Rising and bowing to the* JUDGE.] If it please your lordship and gentlemen of the jury. I am not going to dispute the fact that the prisoner altered this cheque, but I am going to put before you evidence as to the condition of his mind, and to submit that you would not be justified in finding that he was responsible for his actions at the time. I am going to show you, in fact, that he did this in a moment of aberration, amounting to temporary insanity, caused by the violent distress under which he was labouring. Gentlemen, the prisoner is only twenty-three years old. I shall call before you a woman from whom you will learn the events that led up to this act. You will hear from her own lips the tragic circumstances of her life, the still more tragic infatuation with which she has inspired the prisoner. This woman, gentlemen, has been leading a miserable existence with a husband who habitually ill-uses her, from whom she actually goes in terror of her life. I am not, of course, saying that it's either right or desirable for a young man to fall in love with a married woman, or that it's his business to rescue her from an ogre-like husband. I'm not saying anything of the sort. But we all know the power of the passion of love; and I would ask you to remember, gentlemen, in listening to her evidence, that, married to a drunken and violent husband, she has no power to get rid of him; for, as you know, another offence besides violence is necessary to enable a woman to obtain a divorce;

JUSTICE

and of this offence it does not appear that her husband is guilty.

JUDGE. Is this relevant, Mr. Frome?

FROME. My lord, I submit, extremely—I shall be able to show your lordship that directly.

JUDGE. Very well.

FROME. In these circumstances, what alternatives were left to her? She could either go on living with this drunkard, in terror of her life; or she could apply to the Court for a separation order. Well, gentlemen, my experience of such cases assures me that this would have given her very insufficient protection from the violence of such a man; and even if effectual would very likely have reduced her either to the workhouse or the streets—for it's not easy, as she is now finding, for an unskilled woman without means of livelihood to support herself and her children without resorting either to the Poor Law or—to speak quite plainly—to the sale of her body.

JUDGE. You are ranging rather far, Mr. Frome.

FROME. I shall fire point-blank in a minute, my lord.

JUDGE. Let us hope so.

FROME. Now, gentlemen, mark—and this is what I have been leading up to—this woman will tell you, and the prisoner will confirm her, that, confronted with such alternatives, she set her whole hopes on himself, knowing the feeling with which she had inspired him. She saw a way out of her misery by going with him to a new country, where they would both be unknown, and might pass as husband and wife. This was a desperate and, as my friend Mr. Cleaver will no doubt call it, an immoral resolution; but, as a fact, the minds of both of them were constantly turned towards it. One wrong is no excuse for another, and those who are never likely to be faced by such a situation possibly have the right to hold up their hands—

as to that I prefer to say nothing. But whatever view you take, gentlemen, of this part of the prisoner's story—whatever opinion you form of the right of these two young people under such circumstances to take the law into their own hands—the fact remains that this young woman in her distress, and this young man, little more than a boy, who was so devotedly attached to her, *did* conceive this—if you like—reprehensible design of going away together. Now, for that, of course, they required money, and—they had none. As to the actual events of the morning of July 7th, on which this cheque was altered, the events on which I rely to prove the defendant's irresponsibility—I shall allow those events to speak for themselves, through the lips of my witnesses. Robert Cokeson. [*He turns, looks round, takes up a sheet of paper, and waits.*]

> [COKESON *is summoned into court, and goes into the witness-box, holding his hat before him. The oath is administered to him.*]

FROME. What is your name?

COKESON. Robert Cokeson.

FROME. Are you managing clerk to the firm of solicitors who employ the prisoner?

COKESON. Ye-es.

FROME. How long had the prisoner been in their employ?

COKESON. Two years. No, I'm wrong there—all but seventeen days.

FROME. Had you him under your eye all that time?

COKESON. Except Sundays and holidays.

FROME. Quite so. Let us hear, please, what you have to say about his general character during those two years.

COKESON. [*Confidentially to the jury, and as if a little surprised at being asked.*] He was a nice, pleasant-spoken young man. I'd no fault to find with him—quite the contrary. It was a *great* surprise to me when he did a thing like that.

FROME. Did he ever give you reason to suspect his honesty?

COKESON. No! To have dishonesty in our office, that'd never do.

FROME. I'm sure the jury fully appreciate that, Mr. Cokeson.

COKESON. Every man of business knows that honesty's the sign qua non.

FROME. Do you give him a good character all round, or do you not?

COKESON. [*Turning to the* JUDGE.] Certainly. We were all very jolly and pleasant together, until this happened. Quite upset me.

FROME. Now, coming to the morning of the 7th of July, the morning on which the cheque was altered. What have you to say about his demeanour that morning?

COKESON. [*To the jury.*] If you ask me, I don't think he was quite compos when he did it.

THE JUDGE. [*Sharply.*] Are you suggesting that he was insane?

COKESON. Not compos.

THE JUDGE. A little more precision, please.

FROME. [*Smoothly.*] Just tell us, Mr. Cokeson.

COKESON. [*Somewhat outraged.*] Well, in my opinion —[*looking at the* JUDGE.]—such as it is—he was jumpy at the time. The jury will understand my meaning.

FROME. Will you tell us how you came to that conclusion?

COKESON. Ye-es, I will. I have my lunch in from the restaurant, a chop and a potato—saves time. That day it happened to come just as Mr. Walter How handed me the cheque. Well, I like it hot; so I went into the clerks' office and I handed the cheque to Davis, the other clerk, and told him to get change. I noticed young Falder was walking up and down. I said to him: "This is not the Zoological Gardens, Falder."

FROME. Do you remember what he answered?

COKESON. Ye-es: "I wish to God it were!" Struck me as funny.

FROME. Did you notice anything else peculiar?

COKESON. I did.

FROME. What was that?

COKESON. His collar was unbuttoned. Now, I like a young man to be neat. I said to him: "Your collar's unbuttoned."

FROME. And what did he answer?

COKESON. Stared at me. It wasn't nice.

THE JUDGE. Stared at you? Isn't that a very common practice?

COKESON. Ye-es, but it was the look in his eyes. I can't explain my meaning—it was funny.

FROME. Had you ever seen such a look in his eyes before?

COKESON. No. If I had I should have spoken to the partners. We can't have anything eccentric in our profession.

THE JUDGE. Did you speak to them on that occasion?

COKESON. [*Confidentially.*] Well, I didn't like to trouble them about prime facey evidence.

FROME. But it made a very distinct impression on your mind?

COKESON. Ye-es. The clerk Davis could have told you the same.

FROME. Quite so. It's very unfortunate that we've not got him here. Now can you tell me of the morning on which the discovery of the forgery was made? That would be the 18th. Did anything happen that morning?

COKESON. [*With his hand to his ear.*] I'm a little deaf.

FROME. Was there anything in the course of that morning—I mean before the discovery—that caught your attention?

COKESON. Ye-es—a woman.

THE JUDGE. How is *this* relevant, Mr. Frome?

FROME. I am trying to establish the state of mind in which the prisoner committed this act, my lord.

THE JUDGE. I quite appreciate that. But this was long after the act.

FROME. Yes, my lord, but it contributes to my contention.

THE JUDGE. Well!

FROME. You say a woman. Do you mean that she came to the office?

COKESON. Ye-es.

FROME. What for?

COKESON. Asked to see young Falder; he was out at the moment.

FROME. Did you see her?

COKESON. I did.

FROME. Did she come alone?

COKESON. [*Confidentially.*] Well, there you put me in a difficulty. I mustn't tell you what the office-boy told me.

FROME. Quite so, Mr. Cokeson, quite so——

COKESON. [*Breaking in with an air of "You are young—leave it to me."*] But I think we can get round it. In answer to a question put to her by a third party the woman said to me: "They're mine, sir."

THE JUDGE. What are? What were?

COKESON. Her children. They were outside.

THE JUDGE. How do you know?

COKESON. Your lordship mustn't ask me that, or I shall have to tell you what I was told—and that'd never do.

THE JUDGE. [*Smiling.*] The office-boy made a statement.

COKESON. Egg-zactly.

FROME. What I want to ask you, Mr. Cokeson, is this. In the course of her appeal to see Falder, did the woman say anything that you specially remember?

COKESON. [*Looking at him as if to encourage him to complete the sentence.*] A leetle more, sir.

FROME. Or did she not?

COKESON. She did. I shouldn't like you to have led me to the answer.

FROME. [*With an irritated smile.*] Will you tell the jury what it was?

COKESON. "It's a matter of life and death."

FOREMAN OF THE JURY. Do you mean the woman said that?

COKESON. [*Nodding.*] It's not the sort of thing you like to have said to you.

FROME. [*A little impatiently.*] Did Falder come in while she was there? [COKESON *nods.*] And she saw him, and went away?

COKESON. Ah! there I can't follow you. I didn't see her go.

FROME. Well, is she there now?

COKESON. [*With an indulgent smile.*] No!

FROME. Thank you, Mr. Cokeson. [*He sits down.*

CLEAVER. [*Rising.*] You say that on the morning of the forgery the prisoner was jumpy. Well, now, sir, what precisely do you mean by that word?

COKESON. [*Indulgently.*] I *want* you to understand. Have you ever seen a dog that's lost its master? He was kind of everywhere at once with his eyes.

CLEAVER. Thank you; I was coming to his eyes. You called them "funny." What are we to understand by that? Strange, or what?

COKESON. Ye-es, funny.

CLEAVER. [*Sharply.*] Yes, sir, but what may be funny to you may not be funny to me, or to the jury. Did they look frightened, or shy, or fierce, or what?

COKESON. You make it very hard for me. I give you the word, and you want me to give you another.

CLEAVER. [*Rapping his desk.*] Does "funny" mean mad?

COKESON. Not mad, fun——

CLEAVER. Very well! Now you say he had his collar unbuttoned? Was it a hot day?

COKESON. Ye-es; I think it was.

CLEAVER. And did he button it when you called his attention to it?

COKESON. Ye-es. I think he did.

CLEAVER. Would you say that that denoted insanity?

[*He sits down.* COKESON, *who has opened his mouth to reply, is left gaping.*]

FROME. [*Rising hastily.*] Have you ever caught him in that dishevelled state before?

COKESON. No! He was *always* clean and quiet.

FROME. That will do, thank you.

[COKESON *turns blandly to the* JUDGE, *as though to rebuke counsel for not remembering that the* JUDGE *might wish to have a chance; arriving at the conclusion that he is to be asked nothing further, he turns and descends from the box, and sits down next to* JAMES *and* WALTER.]

FROME. Ruth Honeywill.

[*Ruth comes into court, and takes her stand stoically in the witness-box. She is sworn.*]

FROME. What is your name, please?

RUTH. Ruth Honeywill.

FROME. How old are you?

RUTH. Twenty-six.

FROME. You are a married woman, **living with your husband?** A little louder.

RUTH. No, sir; not since July.

FROME. Have you any children?

RUTH. Yes, sir, two.

FROME. Are they living with you?

RUTH. Yes, sir.

FROME. You know the prisoner?

RUTH. [*Looking at him.*] Yes.

FROME. What was the nature of your relations with him?

RUTH. We were friends.

THE JUDGE. Friends?

RUTH. [*Simply.*] Lovers, sir.

THE JUDGE. [*Sharply.*] In what sense do you use that word?

RUTH. We love each other.

THE JUDGE. Yes, but——

RUTH. [*Shaking her head.*] No, your lordship, not yet.

THE JUDGE. Not yet! H'm! [*He looks from* RUTH *to* FALDER.] Well!

FROME. What is your husband?

RUTH. Traveller.

FROME. And what was the nature of your married life?

RUTH. [*Shaking her head.*] It don't bear talking about.

FROME. Did he ill-treat you, or what?

RUTH. Ever since my first was born.

FROME. In what way?

RUTH. I'd rather not say. All sorts of ways.

THE JUDGE. I am afraid I must stop this, you know.

RUTH. [*Pointing to* FALDER.] He offered to take me out of it, sir. We were going to South America.

JUSTICE 191

FROME. [*Hastily.*] Yes, quite—and what prevented you?

RUTH. I was outside his office when he was taken away. It nearly broke my heart.

FROME. You knew, then, that he had been arrested?

RUTH. Yes, sir. I called at his office afterwards, and [*pointing to* COKESON] that gentleman told me all about it.

FROME. Now, do you remember the morning of Friday, July 7th?

RUTH. Yes.

FROME. Why?

RUTH. My husband nearly strangled me that morning.

THE JUDGE. Nearly strangled you!

RUTH. [*Bowing her head.*] Yes, my lord.

FROME. With his hands, or——?

RUTH. Yes, I just managed to get away from him. I went straight to my friend. It was eight o'clock.

THE JUDGE. In the morning? Your husband was not under the influence of liquor then?

RUTH. It wasn't always that.

FROME. In what condition were you?

RUTH. In very bad condition, sir. My dress was torn, and I was half choking.

FROME. Did you tell your friend what had happened?

RUTH. Yes. I wish I never had.

FROME. It upset him?

RUTH. Dreadfully.

FROME. Did he ever speak to you about a cheque?

RUTH. Never.

FROME. Did he ever give you any money?

RUTH. Yes.

FROME. When was that?

RUTH. On Saturday.

FROME. The 8th?

RUTH. To buy an outfit for me and the children and get all ready to start.

FROME. Did that surprise you, or not?

RUTH. What, sir?

FROME. That he had money to give you.

RUTH. Yes, because on the morning when my husband nearly killed me my friend cried because he hadn't the money to get me away. He told me afterwards he'd come into a windfall.

FROME. And when did you last see him?

RUTH. The day he was taken away, sir. It was the day we were to have started.

FROME. Oh, yes, the morning of the arrest. Well, did you see him at all between the Friday and that morning? [RUTH *nods*.] What was his manner then?

RUTH. Dumb-like—sometimes he didn't seem able to say a word.

FROME. As if something unusual had happened to him?

RUTH. Yes.

FROME. Painful, or pleasant, or what?

RUTH. Like a fate hanging over him.

FROME. [*Hesitating*.] Tell me, did you love the prisoner very much?

RUTH. [*Bowing her head*.] Yes.

FROME. And had he a very great affection for you?

RUTH. [*Looking at* FALDER.] Yes, sir.

FROME. Now, ma'am, do you or do you not think that your danger and unhappiness would seriously affect his balance, his control over his actions?

RUTH. Yes.

FROME. His reason, even?

RUTH. For a moment like, I think it would.

FROME. Was he very much upset that Friday morning, or was he fairly calm?

JUSTICE

RUTH. Dreadfully upset. I could hardly bear to let him go from me.

FROME. Do you still love him?

RUTH. [*With her eyes on* FALDER.] He's ruined himself for me.

FROME. Thank you.

> [*He sits down.* RUTH *remains stoically upright in the witness-box.*]

CLEAVER. [*In a considerate voice.*] When you left him on the morning of Friday the 7th you would not say that he was out of his mind, I suppose?

RUTH. No, sir.

CLEAVER. Thank you; I've no further questions to ask you.

RUTH. [*Bending a little forward to the jury.*] I would have done the same for him; I would indeed.

THE JUDGE. Please, please! You say your married life is an unhappy one? Faults on both sides?

RUTH. Only that I never bowed down to him. I don't see why I should, sir, not to a man like that.

THE JUDGE. You refused to obey him?

RUTH. [*Avoiding the question.*] I've always studied him to keep things nice.

THE JUDGE. Until you met the prisoner—was that it?

RUTH. No; even after that.

THE JUDGE. I ask, you know, because you seem to me to glory in this affection of yours for the prisoner.

RUTH. [*Hesitating.*] I—I do. It's the only thing in my life now.

THE JUDGE. [*Staring at her hard.*] Well, step down, please.

> [Ruth *looks at* FALDER, *then passes quietly down and takes her seat among the witnesses.*]

FROME. I call the prisoner, my lord.

[FALDER *leaves the dock; goes into the witness-box, and is duly sworn.*]

FROME. What is your name?

FALDER. William Falder.

FROME. And age?

FALDER. Twenty-three.

FROME. You are not married?

[FALDER *shakes his head.*

FROME. How long have you known the last witness?

FALDER. Six months.

FROME. Is her account of the relationship between you a correct one?

FALDER. Yes.

FROME. You became devotedly attached to her, however?

FALDER. Yes.

THE JUDGE. Though you knew she was a married woman?

FALDER. I couldn't help it, your lordship.

THE JUDGE. Couldn't help it?

FALDER. I didn't seem able to.

[*The* JUDGE *slightly shrugs his shoulders.*

FROME. How did you come to know her?

FALDER. Through my married sister.

FROME. Did you know whether she was happy with her husband?

FALDER. It was trouble all the time.

FROME. You knew her husband?

FALDER. Only through her—he's a brute.

THE JUDGE. I can't allow indiscriminate abuse of a person not present.

FROME. [*Bowing.*] If your lordship pleases. [*To* FALDER.] You admit altering this cheque?

[FALDER *bows his head.*

FROME. Carry your mind, please, to the morning of Friday, July the 7th, and tell the jury what happened.

FALDER. [*Turning to the jury.*] I was having my breakfast when she came. Her dress was all torn, and she was gasping and couldn't seem to get her breath at all; there were the marks of his fingers round her throat; her arm was bruised, and the blood had got into her eyes dreadfully. It frightened me, and then when she told me, I felt—I felt—well—it was too much for me! [*Hardening suddenly.*] If you'd seen it, having the feelings for her that I had, you'd have felt the same, I know.

FROME. Yes?

FALDER. When she left me—because I had to go to the office—I was out of my senses for fear that he'd do it again, and thinking what I could do. I couldn't work—all the morning I was like that—simply couldn't fix my mind on anything. I couldn't think at all. I seemed to have to keep moving. When Davis—the other clerk—gave me the cheque—he said: "It'll do you good, Will, to have a run with this. You seem half off your chump this morning." Then when I had it in my hand—I don't know how it came, but it just flashed across me that if I put the t y and the nought there would be the money to get her away. It just came and went—I never thought of it again. Then Davis went out to his luncheon, and I don't really remember what I did till I'd pushed the cheque through to the cashier under the rail. I remember his saying "Gold or notes?" Then I suppose I knew what I'd done. Anyway, when I got outside I wanted to chuck myself under a 'bus; I wanted to throw the money away; but it seemed I was in for it, so I thought at any rate I'd save her. Of course the tickets I took for the passage and the little I gave her's been wasted, and all, except what I was obliged to spend myself, I've restored. I keep thinking over and over however it was I came to do it, and how I can't have it all again to do differently.

[FALDER *is silent, twisting his hands before him.*]

FROME. How far is it from your office to the bank?

FALDER. Not more than fifty yards, sir.

FROME. From the time Davis went out to lunch to the time you cashed the cheque, how long do you say it must have been?

FALDER. It couldn't have been four minutes, sir, because I ran all the way.

FROME. During those four minutes you say you remember nothing?

FALDER. No, sir; only that I ran.

FROME. Not even adding the t y and the nought?

FALDER. No, sir. I don't really.

[FROME *sits down, and* CLEAVER *rises.*]

CLEAVER. But you remember running, do you?

FALDER. I was all out of breath when I got to the bank.

CLEAVER. And you don't remember altering the cheque?

FALDER. [*Faintly.*] No, sir.

CLEAVER. Divested of the romantic glamour which my friend is casting over the case, is this anything but an ordinary forgery? Come.

FALDER. I was half frantic all that morning, sir.

CLEAVER. Now, now! You don't deny that the t y and the nought were so like the rest of the handwriting as to thoroughly deceive the cashier?

FALDER. It was an accident.

CLEAVER. [*Cheerfully.*] Queer sort of accident, wasn't it? On which day did you alter the counterfoil?

FALDER. [*Hanging his head.*] On the Wednesday morning.

CLEAVER. Was that an accident too?

FALDER. [*Faintly.*] No.

JUSTICE

CLEAVER. To do that you had to watch your opportunity, I suppose?

FALDER. [*Almost inaudibly.*] Yes.

CLEAVER. You don't suggest that you were suffering under great excitement when you did that?

FALDER. I was haunted.

CLEAVER. With the fear of being found out?

FALDER. [*Very low.*] Yes.

THE JUDGE. Didn't it occur to you that the only thing for you to do was to confess to your employers, and restore the money?

FALDER. I was afraid. [*There is silence.*

CLEAVER. You desired, too, no doubt, to complete your design of taking this woman away?

FALDER. When I found I'd done a thing like that, to do it for nothing seemed so dreadful. I might just as well have chucked myself into the river.

CLEAVER. You knew that the clerk Davis was about to leave England—didn't it occur to you when you altered this cheque that suspicion would fall on him?

FALDER. It was all done in a moment. I thought of it afterwards.

CLEAVER. And that didn't lead you to avow what you'd done?

FALDER. [*Sullenly.*] I meant to write when I got out there—I would have repaid the money.

THE JUDGE. But in the meantime your innocent fellow clerk might have been prosecuted.

FALDER. I knew he was a long way off, your lordship. I thought there'd be time. I didn't think they'd find it out so soon.

FROME. I might remind your lordship that as Mr. Walter How had the cheque-book in his pocket till after Davis had sailed, if the discovery had been made only one day later

Falder himself would have left, and suspicion would have attached to him, and not to Davis, from the beginning.

THE JUDGE. The question is whether the prisoner knew that suspicion would light on himself, and not on Davis. [*To* FALDER *sharply.*] Did you know that Mr. Walter How had the cheque-book till after Davis had sailed?

FALDER. I—I—thought—he——

THE JUDGE. Now speak the truth—yes or no!

FALDER. [*Very low.*] No, my lord. I had no means of knowing.

THE JUDGE. That disposes of your point, Mr. Frome.

[FROME *bows to the Judge.*

CLEAVER. Has any aberration of this nature ever attacked you before?

FALDER. [*Faintly.*] No, sir.

CLEAVER. You had recovered sufficiently to go back to your work that afternoon?

FALDER. Yes, I had to take the money back.

CLEAVER. You mean the *nine* pounds. Your wits were sufficiently keen for you to remember that. And you still persist in saying you don't remember altering this cheque.

[*He sits down.*

FALDER. If I hadn't been mad I should never have had the courage.

FROME. [*Rising.*] Did you have your lunch before going back?

FALDER. I never ate a thing all day; and at night I couldn't sleep.

FROME. Now, as to the four minutes that elapsed between Davis's going out and your cashing the cheque: do you say that you recollect *nothing* during those four minutes?

FALDER. [*After a moment.*] I remember thinking of Mr. Cokeson's face.

JUSTICE

FROME. Of Mr. Cokeson's face! Had that any connection with what you were doing?

FALDER. No, sir.

FROME. Was that in the office, before you ran out?

FALDER. Yes, and while I was running.

FROME. And that lasted till the cashier said: "Will you have gold or notes?"

FALDER. Yes, and then I seemed to come to myself—and it was too late.

FROME. Thank you. That closes the evidence for the defence, my lord.

[*The* JUDGE *nods, and* FALDER *goes back to his seat in the dock.*]

FROME. [*Gathering up notes.*] If it please your lordship—Gentlemen of the Jury,—My friend in cross-examination has shown a disposition to sneer at the defence which has been set up in this case, and I am free to admit that nothing I can say will move you, if the evidence has not already convinced you that the prisoner committed this act in a moment when to all practical intents and purposes he was not responsible for his actions; a moment of such mental and moral vacuity, arising from the violent emotional agitation under which he had been suffering, as to amount to temporary madness. My friend has alluded to the "romantic glamour" with which I have sought to invest this case. Gentlemen, I have done nothing of the kind. I have merely shown you the background of "life"—that palpitating life which, believe me—whatever my friend may say—always lies behind the commission of a crime. Now gentlemen, we live in a highly civilized age, and the sight of brutal violence disturbs us in a very strange way, even when we have no personal interest in the matter. But when we see it inflicted on a woman whom we love—what then? Just think of what your own feelings would have been, each of you, at the prisoner's age; and then look at him. Well! he is hardly the comfortable, shall we say bucolic, person likely to contemplate with equanimity marks of gross violence on a woman to whom he was devotedly attached. Yes, gentlemen, look at him! He has not a strong face; but neither has he a vicious face. He is just the sort of man who would easily become the prey of his emotions. You have heard the description of his eyes. My friend may laugh at the word "funny"—*I* think it better describes the peculiar uncanny look of those who are strained to breaking-point than any other word which could have been used. I don't pretend, mind you, that his mental irresponsibility was more than a flash of darkness, in which all sense of proportion became lost; but I do contend, that, just as a man who destroys himself at such a moment may be, and often is, absolved from the stigma attaching to the crime of selfmurder, so he may, and frequently does, commit other crimes while in this irresponsible condition, and that he may as justly be acquitted of criminal intent and treated as a patient. I admit that this is a plea which might well be abused. It is a matter for discretion. But here you have a case in which there is every reason to give the benefit of the doubt. You heard me ask the prisoner what he thought of during those four fatal minutes. What was his answer? "I thought of Mr. Cokeson's face!" Gentlemen, no man could invent an answer like that; it is absolutely stamped with truth. You have seen the great affection (legitimate or not) existing between him and this woman, who came here to give evidence for him at the risk of her life. It is impossible for you to doubt his distress on the morning when he committed this act. We well know what terrible havoc such distress can make in weak and highly nervous people. It was all the work of a moment. The rest has followed, as death follows a stab to the heart, or water drops

JUSTICE

if you hold up a jug to empty it. Believe me, gentlemen, there is nothing more tragic in life than the utter impossibility of changing what you have done. Once this cheque was altered and presented, the work of four minutes—four mad minutes—the rest has been silence. But in those four minutes the boy before you has slipped through a door, hardly opened, into that great cage which never again quite lets a man go—the cage of the Law. His further acts, his failure to confess, the alteration of the counterfoil, his preparations for flight, are all evidence—not of deliberate and guilty intention when he committed the prime act from which these subsequent acts arose; no—they are merely evidence of the weak character which is clearly enough his misfortune. But is a man to be lost because he is bred and born with a weak character? Gentlemen, men like the prisoner are destroyed daily under our law for want of that human insight which sees them as they are, patients, and not criminals. If the prisoner be found guilty, and treated as though he were a criminal type, he will, as all experience shows, in all probability become one. I beg you not to return a verdict that may thrust him back into prison and brand him for ever. Gentlemen, Justice is a machine that, when some one has once given it the starting push, rolls on of itself. Is this young man to be ground to pieces under this machine for an act which at the worst was one of weakness? Is he to become a member of the luckless crews that man those dark, ill-starred ships called prisons? Is that to be his voyage—from which so few return? Or is he to have another chance, to be still looked on as one who has gone a little astray, but who will come back? I urge you, gentlemen, do not ruin this young man! For, as a result of those four minutes, ruin, utter and irretrievable, stares him in the face. He can be saved now. Imprison him as a criminal, and I affirm to you that he will be lost. He has neither the face nor the manner of one who can survive that terrible ordeal. Weigh in the scales his criminality and the suffering he has undergone. The latter is ten times heavier already. He has lain in prison under this charge for more than two months. Is he likely ever to forget that? Imagine the anguish of his mind during that time. He has had his punishment, gentlemen, you may depend. The rolling of the chariot-wheels of Justice over this boy began when it was decided to prosecute him. We are now already at the second stage. If you permit it to go on to the third I would not give—that for him.

> [*He holds up finger and thumb in the form of a circle, drops his hand, and sits down. The jury stir, and consult each other's faces; then they turn towards the counsel for the Crown, who rises, and, fixing his eyes on a spot that seems to give him satisfaction, slides them every now and then towards the jury.*]

CLEAVER. May it please your lordship [*Rising on his toes.*] Gentlemen of the Jury,—The facts in this case are not disputed, and the defence, if my friend will allow me to say so, is so thin that I don't propose to waste the time of the Court by taking you over the evidence. The plea is one of temporary insanity. Well, gentlemen, I daresay it is clearer to me than it is to you why this rather—what shall we call it?—bizarre defence has been set up. The alternative would have been to plead guilty. Now, gentlemen, if the prisoner had pleaded guilty my friend would have had to rely on a simple appeal to his lordship. Instead of that, he has gone into the byways and hedges and found this—er—peculiar plea, which has enabled him to show you the proverbial woman, to put her in the box—to give, in fact, a romantic glow to this affair. I compliment my friend; I think it highly ingenious of him. By these means, he has—

to a certain extent—got round the Law. He has brought the whole story of motive and stress out in court, at first hand, in a way that he would not otherwise have been able to do. But when you have once grasped that fact, gentlemen, you have grasped everything. [*With good-humoured contempt.*] For look at this plea of insanity; we can't put it lower than that. You have heard the woman. She has every reason to favour the prisoner, but what did she say? She said that the prisoner was *not* insane when she left him in the morning. If he were going out of his mind through distress, that was obviously the moment when insanity would have shown itself. You have heard the managing clerk, another witness for the defence. With some difficulty I elicited from him the admission that the prisoner, though jumpy (a word that he seemed to think you would understand, gentlemen, and I'm sure I hope you do), was *not* mad when the cheque was handed to Davis. I agree with my friend that it's unfortunate that we have not got Davis here, but the prisoner has told you the words with which Davis in turn handed him the cheque; he obviously, therefore, was *not* mad when he received it, or he would not have remembered those words. The cashier has told you that he was certainly in his senses when he cashed it. We have therefore the plea that a man who is sane at ten minutes past one, and sane at fifteen minutes past, may, for the purposes of avoiding the consequences of a crime, call himself insane between those points of time. Really, gentlemen, this is so peculiar a proposition that I am not disposed to weary you with further argument. You will form your own opinion of its value. My friend has adopted this way of saying a great deal to you—and very eloquently—on the score of youth, temptation, and the like. I might point out, however, that the offence with which the prisoner is charged is one of the most serious known to our law; and there are certain features in this case, such as the suspicion which he allowed to rest on his innocent fellow-clerk, and his relations with this married woman, which will render it difficult for you to attach too much importance to such pleading. I ask you, in short, gentlemen, for that verdict of guilty which, in the circumstances, I regard you as, unfortunately, bound to record.

> [*Letting his eyes travel from the* JUDGE *and the jury to* FROME, *he sits down.*]

THE JUDGE. [*Bending a little towards the jury, and speaking in a business-like voice.*] Gentlemen, you have heard the evidence, and the comments on it. My only business is to make clear to you the issues you have to try. The facts are admitted, so far as the alteration of this cheque and counterfoil by the prisoner. The defence set up is that he was not in a responsible condition when he committed the crime. Well, you have heard the prisoner's story, and the evidence of the other witnesses—so far as it bears on the point of insanity. If you think that what you have heard establishes the fact that the prisoner was insane at the time of the forgery, you will find him guilty, but insane. If, on the other hand, you conclude from what you have seen and heard that the prisoner was sane—and nothing short of insanity will count—you will find him guilty. In reviewing the testimony as to his mental condition you must bear in mind very carefully the evidence as to his demeanour and conduct both before and after the act of forgery—the evidence of the prisoner himself, of the woman, of the witness—er—Cokeson, and—er—of the cashier. And in regard to that I especially direct your attention to the prisoner's admission that the idea of adding the t y and the nought did come into his mind at the moment when the cheque was handed to him; and also to the alteration of the counterfoil, and to his subsequent conduct generally. The bearing of all this on the question of premeditation (and premeditation will imply sanity) is very obvious. You must not allow any considerations of age or temptation to weigh with you in the finding of your verdict. Before you can come to a verdict of guilty but insane you must be well and thoroughly convinced that the condition of his mind was such as would have qualified him at the moment for a lunatic asylum. [*He pauses; then, seeing that the jury are doubtful whether to retire or no, adds*:] You may retire, gentlemen, if you wish to do so.

> [*The jury retire by a door behind the* JUDGE. *The* JUDGE *bends over his notes.* FALDER, *leaning from the dock, speaks excitedly to his solicitor, pointing down at* RUTH. *The solicitor in turn speaks to* FROME.]

FROME. [*Rising.*] My lord. The prisoner is very anxious that I should ask you if your lordship would kindly request the reporters not to disclose the name of the woman witness in the Press reports of these proceedings. Your lordship will understand that the consequences might be extremely serious to her.

THE JUDGE. [*Pointedly—with the suspicion of a smile.*] Well, Mr. Frome, you deliberately took this course which involved bringing her here.

FROME. [*With an ironic bow.*] If your lordship thinks I could have brought out the full facts in any other way?

THE JUDGE. H'm! Well.

FROME. There is very real danger to her, your lordship.

THE JUDGE. You see, I have to take your word for all that.

FROME. If your lordship would be so kind. I can assure your lordship that I am not exaggerating.

THE JUDGE. It goes very much against the grain with me that the name of a witness should ever be suppressed.

[*With a glance at* FALDER, *who is gripping and clasping his hands before him, and then at* RUTH, *who is sitting perfectly rigid with her eyes fixed on* FALDER.] I'll consider your application. It must depend. I have to remember that she may have come here to commit perjury on the prisoner's behalf.

FROME. Your lordship, I really——

THE JUDGE. Yes, yes—I don't suggest anything of the sort, Mr. Frome. Leave it at that for the moment.

[*As he finishes speaking, the jury return, and file back into the box.*]

CLERK OF ASSIZE. Gentlemen, are you agreed on your verdict?

FOREMAN. We are.

CLERK OF ASSIZE. Is it Guilty, or Guilty but insane?

FOREMAN. Guilty.

[*The* JUDGE *nods; then, gathering up his notes, sits looking at* FALDER, *who stands motionless.*]

FROME. [*Rising.*] If your lordship would allow me to address you in mitigation of sentence. I don't know if your lordship thinks I can add anything to what I have said to the jury on the score of the prisoner's youth, and the great stress under which he acted.

THE JUDGE. I don't think you can, Mr. Frome.

FROME. If your lordship says so—I do most earnestly beg your lordship to give the utmost weight to my plea.

[*He sits down.*

THE JUDGE. [*To the* CLERK.] Call upon him.

THE CLERK. Prisoner at the Bar, you stand convicted of felony. Have you anything to say for yourself, why the Court should not give you judgment according to law?

[FALDER *shakes his head.*

THE JUDGE. William Falder, you have been given fair trial and found guilty, in my opinion rightly found guilty,

JUSTICE

of forgery. [*He pauses; then, consulting his notes, goes on.*] The defence was set up that you were not responsible for your actions at the moment of committing this crime. There is no doubt, I think, that this was a device to bring out at first hand the nature of the temptation to which you succumbed. For throughout the trial your counsel was in reality making an appeal for mercy. The setting up of this defence of course enabled him to put in some evidence that might weigh in that direction. Whether he was well advised to do so is another matter. He claimed that you should be treated rather as a patient than as a criminal. And this plea of his, which in the end amounted to a passionate appeal, he based in effect on an indictment of the march of Justice, which he practically accused of confirming and completing the process of criminality. Now, in considering how far I should allow weight to his appeal, I have a number of factors to take into account. I have to consider on the one hand the grave nature of your offence, the deliberate way in which you subsequently altered the counterfoil, the danger you caused to an innocent man—and that, to my mind, is a very grave point—and finally I have to consider the necessity of deterring others from following your example. On the other hand, I have to bear in mind that you are young, that you have hitherto borne a good character, that you were, if I am to believe your evidence and that of your witnesses, in a state of some emotional excitement when you committed this crime. I have every wish, consistently with my duty—not only to you, but to the community—to treat you with leniency. And this brings me to what are the determining factors in my mind in my consideration of your case. You are a clerk in a lawyer's office—that is a very serious element in this case; there can be no possible excuse for you on the ground that you were not fully conversant with the nature of the crime you were committing, and the penalties that attach to it. It is said, however, that you were carried away by your emotions. The story has been told here to-day of your relations with this—er—Mrs. Honeywill; on that story both the defence and the plea for mercy were in effect based. Now what is that story? It is that you, a young man, and she, a young woman, unhappily married, had formed an attachment, which you both say—with what truth I am unable to gauge—had not yet resulted in immoral relations, but which you both admit was about to result in such relationship. Your counsel has made an attempt to palliate this, on the ground that the woman is in what he describes, I think, as "a hopeless position." As to that I can express no opinion. She is a married woman, and the fact is patent that you committed this crime with the view of furthering an immoral design. Now, however I might wish, I am not able to justify to my conscience a plea for mercy which has a basis inimical to morality. It is vitiated *ab initio,* and would, if successful, free you for the completion of this immoral project. Your counsel has made an attempt to trace your offence back to what he seems to suggest is a defect in the marriage law; he has made an attempt also to show that to punish you with further imprisonment would be unjust. I do not follow him in these flights. *The Law is what it is*— a majestic edifice, sheltering all of us, each stone of which rests on another. I am concerned only with its administration. The crime you have committed is a very serious one. I cannot feel it in accordance with my duty to Society to exercise the powers I have in your favour. You will go to penal servitude for three years.

> [FALDER, *who throughout the* JUDGE's *speech has looked at him steadily, lets his head fall forward on his breast.* RUTH *starts up from her seat*

as he is taken out by the warders. There is a bustle in court.]

THE JUDGE. [*Speaking to the reporters.*] Gentlemen of the Press, I think that the name of the female witness should not be reported.

[*The reporters bow their acquiescence.*

THE JUDGE. [*To* RUTH, *who is staring in the direction in which* FALDER *has disappeared.*] Do you understand, your name will not be mentioned?

COKESON. [*Pulling her sleeve.*] The judge is speaking to you.

[RUTH *turns, stares at the* JUDGE, *and turns away.*]

THE JUDGE. I shall sit rather late to-day. Call the next case.

CLERK OF ASSIZE. [*To a warder.*] Put up John Booley.

[*To cries of "Witnesses in the case of Booley:"*

The curtain falls.

ACT III

SCENE I

A prison. A plainly furnished room, with two large barred windows, overlooking the prisoner's exercise yard, where men, in yellow clothes marked with arrows, and yellow brimless caps, are seen in single file at a distance of four yards from each other, walking rapidly on serpentine white lines marked on the concrete floor of the yard. Two warders in blue uniforms, with peaked caps and swords, are stationed amongst them. The room has distempered walls, a bookcase with numerous official-looking books, a cupboard between the windows, a plan of the prison on the walls, a writing-table covered with documents. It is Christmas Eve.

The GOVERNOR, *a neat, grave-looking man, with a trim, fair moustache, the eyes of a theorist, and grizzled hair, receding from the temples, is standing close to this writing-table looking at a sort of rough saw made out of a piece of metal. The hand in which he holds it is gloved, for two fingers are missing. The chief warder,* WOODER, *a tall, thin, military-looking man of sixty, with grey moustache and melancholy, monkey-like eyes, stands very upright two paces from him.*

THE GOVERNOR. [*With a faint, abstracted smile.*] Queer-looking affair, Mr. Wooder! Where did you find it?

WOODER. In his mattress, sir. Haven't come across such a thing for two years now.

THE GOVERNOR. [*With curiosity.*] Had he any set plan?

WOODER. He'd sawed his window-bar about that much.
  [*He holds up his thumb and finger a quarter of an inch apart.*]

THE GOVERNOR. I'll see him this afternoon. What's his name? Moaney! An old hand, I think?

WOODER. Yes, sir—fourth spell of penal. You'd think an old lag like him would have more sense by now. [*With pitying contempt.*] Occupied his mind, he said. Breaking in and breaking out—that's all they think about.

THE GOVERNOR. Who's next him?

WOODER. O'Cleary, sir.

THE GOVERNOR. The Irishman.

WOODER. Next him again there's that young fellow, Falder—star class—and next him old Clipton.

JUSTICE

THE GOVERNOR. Ah, yes! "The philosopher." I want to see him about his eyes.

WOODER. Curious thing, sir: they seem to know when there's one of these tries at escape going on. It makes them restive—there's a regular wave going through them just now.

THE GOVERNOR. [*Meditatively.*] Odd things—those waves. [*Turning to look at the prisoners exercising.*] Seem quiet enough out here!

WOODER. That Irishman, O'Cleary, began banging on his door this morning. Little thing like that's quite enough to upset the whole lot. They're just like dumb animals at times.

THE GOVERNOR. I've seen it with horses before thunder—it'll run right through cavalry lines.

[*The prison* CHAPLAIN *has entered. He is a dark-haired, ascetic man, in clerical undress, with a peculiarly steady, tight-lipped face and slow, cultured speech.*]

THE GOVERNOR. [*Holding up the saw.*] Seen this, Miller?

THE CHAPLAIN. Useful-looking specimen.

THE GOVERNOR. Do for the Museum, eh! [*He goes to the cupboard and opens it, displaying to view a number of quaint ropes, hooks, and metal tools with labels tied on them.*] That'll do, thanks, Mr. Wooder.

WOODER. [*Saluting.*] Thank you, sir. [*He goes out.*

THE GOVERNOR. Account for the state of the men last day or two, Miller? Seems going through the whole place.

THE CHAPLAIN. No. I don't know of anything.

THE GOVERNOR. By the way, will you dine with us on Christmas Day?

THE CHAPLAIN. To-morrow. Thanks very much.

THE GOVERNOR. Worries me to feel the men discontented. [*Gazing at the saw.*] Have to punish this poor devil. Can't help liking a man who tries to escape. [*He places the saw in his pocket and locks the cupboard again.*]

THE CHAPLAIN. Extraordinary perverted will-power—some of them. Nothing to be done till it's broken.

THE GOVERNOR. And not much afterwards, I'm afraid. Ground too hard for golf?

[WOODER *comes in again.*

WOODER. Visitor who's been seeing Q 3007 asks to speak to you, sir. I told him it wasn't usual.

THE GOVERNOR. What about?

WOODER. Shall I put him off, sir?

THE GOVERNOR. [*Resignedly.*] No, no. Let's see him. Don't go, Miller.

[WOODER *motions to some one without, and as the visitor comes in withdraws. The visitor is* COKESON, *who is attired in a thick overcoat to the knees, woollen gloves, and carries a top hat.*]

COKESON. I'm sorry to trouble you. I've been talking to the young man.

THE GOVERNOR. We have a good many here.

COKESON. Name of Falder, forgery. [*Producing a card, and handing it to the* GOVERNOR.] Firm of James and Walter How. Well known in the law.

THE GOVERNOR. [*Receiving the card—with a faint smile.*] What do you want to see me about, sir?

COKESON. [*Suddenly seeing the prisoners at exercise.*] Why! what a sight!

THE GOVERNOR. Yes, we have that privilege from here; my office is being done up. [*Sitting down at his table.*] Now, please!

COKESON. [*Dragging his eyes with difficulty from the window.*] I *wanted* to say a word with you; I shan't keep

JUSTICE

you long. [*Confidentially.*] Fact is, I oughtn't to be here by rights. His sister came to me—he's got no father and mother—and she was in some distress. "My husband won't let me go and see him," she said; "says he's disgraced the family. And his other sister," she said, "is an invalid." And she asked me to come. Well, I take an interest in him. He was our junior—I go to the same chapel—and I didn't like to refuse. And what I wanted to tell you was, he seems lonely here.

THE GOVERNOR. Not unnaturally.

COKESON. I'm afraid it'll prey on my mind. I see a lot of them about working together.

THE GOVERNOR. Those are local prisoners. The convicts serve their three months here in separate confinement, sir.

COKESON. But we don't want to be unreasonable. He's quite downhearted. I wanted to ask you to let him run about with the others.

THE GOVERNOR. [*With faint amusement.*] Ring the bell —would you, Miller? [*To* COKESON.] You'd like to hear what the doctor says about him, perhaps.

THE CHAPLAIN. [*Ringing the bell.*] You are not accustomed to prisons, it would seem, sir.

COKESON. No. But it's a pitiful sight. He's quite a young fellow. I said to him: "Before a month's up," I said, "you'll be out and about with the others; it'll be a nice change for you." "A month!" he said—like that! "Come!" I said, "we mustn't exaggerate. What's a month? Why, it's nothing!" "A day," he said, "shut up in your cell thinking and brooding as I do, it's longer than a year outside. I can't help it," he said; "I try—but I'm built that way, Mr. Cokeson." And he held his hand up to his face. I could see the tears trickling through his fingers. It wasn't nice.

THE CHAPLAIN. He's a young man with large, rather peculiar eyes, isn't he? Not Church of England, I think?

COKESON. No.

THE CHAPLAIN. I know.

THE GOVERNOR. [*To* WOODER, *who has come in.*] Ask the doctor to be good enough to come here for a minute. [WOODER *salutes, and goes out.*] Let's see, he's not married?

COKESON. No. [*Confidentially.*] But there's a party he's very much attached to, not altogether com-il-fo. It's a sad story.

THE CHAPLAIN. If it wasn't for drink and women, sir, this prison might be closed.

COKESON. [*Looking at the* CHAPLAIN *over his spectacles.*] Ye-es, but I wanted to tell you about that, special. He had hopes they'd have let her come and see him, but they haven't. Of course he asked me questions. I did my best, but I couldn't tell the poor young fellow a lie, with him in here—seemed like hitting him. But I'm afraid it's made him worse.

THE GOVERNOR. What was this news then?

COKESON. Like this. The woman has a nahsty, spiteful feller for a husband, and she'd left him. Fact is, she was going away with our young friend. It's not nice—but I've looked over it. Well, when he was put in here she said she'd earn her living apart, and wait for him to come out. That was a great consolation to him. But after a month she came to me—I *don't* know her personally—and she said: "I can't earn the children's living, let alone my own—I've got no friends. I'm obliged to keep out of everybody's way, else my husband'd get to know where I was. I'm very much reduced," she said. And she has lost flesh. "I'll have to go in the workhouse!" It's a painful story. I said to her: "No," I said, "not that! I've got a wife

JUSTICE

an' family, but sooner than you should do that I'll spare you a little myself." "Really," she said—she's a nice creature—"I don't like to take it from you. I think I'd better go back to my husband." Well, I know he's a nahsty, spiteful feller—drinks—but I didn't like to persuade her not to.

THE CHAPLAIN. Surely, no.

COKESON. Ye-es, but I'm sorry now; it's upset the poor young fellow dreadfully. And what I wanted to say was: He's got his three years to serve. I *want* things to be pleasant for him.

THE CHAPLAIN. [*With a touch of impatience.*] The Law hardly shares your view, I'm afraid.

COKESON. But I can't help thinking that to shut him up there by himself'll turn him silly. And nobody wants that, I s'pose. I *don't* like to see a man cry.

THE CHAPLAIN. It's a very rare thing for them to give way like that.

COKESON. [*Looking at him—in a tone of sudden dogged hostility.*] I keep dogs.

THE CHAPLAIN. Indeed?

COKESON. Ye-es. And I say this: I wouldn't shut one of them up all by himself, month after month, not if he'd bit me all over.

THE CHAPLAIN. Unfortunately, the criminal is not a dog; he has a sense of right and wrong.

COKESON. But that's not the way to make him feel it.

THE CHAPLAIN. Ah! there I'm afraid we must differ.

COKESON. It's the same with dogs. If you treat 'em with kindness they'll do anything for you; but to shut 'em up alone, it only makes 'em savage.

THE CHAPLAIN. Surely you should allow those who have had a little more experience than yourself to know what is best for prisoners.

COKESON. [*Doggedly.*] I know this young feller, I've

watched him for years. He's eurotic—got no stamina. His father died of consumption. I'm thinking of his future. If he's to be kept there shut up by himself, without a cat to keep him company, it'll do him harm. I said to him: "Where do you feel it?" "I can't tell you, Mr. Cokeson," he said, "but sometimes I could beat my head against the wall." It's not nice.

> [*During this speech the* DOCTOR *has entered. He is a medium-sized, rather good-looking man, with a quick eye. He stands leaning against the window.*]

THE GOVERNOR. This gentleman thinks the separate is telling on Q 3007—Falder, young thin fellow, star class. What do you say, Doctor Clements?

THE DOCTOR. He doesn't like it, but it's not doing him any harm.

COKESON. But he's told me.

THE DOCTOR. Of course he'd say so, but we can always tell. He's lost no weight since he's been here.

COKESON. It's his state of mind I'm speaking of.

THE DOCTOR. His mind's all right so far. He's nervous, rather melancholy. I don't see signs of anything more. I'm watching him carefully.

COKESON. [*Nonplussed.*] I'm glad to hear you say that.

THE CHAPLAIN. [*More suavely.*] It's just at this period that we are able to make some impression on them, sir. I am speaking from my special standpoint.

COKESON. [*Turning bewildered to the* GOVERNOR.] I *don't* want to be unpleasant, but having given him this news, I do feel it's awkward.

THE GOVERNOR. I'll make a point of seeing him to-day.

COKESON. I'm much obliged to you. I thought perhaps seeing him every day you wouldn't notice it.

THE GOVERNOR. [*Rather sharply.*] If any sign of

JUSTICE

injury to his health shows itself his case will be reported at once. That's fully provided for. [*He rises.*

COKESON. [*Following his own thoughts.*] Of course, what you don't see doesn't trouble you; but having seen him, I don't want to have him on my mind.

THE GOVERNOR. I think you may safely leave it to us, sir.

COKESON. [*Mollified and apologetic.*] I thought you'd understand me. I'm a plain man—never set myself up against authority. [*Expanding to the* CHAPLAIN.] Nothing personal meant. *Good*-morning.

> [*As he goes out the three officials do not look at each other, but their faces wear peculiar expressions.*]

THE CHAPLAIN. Our friend seems to think that prison is a hospital.

COKESON. [*Returning suddenly with an apologetic air.*] There's just one little thing. This woman—I suppose I mustn't ask you to let him see her. It'd be a rare treat for them both. He's thinking about her all the time. Of course she's not his wife. But he's quite safe in here. They're a pitiful couple. You couldn't make an exception?

THE GOVERNOR. [*Wearily.*] As you say, my dear sir, I couldn't make an exception; he won't be allowed another visit of any sort till he goes to a convict prison.

COKESON. I see. [*Rather coldly.*] Sorry to have troubled you. [*He again goes out.*

THE CHAPLAIN. [*Shrugging his shoulders.*] The plain man indeed, poor fellow. Come and have some lunch, Clements. [*He and the* DOCTOR *go out talking.*

> [*The* GOVERNOR, *with a sigh, sits down at his table and takes up a pen.*]

The curtain falls.

SCENE II

Part of the ground corridor of the prison. The walls are coloured with greenish distemper up to a stripe of deeper green about the height of a man's shoulder, and above this line are whitewashed. The floor is of blackened stones. Daylight is filtering through a heavily barred window at the end. The doors of four cells are visible. Each cell door has a little round peephole at the level of a man's eye, covered by a little round disc, which, raised upwards, affords a view of the cell. On the wall, close to each cell door, hangs a little square board with the prisoner's name, number, and record.

Overhead can be seen the iron structures of the first-floor and second-floor corridors.

The WARDER INSTRUCTOR, *a bearded man in blue uniform, with an apron, and some dangling keys, is just emerging from one of the cells.*

INSTRUCTOR. [*Speaking from the door into the cell.*] I'll have another bit for you when that's finished.

O'CLEARY. [*Unseen—in an Irish voice.*] Little doubt o' that, sirr.

INSTRUCTOR. [*Gossiping.*] Well, you'd rather have it than nothing, I s'pose.

O'CLEARY. An' that's the blessed truth.

[*Sounds are heard of a cell door being closed and locked, and of approaching footsteps.*]

INSTRUCTOR. [*In a sharp, changed voice.*] Look alive over it!

[*He shuts the cell door, and stands at attention. The* GOVERNOR *comes walking down the corridor, followed by* WOODER.]

THE GOVERNOR. Anything to report?

JUSTICE   219

INSTRUCTOR. [*Saluting.*] Q 3007 [*he points to a cell*] is behind with his work, sir. He'll lose marks to-day.

[*The* GOVERNOR *nods and passes on to the end cell. The* INSTRUCTOR *goes away.*]

THE GOVERNOR. This is our maker of saws, isn't it?

[*He takes the saw from his pocket as* WOODER *throws open the door of the cell. The convict* MOANEY *is seen lying on his bed, athwart the cell, with his cap on. He springs up and stands in the middle of the cell. He is a raw-boned fellow, about fifty-six years old, with outstanding bat's ears and fierce, staring, steel-coloured eyes.*]

WOODER. Cap off! [MOANEY *removes his cap.*] Out here! [MOANEY *comes to the door.*

THE GOVERNOR. [*Beckoning him out into the corridor, and holding up the saw—with the manner of an officer speaking to a private.*] Anything to say about this, my man? [MOANEY *is silent.*] Come!

MOANEY. It passed the time.

THE GOVERNOR. [*Pointing into his cell.*] Not enough to do, eh?

MOANEY. It don't occupy your mind.

THE GOVERNOR. [*Tapping the saw.*] You might find a better way than this.

MOANEY. [*Sullenly.*] Well! What way? I must keep my hand in against the time I get out. What's the good of anything else to me at my time of life? [*With a gradual change to civility as his tongue warms.*] Ye know that, sir. I'll be in again within a year or two, after I've done this lot. I don't want to disgrace meself when I'm out. *You've* got your pride keeping the prison smart; well, I've got mine. [*Seeing that the* GOVERNOR *is listening with interest, he goes on, pointing to the saw.*] I *must* be doin' a little o' this. It's no harm to any one. I was five weeks makin' that saw—a bit of all right it is, too; now I'll get cells, I suppose, or seven days' bread and water. You can't help it, sir, I know that—I quite put meself in your place.

THE GOVERNOR. Now, look here, Moaney, if I pass it over will you give me your word not to try it on again? Think! [*He goes into the cell, walks to the end of it, mounts the stool, and tries the window-bars.*]

THE GOVERNOR. [*Returning.*] Well?

MOANEY. [*Who has been reflecting.*] I've got another six weeks to do in here, alone. I can't do it and think o' nothing. I must have something to interest me. You've made me a sporting offer, sir, but I can't pass my word about it. I shouldn't like to deceive a gentleman. [*Pointing into the cell.*] Another four hours' steady work would have done it.

THE GOVERNOR. Yes, and what then? Caught, brought back, punishment. Five weeks' hard work to make this, and cells at the end of it, while they put a new bar to your window. Is it worth it, Moaney?

MOANEY. [*With a sort of fierceness.*] Yes, it is.

THE GOVERNOR. [*Putting his hand to his brow.*] Oh, well! Two days' cells—bread and water.

MOANEY. Thank 'e, sir.

> [*He turns quickly like an animal and slips into his cell. The* GOVERNOR *looks after him and shakes his head as* WOODER *closes and locks the cell door.*]

THE GOVERNOR. Open Clipton's cell.

> [WOODER *opens the door of* CLIPTON's *cell.* CLIPTON *is sitting on a stool just inside the door, at work on a pair of trousers. He is a small, thick, oldish man, with an almost shaven head,*

and smouldering little dark eyes behind smoked spectacles. He gets up and stands motionless in the doorway, peering at his visitors.]

THE GOVERNOR. [*Beckoning.*] Come out here a minute, Clipton.

> [CLIPTON, *with a sort of dreadful quietness, comes into the corridor, the needle and thread in his hand. The* GOVERNOR *signs to* WOODER, *who goes into the cell and inspects it carefully.*]

THE GOVERNOR. How are your eyes?

CLIPTON. I don't complain of them. I don't see the sun here. [*He makes a stealthy movement, protruding his neck a little.*] There's just one thing, Mr. Governor, as you're speaking to me. I wish you'd ask the cove next door here to keep a bit quieter.

THE GOVERNOR. What's the matter? I don't want any tales, Clipton.

CLIPTON. He keeps me awake. I don't know who he is. [*With contempt.*] One of this *star* class, I expect. Oughtn't to be here with *us*.

THE GOVERNOR. [*Quietly.*] Quite right, Clipton. He'll be moved when there's a cell vacant.

CLIPTON. He knocks about like a wild beast in the early morning. I'm not used to it—stops me getting my sleep out. In the evening too. It's not fair, Mr. Governor, as you're speaking to me. Sleep's the comfort I've got here; I'm entitled to take it out full.

> [WOODER *comes out of the cell, and instantly, as though extinguished,* CLIPTON *moves with stealthy suddenness back into his cell.*]

WOODER. All right, sir.

> [*The Governor nods. The door is closed and locked.*]

THE GOVERNOR. Which is the man who banged on his door this morning?

WOODER. [*Going towards* O'CLEARY's *cell.*] This one, sir; O'Cleary.

> [*He lifts the disc and glances through the peep hole.*]

THE GOVERNOR. Open.

> [WOODER *throws open the door.* O'CLEARY, *who is seated at a little table by the door as if listening, springs up and stands at attention just inside the doorway. He is a broad-faced, middle-aged man, with a wide, thin, flexible mouth, and little holes under his high cheek-bones.*]

THE GOVERNOR. Where's the joke, O'Cleary.

O'CLEARY. The joke, your honour? I've not seen one for a long time.

THE GOVERNOR. Banging on your door?

O'CLEARY. Oh! that!

THE GOVERNOR. It's womanish.

O'CLEARY. An' it's that I'm becoming this two months past.

THE GOVERNOR. Anything to complain of?

O'CLEARY. No, sirr.

THE GOVERNOR. You're an old hand; you ought to know better.

O'CLEARY. Yes, I've been through it all.

THE GOVERNOR. You've got a youngster next door; you'll upset him.

O'CLEARY. It cam' over me, your honour. I can't always be the same steady man.

THE GOVERNOR. Work all right?

O'CLEARY. [*Taking up a rush mat he is making.*] Oh! I can do it on me head. It's the miserablest stuff—don't take the brains of a mouse. [*Working his mouth.*] It's

JUSTICE

here I feel it—the want of a little noise—a terrible little wud ease me.

THE GOVERNOR. You know as well as I do that if you were out in the shops you wouldn't be allowed to talk.

O'CLEARY. [*With a look of profound meaning.*] Not with my mouth.

THE GOVERNOR. Well, then?

O'CLEARY. But it's the great conversation I'd have.

THE GOVERNOR. [*With a smile.*] Well, no more conversation on your door.

O'CLEARY. No, sirr, I wud not have the little wit to repeat meself.

THE GOVERNOR. [*Turning.*] Good-night.

O'CLEARY. Good-night, your honour.

[*He turns into his cell. The* GOVERNOR *shuts the door.*]

THE GOVERNOR. [*Looking at the record card.*] Can't help liking the poor blackguard.

WOODER. He's an amiable man, sir.

THE GOVERNOR. [*Pointing down the corridor.*] Ask the doctor to come here, Mr. Wooder.

[WOODER *salutes and goes away down the corridor. The* GOVERNOR *goes to the door of* FALDER's *cell. He raises his uninjured hand to uncover the peep-hole; but, without uncovering it, shakes his head and drops his hand; then, after scrutinising the record board, he opens the cell door.* FALDER, *who is standing against it, lurches forward.*]

THE GOVERNOR. [*Beckoning him out.*] Now tell me: can't you settle down, Falder?

FALDER. [*In a breathless voice.*] Yes, sir.

THE GOVERNOR. You know what I mean? It's no good running your head against a stone wall, is it?

FALDER. No, sir.

THE GOVERNOR. Well, come.

FALDER. I try, sir.

THE GOVERNOR. Can't you sleep?

FALDER. Very little. Between two o'clock and getting up's the worst time.

THE GOVERNOR. How's that?

FALDER. [*His lips twitch with a sort of smile.*] I don't know, sir. I was always nervous. [*Suddenly voluble.*] Everything seems to get such a size then. I feel I'll never get out as long as I live.

THE GOVERNOR. That's morbid, my lad. Pull yourself together.

FALDER. [*With an equally sudden dogged resentment.*] Yes—I've got to——

THE GOVERNOR. Think of all these other fellows!

FALDER. They're used to it.

THE GOVERNOR. They all had to go through it once for the first time, just as you're doing now.

FALDER. Yes, sir, I shall get to be like them in time, I suppose.

THE GOVERNOR. [*Rather taken aback.*] H'm! Well! That rests with you. Now come. Set your mind to it, like a good fellow. You're still quite young. A man can make himself what he likes.

FALDER. [*Wistfully.*] Yes, sir.

THE GOVERNOR. Take a good hold of yourself. Do you read?

FALDER. I don't take the words in. [*Hanging his head.*] I know it's no good; but I can't help thinking of what's going on outside. In my cell I can't see out at all. It's thick glass, sir.

THE GOVERNOR. You've had a visitor. Bad news?

FALDER. Yes.

JUSTICE

THE GOVERNOR. You must'nt think about it.

FALDER. [*Looking back at his cell.*] How can I help it, sir?

> [*He suddenly becomes motionless as* WOODER *and the* DOCTOR *approach. The* GOVERNOR *motions to him to go back into his cell.*]

FALDER. [*Quick and low.*] I'm quite right in my head, sir. [*He goes back into his cell.*

THE GOVERNOR. [*To the* DOCTOR.] Just go in and see him, Clements.

> [*The* DOCTOR *goes into the cell. The* GOVERNOR *pushes the door to, nearly closing it, and walks towards the window.*]

WOODER. [*Following.*] Sorry you should be troubled like this, sir. Very contented lot of men, on the whole.

THE GOVERNOR. [*Shortly.*] You think so?

WOODER. Yes, sir. It's Christmas doing it, in my opinion.

THE GOVERNOR. [*To himself.*] Queer, that!

WOODER. Beg pardon, sir?

THE GOVERNOR. Christmas!

> [*He turns towards the window, leaving* WOODER *looking at him with a sort of pained anxiety.*]

WOODER. [*Suddenly.*] Do you think we make show enough, sir? If you'd like us to have more holly?

THE GOVERNOR. Not at all, Mr. Wooder.

WOODER. Very good, sir.

> [*The* DOCTOR *has come out of* FALDER's *cell, and the* GOVERNOR *beckons to him.*]

THE GOVERNOR. Well?

THE DOCTOR. I can't make anything much of him. He's nervous, of course.

THE GOVERNOR. Is there any sort of case to report? Quite frankly, Doctor.

THE DOCTOR. Well, I don't think the separate's doing

him any good; but then I could say the same of a lot of them—they'd get on better in the shops, there's no doubt.

THE GOVERNOR. You mean you'd have to recommend others?

THE DOCTOR. A dozen at least. It's on his nerves. There's nothing tangible. That fellow there [*pointing to* O'CLEARY's *cell*], for instance—feels it just as much, in his way. If I once get away from physical facts—I shan't know where I am. Conscientiously, sir, I don't know how to differentiate him. He hasn't lost weight. Nothing wrong with his eyes. His pulse is good. Talks all right.

THE GOVERNOR. It doesn't amount to melancholia?

THE DOCTOR. [*Shaking his head.*] I can report on him if you like; but if I do I ought to report on others.

THE GOVERNOR. I see. [*Looking towards* FALDER's *cell.*] The poor devil must just stick it then.

[*As he says this he looks absently at* WOODER.]

WOODER. Beg pardon, sir?

[*For answer the* GOVERNOR *stares at him, turns on his heel, and walks away. There is a sound as of beating on metal.*]

THE GOVERNOR. [*Stopping.*] Mr. Wooder?

WOODER. Banging on his door, sir. I thought we should have more of that.

[*He hurries forward, passing the* GOVERNOR, *who follows closely.*]

The curtain falls.

SCENE III

FALDER's *cell, a whitewashed space thirteen feet broad by seven deep, and nine feet high, with a rounded ceiling.*

JUSTICE

The floor is of shiny blackened bricks. The barred window of opaque glass, with a ventilator, is high up in the middle of the end wall. In the middle of the opposite end wall is the narrow door. In a corner are the mattress and bedding rolled up (two blankets, two sheets, and a coverlet). Above them is a quarter-circular wooden shelf, on which is a Bible and several little devotional books, piled in a symmetrical pyramid; there are also a black hair-brush, tooth-brush, and a bit of soap. In another corner is the wooden frame of a bed, standing on end. There is a dark ventilator under the window, and another over the door. FALDER'S work (a shirt to which he is putting buttonholes) is hung to a nail on the wall over a small wooden table, on which the novel "Lorna Doone" lies open. Low down in the corner by the door is a thick glass screen, about a foot square, covering the gas-jet let into the wall. There is also a wooden stool, and a pair of shoes beneath it. Three bright round tins are set under the window.

In fast-failing daylight, FALDER, *in his stockings, is seen standing motionless, with his head inclined towards the door, listening. He moves a little closer to the door, his stockinged feet making no noise. He stops at the door. He is trying harder and harder to hear something, any little thing that is going on outside. He springs suddenly upright—as if at a sound—and remains perfectly motionless. Then, with a heavy sigh, he moves to his work, and stands looking at it, with his head down; he does a stitch or two, having the air of a man so lost in sadness that each stitch is, as it were, a coming to life. Then turning abruptly, he begins pacing the cell, moving his head, like an animal pacing his cage. He stops again at the door, listens, and, placing the palms of his hands against it with his fingers spread out, leans his forehead against the iron. Turning from it, presently, he moves slowly back towards the window, tracing his way with his finger along the top line of the distemper that runs round the wall. He stops under the window, and, picking up the lid of one of the tins, peers into it. It has grown very nearly dark. Suddenly the lid falls out of his hand with a clatter—the only sound that has broken the silence—and he stands staring intently at the wall where the stuff of the shirt is hanging rather white in the darkness—he seems to be seeing somebody or something there. There is a sharp tap and click; the cell light behind the glass screen has been turned up. The cell is brightly lighted.* FALDER *is seen gasping for breath.*

A sound from far away, as of distant, dull beating on thick metal, is suddenly audible. FALDER *shrinks back, not able to bear this sudden clamour. But the sound grows, as though some great tumbril were rolling towards the cell. And gradually it seems to hypnotise him. He begins creeping inch by inch nearer to the door. The banging sound, travelling from cell to cell, draws closer and closer;* FALDER'S *hands are seen moving as if his spirit had already joined in this beating, and the sound swells till it seems to have entered the very cell. He suddenly raises his clenched fists. Panting violently, he flings himself at his door, and beats on it.*

The curtain falls.

JUSTICE 229

ACT IV

The scene is again COKESON's *room, at a few minutes to ten of a March morning, two years later. The doors are all open.* SWEEDLE, *now blessed with a sprouting moustache, is getting the offices ready. He arranges papers on* COKESON's *table; then goes to a covered washstand, raises the lid, and looks at himself in the mirror. While he is gazing his fill* RUTH HONEYWILL *comes in through the outer office and stands in the doorway. There seems a kind of exultation and excitement behind her habitual impassivity.*

SWEEDLE. [*Suddenly seeing her, and dropping the lid of the washstand with a bang.*] Hello! It's you!

RUTH. Yes.

SWEEDLE. There's only me here! They don't waste their time hurrying down in the morning. Why, it must be two years since we had the pleasure of seeing you. [*Nervously.*] What have you been doing with yourself?

RUTH. [*Sardonically.*] Living.

SWEEDLE. [*Impressed.*] If you want to see *him* [*he points to* COKESON's *chair*], he'll be here directly—never misses—not much. [*Delicately.*] I hope our friend's back from the country. His time's been up these three months, if I remember. [RUTH *nods.*] I was awful sorry about that. The governor made a mistake—if you ask me.

RUTH. He did.

SWEEDLE. He ought to have given him a chanst. And, *I* say, the judge ought to ha' let him go after that. They've forgot what human nature's like. Whereas *we* know.

[RUTH *gives him a honeyed smile.*

SWEEDLE. They come down on you like a cartload of bricks, flatten you out, and when you don't swell up again they complain of it. I know 'em—seen a lot of that sort of thing in my time. [*He shakes his head in the plenitude of wisdom.*] Why, only the other day the governor——

[*But* COKESON *has come in through the outer office; brisk with east wind, and decidedly greyer.*]

COKESON. [*Drawing off his coat and gloves.*] Why! it's you! [*Then motioning* SWEEDLE *out, and closing the door.*] Quite a stranger! Must be two years. D'you want to see me? I can give you a minute. Sit down! Family well?

RUTH. Yes. I'm not living where I was.

COKESON. [*Eyeing her askance.*] I hope things are more comfortable at home.

RUTH. I couldn't stay with Honeywill, after all.

COKESON. You haven't done anything rash, I hope. I should be sorry if you'd done anything rash.

RUTH. I've kept the children with me.

COKESON. [*Beginning to feel that things are not so jolly as he had hoped.*] Well, I'm glad to have seen you. You've not heard from the young man, I suppose, since he came out?

RUTH. Yes, I ran across him yesterday.

COKESON. I hope he's well.

RUTH. [*With sudden fierceness.*] He can't get anything to do. It's dreadful to see him. He's just skin and bone.

COKESON. [*With genuine concern.*] Dear me! I'm sorry to hear that. [*On his guard again.*] Didn't they find him a place when his time was up?

RUTH. He was only there three weeks. It got out.

COKESON. I'm sure I don't know what I can do for you. I don't like to be snubby.

RUTH. I can't bear his being like that.

COKESON. [*Scanning her not unprosperous figure.*] I know his relations aren't very forthy about him. Perhaps *you* can do something for him, till he finds his feet.

JUSTICE

RUTH. Not now. I could have—but not *now*.

COKESON. I don't understand.

RUTH. [*Proudly.*] I've seen him again—that's all over.

COKESON. [*Staring at her—disturbed.*] I'm a family man—I don't want to hear anything unpleasant. Excuse me—I'm very busy.

RUTH. I'd have gone home to my people in the country long ago, but they've never got over me marrying Honeywill. I never was waywise, Mr. Cokeson, but I'm proud. I was only a girl, you see, when I married him. I thought the world of him, of course . . . he used to come travelling to our farm.

COKESON. [*Regretfully.*] I did hope you'd have got on better, after you saw me.

RUTH. He used me worse than ever. He couldn't break my nerve, but I lost my health; and then he began knocking the children about. . . . I couldn't stand that. I wouldn't go back now, if he were dying.

COKESON. [*Who has risen and is shifting about as though dodging a stream of lava.*] We mustn't be violent, must we?

RUTH. [*Smouldering.*] A man that can't behave better than that—— [*There is silence.*

COKESON. [*Fascinated in spite of himself.*] Then there you were! And what did you do then?

RUTH. [*With a shrug.*] Tried the same as when I left him before . . . making skirts . . . cheap things. It was the best I could get, but I never made more than ten shillings a week, buying my own cotton and working all day; I hardly ever got to bed till past twelve. I kept at it for nine months. [*Fiercely.*] Well, I'm not fit for that; I wasn't made for it. I'd rather die.

COKESON. My dear woman! We mustn't talk like that.

RUTH. It was starvation for the children too—after

what they'd always had. I soon got not to care. I used to be too tired. [*She is silent.*

COKESON. [*With fearful curiosity.*] Why, what happened then?

RUTH. [*With a laugh.*] My employer happened then—he's happened ever since.

COKESON. Dear! Oh dear! I never came across a thing like this.

RUTH. [*Dully.*] He's treated me all right. But I've done with that. [*Suddenly her lips begin to quiver, and she hides them with the back of her hand.*] I never thought I'd see *him* again, you see. It was just a chance I met him by Hyde Park. We went in there and sat down, and he told me all about himself. Oh! Mr. Cokeson, give him another chance.

COKESON. [*Greatly disturbed.*] Then you've both lost your livings! What a horrible position!

RUTH. If he could only get here—where there's nothing to find out about him!

COKESON. We can't have anything derogative to the firm.

RUTH. I've no one else to go to.

COKESON. I'll speak to the partners, but I don't think they'll take him, under the circumstances. I don't really.

RUTH. He came with me; he's down there in the street. [*She points to the window.*

COKESON. [*On his dignity.*] He shouldn't have done that until he's sent for. [*Then softening at the look on her face.*] We've got a vacancy, as it happens, but I can't promise anything.

RUTH. It would be the saving of him.

COKESON. Well, I'll do what I can, but I'm not sanguine. Now tell him that I don't want him till I see how things are. Leave your address? [*Repeating her.*] 83 Mullingar Street? [*He notes it on blotting-paper.*] Good-morning.

JUSTICE

RUTH. Thank you.

[*She moves towards the door, turns as if to speak, but does not, and goes away.*]

COKESON. [*Wiping his head and forehead with a large white cotton handkerchief.*] What a business! [*Then looking amongst his papers, he sounds his bell.* SWEEDLE *answers it.*]

COKESON. Was that young Richards coming here to-day after the clerk's place?

SWEEDLE. Yes.

COKESON. Well, keep him in the air; I don't want to see him yet.

SWEEDLE. What shall I tell him, sir?

COKESON. [*With asperity.*] Invent something. Use your brains. Don't stump him off altogether.

SWEEDLE. Shall I tell him that we've got illness, sir?

COKESON. No! Nothing untrue. Say I'm not here to-day.

SWEEDLE. Yes, sir. Keep him hankering?

COKESON. Exactly. And look here. You remember Falder? I may be having him round to see me. Now, treat him like you'd have him treat you in a similar position.

SWEEDLE. I naturally should do.

COKESON. That's right. When a man's down never hit 'im. 'Tisn't necessary. Give him a hand up. That's a metaphor I recommend to you in life. It's sound policy.

SWEEDLE. Do you think the governors will take him on again, sir?

COKESON. Can't say anything about that. [*At the sound of some one having entered the outer office.*] Who's there?

SWEEDLE. [*Going to the door and looking.*] It's Falder, sir.

COKESON. [*Vexed.*] Dear me! That's very naughty of her. Tell him to call again. I don't want——

[*He breaks off as* FALDER *comes in.* FALDER *is*

thin, pale, older, his eyes have grown more restless. His clothes are very worn and loose.
SWEEDLE, *nodding cheerfully, withdraws.*

COKESON. Glad to see you. You're rather previous. [*Trying to keep things pleasant.*] Shake hands! She's striking while the iron's hot. [*He wipes his forehead.*] I don't blame her. She's anxious.

[FALDER *timidly takes* COKESON's *hand and glances towards the partners' door.*]

COKESON. No—not yet! Sit down! [FALDER *sits in the chair at the side of* COKESON's *table, on which he places his cap.*] Now you are here I'd like you to give me a little account of yourself. [*Looking at him over his spectacles.*] How's your health?

FALDER. I'm alive, Mr. Cokeson.

COKESON. [*Preoccupied.*] I'm glad to hear that. About this matter. I don't like doing anything out of the ordinary; it's not my habit. I'm a plain man, and I want everything smooth and straight. But I promised your friend to speak to the partners, and I always keep my word.

FALDER. I just want a chance, Mr. Cokeson. I've paid for that job a thousand times and more. I have, sir. No one knows. They say I weighed more when I came out than when I went in. They couldn't weigh me here [*He touches his head*], or here [*He touches his heart, and gives a sort of laugh*]. Till last night I'd have thought there was nothing in here at all.

COKESON. [*Concerned.*] You've not got heart disease?

FALDER. Oh! they passed me sound enough.

COKESON. But they got you a place, didn't they?

FALDER. Yes; very good people, knew all about it—very kind to me. I thought I was going to get on first rate. But one day, all of a sudden, the other clerks got wind of it. . . . I couldn't stick it, Mr. Cokeson, I couldn't, sir.

COKESON. Easy, my dear fellow, easy!

FALDER. I had one small job after that, but it didn't last.

COKESON. How was that?

FALDER. It's no good deceiving you, Mr. Cokeson. The fact is, I seem to be struggling against a thing that's all round me. I can't explain it: it's as if I was in a net; as fast as I cut it here, it grows up there. I didn't act as I ought to have, about references; but what are you to do? You must have them. And that made me afraid, and I left. In fact, I'm—I'm afraid all the time now.

[*He bows his head and leans dejectedly silent over the table.*]

COKESON. I feel for you—I do really. Aren't your sisters going to do anything for you?

FALDER. One's in consumption. And the other——

COKESON. Ye . . . es. She told me her husband wasn't quite pleased with you.

FALDER. When I went there—they were at supper—my sister wanted to give me a kiss—I know. But he just looked at her, and said: "What have you come for?" Well, I pocketed my pride and I said: "Aren't you going to give me your hand, Jim? Cis is, I know," I said. "Look here!" he said, "that's all very well, but we'd better come to an understanding. I've been expecting you, and I've made up my mind. I'll give you fifteen pounds to go to Canada with." "I see," I said—"good riddance! No, thanks; keep your fifteen pounds." Friendship's a queer thing when you've been where I have.

COKESON. I understand. Will you take the fifteen pound from me? [*Flustered, as* FALDER *regards him with a queer smile.*] Quite without prejudice; I meant it kindly.

FALDER. I'm not allowed to leave the country.

COKESON. Oh! ye . . . es—ticket-of-leave? You aren't looking the thing.

FALDER. I've slept in the Park three nights this week. The dawns aren't all poetry there. But meeting her—I feel a different man this morning. I've often thought the being fond of her's the best thing about me; it's sacred, somehow—and yet it did for me. That's queer, isn't it?

COKESON. I'm sure we're all very sorry for you.

FALDER. That's what I've found, Mr. Cokeson. Awfully sorry for me. [*With quiet bitterness.*] But it doesn't do to associate with criminals!

COKESON. Come, come, it's no use calling yourself names. That never did a man any good. Put a face on it.

FALDER. It's easy enough to put a face on it, sir, when you're independent. Try it when you're down like me. They talk about giving you your deserts. Well, I think I've had just a bit over.

COKESON. [*Eyeing him askance over his spectacles.*] I hope they haven't made a Socialist of you.

[FALDER *is suddenly still, as if brooding over his past self; he utters a peculiar laugh.*]

COKESON. You must give them credit for the best intentions. Really you must. Nobody wishes you harm, I'm sure.

FALDER. I believe that, Mr. Cokeson. Nobody wishes you harm, but they down you all the same. This feeling ——[*He stares round him, as though at something closing in.*] It's crushing me. [*With sudden impersonality.*] I know it is.

COKESON. [*Horribly disturbed.*] There's nothing there! We must try and take it quiet. I'm sure I've often had you in my prayers. Now leave it to me. I'll use my gumption and take 'em when they're jolly.

[*As he speaks the two partners come in.*

COKESON. [*Rather disconcerted, but trying to put them all at ease.*] I didn't expect you quite so soon. I've just

JUSTICE

been having a talk with this young man. I think you'll remember him.

JAMES. [*With a grave, keen look.*] Quite well. How are you, Falder?

WALTER. [*Holding out his hand almost timidly.*] Very glad to see you again, Falder.

FALDER. [*Who has recovered his self-control, takes the hand.*] Thank you, sir.

COKESON. Just a word, Mr. James. [*To* FALDER, *pointing to the clerks' office.*] You might go in there a minute. You know your way. Our junior won't be coming this morning. His wife's just had a little family.

[FALDER *goes uncertainly out into the clerks' office.*

COKESON. [*Confidentially.*] I'm bound to tell you all about it. He's quite penitent. But there's a prejudice against him. And you're not seeing him to advantage this morning; he's under-nourished. It's very trying to go without your dinner.

JAMES. Is that so, Cokeson?

COKESON. I wanted to ask you. He's had his lesson. Now *we* know all about him, and we want a clerk. There is a young fellow applying, but I'm keeping him in the air.

JAMES. A gaol-bird in the office, Cokeson? I don't see it.

WALTER. "The rolling of the chariot-wheels of Justice!" I've never got that out of my head.

JAMES. I've nothing to reproach myself with in this affair. What's he been doing since he came out?

COKESON. He's had one or two places, but he hasn't kept them. He's sensitive—quite natural. Seems to fancy everybody's down on him.

JAMES. Bad sign. Don't like the fellow—never did from the first. "Weak character" 's written all over him.

WALTER. I think we owe him a leg up.

JAMES. He brought it all on himself.

WALTER. The doctrine of full responsibility doesn't quite hold in these days.

JAMES. [*Rather grimly.*] You'll find it safer to hold it for all that, my boy.

WALTER. For oneself, yes—not for other people, thanks.

JAMES. Well! I don't want to be hard.

COKESON. I'm glad to hear you say that. He seems to see something [*Spreading his arms.*] round him. 'Tisn't healthy.

JAMES. What about that woman he was mixed up with? I say some one uncommonly like her outside as we came in.

COKESON. *That!* Well, I can't keep anything from you. He has met her.

JAMES. Is she with her husband?

COKESON. No.

JAMES. Falder living with her, I suppose?

COKESON. [*Desperately trying to retain the new-found jollity.*] I don't know that of my own knowledge. 'Tisn't my business.

JAMES. It's *our* business, if we're going to engage him, Cokeson.

COKESON. [*Reluctantly.*] I ought to tell you, perhaps. I've had the party here this morning.

JAMES. I thought so. [*To* WALTER.] No, my dear boy, it won't do. Too shady altogether.

COKESON. The two things together make it very awkward for you—I see that.

WALTER. [*Tentatively.*] I don't quite know what we have to do with his private life.

JAMES. No, no! He must make a clean sheet of it, or he can't come here.

WALTER. Poor devil!

COKESON. Will you have him in? [*And as* JAMES *nods.*] I think I can get him to see reason.

JUSTICE

JAMES. [*Grimly.*] You can leave that to me, Cokeson.

WALTER. [*To* JAMES, *in a low voice, while* COKESON *is summoning* FALDER.] His whole future may depend on what we do, dad.

[FALDER *comes in. He has pulled himself together, and presents a steady front.*]

JAMES. Now look here, Falder. My son and I want to give you another chance; but there are two things I must say to you. In the first place: It's no good coming here as a victim. If you've any notion that you've been unjustly treated—get rid of it. You can't play fast and loose with morality and hope to go scot-free. If Society didn't take care of itself, nobody would—the sooner you realise that the better.

FALDER. Yes, sir; but—may I say something?

JAMES. Well?

FALDER. I had a lot of time to think it over in prison.
[*He stops.*

COKESON. [*Encouraging him.*] I'm sure you did.

FALDER. There were all sorts there. And what I mean, sir, is, that if we'd been treated differently the first time, and put under somebody that could look after us a bit, and not put in prison, not a quarter of us would ever have got there.

JAMES. [*Shaking his head.*] I'm afraid I've very grave doubts of that, Falder.

FALDER. [*With a gleam of malice.*] Yes, sir, so I found.

JAMES. My good fellow, don't forget that you began it.

FALDER. I never wanted to do wrong.

JAMES. Perhaps not. But you did.

FALDER. [*With all the bitterness of his past suffering.*] It's knocked me out of time. [*Pulling himself up.*] That is, I mean, I'm not what I was.

JAMES. This isn't encouraging for us, Falder.

COKESON. He's putting it awkwardly, Mr. James.

FALDER. [*Throwing over his caution from the intensity of his feeling.*] I mean it, Mr. Cokeson.

JAMES. Now, lay aside all those thoughts, Falder, and look to the future.

FALDER. [*Almost eagerly.*] Yes, sir, but you don't understand what prison is. It's here it gets you.

[*He grips his chest.*

COKESON. [*In a whisper to* JAMES.] I told you he wanted nourishment.

WALTER. Yes, but, my dear fellow, that'll pass away. Time's merciful.

FALDER. [*With his face twitching.*] I hope so, sir.

JAMES. [*Much more gently.*] Now, my boy, what you've got to do is to put all the past behind you and build yourself up a steady reputation. And that brings me to the second thing. This woman you were mixed up with—you must give us your word, you know, to have done with that. There's no chance of your keeping straight if you're going to begin your future with such a relationship.

FALDER. [*Looking from one to the other with a hunted expression.*] But sir . . . but sir . . . it's the one thing I looked forward to all that time. And she too . . . I couldn't find her before last night.

[*During this and what follows* COKESON *becomes more and more uneasy.*]

JAMES. This is painful, Falder. But you must see for yourself that it's impossible for a firm like this to close its eyes to everything. Give us this proof of your resolve to keep straight, and you can come back—not otherwise.

FALDER. [*After staring at* JAMES, *suddenly stiffens himself.*] I couldn't give her up. I couldn't! Oh, sir! I'm all she's got to look to. And I'm sure she's all I've got.

JAMES. I'm very sorry, Falder, but I must be firm. It's

for the benefit of you both in the long run. No good can come of this connection. It was the cause of all your disaster.

FALDER. But sir, it means—having gone through all that—getting broken up—my nerves are in an awful state—for nothing. I did it for her.

JAMES. Come! If she's anything of a woman she'll see it for herself. She won't want to drag you down further. If there were a prospect of your being able to marry her— it might be another thing.

FALDER. It's not my fault, sir, that she couldn't get rid of him—she would have if she could. That's been the whole trouble from the beginning. [*Looking suddenly at* WALTER.] . . . If anybody would help her! It's only money wanted now, I'm sure.

COKESON. [*Breaking in, as* WALTER *hesitates, and is about to speak.*] I don't think we need consider that— it's rather far-fetched.

FALDER. [*To* WALTER, *appealing.*] He must have given her full cause since; she could prove that he drove her to leave him.

WALTER. I'm inclined to do what you say, Falder, if it can be managed.

FALDER. Oh, sir!

[*He goes to the window and looks down into the street.*]

COKESON. [*Hurriedly.*] You don't take me, Mr. Walter. I have my reasons.

FALDER. [*From the window.*] She's down there, sir. Will you see her? I can beckon to her from here.

[WALTER *hesitates, and looks from* COKESON *to* JAMES.]

JAMES. [*With a sharp nod.*] Yes, let her come.

[FALDER *beckons from the window.*

COKESON. [*In a low fluster to* JAMES *and* WALTER.] No, Mr. James. She's not been quite what she ought to ha' been, while this young man's been away. She's lost her chance. We can't consult how to swindle the Law.

> [FALDER *has come from the window. The three men look at him in a sort of awed silence.*]

FALDER. [*With instinctive apprehension of some change—looking from one to the other.*] There's been nothing between us, sir, to prevent it. . . . What I said at the trial was true. And last night we only just sat in the Park.

> [SWEEDLE *comes in from the outer office.*]

COKESON. What is it?

SWEEDLE. Mrs. Honeywill. [*There is silence.*

JAMES. Show her in.

> [RUTH *comes slowly in, and stands stoically with* FALDER *on one side and the three men on the other. No one speaks.* COKESON *turns to his table, bending over his papers as though the burden of the situation were forcing him back into his accustomed groove.*]

JAMES. [*Sharply.*] Shut the door there. [SWEEDLE *shuts the door.*] We've asked you to come up because there are certain facts to be faced in this matter. I understand you have only just met Falder again.

RUTH. Yes—only yesterday.

JAMES. He's told us about himself, and we're very sorry for him. I've promised to take him back here if he'll make a fresh start. [*Looking steadily at* RUTH.] This is a matter that requires courage, ma'am.

> [RUTH, *who is looking at* FALDER, *begins to twist her hands in front of her as though prescient of disaster.*]

FALDER. Mr. Walter How is good enough to say that he'll help us to get you a divorce.

JUSTICE

[RUTH *flashes a startled glance at* JAMES *and* WALTER.]

JAMES. I don't think that's practicable, Falder.

FALDER. But, sir——!

JAMES. [*Steadily.*] Now, Mrs. Honeywill. You're fond of him.

RUTH. Yes, sir; I love him.

[*She looks miserably at* FALDER.

JAMES. Then you don't want to stand in his way, do you?

RUTH. [*In a faint voice.*] I could take care of him.

JAMES. The best way you can take care of him will be to give him up.

FALDER. Nothing shall make me give you up. You can get a divorce. There's been nothing between us, has there?

RUTH. [*Mournfully shaking her head—without looking at him.*] No.

FALDER. We'll keep apart till it's over, sir; if you'll only help us—we promise.

JAMES. [*To Ruth.*] You see the thing plainly, don't you? You see what I mean?

RUTH. [*Just above a whisper.*] Yes.

COKESON. [*To himself.*] There's a dear woman.

JAMES. The situation is impossible.

RUTH. Must I, sir?

JAMES. [*Forcing himself to look at her.*] I put it to you, ma'am. His future is in your hands.

RUTH. [*Miserably.*] I want to do the best for him.

JAMES. [*A little huskily.*] That's right, that's right!

FALDER. I don't understand. You're not going to give me up—after all this? There's something—— [*Starting forward to* JAMES.] Sir, I swear solemnly there's been nothing between us.

JAMES. I believe, you, Falder. Come, my lad, be as plucky as she is.

FALDER. Just now you were going to help us. [*He stares at* RUTH, *who is standing absolutely still; his face and hands twitch and quiver as the truth dawns on him.*] What is it? You've not been——

WALTER. Father!

JAMES. [*Hurriedly.*] There, there! That'll do, that'll do! I'll give you your chance, Falder. Don't let me know what you do with yourselves, that's all.

FALDER. [*As if he has not heard.*] Ruth?

> [RUTH *looks at him; and* FALDER *covers his face with his hands. There is silence.*]

COKESON. [*Suddenly.*] There's some one out there. [*To* Ruth.] Go in here. You'll feel better by yourself for a minute.

> [*He points to the clerks' room and moves towards the outer office.* FALDER *does not move.* RUTH *puts out her hand timidly. He shrinks back from the touch. She turns and goes miserably into the clerks' room. With a brusque movement he follows, seizing her by the shoulder just inside the doorway.* COKESON *shuts the door.*]

JAMES. [*Pointing to the outer office.*] Get rid of that, whoever it is.

SWEEDLE. [*Opening the office door, in a scared voice.*] Detective-Sergeant Wister.

> [*The detective enters, and closes the door behind him.*]

WISTER. Sorry to disturb you, sir. A clerk you had here, two years and a half ago. I arrested him in this room.

JAMES. What about him?

WISTER. I thought perhaps I might get his whereabouts from you. [*There is an awkward silence.*

JUSTICE

COKESON. [*Pleasantly, coming to the rescue.*] We're not responsible for his movements; you know that.

JAMES. What do you want with him?

WISTER. He's failed to report himself this last four weeks.

WALTER. How d'you mean?

WISTER. Ticket-of-leave won't be up for another six months, sir.

WALTER. Has he to keep in touch with the police till then?

WISTER. We're bound to know where he sleeps every night. I dare say we shouldn't interfere, sir, even though he hasn't reported himself. But we've just heard there's a serious matter of obtaining employment with a forged reference. What with the two things together—we must have him.

[*Again there is silence. WALTER and COKESON steal glances at JAMES, who stands staring steadily at the detective.*]

COKESON. [*Expansively.*] We're very busy at the moment. If you could make it convenient to call again we might be able to tell you then.

JAMES. [*Decisively.*] I'm a servant of the Law, but I dislike peaching. In fact, I can't do such a thing. If you want him you must find him without us.

[*As he speaks his eye falls on FALDER's cap, still lying on the table, and his face contracts.*]

WISTER. [*Noting the gesture—quietly.*] Very good, sir. I ought to warn you that, having broken the terms of his license, he's still a convict, and sheltering a convict——

JAMES. I shelter no one. But you mustn't come here and ask questions which it's not my business to answer.

WISTER. [*Drily.*] I won't trouble you further then, gentlemen.

COKESON. I'm sorry we couldn't give you the information. You quite understand, don't you? Good-morning!

> [WISTER *turns to go, but instead of going to the door of the outer office he goes to the door of the clerks' room.*]

COKESON. The other door . . . the other door!

> [WISTER *opens the clerks' door.* RUTH'S *voice is heard:* "Oh, do!" *and* FALDER'S: "I can't!" *There is a little pause; then, with sharp fright,* RUTH *says:* "Who's that?" WISTER *has gone in.*]
>
> [*The three men look aghast at the door.*]

WISTER. [*From within.*] Keep back, please!

> [*He comes swiftly out with his arm twisted in* FALDER'S. *The latter gives a white, staring look at the three men.*]

WALTER. Let him go this time, for God's sake!

WISTER. I couldn't take the responsibility, sir.

FALDER. [*With a queer, desperate laugh.*] Good!

> [*Flinging a look back at* RUTH, *he throws up his head, and goes out through the outer office, half dragging* WISTER *after him.*]

WALTER. [*With despair.*] That finishes him. It'll go on for ever now.

> [SWEEDLE *can be seen staring through the outer door. There are sounds of footsteps descending the stone stairs; suddenly a dull thud, a faint* "My God!" *in* WISTER'S *voice.*]

JAMES. What's that?

> [SWEEDLE *dashes forward. The door swings to behind him. There is dead silence.*]

WALTER. [*Starting forward to the inner room.*] The woman—she's fainting!

> [*He and* COKESON *support the fainting* RUTH *from the doorway of the clerks' room.*]

JUSTICE

COKESON. [*Distracted.*] Here, my dear! There, there!

WALTER. Have you any brandy?

COKESON. I've got sherry.

WALTER. Get it, then. Quick!

> [*He places* RUTH *in a chair—which* JAMES *has dragged forward.*]

COKESON. [*With sherry.*] Here! It's good strong sherry.

> [*They try to force the sherry between her lips. There is the sound of feet, and they stop to listen. The outer door is reopened—*WISTER *and* SWEEDLE *are seen carrying some burden.*]

JAMES. [*Hurrying forward.*] What is it?

> [*They lay the burden down in the outer office, out of sight, and all but* RUTH *cluster round it, speaking in hushed voices.*]

WISTER. He jumped—neck's broken.

WALTER. Good God!

WISTER. He must have been mad to think he could give me the slip like that. And what was it—just a few months!

WALTER. [*Bitterly.*] Was that all?

JAMES. What a desperate thing! [*Then, in a voice unlike his own.*] Run for a doctor—you! [SWEEDLE *rushes from the outer office.*] An ambulance!

> [WISTER *goes out. On* RUTH'S *face an expression of fear and horror has been seen growing, as if she dared not turn towards the voices. She now rises and steals towards them.*]

WALTER. [*Turning suddenly.*] Look!

> [*The three men shrink back out of her way, one by one, into* COKESON'S *room.* RUTH *drops on her knees by the body.*]

RUTH. [*In a whisper.*] What is it? He's not breathing. [*She crouches over him.*] My dear! My pretty!

[*In the outer office doorway the figures of men are seen standing.*]

RUTH. [*Leaping to her feet.*] No, no! No, no! He's dead! [*The figures of the men shrink back.*

COKESON. [*Stealing forward. In a hoarse voice.*] There, there, poor dear woman!

[*At the sound behind her* RUTH *faces round at him.*]

COKESON. No one'll touch him now! Never again! He's safe with gentle Jesus!

[RUTH *stands as though turned to stone in the doorway staring at* COKESON, *who, bending humbly before her, holds out his hand as one would to a lost dog.*]

The curtain falls.

THE PIGEON

A DRAMA IN THREE ACTS

PERSONS OF THE PLAY

CHRISTOPHER WELLWYN, *an artist*
ANN, *his daughter*
GUINEVERE MEGAN, *a flower-seller*
RORY MEGAN, *her husband*
FERRAND, *an alien*
TIMSON, *once a cabman*
EDWARD BERTLEY, *a Canon*
ALFRED CALWAY, *a Professor*
SIR THOMAS HOXTON, *A Justice of the Peace*
Also a police constable, three humble-men, and some curious persons

The action passes in Wellwyn's Studio, and the street outside.

ACT   I. Christmas Eve.
ACT II. New Year's Day.
ACT III. The First of April.

ACT I

It is the night of Christmas Eve, the SCENE *is a Studio, flush with the street, having a skylight darkened by a fall of snow. There is no one in the room, the walls of which are whitewashed, above a floor of bare dark boards. A fire is cheerfully burning. On a model's platform stands an easel and canvas. There are busts and pictures; a screen, a little stool, two arm-chairs, and a long, old-fashioned settle under the window. A door in one wall leads to the house, a door in the opposite wall to the model's dressing-room, and the street door is in the centre of the wall between. On a low table a Russian samovar is hissing, and beside it on a tray stands a teapot, with glasses, lemon, sugar, and a decanter of rum. Through a huge uncurtained window close to the street door the snowy lamp-lit street can be seen, and beyond it the river and a night of stars.*

The sound of a latchkey turned in the lock of the street door, and ANN WELLWYN *enters, a girl of seventeen, with hair tied in a ribbon and covered by a scarf. Leaving the door open, she turns up the electric light and goes to the fire. She throws off her scarf and long red cloak. She is dressed in a high evening frock of some soft white material. Her movements are quick and substantial. Her face, full of no nonsense, is decided and sincere, with deep-set eyes, and a capable, well-shaped forehead. Shredding off her gloves she warms her hands.*

In the doorway appear the figures of two men. The first is rather short and slight, with a soft short beard, bright soft eyes, and a crumply face. Under his squash hat his hair is rather plentiful and rather grey. He wears an old brown ulster and woollen gloves, and is puffing at a hand-made cigarette. He is ANN's *father,* WELLWYN, *the artist. His companion is a well-wrapped clergyman of medium height and stoutish build, with a pleasant, rosy face, rather shining eyes, and rather chubby clean-shaped lips; in appearance, indeed, a grown-up boy. He is the Vicar of the parish* —CANON BERTLEY.

BERTLEY. My dear Wellwyn, the whole question of reform is full of difficulty. When you have two men like Professor Calway and Sir Thomas Hoxton taking diametrically opposite points of view, as we've seen to-night, I confess, I——

WELLWYN. Come in, Vicar, and have some grog.

BERTLEY. Not to-night, thanks! Christmas to-morrow! Great temptation, though, this room! Good-night, Wellwyn; good-night, Ann!

ANN. [*Coming from the fire towards the tea table.*] Good-night, Canon Bertley.

[*He goes out, and* WELLWYN, *shutting the door after him, approaches the fire.*]

ANN. [*Sitting on the little stool, with her back to the fire, and making tea.*] Daddy!

WELLWYN. My dear?

ANN. You say you liked Professor Calway's lecture. Is it going to do you any good, that's the question?

WELLWYN. I—I hope so, Ann.

ANN. I took you on purpose. Your charity's getting

THE PIGEON

simply awful. Those two this morning cleared out all my housekeeping money.

WELLWYN. Um! Um! I quite understand your feeling.

ANN. They both had your card, so I couldn't refuse—didn't know what you'd said to them. Why don't you make it a rule never to give your card to anyone except really decent people, and—picture dealers, of course.

WELLWYN. My dear, I have—often.

ANN. Then why don't you keep it? It's a frightful habit. You *are* naughty, Daddy. One of these days you'll get yourself into most fearful complications.

WELLWYN. My dear, when they—when they look at you?

ANN. You know the house wants all sorts of things. Why do you speak to them at all?

WELLWYN. I don't—they speak to me.

[*He takes off his ulster and hangs it over the back of an arm-chair.*]

ANN. They see you coming. Anybody can see *you* coming, Daddy. That's why you ought to be so careful. I shall make you wear a hard hat. Those squashy hats of yours are hopelessly inefficient.

WELLWYN. [*Gazing at his hat.*] Calway wears one.

ANN. As if anyone would beg of Professor Calway.

WELLWYN. Well—perhaps not. You know, Ann, I admire that fellow. Wonderful power of—of—theory! How a man can be so absolutely tidy in his mind! It's most exciting.

ANN. Has any one begged of you to-day?

WELLWYN. [*Doubtfully.*] No—no.

ANN. [*After a long, severe look.*] Will you have rum in your tea?

WELLWYN. [*Crestfallen.*] Yes, my dear—a good deal.

ANN. [*Pouring out the rum, and handing him the glass.*] Well, who was it?

WELLWYN. He didn't beg of me. [*Losing himself in recollection.*] Interesting old creature, Ann—real type. Old cabman.

ANN. Where?

WELLWYN. Just on the Embankment.

ANN. Of course! Daddy, you know the Embankment ones are *always* rotters.

WELLWYN. Yes, my dear; but this wasn't.

ANN. Did you give him your card?

WELLWYN. I—I—don't——

ANN. *Did* you, Daddy?

WELLWYN. I'm rather afraid I may have!

ANN. May have! It's simply immoral.

WELLWYN. Well, the old fellow was so awfully human, Ann. Besides, I didn't give him any money—hadn't got any.

ANN. Look here, Daddy! Did you ever ask anybody for anything? You know you never did, you'd starve first. So would anybody decent. Then, why won't you see that people who beg are rotters?

WELLWYN. But, my dear, we're not all the same. They wouldn't do it if it wasn't natural to them. One likes to be friendly. What's the use of being alive if one isn't?

ANN. Daddy, you're hopeless.

WELLWYN. But, look here, Ann, the whole thing's so jolly complicated. According to Calway, we're to give the State all we can spare, to make the undeserving deserving. He's a Professor; he ought to know. But old Hoxton's always dinning it into me that we ought to support private organizations for helping the deserving, and damn the undeserving. Well, that's just the opposite. And he's a J. P. Tremendous experience. And the Vicar seems to be

THE PIGEON

for a little bit of both. Well, what the devil—? My trouble is, whichever I'm with, he always converts me. [*Ruefully.*] And there's no fun in any of them.

ANN. [*Rising.*] Oh! Daddy, you are so—don't you know that you're the despair of all social reformers? [*She envelops him.*] There's a tear in the left knee of your trousers. You're not to wear them again.

WELLWYN. Am I likely to?

ANN. I shouldn't be a bit surprised if it isn't your only pair. D'you know what I live in terror of?

[WELLWYN *gives her a queer and apprehensive look.*

ANN. That you'll take them off some day, and give them away in the street. Have you got any money? [*She feels in his coat, and he in his trousers—they find nothing.*] Do you know that your pockets are one enormous hole?

WELLWYN. No!

ANN. Spiritually.

WELLWYN. Oh! Ah! H'm!

ANN. [*Severely.*] Now, look here, Daddy! [*She takes him by his lapels.*] Don't imagine that it isn't the most disgusting luxury on your part to go on giving away things as you do! You know what you really are, I suppose—a sickly sentimentalist!

WELLWYN. [*Breaking away from her, disturbed.*] It isn't sentiment. It's simply that they seem to me so—so—jolly. If I'm to give up feeling sort of—nice in here [*he touches his chest*] about people—it doesn't matter *who* they are—then I don't know what I'm to do. I shall have to sit with my head in a bag.

ANN. I think you ought to.

WELLWYN. I suppose they see I like them—then they tell me things. After that, of course you can't help doing what you can.

ANN. Well, if you *will* love them up!

WELLWYN. My dear, I don't want to. It isn't *them* especially—why, I feel it even with old Calway sometimes. It's only Providence that he doesn't want anything of me—except to make me like himself—confound him!

ANN. [*Moving towards the door into the house—impressively.*] What you don't see is that other people aren't a bit like *you*.

WELLWYN. Well, thank God!

ANN. It's so old-fashioned too! I'm going to bed—I just leave you to your conscience.

WELLWYN. Oh!

ANN. [*Opening the door—severely.*] Good-night—[*with a certain weakening*] you old—Daddy!

> [*She jumps at him, gives him a hug, and goes out. WELLWYN stands perfectly still. He first gazes up at the skylight, then down at the floor. Slowly he begins to shake his head, and mutter, as he moves towards the fire.*]

WELLWYN. Bad lot. . . . Low type—no backbone, no stability!

> [*There comes a fluttering knock on the outer door. As the sound slowly enters his consciousness, he begins to wince, as though he knew, but would not admit its significance. Then he sits down, covering his ears. The knocking does not cease. WELLWYN drops first one, then both hands, rises, and begins to sidle towards the door. The knocking becomes louder.*]

WELLWYN. Ah dear! Tt! Tt! Tt!

> [*After a look in the direction of* ANN's *disappearance, he opens the street door a very little way. By the light of the lamp there can be seen a young girl in dark clothes, huddled in a shawl*

THE PIGEON

> to which the snow is clinging. She has on her
> arm a basket covered with a bit of sacking.]

WELLWYN. I can't, you know; it's impossible.

> [*The girl says nothing, but looks at him with
> dark eyes.*]

WELLWYN. [*Wincing.*] Let's see—I don't know you—do I?

> [*The girl, speaking in a soft, hoarse voice, with a
> faint accent of reproach*: "Mrs. Megan—you
> give me this—" *She holds out a dirty visiting
> card.*]

WELLWYN. [*Recoiling from the card.*] Oh! Did I? Ah! When?

MRS. MEGAN. You 'ad some vi'lets off of me last spring. You give me 'arf a crown. [*A smile tries to visit her face.*

WELLWYN. [*Looking stealthily round.*] Ah! Well, come in—just for a minute—it's very cold—and tell us what it is.

> [*She comes in stolidly, a sphinx-like figure, with
> her pretty tragic little face.*]

WELLWYN. I don't remember you. [*Looking closer.*] Yes, *I do.* Only—you weren't the same—were you?

MRS. MEGAN. [*Dully.*] I seen trouble since.

WELLWYN. Trouble! Have some tea?

> [*He looks anxiously at the door into the house,
> then goes quickly to the table, and pours out a
> glass of tea, putting rum into it.*]

WELLWYN. [*Handing her the tea.*] Keeps the cold out! Drink it off!

> [MRS. MEGAN *drinks it off, chokes a little, and
> almost immediately seems to get a size larger.*
> WELLWYN *watches her with his head held on
> one side, and a smile broadening on his face.*]

WELLWYN. Cure for all evils, um?

Mrs. Megan. It warms you. [*She smiles.*

Wellwyn. [*Smiling back, and catching himself out.*] Well! You know, I oughtn't.

Mrs. Megan. [*Conscious of the disruption of his personality, and withdrawing into her tragic abyss.*] I wouldn't 'a come, but you told me if I wanted an 'and——

Wellwyn. [*Gradually losing himself in his own nature.*] Let me see—corner of Flight Street, wasn't it?

Mrs. Megan. [*With faint eagerness.*] Yes, sir, an' I told you about me vi'lets—it was a luvly spring day.

Wellwyn. Beautiful! Beautiful! Birds singing, and the trees, &c.! We had quite a talk. You had a baby with you.

Mrs. Megan. Yes. I got married since then.

Wellwyn. Oh! Ah! Yes! [*Cheerfully.*] And how's the baby?

Mrs. Megan. [*Turning to stone.*] I lost her.

Wellwyn. Oh! poor— Um!

Mrs. Megan. [*Impassive.*] You said something abaht makin' a picture of me. [*With faint eagerness.*] So I thought I might come, in case you'd forgotten.

Wellwyn. [*Looking at her intently.*] Things going badly?

Mrs. Megan. [*Stripping the sacking off her basket.*] I keep 'em covered up, but the cold gets to 'em. Thruppence—that's all I've took.

Wellwyn. Ho! Tt! Tt! [*He looks into the basket.*] Christmas, too!

Mrs. Megan. They're dead.

Wellwyn. [*Drawing in his breath.*] Got a *good* husband?

Mrs. Megan. He plays cards.

Wellwyn. Oh, Lord! And what are you doing out— with a cold like that? [*He taps his chest.*

THE PIGEON

Mrs. Megan. We was sold up this morning—he's gone off with 'is mates. Haven't took enough yet for a night's lodgin'.

Wellwyn. [*Correcting a spasmodic dive into his pockets.*] But who buys *flowers* at this time of night?

[*Mrs. Megan looks at him, and faintly smiles.*]

Wellwyn. [*Rumpling his hair.*] Saints above us! Here! Come to the fire!

[*She follows him to the fire. He shuts the street door.*]

Wellwyn. Are your feet wet? [*She nods.*] Well, sit down here, and take them off. That's right.

[*She sits on the stool. And after a slow look up at him, which has in it a deeper knowledge than belongs of right to her years, begins taking off her shoes and stockings. Wellwyn goes to the door into the house, opens it, and listens with a sort of stealthy casualness. He returns whistling, but not out loud. The girl has finished taking off her stockings, and turned her bare toes to the flames. She shuffles them back under her skirt.*]

Wellwyn. How old are you, my child?

Mrs. Megan. Nineteen, come Candlemas.

Wellwyn. And what's your name?

Mrs. Megan. Guinevere.

Wellwyn. What? Welsh?

Mrs. Megan. Yes—from Battersea.

Wellwyn. And your husband?

Mrs. Megan. No. Irish, 'e is. Notting Dale, 'e comes from.

Wellwyn. Roman Catholic?

Mrs. Megan. Yes. My 'usband's an atheist as well.

WELLWYN. I see. [*Abstractedly.*] How jolly! And how old is he—this young man of yours?

MRS. MEGAN. 'E'll be twenty soon.

WELLWYN. Babes in the wood! Does he treat you badly?

MRS. MEGAN. No.

WELLWYN. Nor drink?

MRS. MEGAN. No. He's not a bad one. Only he gets playin' cards—then 'e'll fly the kite.

WELLWYN. I see. And when he's not flying it, what does he do?

MRS. MEGAN. [*Touching her basket.*] Same as me. Other jobs tires 'im.

WELLWYN. That's very nice! [*He checks himself.*] Well, what am I to do with you?

MRS. MEGAN. Of course, I could get me night's lodging if I like to do—the same as some of them.

WELLWYN. No! no! Never, my child! Never!

MRS. MEGAN. It's easy that way.

WELLWYN. Heavens! But your husband! Um?

MRS. MEGAN. [*With stoical vindictiveness.*] He's after one I know of.

WELLWYN. Tt! What a pickle!

MRS. MEGAN. I'll 'ave to walk about the streets.

WELLWYN. [*To himself.*] Now how can I?

[MRS. MEGAN *looks up and smiles at him, as if she had already discovered that he is peculiar.*]

WELLWYN. You see, the fact is, I mustn't give you anything—because—well, for one thing I haven't got it. There are other reasons, but that's the—real one. But, now, there's a little room where my models dress. I wonder if you could sleep there. Come, and see.

[*The Girl gets up lingeringly, loth to leave the warmth. She takes up her wet stockings.*]

THE PIGEON

MRS. MEGAN. Shall I put them on again?

WELLWYN. No, no; there's a nice warm pair of slippers. [*Seeing the steam rising from her.*] Why, you're wet all over. Here, wait a little!

> [*He crosses to the door into the house, and after stealthy listening, steps through. The Girl, like a cat, steals back to the warmth of the fire.* WELLWYN *returns with a candle, a canary-coloured bath gown, and two blankets.*]

WELLWYN. Now then! [*He precedes her towards the door of the model's room.*] Hsssh! [*He opens the door and holds up the candle to show her the room.*] Will it do? There's a couch. You'll find some washing things. Make yourself quite at home. See!

> [*The Girl, perfectly dumb, passes through with her basket—and her shoes and stockings.* WELLWYN *hands her the candle, blankets, and bath gown.*]

WELLWYN. Have a good sleep, child! Forget that you're alive! [*He closes the door, mournfully.*] Done it again! [*He goes to the table, cuts a large slice of cake, knocks on the door, and hands it in.*] Chow-chow! [*Then, as he walks away, he sights the opposite door.*] Well—damn it, what *could* I have done? Not a farthing on me! [*He goes to the street door to shut it, but first opens it wide to confirm himself in his hospitality.*] Night like this!

> [*A sputter of snow is blown in his face. A voice says:* "Monsieur, pardon!" WELLWYN *recoils spasmodically. A figure moves from the lamp-post to the doorway. He is seen to be young and to have ragged clothes. He speaks again:* "You do not remember me, Monsieur? My name is Ferrand—it was in Paris, in the Champs-Elysées — by the fountain. . . .

When you came to the door, Monsieur—I am not made of iron. . . . Tenez, here is your card—I have never lost it." *He holds out to* WELLWYN *an old and dirty visiting card. As inch by inch he has advanced into the doorway, the light from within falls on him, a tall gaunt young pagan with fair hair and reddish golden stubble of beard, a long ironical nose a little to one side, and large, grey, rather prominent eyes. There is a certain grace in his figure and movement; his clothes are nearly dropping off him.*]

WELLWYN. [*Yielding to a pleasant memory.*] Ah! yes. By the fountain. I was sitting there, and you came and ate a roll, and drank the water.

FERRAND. [*With faint eagerness.*] My breakfast. I was in poverty—veree bad off. You gave me ten francs. I thought I had a little the right [WELLWYN *makes a movement of disconcertion*], seeing you said that if I came to England——

WELLWYN. Um! And so you've come?

FERRAND. It was time that I consolidated my fortunes, Monsieur.

WELLWYN. And you—have——

[*He stops embarrassed.*

FERRAND. [*Shrugging his ragged shoulders.*] One is not yet Rothschild.

WELLWYN. [*Sympathetically.*] No. [*Yielding to memory.*] We talked philosophy.

FERRAND. I have not yet changed my opinion. We other vagabonds, we are exploited by the bourgeois. This is always my idea, Monsieur.

WELLWYN. Yes—not quite the general view, perhaps! Well— [*Heartily.*] Come in! Very glad to see you again.

FERRAND. [*Brushing his arms over his eyes.*] Pardon,

THE PIGEON

Monsieur—your goodness—I am a little weak. [*He opens his coat, and shows a belt drawn very tight over his ragged shirt.*] I tighten him one hole for each meal, during two days now. That gives you courage.

WELLWYN. [*With cooing sounds, pouring out tea, and adding rum.*] Have some of this. It'll buck you up.

[*He watches the young man drink.*

FERRAND. [*Becoming a size larger.*] Sometimes I think that I will never succeed to dominate my life, Monsieur—though I have no vices, except that I guard always the aspiration to achieve success. But I will not roll myself under the machine of existence to gain a nothing every day. I must find with what to fly a little.

WELLWYN. [*Delicately.*] Yes; yes—I remember, you found it difficult to stay long in any particular—yes.

FERRAND. [*Proudly.*] In one little corner? No—Monsieur—never! That is not in my character. I must see life.

WELLWYN. Quite, quite! Have some cake?

[*He cuts cake.*

FERRAND. In your country they say you cannot eat the cake and have it. But one must always try, Monsieur; one must never be content. [*Refusing the cake.*] Grand merci, but for the moment I have no stomach—I have lost my stomach now for two days. If I could smoke, Monsieur! [*He makes the gesture of smoking.*]

WELLWYN. Rather! [*Handing his tobacco pouch.*] Roll yourself one.

FERRAND. [*Rapidly rolling a cigarette.*] If I had not found you, Monsieur—I would have been a little hole in the river tonight—I was so discouraged. [*He inhales and puffs a long luxurious whiff of smoke. Very bitterly.*] Life! [*He disperses the puff of smoke with his finger, and stares before him.*] And to think that in a few minutes HE will be born! Monsieur! [*He gazes intently at* WELLWYN.] The world would reproach you for your goodness to me.

WELLWYN. [*Looking uneasily at the door into the house.*] You think so? Ah!

FERRAND. Monsieur, if HE himself were on earth now, there would be a little heap of gentlemen writing to the journals every day to call Him sloppee sentimentalist! And what is veree funny, these gentlemen they would all be most strong Christians. [*He regards* WELLWYN *deeply.*] But that will not trouble you, Monsieur; I saw well from the first that you are no Christian. You have so kind a face.

WELLWYN. Oh! Indeed!

FERRAND. You have not enough the Pharisee in your character. You do not judge, and you are judged.

[*He stretches his limbs as if in pain.*

WELLWYN. Are you in pain?

FERRAND. I 'ave a little the rheumatism.

WELLWYN. Wet through, of course! [*Glancing towards the house.*] Wait a bit! I wonder if you'd like these trousers; they've——er——they're not quite——

> [*He passes through the door into the house.* FERRAND *stands at the fire, with his limbs spread as it were to embrace it, smoking with abandonment.* WELLWYN *returns stealthily, dressed in a Jaeger dressing-gown, and bearing a pair of drawers, his trousers, a pair of slippers, and a sweater.*]

WELLWYN. [*Speaking in a low voice, for the door is still open.*] Can you make these do for the moment?

FERRAND. *Je vous remercie, Monsieur.* [*Pointing to the screen.*] May I retire?

WELLWYN. Yes, yes.

> [FERRAND *goes behind the screen.* WELLWYN *closes the door into the house, then goes to the*

THE PIGEON

window to draw the curtains. He suddenly recoils and stands petrified with doubt.]

WELLWYN. Good Lord!

[*There is the sound of tapping on glass. Against the window-pane is pressed the face of a man.* WELLWYN *motions to him to go away. He does not go, but continues tapping.* WELLWYN *opens the door. There enters a square old man, with a red, pendulous-jawed, shaking face under a snow-besprinkled bowler hat. He is holding out a visiting card with tremulous hand.*]

WELLWYN. Who's that? Who are you?

TIMSON. [*In a thick, hoarse, shaking voice.*] 'Appy to see you, sir; we 'ad a talk this morning. Timson—I give you me name. You invited of me, if ye remember.

WELLWYN. It's a little late, really.

TIMSON. Well, ye see, I never expected to 'ave to call on yer. I was 'itched up all right when I spoke to yer this mornin', but bein' Christmas, things 'ave took a turn with me to-day. [*He speaks with increasing thickness.*] I'm reg'lar disgusted—not got the price of a bed abaht me. Thought you wouldn't like me to be delicate—not at my age.

WELLWYN. [*With a mechanical and distracted dive of his hands into his pockets.*] The fact is, it so happens I haven't a copper on me.

TIMSON. [*Evidently taking this for professional refusal.*] Wouldn't arsk you if I could 'elp it. 'Ad to do with 'orses all me life. It's this 'ere cold I'm frightened of. I'm afraid I'll go to sleep.

WELLWYN. Well, really, I——

TIMSON. To be froze to death—I mean—it's awkward.

WELLWYN. [*Puzzled and unhappy.*] Well—come in a moment, and let's—think it out. Have some tea!

[*He pours out the remains of the tea, and finding*

there is not very much, adds rum rather liberally. TIMSON, *who walks a little wide at the knees, steadying his gait, has followed.*]

TIMSON. [*Receiving the drink.*] Yer 'ealth. 'Ere's—sobriety! [*He applies the drink to his lips with shaking hand. Agreeably surprised.*] Blimey! Thish yer tea's foreign, ain't it?

FERRAND. [*Reappearing from behind the screen in his new clothes of which the trousers stop too soon.*] With a needle, Monsieur, I would soon have with what to make face against the world.

WELLWYN. Too short! Ah!

[*He goes to the dais on which stands* ANN's *work-basket, and takes from it a needle and cotton. While he is so engaged* FERRAND *is sizing up old* TIMSON, *as one dog will another. The old man, glass in hand, seems to have lapsed into coma.*]

FERRAND. [*Indicating* TIMSON.] Monsieur!

[*He makes the gesture of one drinking, and shakes his head.*]

WELLWYN. [*Handing him the needle and cotton.*] Um! Afraid so!

[*They approach* TIMSON, *who takes no notice.*

FERRAND. [*Gently.*] It is an old cabby, is it not, Monsieur? *Ceux sont tous des buveurs.*

WELLWYN. [*Concerned at the old man's stupefaction.*] Now, my old friend, sit down a moment. [*They manœuvre* TIMSON *to the settle.*] Will you smoke?

TIMSON. [*In a drowsy voice.*] Thank 'ee—smoke pipe of 'baccer. Old 'orse—standin' abaht in th' cold.

[*He relapses into coma.*

FERRAND. [*With a click of his tongue.*] *Il est parti.*

WELLWYN. [*Doubtfully.*] He hasn't really left a horse outside, do you think?

THE PIGEON

FERRAND. *Non, non, Monsieur*—no 'orse. He is dreaming. I know very well that state of him—that catches you sometimes. It is the warmth sudden on the stomach. He will speak no more sense tonight. At the most, drink, and fly a little in his past.

WELLWYN. Poor old buffer!

FERRAND. Touching, is it not, Monsieur? There are many brave gents among the old cabbies—they have philosophy—that comes from 'orses, and from sitting still.

WELLWYN. [*Touching* TIMSON'S *shoulder.*] Drenched!

FERRAND. That will do 'im no 'arm, Monsieur—no 'arm at all. He is well wet inside, remember—it is Christmas to-morrow. Put him a rug, if you will, he will soon steam.

[WELLWYN *takes up* ANN'S *long red cloak, and wraps it round the old man.*]

TIMSON. [*Faintly roused.*] Tha's right. Put—the rug on th' old 'orse.

[*He makes a strange noise, and works his head and tongue.*]

WELLWYN. [*Alarmed.*] What's the matter with him?

FERRAND. It is nothing, Monsieur; for the moment he thinks 'imself a 'orse. *Il joue "cache-cache,"* 'ide and seek, with what you call—'is bitt.

WELLWYN. But what's to be done with him? One can't turn him out in this state.

FERRAND. If you wish to leave him 'ere, Monsieur, have no fear. I charge myself with him.

WELLWYN. Oh! [*Dubiously.*] You—er—I really don't know, I—hadn't contemplated—You think you could manage if I—if I went to bed?

FERRAND. But certainly, Monsieur.

WELLWYN. [*Still dubiously.*] You—you're sure you've everything you want?

FERRAND. [*Bowing.*] *Mais oui, Monsieur.*

WELLWYN. I don't know what I can do by staying.

FERRAND. There is nothing you can do, Monsieur. Have confidence in me.

WELLWYN. Well—keep the fire up quietly—very quietly. You'd better take this coat of mine, too. You'll find it precious cold, I expect, about three o'clock.

[*He hands* FERRAND *his ulster.*

FERRAND. [*Taking it.*] I shall sleep in praying for you, Monsieur.

WELLWYN. Ah! Yes! Thanks! Well—good-night! By the way, I shall be down rather early. Have to think of my household a bit, you know.

FERRAND. *Très bien, Monsieur.* I comprehend. One must well be regular in this life.

WELLWYN. [*With a start.*] Lord! [*He looks at the door of the model's room.*] I'd forgotten——

FERRAND. Can I undertake anything, Monsieur?

WELLWYN. *No, no!* [*He goes to the electric light switch by the outer door.*] You won't want this, will you?

FERRAND. *Merci, Monsieur.*

[WELLWYN *switches off the light.*

FERRAND. *Bon soir, Monsieur!*

WELLWYN. The devil! Er—good-night!

[*He hesitates, rumples his hair, and passes rather suddenly away.*]

FERRAND. [*To himself.*] Poor pigeon! [*Looking long at old* TIMSON.] *Espèce de type anglais!*

[*He sits down in the firelight, curls up a foot on his knee, and taking out a knife, rips the stitching of a turned-up end of trouser, pinches the cloth double, and puts in the preliminary stitch of a new hem—all with the swiftness of one well accustomed. Then, as if hearing a sound behind him, gets up quickly and slips behind the*

THE PIGEON

screen. MRS. MEGAN, attracted by the cessation of voices, has opened the door, and is creeping from the model's room towards the fire. She has almost reached it before she takes in the torpid crimson figure of old TIMSON. She halts and puts her hand to her chest—a queer figure in the firelight, garbed in the canary-coloured bath gown and rabbit's-wool slippers, her black matted hair straggling down on her neck. Having quite digested the fact that the old man is in a sort of stupor, MRS. MEGAN goes close to the fire, and sits on the little stool, smiling sideways at old TIMSON. FERRAND, coming quietly up behind, examines her from above, drooping his long nose as if enquiring with it as to her condition in life; then he steps back a yard or two.]

FERRAND. [*Gently.*] Pardon, Ma'moiselle.

MRS. MEGAN. [*Springing to her feet.*] Oh!

FERRAND. All right, all right! We are brave gents!

TIMSON. [*Faintly roused.*] 'Old up, there!

FERRAND. Trust in me, Ma'moiselle!

[MRS. MEGAN *responds by drawing away.*

FERRAND. [*Gently.*] We must be good comrades. This asylum—it is better than a doss-'ouse.

[*He pushes the stool over towards her, and seats himself. Somewhat reassured,* MRS. MEGAN *again sits down.*]

MRS. MEGAN. You frightened me.

TIMSON. [*Unexpectedly—in a drowsy tone.*] Purple foreigners!

FERRAND. Pay no attention, Ma'moiselle. He is a philosopher.

Mrs. Megan. Oh! I thought 'e was boozed.

[*They both look at* Timson.

Ferrand. It is the same—veree 'armless.

Mrs. Megan. What's that he's got on 'im?

Ferrand. It's a coronation robe. Have no fear, Ma'moiselle. Veree docile potentate.

Mrs. Megan. I wouldn't be afraid of him. [*Challenging* Ferrand.] I'm afraid o' *you*.

Ferrand. It is because you do not know me, Ma'moiselle. You are wrong, it is always the unknown you should love.

Mrs. Megan. I don't like the way you—speaks to me.

Ferrand. Ah! You are a Princess in disguise?

Mrs. Megan. No fear!

Ferrand. No? What is it then you do to make face against the necessities of life? A living?

Mrs. Megan. Sells flowers.

Ferrand. [*Rolling his eyes.*] It is not a career.

Mrs. Megan. [*With a touch of deviltry.*] You don't know what I do.

Ferrand. Ma'moiselle, whatever you do is charming.

[Mrs. Megan *looks at him, and slowly smiles.*

Mrs. Megan. You're a foreigner.

Ferrand. It is true.

Mrs. Megan. What do *you* do for a livin'?

Ferrand. I am an interpreter.

Mrs. Megan. You ain't very busy, are you?

Ferrand. [*With dignity.*] At present I am resting.

Mrs. Megan. [*Looking at him and smiling.*] How did you and 'im come here?

Ferrand. Ma'moiselle, we would ask you the same question.

Mrs. Megan. The gentleman let me. 'E's funny.

THE PIGEON

FERRAND. *C'est un ange!* [*At* MRS. MEGAN'S *blank stare he interprets.*] An angel!

MRS. MEGAN. Me luck's out—that's why I come.

FERRAND. [*Rising.*] Ah! Ma'moiselle! Luck! There is the little God who dominates us all. Look at this old! [*He points to* TIMSON.] He is finished. In his day that old would be doing good business. He could afford himself — [*He makes a sign of drinking.*] Then come the motor cars. All goes—he has nothing left, only 'is 'abits of a cocher! Luck!

TIMSON. [*With a vague gesture—drowsily.*] Kick the foreign beggars out.

FERRAND. A real Englishman. . . . And look at me! My father was merchant of ostrich feathers in Brussels. If I had been content to go in his business, I would 'ave been rich. But I was born to roll—"rolling stone"—to voyage is stronger than myself. Luck! . . . And you, Ma'moiselle, shall I tell your fortune? [*He looks in her face.*] You were born for *la joie de vivre*—to drink the wines of life. *Et vous voilà!* Luck!

> [*Though she does not in the least understand what he has said, her expression changes to a sort of glee.*]

FERRAND. Yes. You were born loving pleasure. Is it not? You see, you cannot say, No. All of us, we have our fates. Give me your hand. [*He kneels down and takes her hand.*] In each of us there is that against which we cannot struggle. Yes, yes!

> [*He holds her hand, and turns it over between his own.* MRS. MEGAN *remains stolid, half-fascinated, half-reluctant.*]

TIMSON. [*Flickering into consciousness.*] Be'ave yourselves! Yer crimson canary birds!

> [MRS. MEGAN *would withdraw her hand, but cannot.*

FERRAND. Pay no attention, Ma'moiselle. He is a Puritan.

> [TIMSON *relapses into comatosity, upsetting his glass, which falls with a crash.*]

MRS. MEGAN. Let go my hand, please!

FERRAND. [*Relinquishing it, and staring into the fire gravely.*] There is one thing I have never done—'urt a woman—that is hardly in my character. [*Then, drawing a little closer, he looks into her face.*] Tell me, Ma'moiselle, what is it you think of all day long?

MRS. MEGAN. I dunno—lots, I thinks of.

FERRAND. Shall I tell you? [*Her eyes remain fixed on his, the strangeness of him preventing her from telling him to "get along." He goes on in his ironic voice.*] It is of the streets—the lights—the faces—it is of all which moves, and is warm—it is of colour—it is [*he brings his face quite close to hers*] of Love. That is for you what the road is for me. That is for you what the rum is for that old— [*He jerks his thumb back at* TIMSON. *Then bending swiftly forward to the girl.*] See! I kiss you—Ah!

> [*He draws her forward off the stool. There is a little struggle, then she resigns her lips. The little stool, overturned, falls with a clatter. They spring up, and move apart. The door opens and* ANN *enters from the house in a blue dressing-gown, with her hair loose, and a candle held high above her head. Taking in the strange half-circle round the stove, she recoils. Then, standing her ground, calls in a voice sharpened by fright:* "Daddy—Daddy!"]

TIMSON. [*Stirring uneasily, and struggling to his feet.*] All ri——! *I'm* comin'!

FERRAND. Have no fear, Madame!

> [*In the silence that follows, a clock begins loudly*

*striking twelve. ANN remains, as if carved in
stone, her eyes fastened on the strangers. There
is the sound of someone falling downstairs, and
WELLWYN appears, also holding a candle above
his head.*]

ANN. Look!

WELLWYN. Yes, yes, my dear! It—it happened.

ANN. [*With a sort of groan.*] Oh! Daddy!

[*In the renewed silence, the church clock ceases
to chime.*]

FERRAND. [*Softly, in his ironic voice.*] HE is come,
Monsieur! 'Appy Christmas! Bon Noël!

[*There is a sudden chime of bells.
The stage is blotted dark.*

The curtain falls.

ACT II

*It is four o'clock in the afternoon of New Year's Day. On
the raised dais MRS. MEGAN is standing, in her rags;
with bare feet and ankles, her dark hair as if blown
about, her lips parted, holding out a dishevelled bunch
of violets. Before his easel, WELLWYN is painting her.
Behind him, at a table between the cupboard and the
door to the model's room, TIMSON is washing brushes,
with the movements of one employed upon relief works.
The samovar is hissing on the table by the stove, the
tea things are set out.*

WELLWYN. Open your mouth.

[MRS. MEGAN *opens her mouth.*

ANN. [*In hat and coat, entering from the house.*]
Daddy!

[WELLWYN *goes to her; and, released from restraint,* MRS. MEGAN *looks round at* TIMSON *and grimaces.*]

WELLWYN. Well, my dear?

[*They speak in low voices.*

ANN. [*Holding out a note.*] This note from Canon Bertley. He's going to bring her husband here this afternoon. [*She looks at* MRS. MEGAN.

WELLWYN. Oh! [*He also looks at* MRS. MEGAN.

ANN. And I met Sir Thomas Hoxton at church this morning, and spoke to him about Timson.

WELLWYN. Um!

[*They look at* TIMSON. *Then* ANN *goes back to the door, and* WELLWYN *follows her.*]

ANN. [*Turning.*] I'm going round now, Daddy, to ask Professor Calway what we're to do with that Ferrand.

WELLWYN. Oh! One each! I wonder if they'll like it.

ANN. They'll have to lump it.

[*She goes out into the house.*

WELLWYN. [*Back at his easel.*] You can shut your mouth now.

[MRS. MEGAN *shuts her mouth, but opens it immediately to smile.*]

WELLWYN. [*Spasmodically.*] Ah! Now that's what I want. [*He dabs furiously at the canvas. Then standing back, runs his hands through his hair and turns a painter's glance towards the skylight.*] Dash! Light's gone! Off you get, child—don't tempt me!

[MRS. MEGAN *descends. Passing towards the door of the model's room she stops, and stealthily looks at the picture.*]

TIMSON. Ah! Would yer!

WELLWYN. [*Wheeling round.*] Want to have a look? Well—come on!

THE PIGEON

[*He takes her by the arm, and they stand before the canvas. After a stolid moment, she giggles.*]

WELLWYN. Oh! You think so?

MRS. MEGAN. [*Who has lost her hoarseness.*] It's not like my picture that I had on the pier.

WELLWYN. No—it wouldn't be.

MRS. MEGAN. [*Timidly.*] If I had an 'at on, I'd look better.

WELLWYN. With feathers?

MRS. MEGAN. Yes.

WELLWYN. Well, you can't! I don't like hats, and I don't like feathers.

[*MRS. MEGAN timidly tugs his sleeve. TIMSON, screened as he thinks by the picture, has drawn from his bulky pocket a bottle and is taking a stealthy swig.*]

WELLWYN. [*To MRS. MEGAN, affecting not to notice.*] How much do I owe you?

MRS. MEGAN. [*A little surprised.*] You paid me for to-day—all 'cept a penny.

WELLWYN. Well! Here it is. [*He gives her a coin.*] Go and get your feet on!

MRS. MEGAN. You've given me 'arf a crown.

WELLWYN. Cut away now!

[*MRS. MEGAN, smiling at the coin, goes towards the model's room. She looks back at WELLWYN, as if to draw his eyes to her, but he is gazing at the picture; then, catching old TIMSON'S sour glance, she grimaces at him, kicking up her feet with a little squeal. But when WELLWYN turns to the sound, she is demurely passing through the doorway.*]

TIMSON. [*In his voice of dubious sobriety.*] I've finished

these yer brushes, sir. It's not a man's work. I've been thinkin' if you'd keep an 'orse, I could give yer satisfaction.

WELLWYN. Would the horse, Timson?

TIMSON. [*Looking him up and down.*] I knows of one that would just suit yer. Reel 'orse, you'd like 'im.

WELLWYN. [*Shaking his head.*] Afraid not, Timson! Awfully sorry, though, to have nothing better for you than this, at present.

TIMSON. [*Faintly waving the brushes.*] Of course, if you can't afford it, I don't press you—it's only that I feel I'm not doing meself justice. [*Confidentially.*] There's just one thing, sir; I can't bear to see a gen'leman imposed on. That foreigner—'e's not the sort to 'ave about the place. Talk? Oh! ah! But 'e'll never do any good with 'imself. He's a alien.

WELLWYN. Terrible misfortune to a fellow, Timson.

TIMSON. Don't you believe it, sir; it's his fault I says to the young lady yesterday: Miss Ann, your father's a gen'leman [*with a sudden accent of hoarse sincerity*], and so you are—I don't mind sayin' it—*but,* I said, he's too easy-goin'.

WELLWYN. Indeed!

TIMSON. Well, see that girl now! [*He shakes his head.*] I never did believe in goin' behind a person's back—I'm an Englishman—but [*lowering his voice*] she's a bad hat, sir. Why, look at the street she comes from!

WELLWYN. Oh! you know it.

TIMSON. Lived there meself larst three years. See the difference a few days' corn's made in her. She's that saucy you can't touch 'er head.

WELLWYN. Is there any necessity, Timson?

TIMSON. Artful too. Full o' vice, I call 'er. Where's 'er 'usband?

THE PIGEON

WELLWYN. [*Gravely.*] Come, Timson! You wouldn't like *her* to——

TIMSON. [*With dignity, so that the bottle in his pocket is plainly visible.*] I'm a man as always beared inspection.

WELLWYN. [*With a well-directed smile.*] So I see.

TIMSON. [*Curving himself round the bottle.*] It's not for me to say nothing—but I can tell a gen'leman as quick as ever I can tell an 'orse.

WELLWYN. [*Painting.*] I find it safest to assume that every man is a gentleman, and every woman a lady. Saves no end of self-contempt. Give me the little brush.

TIMSON. [*Handing him the brush—after a considerable introspective pause.*] Would yer like me to stay and wash it for yer again? [*With great resolution.*] I will—I'll do it for you—never grudged workin' for a gen'leman.

WELLWYN. [*With sincerity.*] Thank you, Timson—very good of you, I'm sure. [*He hands him back the brush.*] Just lend us a hand with this. [*Assisted by* TIMSON *he pushes back the dais.*] Let's see! What do I owe you?

TIMSON. [*Reluctantly.*] It so 'appens, you advanced me to-day's yesterday.

WELLWYN. Then I suppose you want to-morrow's?

TIMSON. Well, I 'ad to spend it, lookin' for a permanent job. When you've got to do with 'orses, you can't neglect the publics, or you might as well be dead.

WELLWYN. Quite so!

TIMSON. It mounts up in the course o' the year.

WELLWYN. It would. [*Passing him a coin.*] This is for an exceptional purpose—Timson—see. Not——

TIMSON. [*Touching his forehead.*] Certainly, sir. I quite understand. I'm not that sort, as I think I've proved to yer, comin' here regular day after day, all the week. There's one thing, I ought to warn you perhaps—I might 'ave to give this job up any day.

[*He makes a faint demonstration with the little brush, then puts it, absent-mindedly, into his pocket.*]

WELLWYN. [*Gravely.*] I'd never stand in the way of your bettering yourself, Timson. And, by the way, my daughter spoke to a friend about you to-day. I think something may come of it.

TIMSON. Oh! Oh! She did! Well, it might do me a bit o' good. [*He makes for the outer door, but stops.*] That foreigner! 'E sticks in my gizzard. It's not as if there wasn't plenty o' pigeons for 'im to pluck in 'is own Gawd-forsaken country. Reg-lar jay, that's what I calls 'im. I could tell yer something——

[*He has opened the door, and suddenly sees that* FERRAND *himself is standing there. Sticking out his lower lip,* TIMSON *gives a roll of his jaw and lurches forth into the street. Owing to a slight miscalculation, his face and raised arms are plainly visible through the window, as he fortifies himself from his battle against the cold.* FERRAND, *having closed the door, stands with his thumb acting as pointer towards this spectacle. He is now remarkably dressed in an artist's squashy green hat, a frock coat too small for him, a bright blue tie of knitted silk, the grey trousers that were torn, well-worn brown boots, and a tan waistcoat.*]

WELLWYN. What luck today?

FERRAND. [*With a shrug.*] Again I have beaten all London, Monsieur—not one bite. [*Contemplating himself.*] I think perhaps, that, for the bourgeoisie, there is a little too much colour in my costume.

WELLWYN. [*Contemplating him.*] Let's see—I believe I've an old top hat somewhere.

FERRAND. Ah! Monsieur, *merci,* but *that* I could not. It is scarcely in my character.

WELLWYN. True!

FERRAND. I have been to merchants of wine, of *tabac,* to hotels, to Leicester Square. I have been to a—Society for spreading Christian knowledge—I thought there I would have a chance perhaps as interpreter. *Toujours hême chose*—we regret, we have no situation for you—same thing everywhere. It seems there is nothing doing in this town.

WELLWYN. I've noticed, there never is.

FERRAND. I was thinking, Monsieur, that in aviation there might be a career for me—but it seems one must be trained.

WELLWYN. Afraid so, Ferrand.

FERRAND. [*Approaching the picture.*] Ah! You are always working at this. You will have something of very good there, Monsieur. You wish to fix the type of wild savage existing ever amongst our high civilisation. *C'est très chic ça!* [WELLWYN *manifests the quiet delight of an English artist actually understood.*] In the figures of these good citizens, to whom she offers her flower, you would give the idea of all the cage doors open to catch and make tame the wild bird, that will surely die within. *Très gentil!* Believe me, Monsieur, you have there the greatest comedy of life! How anxious are the tame birds to do the wild birds good. [*His voice changes.*] For the wild birds it is not funny. There is in some human souls, Monsieur, what cannot be made tame.

WELLWYN. I believe you, Ferrand.

> [*The face of a young man appears at the window, unseen. Suddenly* ANN *opens the door leading to the house.*]

ANN. Daddy—I want you.

WELLWYN. [*To* FERRAND.] Excuse me a minute!

> [*He goes to his daughter, and they pass out.* FERRAND *remains at the picture.* MRS. MEGAN *dressed in some of* ANN's *discarded garments, has come out of the model's room. She steals up behind* FERRAND *like a cat, reaches an arm up, and curls it round his mouth. He turns, and tries to seize her; she disingenuously slips away. He follows. The chase circles the tea table. He catches her, lifts her up, swings round with her, so that her feet fly out; kisses her bent-back face, and sets her down. She stands there smiling. The face at the window darkens.*]

FERRAND. La Valse!

> [*He takes her with both hands by the waist, she puts her hands against his shoulders to push him off—and suddenly they are whirling. As they whirl, they bob together once or twice, and kiss. Then, with a warning motion towards the door, she wrenches herself free, and stops beside the picture, trying desperately to appear demure.* WELLWYN *and* ANN *have entered. The face has vanished.*]

FERRAND. [*Pointing to the picture.*] One does not comprehend all this, Monsieur, without well studying. I was in train to interpret for Ma'moiselle the chiaroscuro.

WELLWYN. [*With a queer look.*] Don't take it *too* seriously, Ferrand.

FERRAND. It is a masterpiece.

WELLWYN. My daughter's just spoken to a friend, Professor Calway. He'd like to meet you. Could you come back a little later?

FERRAND. Certainly, Ma'moiselle. That will be an opening for me, I trust. [*He goes to the street door.*

THE PIGEON

ANN. [*Paying no attention to him.*] Mrs. Megan, will you too come back in half an hour?

FERRAND. *Très bien, Ma'moiselle!* I will see that she does. We will take a little promenade together. That will do us good.

> [*He motions towards the door;* MRS. MEGAN, *all eyes, follows him out.*]

ANN. Oh! Daddy, they *are* rotters. Couldn't you *see* they were having the most high jinks?

WELLWYN. [*At his picture.*] I seemed to have noticed something.

ANN. [*Preparing for tea.*] They were kissing.

WELLWYN. Tt! Tt!

ANN. They're hopeless, all three—especially her. Wish I hadn't given her my clothes now.

WELLWYN. [*Absorbed.*] Something of wild-savage.

ANN. Thank goodness it's the Vicar's business to see that married people live together in his parish.

WELLWYN. Oh! [*Dubiously.*] The Megans are Roman Catholic-Atheists, Ann.

ANN. [*With heat.*] Then they're all the more bound.

> [WELLWYN *gives a sudden and alarmed whistle.*]

ANN. What's the matter?

WELLWYN. Didn't you say you spoke to Sir Thomas, too. Suppose he comes in while the Professor's here. They're cat and dog.

ANN. [*Blankly.*] Oh! [*As* WELLWYN *strikes a match.*] The samovar *is* lighted. [*Taking up the nearly empty decanter of rum and going to the cupboard.*] It's all right. He won't.

WELLWYN. We'll hope not.

> [*He turns back to his picture.*]

ANN. [*At the cupboard.*] Daddy!

WELLWYN. Hi!

ANN. There were *three* bottles.

WELLWYN. Oh!

ANN. Well! Now there aren't any.

WELLWYN. [*Abstracted.*] That'll be Timson.

ANN. [*With real horror.*] But it's awful!

WELLWYN. It is, my dear.

ANN. In seven days. To say nothing of the stealing.

WELLWYN. [*Vexed.*] I blame myself—very much. Ought to have kept it locked up.

ANN. You ought to keep *him* locked up!

[*There is heard a mild but authoritative knock.*]

WELLWYN. Here's the Vicar!

ANN. What are you going to do about the rum?

WELLWYN. [*Opening the door to* CANON BERTLEY.] Come in, Vicar! Happy New Year!

BERTLEY. Same to you! Ah! Ann! I've got into touch with her young husband—he's coming round.

ANN. [*Still a little out of her plate.*] Thank Go—— Moses!

BERTLEY. [*Faintly surprised.*] From what I hear he's not really a bad youth. Afraid he bets on horses. The great thing, Wellwyn, with those poor fellows is to put your finger on the weak spot.

ANN. [*To herself—gloomily.*] That's not difficult. What would you do, Canon Bertley, with a man who's been drinking father's rum?

BERTLEY. Remove the temptation, of course.

WELLWYN. He's done that.

BERTLEY. Ah! Then— [WELLWYN *and* ANN *hang on his words*] then I should—er——

ANN. [*Abruptly.*] Remove *him*.

BERTLEY. Before I say that, Ann, I must certainly see the individual.

WELLWYN. [*Pointing to the window.*] There he is!

THE PIGEON

[*In the failing light* TIMSON's *face is indeed to be seen pressed against the window pane.*]

ANN. Daddy, I do wish you'd have thick glass put in. It's so disgusting to be spied at! [WELLWYN *going quickly to the door, has opened it.*] What do you want?

[TIMSON *enters with dignity. He is fuddled.*

TIMSON. [*Slowly.*] Arskin' yer pardon—thought it me duty to come back—found thish yer little brishel on me.

[*He produces the little paint brush.*

ANN. [*In a deadly voice.*] Nothing else?

[TIMSON *accords her a glassy stare.*

WELLWYN. [*Taking the brush hastily.*] That'll do, Timson, thanks!

TIMSON. As I am 'ere, can I do anything for yer?

ANN. Yes, you can sweep out that little room. [*She points to the model's room.*] There's a broom in there.

TIMSON. [*Disagreeably surprised.*] Certainly; never make bones about a little extra—never 'ave in all me life. Do it at onsh, I will. [*He moves across to the model's room at that peculiar broad gait so perfectly adjusted to his habits.*] You quite understand me—couldn't bear to 'ave anything on me that wasn't mine. [*He passes out.*

ANN. Old fraud!

WELLWYN. "In" and "on." Mark my words, he'll restore the—bottles.

BERTLEY. But, my dear Wellwyn, that *is* stealing.

WELLWYN. We all have our discrepancies, Vicar.

ANN. Daddy! Discrepancies!

WELLWYN. Well, Ann, my theory is that as regards solids Timson's an Individualist, but as regards liquids he's a Socialist . . . or *vice versa,* according to taste.

BERTLEY. No, no, we mustn't joke about it. [*Gravely.*] I do think he should be spoken to.

WELLWYN. Yes, but not by me.

BERTLEY. Surely you're the proper person.

WELLWYN. [*Shaking his head.*] It was my rum, Vicar. Look so personal.

[*There sound a number of little tat-tat knocks.*]

WELLWYN. Isn't that the Professor's knock?

[*While Ann sits down to make tea, he goes to the door and opens it. There, dressed in an ulster, stands a thin, clean-shaved man, with a little hollow sucked into either cheek, who, taking off a grey squash hat, discloses a majestically bald forehead, which completely dominates all that comes below it.*]

WELLWYN. Come in, Professor! So awfully good of you! You know Canon Bertley, I think?

CALWAY. Ah! How d'you do?

WELLWYN. Your opinion will be invaluable, Professor.

ANN. Tea, Professor Calway?

[*They have assembled round the tea table.*]

CALWAY. Thank you; no tea; milk.

WELLWYN. Rum?

[*He pours rum into* CALWAY'S *milk.*]

CALWAY. A little—thanks! [*Turning to* ANN.] You were going to show me some one you're trying to rescue, or something, I think.

ANN. Oh! Yes. He'll be here directly—simply perfect rotter.

CALWAY. [*Smiling.*] Really! Ah! I think you said he was a congenital?

WELLWYN. [*With great interest.*] What!

ANN. [*Low.*] Daddy! [*To* CALWAY.] Yes; I—I think that's what you call him.

CALWAY. Not old?

ANN. No; and quite healthy—a vagabond.

CALWAY. [*Sipping.*] I see! Yes. Is it, do you think

THE PIGEON

chronic unemployment with a vagrant tendency? Or would it be nearer the mark to say: Vagrancy——

WELLWYN. Pure! Oh! pure! Professor. Awfully human.

CALWAY. [*With a smile of knowledge.*] Quite! And— er——

ANN. [*Breaking in.*] Before he comes, there's another——

BERTLEY. [*Blandly.*] Yes, when you came in, we were discussing what should be done with a man who drinks rum— [CALWAY *pauses in the act of drinking*] that doesn't belong to him.

CALWAY. Really! Dipsomaniac?

BERTLEY. Well—perhaps you could tell us—drink certainly changing thine to mine. The Professor could see him, Wellwyn?

ANN. [*Rising.*] Yes, do come and look at him, Professor Calway. He's in there.

> [*She points towards the model's room. CALWAY smiles deprecatingly.*]

ANN. No, *really;* we needn't open the door. You can see him through the glass. He's more than half——

CALWAY. Well, I hardly——

ANN. Oh! Do! Come on, Professor Calway! We *must* know what to do with him. [CALWAY *rises.*] You can stand on a chair. It's all science.

> [*She draws* CALWAY *to the model's room, which is lighted by a glass panel in the top of the high door.* CANON BERTLEY *also rises and stands watching.* WELLWYN *hovers, torn between respect for science and dislike of espionage.*]

ANN. [*Drawing up a chair.*] Come on!

CALWAY. Do you seriously wish me to?

ANN. Rather! It's quite safe; he can't see you.

CALWAY. But he might come out.

[ANN *puts her back against the door.* CALWAY *mounts the chair dubiously, and raises his head cautiously, bending it more and more downwards.*]

ANN. Well?

CALWAY. He appears to be—sitting on the floor.

WELLWYN. Yes, that's all right!

[BERTLEY *covers his lips.*

CALWAY. [*To* ANN—*descending.*] By the look of his face, as far as one can see it, I should say there was a leaning towards mania. I know the treatment.

[*There come three loud knocks on the door.* WELLWYN *and* ANN *exchange a glance of consternation.*]

ANN. Who's that?

WELLWYN. It sounds like Sir Thomas.

CALWAY. Sir Thomas Hoxton?

WELLWYN. [*Nodding.*] Awfully sorry, Professor. You see, we——

CALWAY. Not at all. Only I must decline to be involved in argument with him, please.

BERTLEY. He has experience. We might get his opinion, don't you think?

CALWAY. On a point of reform? A J.P.!

BERTLEY. [*Deprecating.*] My dear Sir—we needn't take it.

[*The three knocks resound with extraordinary fury.*

ANN. You'd better open the door, Daddy.

[WELLWYN *opens the door.* SIR THOMAS HOXTON *is disclosed in a fur overcoat and top hat. His square, well-coloured face is remarkable for a massive jaw, dominating all that comes above it. His voice is resolute.*]

THE PIGEON 287

HOXTON. Afraid I didn't make myself heard.

WELLWYN. So good of you to come, Sir Thomas. Canon Bertley! [*They greet.*] Professor Calway you know, I think.

HOXTON. [*Ominously.*] I do.

[*They almost greet. An awkward pause.*

ANN. [*Blurting it out.*] That old cabman I told you of's been drinking father's rum.

BERTLEY. We were just discussing what's to be done with him, Sir Thomas. One wants to do the very best, of course. The question of reform is always delicate.

CALWAY. I beg your pardon. There *is* no question here.

HOXTON. [*Abruptly.*] Oh! Is he in the house?

ANN. In there.

HOXTON. Works for you, eh?

WELLWYN. Er—yes.

HOXTON. Let's have a look at him!

[*An embarrassed pause.*

BERTLEY. Well—the fact is, Sir Thomas——

CALWAY. When last under observation——

ANN. He was sitting on the floor.

WELLWYN. I don't want the old fellow to feel he's being made a show of. Disgusting to be spied at, Ann.

ANN. You can't, Daddy! He's drunk.

HOXTON. Never mind, Miss Wellwyn. Hundreds of these fellows before me in my time. [*At* CALWAY.] The only thing is a sharp lesson!

CALWAY. I disagree. I've seen the man; what he requires is steady control, and the Dobbins treatment.

[WELLWYN *approaches them with fearful interest.*

HOXTON. Not a bit of it! He wants one for his knob! Brace 'em up! It's the only thing.

BERTLEY. Personally, I think that if he were spoken to seriously——

CALWAY. I cannot walk arm in arm with a crab!

HOXTON. [*Approaching* CALWAY.] I beg your pardon?

CALWAY. [*Moving back a little.*] You're moving backwards, Sir Thomas. I've told you before, convinced reactionaryism, in these days——

[*There comes a single knock on the street door.*

BERTLEY. [*Looking at his watch.*] D'you know, I'm rather afraid this may be our young husband, Wellwyn. I told him half-past four.

WELLWYN. Oh! Ah! Yes. [*Going towards the two reformers.*] Shall we go into the house, Professor, and settle the question quietly while the Vicar sees a young man?

CALWAY. [*Pale with uncompleted statement, and gravitating insensibly in the direction indicated.*] The merest sense of continuity—a simple instinct for order——

HOXTON. [*Following.*] The only way to get order, sir, is to bring the disorderly up with a round turn. [CALWAY *turns to him in the doorway.*] You people without practical experience——

CALWAY. If you'll listen to me a minute.

HOXTON. I can show you in a mo——

[*They vanish through the door.*

WELLWYN. I was afraid of it.

BERTLEY. The two points of view. Pleasant to see such keenness. I may want you, Wellwyn. And Ann perhaps had better not be present.

WELLWYN. [*Relieved.*] Quite so! My dear!

[ANN *goes reluctantly.* WELLWYN *opens the street door. The lamp outside has just been lighted, and, by its gleam, is seen the figure of* RORY MEGAN, *thin, pale, youthful.* ANN *turning at the door into the house gives him a long, inquisitive look, then goes.*]

WELLWYN. Is that Megan?

THE PIGEON

MEGAN. Yus.

WELLWYN. Come in.

> [MEGAN *comes in. There follows an awkward silence, during which* WELLWYN *turns up the light, then goes to the tea table and pours out a glass of tea and rum.*]

BERTLEY. [*Kindly.*] Now, my boy, how is it that you and your wife are living apart, like this?

MEGAN. I dunno.

BERTLEY. Well, if *you* don't, none of us are very likely to, are we?

MEGAN. That's what I thought, as I was comin' along.

WELLWYN. [*Twinkling.*] Have some tea, Megan? [*Handing him the glass.*] What d'you think of her picture? 'Tisn't quite finished.

MEGAN. [*After scrutiny.*] I seen her look like it—once,

WELLWYN. Good! When was that?

MEGAN. [*Stoically.*] When she 'ad the measles.

[*He drinks.*

WELLWYN. [*Ruminating.*] I see—yes. I quite see—feverish!

BERTLEY. My dear Wellwyn, let me—— [*To* MEGAN.] Now, I hope you're willing to come together again, and to maintain her?

MEGAN. If she'll maintain me.

BERTLEY. Oh! but—— I see, you mean you're in the same line of business?

MEGAN. Yus.

BERTLEY. And lean on each other. Quite so!

MEGAN. I leans on 'er mostly—with 'er looks.

BERTLEY. Indeed! Very interesting—that!

MEGAN. Yus. Sometimes she'll take 'arf a crown off of a toff. [*He looks at* WELLWYN.

WELLWYN. [*Twinkling.*] I apologize to you, Megan.

MEGAN. [*With a faint smile.*] I could do with a bit more of it.

BERTLEY. [*Dubiously.*] Yes! Yes! Now, my boy, I've heard you bet on horses.

MEGAN. No, I don't.

BERTLEY. Play cards, then? Come! Don't be afraid to acknowledge it.

MEGAN. When I'm 'ard up—yus.

BERTLEY. But don't you know that's ruination?

MEGAN. Depends. Sometimes I wins a lot.

BERTLEY. You know that's not at all what I mean. Come, promise me to give it up.

MEGAN. I dunno abaht that.

BERTLEY. Now, there's a good fellow. Make a big effort and throw the habit off!

MEGAN. Comes over me—same as it might over you.

BERTLEY. Over me! How do you mean, my boy?

MEGAN. [*With a look up.*] To tork!

[WELLWYN, *turning to the picture, makes a funny little noise.*]

BERTLEY. [*Maintaining his good humour.*] A hit! But you forget, you know, to talk's my business. It's not yours to gamble.

MEGAN. You try sellin' flowers. If that ain't a—gamble——

BERTLEY. I'm afraid we're wandering a little from the point. Husband and wife should be together. You were brought up to that. Your father and mother——

MEGAN. Never was.

WELLWYN. [*Turning from the picture.*] The question is, Megan: Will you take your wife home? She's a good little soul.

MEGAN. She never let me know it.

[*There is a feeble knock on the door.*

THE PIGEON

WELLWYN. Well, now come. Here she is!

[*He points to the door, and stands regarding* MEGAN *with his friendly smile.*]

MEGAN. [*With a gleam of responsiveness.*] I might, perhaps, to please *you*, sir.

BERTLEY. [*Appropriating the gesture.*] Capital, I thought we should get on in time.

MEGAN. Yus.

[WELLWYN *opens the door.* MRS. MEGAN *and* FERRAND *are revealed. They are about to enter, but catching sight of* MEGAN, *hesitate.*]

BERTLEY. Come in! Come in!

[MRS. MEGAN *enters stolidly.* FERRAND, *following, stands apart with an air of extreme detachment.* MEGAN, *after a quick glance at them both, remains unmoved. No one has noticed that the door of the model's room has been opened, and that the unsteady figure of old* TIMSON *is standing there.*]

BERTLEY. [*A little awkward in the presence of* FERRAND—*to the* MEGANS.] This begins a new chapter. We won't improve the occasion. No need.

[MEGAN, *turning towards his wife, makes her a gesture as if to say:* "Here! let's get out of this!"]

BERTLEY. Yes, yes, you'll like to get home at once —I know.   [*He holds up his hand mechanically.*

TIMSON. I forbids the banns.

BERTLEY. [*Startled.*] Gracious!

TIMSON. [*Extremely unsteady.*] Just cause and impejiment. There 'e stands.   [*He points to* FERRAND.] The crimson foreigner! The mockin' jay!

WELLWYN. Timson!

TIMSON. You're a gen'leman—I'm aweer o' that—but

I must speak the truth—[*he waves his hand*] an' shame the devil!

BERTLEY. Is this the rum——?

TIMSON. [*Struck by the word.*] I'm a teetotaler.

WELLWYN. Timson, Timson!

TIMSON. Seein' as there's ladies present, I won't be conspicuous. [*Moving away, and making for the door, he strikes against the dais, and mounts upon it.*] But what I do say, is: He's no better than 'er and she's worse.

BERTLEY. This is distressing.

FERRAND. [*Calmly.*] On my honour, Monsieur!

[TIMSON *growls.*

WELLWYN. Now, now, Timson!

TIMSON. That's all right. You're a gen'leman, an' I'm a gen'leman, but he ain't an' she ain't.

WELLWYN. We shall not believe you.

BERTLEY. No, no; we shall not believe you.

TIMSON. [*Heavily.*] Very well, you doubts my word. Will it make any difference, Guv'nor, if I speaks the truth?

BERTLEY. No, certainly not—that is—of course, it will.

TIMSON. Well, then, I see 'em plainer than I see [*pointing at* BERTLEY] the two of you.

WELLWYN. Be quiet, Timson!

BERTLEY. Not even her husband believes you.

MEGAN. [*Suddenly.*] Don't I!

WELLWYN. Come, Megan, you can see the old fellow's in Paradise.

BERTLEY. Do you credit such a—such an object?

[*He points at* TIMSON, *who seems falling asleep.*

MEGAN. Naow!

[*Unseen by anybody,* ANN *has returned.*

BERTLEY. Well, then, my boy?

MEGAN. I seen 'em meself.

THE PIGEON

BERTLEY. Gracious! But just now you were willing

MEGAN. [*Sardonically.*] There wasn't nothing against me honour, then. Now you've took it away between you, comin' aht with it like this. I don't want no more of 'er, and I'll want a good deal more of 'im; as 'e'll soon find.

[*He jerks his chin at* FERRAND, *turns slowly on his heel, and goes out into the street. There follows a profound silence.*]

ANN. What did I say, Daddy? Utter! All three.
[*Suddenly alive to her presence, they all turn.*]

TIMSON. [*Waking up and looking round him.*] Well, p'raps I'd better go.

[*Assisted by* WELLWYN *he lurches gingerly off the dais towards the door, which* WELLWYN *holds open for him.*]

TIMSON. [*Mechanically.*] Where to, sir?

[*Receiving no answer he passes out, touching his hat; and the door is closed.*]

WELLWYN. Ann!

[ANN *goes back whence she came.* BERTLEY, *steadily regarding* MRS. MEGAN, *who has put her arm up in front of her face, beckons to* FERRAND, *and the young man comes gravely forward.*]

BERTLEY. Young people, this is very dreadful. [MRS. MEGAN *lowers her arm a little, and looks at him over it.*] Very sad!

MRS. MEGAN. [*Dropping her arm.*] Megan's no better than what I am.

BERTLEY. Come, come! Here's your home broken up! [MRS. MEGAN *smiles. Shaking his head gravely.*] Surely—surely—you mustn't smile. [MRS. MEGAN *becomes tragic.*] That's better. Now, what is to be done?

FERRAND. Believe me, Monsieur, I greatly regret.

BERTLEY. I'm glad to hear it.

FERRAND. If I had foreseen this disaster.

BERTLEY. Is that your only reason for regret?

FERRAND. [*With a little bow.*] Any reason that you wish, Monsieur. I will do my possible.

MRS. MEGAN. I could get an unfurnished room if [*she slides her eyes round at* WELLWYN] I 'ad the money to furnish it.

BERTLEY. But suppose I can induce your husband to forgive you, and take you back?

MRS. MEGAN. [*Shaking her head.*] 'E'd 'it me.

BERTLEY. I said to forgive.

MRS. MEGAN. That wouldn't make no difference. [*With a flash at* BERTLEY.] An' I ain't forgiven him!

BERTLEY. That is sinful.

MRS. MEGAN. *I'm* a Catholic.

BERTLEY. My good child, what difference does that make?

FERRAND. Monsieur, if I might interpret for her.

[BERTLEY *silences him with a gesture.*

MRS. MEGAN. [*Sliding her eyes towards* WELLWYN.] If I 'ad the money to buy some fresh stock.

BERTLEY. Yes; yes; never mind the money. What I want to find in you both, is repentance.

MRS. MEGAN. [*With a flash up at him.*] I can't get me livin' off of repentin'.

BERTLEY. Now, now! Never say what you know to be wrong.

FERRAND. Monsieur, her soul is very simple.

BERTLEY. [*Severely.*] I do not know, sir, that we shall get any great assistance from your views. In fact, one thing is clear to me, she must discontinue your acquaintanceship at once.

THE PIGEON

FERRAND. Certainly, Monsieur. We have no serious intentions.

BERTLEY. All the more shame to you, then!

FERRAND. Monsieur, I see perfectly your point of view. It is very natural. [*He bows and is silent.*

MRS. MEGAN. I don't want 'im hurt 'cos o' me. Megan'll get his mates to belt him—bein' foreign like he is.

BERTLEY. Yes, never mind that. It's *you* I'm thinking of.

MRS. MEGAN. I'd sooner they'd hit *me*.

WELLWYN. [*Suddenly.*] Well said, my child!

MRS. MEGAN. 'Twasn't his fault.

FERRAND. [*Without irony—to* WELLWYN.] I cannot accept that Monsieur. The blame—it is all mine.

ANN. [*Entering suddenly from the house.*] Daddy, they're having an awful——!

[*The voices of* PROFESSOR CALWAY *and* SIR THOMAS HOXTON *are distinctly heard.*]

CALWAY. The question is a much wider one, Sir Thomas.

HOXTON. As wide as you like, you'll never——

[WELLWYN *pushes* ANN *back into the house and closes the door behind her. The voices are still faintly heard arguing on the threshold.*]

BERTLEY. Let me go in here a minute, Wellwyn. I must finish speaking to her. [*He motions* MRS. MEGAN *towards the model's room.*] We can't leave the matter thus.

FERRAND. [*Suavely.*] Do you desire my company, Monsieur?

[BERTLEY, *with a prohibitive gesture of his hand, shepherds the reluctant* MRS. MEGAN *into the model's room.*]

WELLWYN. [*Sorrowfully.*] You shouldn't have done this, Ferrand. It wasn't the square thing.

FERRAND. [*With dignity.*] Monsieur, I feel that I am in the wrong. It was stronger than me.

[*As he speaks,* SIR THOMAS HOXTON *and* PROFESSOR CALWAY *enter from the house. In the dim light, and the full cry of argument, they do not notice the figures at the fire.* SIR THOMAS HOXTON *leads towards the street door.*]

HOXTON. No sir, I repeat, if the country once commits itself to your views of reform, it's as good as doomed.

CALWAY. I seem to have heard that before, Sir Thomas. And let me say at once that your hitty-missy cart-load of bricks *régime*——

HOXTON. Is a deuced sight better, sir, than your grandmotherly methods. What the old fellow wants is a shock! With all this socialistic molly-coddling, you're losing sight of the individual.

CALWAY. [*Swiftly.*] You, sir, with your "devil take the hindmost," have never even seen him.

[SIR THOMAS HOXTON, *throwing back a gesture of disgust, steps out into the night, and falls heavily.* PROFESSOR CALWAY, *hastening to his rescue, falls more heavily still.* TIMSON, *momentarily roused from slumber on the doorstep, sits up.*]

HOXTON. [*Struggling to his knees.*] Damnation!

CALWAY. [*Sitting.*] How simultaneous!

[WELLWYN *and* FERRAND *approach hastily.*

FERRAND. [*Pointing to* TIMSON.] Monsieur, it was true, it seems. They had lost sight of the individual.

[*A policeman has appeared under the street lamp. He picks up* HOXTON'S *hat.*]

CONSTABLE. Anything wrong, sir?

HOXTON. [*Recovering his feet.*] Wrong? Great Scott! Constable! Why do you let things lie about in the street like this? Look here, Wellwyn!

[*They all scrutinize* TIMSON.

THE PIGEON

WELLWYN. It's only the old fellow whose reform you were discussing.

HOXTON. How did he come here?

CONSTABLE. Drunk, sir. [*Ascertaining* TIMSON *to be in the street.*] Just off the premises, by good luck. Come along, father.

TIMSON. [*Assisted to his feet—drowsily.*] Cert'nly, by no means; take my arm.

> [*They move from the doorway.* HOXTON *and* CALWAY *re-enter, and go towards the fire.*]

ANN. [*Entering from the house.*] What's happened?

CALWAY. Might we have a brush?

HOXTON. [*Testily.*] Let it dry!

> [*He moves to the fire and stands before it.* PROFESSOR CALWAY *following stands a little behind him.* ANN *returning begins to brush the* PROFESSOR's *sleeve.*]

WELLWYN. [*Turning from the door, where he has stood looking after the receding* TIMSON.] Poor old Timson!

FERRAND. [*Softly.*] Must be philosopher, Monsieur! They will but run him in a little.

> [*From the model's room* MRS. MEGAN *has come out, shepherded by* CANON BERTLEY.]

BERTLEY. Let's see, your Christian name is——

MRS. MEGAN. Guinevere.

BERTLEY. Oh! Ah! Ah! Ann, take Gui—— take our little friend into the study a minute: I am going to put her into service. We shall make a new woman of her yet.

ANN. [*Handing* CANON BERTLEY *the brush, and turning to* MRS. MEGAN.] Come on!

> [*She leads into the house, and* MRS. MEGAN *follows stolidly.*]

BERTLEY. [*Brushing* CALWAY's *back.*] Have you fallen?

CALWAY. Yes.

BERTLEY. Dear me! How was that?

HOXTON. That old ruffian drunk on the doorstep. Hope they'll give him a sharp dose! These rag-tags!

> [*He looks round, and his angry eyes light by chance on* FERRAND.]

FERRAND. [*With his eyes on* HOXTON—*softly.*] Monsieur, something tells me it is time I took the road again.

WELLWYN. [*Fumbling out a sovereign.*] Take this, then!

FERRAND. [*Refusing the coin.*] Non, Monsieur. To abuse 'ospitality is not in my character.

BERTLEY. We must not despair of anyone.

HOXTON. Who talked of despairing? Treat him, as I say, and you'll see!

CALWAY. The interest of the State——

HOXTON. The interest of the individual citizen, sir——

BERTLEY. Come! A little of both, a little of both!

> [*They resume their brushing.*

FERRAND. You are now debarrassed of us three, Monsieur. I leave you instead—these sirs. [*He points.*] Au revoir, Monsieur! [*Motioning towards the fire.*] 'Appy New Year!

> [*He slips quietly out.* WELLWYN, *turning, contemplates the three reformers. They are all now brushing away, scratching each other's backs, and gravely hissing. As he approaches them, they speak with a certain unanimity.*]

HOXTON. My theory——!
CALWAY. My theory——!
BERTLEY. My theory——!

> [*They stop surprised.* WELLWYN *makes a gesture of discomfort, as they speak again with still more unanimity.*]

HOXTON. My——!
CALWAY. My——!

THE PIGEON

BERTLEY. My——!

[*They stop in greater surprise.
The stage is blotted dark.*

The curtain falls.

ACT III

It is the first of April—a white spring day of gleams and driving showers. The street door of WELLWYN'S *studio stands wide open, and, past it, in the street, the wind is whirling bits of straw and paper bags. Through the door can be seen the butt end of a stationary furniture van with its flap let down. To this van three humble-men in shirt sleeves and aprons, are carrying out the contents of the studio. The hissing samovar, the tea-pot, the sugar, and the nearly empty decanter of rum stand on the low round table in the fast-being-gutted room.* WELLWYN *in his ulster and soft hat, is squatting on the little stool in front of the blazing fire, staring into it, and smoking a hand-made cigarette. He has a moulting air. Behind him the humble-men pass, embracing busts and other articles of vertu.*

CHIEF H'MAN. [*Stopping, and standing in the attitude of expectation.*] We've about pinched this little lot, sir. Shall we take the—reservoir?

[*He indicates the samovar.*

WELLWYN. Ah! [*Abstractedly feeling in his pockets, and finding coins.*] Thanks—thanks—heavy work, I'm afraid.

H'MAN. [*Receiving the coins—a little surprised and a good deal pleased.*] Thank'ee, sir. Much obliged, I'm sure. We'll 'ave to come back for this. [*He gives the dais a*

vigorous push with his foot.] Not a fixture, as I understand. Perhaps you'd like us to leave these 'ere for a bit.
[*He indicates the tea things.*

WELLWYN. Ah! do.

[*The humble-men go out. There is the sound of horses being started, and the butt end of the van disappears.* WELLWYN *stays on his stool, smoking and brooding over the fire. The open doorway is darkened by a figure.* CANON BERTLEY *is standing there.*]

BERTLEY. Wellwyn! [WELLWYN *turns and rises.*] It's ages since I saw you. No idea you were moving. This is very dreadful.

WELLWYN. Yes, Ann found this—too exposed. That tall house in Flight Street—we're going there. Seventh floor.

BERTLEY. Lift?

[WELLWYN *shakes his head.*

BERTLEY. Dear me! No lift? Fine view, no doubt. [WELLWYN *nods.*] You'll be greatly missed.

WELLWYN. So Ann thinks. Vicar, what's become of that little flower-seller I was painting at Christmas? You took her into service.

BERTLEY. Not we—exactly! Some dear friends of ours. Painful subject!

WELLWYN. Oh!

BERTLEY. Yes. She got the footman into trouble.

WELLWYN. Did she, now?

BERTLEY. Disappointing. I consulted with Calway, and he advised me to try a certain institution. We got her safely in—excellent place; but, d'you know, she broke out three weeks ago. And since—I've heard—[*he holds his hands up*] hopeless, I'm afraid—quite!

THE PIGEON

WELLWYN. I *thought* I saw her last night. You can't tell me her address, I suppose?

BERTLEY. [*Shaking his head.*] The husband too has quite passed out of my ken. He betted on horses, you remember. I'm sometimes tempted to believe there's nothing for some of these poor folk but to pray for death.

[ANN *has entered from the house. Her hair hangs from under a knitted cap. She wears a white wool jersey, and a loose silk scarf.*]

BERTLEY. Ah! Ann. I was telling your father of that poor little Mrs. Megan.

ANN. Is she dead?

BERTLEY. Worse I fear. By the way—what became of her accomplice?

ANN. We haven't seen him since. [*She looks searchingly at* WELLWYN.] At least—have *you*—Daddy?

WELLWYN. [*Rather hurt.*] No, my dear; I have not.

BERTLEY. And the—old gentleman who drank the rum?

ANN. He got fourteen days. It was the fifth time.

BERTLEY. Dear me!

ANN. When he came out he got more drunk than ever. Rather a score for Professor Calway, wasn't it?

BERTLEY. I remember. He and Sir Thomas took a kindly interest in the old fellow.

ANN. Yes, they fell over him. The Professor got him into an Institution.

BERTLEY. Indeed!

ANN. He was perfectly sober all the time he was there.

WELLWYN. My dear, they only allow them milk.

ANN. Well, anyway, he was reformed.

WELLWYN. Ye—yes!

ANN. [*Terribly.*] Daddy! You've been seeing him!

WELLWYN. [*With dignity.*] My dear, I have not.

ANN. How do you know, then?

WELLWYN. Came across Sir Thomas on the Embankment yesterday; told me old Timson had been had up again for sitting down in front of a brewer's dray.

ANN. Why?

WELLWYN. Well, you see, as soon as he came out of the what d'you call 'em, he got drunk for a week, and it left him in low spirits.

BERTLEY. Do you mean he deliberately sat down, with the intention—of—er?

WELLWYN. Said he was tired of life, but they didn't believe him.

ANN. Rather a score for Sir Thomas! I suppose he'd told the Professor? What did *he* say?

WELLWYN. Well, the Professor said [*with a quick glance at* BERTLEY] he felt there was nothing for some of these poor devils but a lethal chamber.

BERTLEY. [*Shocked.*] Did he really!

[*He has not yet caught* WELLWYN'*s glance.*

WELLWYN. And Sir Thomas agreed. Historic occasion. And you, Vicar—H'm!

[BERTLEY *winces.*

ANN. [*To herself.*] Well, there isn't.

BERTLEY. And yet! Some good in the old fellow, no doubt, if one could put one's finger on it. [*Preparing to go.*] You'll let us know, then, when you're settled. What was the address? [WELLWYN *takes out and hands him a card.*] Ah! yes. Good-bye, Ann. Good-bye, Wellwyn. [*The wind blows his hat along the street.*] What a wind!

[*He goes, pursuing.*

ANN. [*Who has eyed the card askance.*] Daddy, have you told those other two where we're going?

WELLWYN. Which other two, my dear?

ANN. The Professor and Sir Thomas.

WELLWYN. Well, Ann, naturally I——

THE PIGEON

ANN. [*Jumping on to the dais with disgust.*] Oh, dear! When I'm trying to get you away from all this atmosphere. I don't so much mind the Vicar knowing, because he's got a weak heart——

[*She jumps off again.*

WELLWYN. [*To himself.*] Seventh floor! I felt there was something.

ANN. [*Preparing to go.*] I'm going round now. But you must stay here till the van comes back. And don't forget you tipped the men after the first load.

WELLWYN. Oh! yes, yes. [*Uneasily.*] Good sorts they look, those fellows!

ANN. [*Scrutinising him.*] What have you done?

WELLWYN. Nothing, my dear, really——!

ANN. What?

WELLWYN. I—I rather think I may have tipped them twice.

ANN. [*Drily.*] Daddy! If it is the first of April, it's not necessary to make a fool of *oneself*. That's the last time you ever do these ridiculous things. [WELLWYN *eyes her askance.*] I'm going to see that you spend your money on yourself. You needn't look at me like that! I *mean* to. As soon as I've got you away from here, and all—these——

WELLWYN. Don't rub it in, Ann!

ANN. [*Giving him a sudden hug—then going to the door—with a sort of triumph.*] Deeds, not words, Daddy!

[*She goes out, and the wind catching her scarf blows it out beneath her firm young chin.* WELLWYN *returning to the fire, stands brooding, and gazing at his extinct cigarette.*]

WELLWYN. [*To himself.*] Bad lot—low type! No method! No theory!

[*In the open doorway appear* FERRAND *and* MRS. MEGAN. *They stand, unseen, looking at him.*

THE PIGEON

FERRAND *is more ragged, if possible, than on Christmas Eve. His chin and cheeks are clothed in a reddish golden beard.* MRS. MEGAN's *dress is not so woe-begone, but her face is white, her eyes dark-circled. They whisper. She slips back into the shadow of the doorway.* WELL-WYN *turns at the sound, and stares at* FERRAND *in amazement.*]

FERRAND. [*Advancing.*] Enchanted to see you, Monsieur. [*He looks round the empty room.*] You are leaving?

WELLWYN. [*Nodding—then taking the young man's hand.*] How goes it?

FERRAND. [*Displaying himself, simply.*] As you see, Monsieur. I have done of my best. It still flies from me.

WELLWYN. [*Sadly—as if against his will.*] Ferrand, it will always fly.

[*The young foreigner shivers suddenly from head to foot; then controls himself with a great effort.*]

FERRAND. Don't say that, Monsieur! It is too much the echo of my heart.

WELLWYN. Forgive me! I didn't mean to pain you.

FERRAND. [*Drawing nearer the fire.*] That old cabby, Monsieur, you remember—they tell me, he nearly succeeded to gain happiness the other day.

[WELLWYN *nods.*

FERRAND. And those Sirs, so interested in him, with their theories? He has worn them out? [WELLWYN *nods.*] That goes without saying. And now they wish for him the lethal chamber.

WELLWYN. [*Startled.*] How did you know that?

[*There is silence.*

FERRAND. [*Staring into the fire.*] Monsieur, while I was on the road this time I fell ill of a fever. It seemed

THE PIGEON

to me in my illness that I saw the truth—how I was wasting in this world—I would never be for any one—nor any one for me—all would go by, and I never of it—fame, and fortune, and peace, even the necessities of life, ever mocking me.

> [*He draws closer to the fire, spreading his fingers to the flame. And while he is speaking, through the doorway* MRS. MEGAN *creeps in to listen.*]

FERRAND. [*Speaking on into the fire.*] And I saw, Monsieur, so plain, that I should be vagabond all my days, and my days short, I dying in the end the death of a dog. I saw it all in my fever—clear as that flame—there was nothing for us others, but the herb of death. [WELLWYN *takes his arm and presses it.*] And so, Monsieur, I *wished* to die. I told no one of my fever. I lay out on the ground—it was veree cold. But they would not let me die on the roads of their parishes—they took me to an Institution, Monsieur, I looked in their eyes while I lay there, and I saw more clear than the blue heaven that they thought it best that I should die, although they would not let me. Then Monsieur, naturally my spirit rose, and I said: "So much the worse for you. I will live a little more." One is made like that! Life is sweet, Monsieur.

WELLWYN. Yes, Ferrand; Life is sweet.

FERRAND. That little girl you had here, Monsieur— [WELLWYN *nods*] in her too there is something of wild-savage. She must have joy of life. I have seen her since I came back. She had embraced the life of joy. It is not quite the same thing. [*He lowers his voice.*] She is lost, Monsieur, as a stone that sinks in water. I can see, if she cannot. [*As* WELLWYN *makes a movement of distress.*] Oh! I am not to blame for that, Monsieur. It had well begun before I knew her.

WELLWYN. Yes, yes—I was afraid of it, at the time.

[MRS. MEGAN *turns silently, and slips away.*

FERRAND. I do my best for her, Monsieur, but look at me! Besides, I am not good for her—it is not good for simple souls to be with those who see things clear. For the great part of mankind, to see anything—is fatal.

WELLWYN. Even for you, it seems.

FERRAND. No, Monsieur. To be so near to death has done me good; I shall not lack courage any more till the wind blows on my grave. Since I saw you, Monsieur, I have been in three Institutions. They are palaces. One may eat upon the floor—though it is true—for Kings—they eat too much of skilly there. One little thing they lack—those palaces. It is understanding of the 'uman heart. In them tame birds pluck wild birds naked.

WELLWYN. They mean well.

FERRAND. Ah! Monsieur, I am loafer, waster—what you like—for all that [*bitterly*] poverty is my only crime. If I were rich, should I not be simply veree original, 'ighly respected, with soul above commerce, travelling to see the world? And that young girl, would she not be "that charming ladee," "veree *chic,* you know!" And the old Tims—good old-fashioned gentleman—drinking his liquor well. *Eh! bien*—what are we now? Dark beasts, despised by all. That is life, Monsieur. [*He stares into the fire.*

WELLWYN. We're our own enemies, Ferrand. I can afford it—you can't. Quite true!

FERRAND. [*Earnestly.*] Monsieur, do you know this? You are the sole being that can do us good—we hopeless ones.

WELLWYN. [*Shaking his head.*] Not a bit of it; I'm hopeless too.

FERRAND. [*Eagerly.*] Monsieur, it is just that. You *understand*. When we are with you we feel something—here—[*he touches his heart.*] If I had one prayer to make,

THE PIGEON

it would be, Good God, give me to understand! Those sirs, with their theories, they can clean our skins and chain our 'abits—that soothes for them the æsthetic sense; it gives them too their good little importance. But our spirits they cannot touch, for they nevare understand. Without that, Monsieur, all is dry as a parched skin of orange.

WELLWYN. Don't be so bitter. Think of all the work they do!

FERRAND. Monsieur, of their industry I say nothing. They do a good work while they attend with their theories to the sick and the tame old, and the good unfortunate deserving. Above all to the little children. But, Monsieur, when all is done, there are always us hopeless ones. What can they do with me, Monsieur, with that girl, or with that old man? Ah! Monsieur, we, too, 'ave our qualities, we others—it wants your courage to undertake a career like mine, or like that young girl's. We wild ones—we know a thousand times more of life than ever will those Sirs. They waste their time trying to make rooks white. Be kind to us if you will, or let us alone like Mees Ann, but do not try to change our skins. Leave us to live, or leave us to die when we like in the free air. If you do not wish of us, you have but to shut your pockets and your doors— we shall die the faster.

WELLWYN. [*With agitation.*] But that, you know—we can't do—now can we?

FERRAND. If you cannot, how is it our fault? The harm we do to others—is it so much? If I am criminal, dangerous —shut me up! I would not pity myself—nevare. But we in whom something moves—like that flame, Monsieur, that *cannot* keep still—we others—we are not many—that must have motion in our lives, do not let them make us prisoners, with their theories, because we are not like them—it is life itself they would enclose! [*He draws up his tattered figure, then bending over the fire again.*] I ask your pardon; I am talking. If I could smoke, Monsieur!

[WELLWYN *hands him a tobacco pouch; and he rolls a cigarette with his yellow-stained fingers.*]

FERRAND. The good God made me so that I would rather walk a whole month of nights, hungry, with the stars, than sit one single day making round business on an office stool! It is not to my advantage. I cannot help it that I am a vagabond. What would you have? It is stronger than me. [*He looks suddenly at* WELLWYN.] Monsieur, I say to you things I have never said.

WELLWYN. [*Quietly.*] Go on, go on. [*There is silence.*

FERRAND. [*Suddenly.*] Monsieur! Are you really English? The English are so civilised.

WELLWYN. And am I not?

FERRAND. You treat me like a brother.

[WELLWYN *has turned towards the street door at a sound of feet, and the clamour of voices.*]

TIMSON. [*From the street.*] Take her in 'ere. I knows 'im.

[*Through the open doorway come a* POLICE CONSTABLE *and a* LOAFER, *bearing between them the limp white-faced form of* MRS. MEGAN, *hatless and with drowned hair, enveloped in the policeman's waterproof. Some curious persons bring up the rear, jostling in the doorway, among whom is* TIMSON *carrying in his hands the policeman's dripping waterproof leg-pieces.*]

FERRAND. [*Starting forward.*] Monsieur, it is that little girl!

WELLWYN. What's happened? Constable! What's happened!

[*The* CONSTABLE *and* LOAFER *have laid the body*

THE PIGEON

down on the dais; with WELLWYN *and* FERRAND *they stand bending over her.*]

CONSTABLE. 'Tempted sooicide, sir; but she hadn't been in the water 'arf a minute when I got hold of her. [*He bends lower.*] Can't understand her collapsin' like this.

WELLWYN. [*Feeling her heart.*] I don't feel anything.

FERRAND. [*In a voice sharpened by emotion.*] Let me try, Monsieur.

CONSTABLE. [*Touching his arm.*] You keep off, my lad.

WELLWYN. No, constable—let him. He's her friend.

CONSTABLE. [*Releasing* FERRAND—*to the* LOAFER.] Here you! Cut off for a doctor—sharp now! [*He pushes back the curious persons.*] Now then, stand away there, please—we can't have you round the body. Keep back—Clear out, now!

[*He slowly moves them back, and at last shepherds them through the door and shuts it on them,* TIMSON *being last.*]

FERRAND. The rum!

[WELLWYN *fetches the decanter. With the little there is left* FERRAND *chafes the girl's hands and forehead, and pours some between her lips. But there is no response from the inert body.*]

FERRAND. Her soul is still away, Monsieur!

[WELLWYN, *seizing the decanter, pours into it tea and boiling water.*]

CONSTABLE. It's never drownin', sir—her head was hardly under; I was on to her like knife.

FERRAND. [*Rubbing her feet.*] She has not yet her philosophy, Monsieur; at the beginning they often try. If she is dead! [*In a voice of awed rapture.*] What fortune!

CONSTABLE. [*With puzzled sadness.*] True enough, sir—that! We'd just begun to know 'er. If she 'as been taken—her best friends couldn't wish 'er better.

WELLWYN. [*Applying the decanter to her lips.*] Poor little thing! I'll try this hot tea.

FERRAND. [*Whispering.*] *La mort—le grand ami!*

WELLWYN. Look! Look at her! She coming round!

> [*A faint tremor passes over* MRS. MEGAN'S *body. He again applies the hot drink to her mouth. She stirs and gulps.*]

CONSTABLE. [*With intense relief.*] That's brave! Good lass! She'll pick up now, sir.

> [*Then, seeing that* TIMSON *and the curious persons have again opened the door, he drives them out, and stands with his back against it.* MRS. MEGAN *comes to herself.*]

WELLWYN. [*Sitting on the dais and supporting her—as if to a child.*] There you are, my dear. There, there—better now! That's right. Drink a little more of this tea.

> [MRS. MEGAN *drinks from the decanter.*

FERRAND. [*Rising.*] Bring her to the fire, Monsieur.

> [*They take her to the fire and seat her on the little stool. From the moment of her restored animation* FERRAND *has resumed his air of cynical detachment, and now stands apart with arms folded, watching.*]

WELLWYN. Feeling better, my child?

MRS. MEGAN. Yes.

WELLWYN. That's good. That's good. Now, how was it? Um?

MRS. MEGAN. I dunno. [*She shivers.*] I was standin' here just now when you was talkin', and when I heard 'im, it cam' over me to do it—like.

WELLWYN. Ah, yes *I* know.

MRS. MEGAN. I didn't seem no good to meself nor any one. But when I got in the water, I didn't want to any more. It was cold in there.

THE PIGEON

WELLWYN. Have you been having such a bad time of it?

MRS. MEGAN. Yes. And listenin' to him upset me. [*She signs with her head at* FERRAND.] I feel better now I've been in the water. [*She smiles and shivers.*

WELLWYN. There, there! Shivery? Like to walk up and down a little?

[*They begin walking together up and down.*

WELLWYN. Beastly when your head goes under?

MRS. MEGAN. Yes. It frightened me. I thought I wouldn't come up again.

WELLWYN. I know—sort of world without end, wasn't it? What did you think of, um?

MRS. MEGAN. I wished I 'adn't jumped—an' I thought of my baby—that died—and—[*in a rather surprised voice*] and I thought of d-dancin'.

[*Her mouth quivers, her face puckers, she gives a choke and a little sob.*]

WELLWYN. [*Stopping and stroking her.*] There, there—there!

[*For a moment her face is buried in his sleeve, then she recovers herself.*]

MRS. MEGAN. Then 'e got hold o' me, an' pulled me out.

WELLWYN. Ah! what a comfort—um?

MRS. MEGAN. Yes. The water got into me mouth. [*They walk again.*] I wouldn't have gone to do it but for *him*. [*She looks towards* FERRAND.] His talk made me feel all funny, as if people wanted me to.

WELLWYN. My dear child! Don't think such things! As if anyone would——!

MRS. MEGAN. [*Stolidly.*] I thought they did. They used to look at me so sometimes, where I was before I ran away—I couldn't stop there, you know.

WELLWYN. Too cooped-up?

THE PIGEON

Mrs. Megan. Yes. No life at all, it wasn't—not after sellin' flowers, I'd rather be doin' what I am.

Wellwyn. Ah! Well—it's all over, now! How d'you feel—eh? Better?

Mrs. Megan. Yes, I feels all right now.

[*She sits up again on the little stool before the fire.*]

Wellwyn. No shivers, and no aches; quite comfy?

Mrs. Megan. Yes.

Wellwyn. That's a blessing. All well, now, Constable —thank you!

Constable. [*Who has remained discreetly apart at the door—cordially.*] First rate, sir! That's capital! [*He approaches and scrutinises* Mrs. Megan.] Right as rain, eh, my girl?

Mrs. Megan. [*Shrinking a little.*] Yes.

Constable. That's fine. Then I think perhaps, for 'er sake, sir, the sooner we move on and get her a change o' clothin', the better.

Wellwyn. Oh! don't bother about that—I'll send round for my daughter—we'll manage for her here.

Constable. Very kind of you, I'm sure, sir. But [*with embarrassment*] she seems all right. She'll get every attention at the station.

Wellwyn. But I assure you, we don't mind at all; we'll take the greatest care of her.

Constable. [*Still more embarrassed.*] Well, sir, of course, I'm thinkin' of—— I'm afraid I can't depart from the usual course.

Wellwyn. [*Sharply.*] What! But—oh! No! No! That'll be all right, Constable! That'll be all right! I assure you.

Constable. [*With more decision.*] I'll have to charge her, sir.

THE PIGEON

WELLWYN. Good God! You don't mean to say the poor little thing has got to be——

CONSTABLE. [*Consulting with him.*] Well, sir, we can't get over the facts, can we? There it is! You know what sooicide amounts to—it's an awkward job.

WELLWYN. [*Calming himself with an effort.*] But look here, Constable, as a reasonable man—— This poor wretched little girl—*you* know what that life means better than anyone! Why! It's to her credit to try and jump out of it!

[*The* CONSTABLE *shakes his head.*

WELLWYN. You said yourself her best friends couldn't wish her better! [*Dropping his voice still more.*] Everybody feels it! The Vicar was here a few minutes ago saying the very same thing—the Vicar, Constable! [*The* CONSTABLE *shakes his head.*] Ah! now, look here, I know something of her. Nothing can be done with her. We all admit it. Don't you see? Well, then hang it—you needn't go and make fools of us all by——

FERRAND. Monsieur, it is the first of April.

CONSTABLE. [*With a sharp glance at him.*] Can't neglect me duty, sir; that's impossible.

WELLWYN. Look here! She—slipped. She's been telling me. Come, Constable, there's a good fellow. May be the making of her, this.

CONSTABLE. I quite appreciate your good 'eart, sir, an' you make it very 'ard for me—but, come now! I put it to you as a gentleman, would you go back on your duty if you was me?

[WELLWYN *raises his hat, and plunges his fingers through and through his hair.*]

WELLWYN. Well! God in heaven! Of all the d——d topsy-turvy——! Not a soul in the world wants her alive—

and now she's to be prosecuted for trying to be where everyone wishes her.

CONSTABLE. Come, sir, come! Be a man!

[*Throughout all this* MRS. MEGAN *has sat stolidly before the fire, but as* FERRAND *suddenly steps forward she looks up at him.*]

FERRAND. Do not grieve, Monsieur! This will give her courage. There is nothing that gives more courage than to see the irony of things. [*He touches* MRS. MEGAN'S *shoulder.*] Go, my child; it will do you good.

[MRS. MEGAN *rises, and looks at him dazedly.*

CONSTABLE. [*Coming forward, and taking her by the hand.*] That's my good lass. Come along! We won't hurt you.

MRS. MEGAN. I don't want to go. They'll stare at me.

CONSTABLE. [*Comforting.*] Not they! I'll see to that.

WELLWYN. [*Very upset.*] Take her in a cab, Constable, if you must—for God's sake! [*He pulls out a shilling.*] Here!

CONSTABLE. [*Taking the shilling.*] I will, sir, certainly. Don't think I want to——

WELLWYN. No, no, I know. You're a good sort.

CONSTABLE. [*Comforting.*] Don't you take on, sir. It's her first try; they won't be hard on 'er. Like as not only bind 'er over in her own recogs not to do it again. Come, my dear.

MRS. MEGAN. [*Trying to free herself from the policeman's cloak.*] I want to take this off. It looks so funny.

[*As she speaks the door is opened by* ANN; *behind whom is dimly seen the form of old* TIMSON, *still heading the curious persons.*]

ANN. [*Looking from one to the other in amaze.*] What is it? What's happened? Daddy!

FERRAND. [*Out of the silence.*] It is nothing, Ma'-

THE PIGEON

moiselle! She has failed to drown herself. They run her in a little.

WELLWYN. Lend her your jacket, my dear; she'll catch her death.

[ANN, *feeling* MRS. MEGAN's *arm, strips off her jacket, and helps her into it without a word.*]

CONSTABLE. [*Donning his cloak.*] Thank you, Miss— very good of you, I'm sure.

MRS. MEGAN. [*Mazed.*] It's warm!

[*She gives them all a last half-smiling look, and passes with the* CONSTABLE *through the doorway.*]

FERRAND. That makes the third of us, Monsieur. We are not in luck. To wish us dead, it seems, is easier than to let us die.

[*He looks at* ANN, *who is standing with her eyes fixed on her father.* WELLWYN *has taken from his pocket a visiting card.*]

WELLWYN. [*To* FERRAND.] Here quick; take this, run after her! When they've done with her tell her to come to us.

FERRAND. [*Taking the card, and reading the address.*] "No. 7, Haven House, Flight Street!" Rely on me, Monsieur—I will bring her myself to call on you. *Au revoir, mon bon Monsieur!*

[*He bends over* WELLWYN's *hand; then, with a bow to* ANN *goes out; his tattered figure can be seen through the window, passing in the wind.* WELLWYN *turns back to the fire. The figure of* TIMSON *advances into the doorway, no longer holding in either hand a waterproof leg-piece.*

TIMSON. [*In a croaky voice.*] Sir!

WELLWYN. What—you, Timson?

TIMSON. On me larst legs, sir. 'Ere! You can see 'em for yerself! Shawn't trouble yer long.

WELLWYN. [*After a long and desperate stare.*] Not now—Timson—not now! Take this! [*He takes out another card, and hands it to* TIMSON.] Some other time.

TIMSON. [*Taking the card.*] Yer new address! You are a gen'leman. [*He lurches slowly away.*

> [ANN *shuts the street door and sets her back against it. The rumble of the approaching van is heard outside. It ceases.*]

ANN. [*In a fateful voice.*] Daddy! [*They stare at each other.*] Do you know what you've done? Given your card to those six rotters.

WELLWYN. [*With a blank stare.*] Six?

ANN. [*Staring round the naked room.*] What was the good of this?

WELLWYN. [*Following her eyes—very gravely.*] Ann! It is stronger than me.

> [*Without a word* ANN *opens the door, and walks straight out. With a heavy sigh,* WELLWYN *sinks down on the little stool before the fire. The three humble-men come in.*]

CHIEF HUMBLE-MAN. [*In an attitude of expectation.*] This is the larst of it, sir.

WELLWYN. Oh! Ah! yes!

> [*He gives them money; then something seems to strike him, and he exhibits certain signs of vexation. Suddenly he recovers, looks from one to the other, and then at the tea things. A faint smile comes on his face.*]

WELLWYN. You can finish the decanter.

[*He goes out in haste.*

CHIEF HUMBLE-MAN. [*Clinking the coins.*] Third time of arskin'! April fool! Not 'arf! Good old pigeon!

THE PIGEON

SECOND HUMBLE-MAN. 'Uman being, *I* call 'im.

CHIEF HUMBLE-MAN. [*Taking the three glasses from the last packing-case, and pouring very equally into them.*] That's right. Tell you wot, I'd never 'a touched this unless 'e'd told me to, I wouldn't—not with 'im.

SECOND HUMBLE-MAN. Ditto to that! This is a bit of orl right! [*Raising his glass.*] Good luck!

THIRD HUMBLE-MAN. Same 'ere!

> [*Simultaneously they place their lips smartly against the liquor, and at once let fall their faces and their glasses.*]

CHIEF HUMBLE-MAN. [*With great solemnity.*] Crikey! Bill! *Tea!* . . . 'E's *got* us!

The stage is blotted dark.

The curtain falls.

A BIT O' LOVE

A PLAY IN THREE ACTS

PERSONS OF THE PLAY

MICHAEL STRANGWAY
BEATRICE STRANGWAY
MRS. BRADMERE
JIM BERE
JACK CREMER
MRS. BURLACOMBE
BURLACOMBE
TRUSTAFORD
JARLAND
CLYST
FREMAN
GODLEIGH
SOL POTTER
MORSE, AND OTHERS

IVY BURLACOMBE
CONNIE TRUSTAFORD
GLADYS FREMAN
MERCY JARLAND
TIBBY JARLAND
BOBBIE JARLAND

SCENE: A VILLAGE OF THE WEST

The action passes on Ascension Day.

ACT I. STRANGWAY'S *rooms at* BURLACOMBES'. *Morning.*

ACT II.
    SCENE I. The Village Inn.
    SCENE II. The same.
    SCENE III. Outside the church.

ACT III.
    SCENE I. STRANGWAY'S *rooms.*
    SCENE II. BURLACOMBES' *barn.*

Evening.

ACT I

*It is Ascension Day in a village of the West. In the
low panelled hall-sitting-room of the* BURLACOMBERS'
farmhouse on the village green, MICHAEL STRANG-
WAY, *a clerical collar round his throat and a dark
Norfolk jacket on his back, is playing the flute before
a very large framed photograph of a woman, which
is the only picture on the walls. His age is about
thirty-five; his figure thin and very upright and his
clean-shorn face thin, upright, narrow, with long and
rather pointed ears; his dark hair is brushed in a cox-
comb off his forehead. A faint smile hovers about his
lips that Nature has made rather full and he has made
thin, as though keeping a hard secret; but his bright
grey eyes, dark round the rim, look out and upwards
almost as if he were being crucified. There is something about the whole of him that makes him seem
not quite present. A gentle creature, burnt within.*
*A low, broad window above a window-seat forms the back-
ground to his figure; and through its lattice panes
are seen the outer gate and yew-trees of a churchyard
and the porch of a church, bathed in May sunlight.
The front door at right angles to the window-seat,
leads to the village green, and a door on the left into
the house.*
It is the third movement of Veracini's violin sonata that
STRANGWAY *plays. His back is turned to the door
into the house, and he does not hear when it is opened,
and* IVY BURLACOMBE, *the farmer's daughter, a girl*

*of fourteen, small and quiet as a mouse, comes in,
a prayer-book in one hand, and in the other a glass
of water, with wild orchis and a bit of deep pink
hawthorn. She sits down on the window-seat, and
having opened her book, sniffs at the flowers. Coming
to the end of the movement* STRANGWAY *stops, and
looking up at the face on the wall, heaves a long sigh.*

IVY. [*From the seat.*] I picked these for yü, Mr. Strangway.

STRANGWAY. [*Turning with a start.*] Ah! Ivy. Thank you. [*He puts his flute down on a chair against the far wall.*] Where are the others?

> [*As he speaks,* GLADYS FREMAN, *a dark gipsyish girl, and* CONNIE TRUSTAFORD, *a fair, stolid, blue-eyed Saxon, both about sixteen, come in through the front door, behind which they have evidently been listening. They too have prayer-books in their hands. They sidle past* IVY, *and also sit down under the window.*]

GLADYS. Mercy's comin', Mr. Strangway.

STRANGWAY. Good morning, Gladys; good morning, Connie.

> [*He turns to a book-case on a table against the far wall, and taking out a book, finds his place in it. While he stands thus with his back to the girls,* MERCY JARLAND *comes in from the green. She also is about sixteen, with fair hair and china-blue eyes. She glides in quickly, hiding something behind her, and sits down on the seat next the door. And at once there is a whispering.*]

STRANGWAY. [*Turning to them.*] Good morning, Mercy.

MERCY. Good morning, Mr. Strangway.

STRANGWAY. Now, yesterday I was telling you what our Lord's coming meant to the world. I want you to understand that before He came there wasn't really love, as we know it. I don't mean to say that there weren't many good people; but there wasn't love for the sake of loving. D'you think you understand what I mean?

[MERCY *fidgets.* GLADYS's *eyes are following a fly.*]

IVY. Yes, Mr. Strangway.

STRANGWAY. It isn't enough to love people because they're good to you, or because in some way or other you're going to get something by it. We have to love because we love loving. That's the great thing—without that we're nothing but Pagans.

GLADYS. Please, what is Pagans?

STRANGWAY. That's what the first Christians called the people who lived in the villages and were not yet Christians, Gladys.

MERCY. We live in a village, but we're Christians.

STRANGWAY. [*With a smile.*] Yes, Mercy; and what is a Christian?

[MERCY *kicks a foot sideways against her neighbour, frowns over her china-blue eyes, is silent; then, as his question passes on, makes a quick little face, wriggles, and looks behind her.*]

STRANGWAY. Ivy?

IVY. 'Tis a man—whü—whü—

STRANGWAY. Yes?—Connie?

CONNIE. [*Who speaks rather thickly, as if she had a permanent slight cold.*] Please, Mr. Strangway, 'tis a man whü goes to church.

GLADYS. He 'as to be baptized—and confirmed; and—and—buried.

IVY. 'Tis a man whü—whü's güde and—

GLADYS. He don't drink, an' he don't beat his horses, an' he don't hit back.

MERCY. [*Whispering.*] 'Tisn't your turn. [*To* STRANGWAY] 'Tis a man like us.

IVY. I know what Mrs. Strangway said it was, 'cause I asked her once, before she went away.

STRANGWAY. [*Startled.*] Yes?

IVY. She said it was a man whü forgave everything.

STRANGWAY. Ah!

> [*The note of cuckoo comes travelling. The girls are gazing at* STRANGWAY, *who seems to have gone off into a dream. They begin to fidget and whisper.*]

CONNIE. Please, Mr. Strangway, father says if yü hit a man and he don't hit yü back, he's no güde at all.

MERCY. When Tommy Morse wouldn't fight, us pinched him—he did squeal! [*She giggles.*] Made me laugh!

STRANGWAY. Did I ever tell you about St. Francis of Assisi?

IVY. [*Clasping her hands.*] No.

STRANGWAY. Well, he was the best Christian, I think, that ever lived—simply full of love and joy.

IVY. I expect he's dead.

STRANGWAY. About seven hundred years, Ivy.

IVY. [*Softly.*] Oh!

STRANGWAY. Everything to him was brother or sister—the sun and the moon, and all that was poor and weak and sad, and animals and birds, so that they even used to follow him about.

MERCY. I know. He had crumbs in his pocket.

STRANGWAY. No; he had love in his eyes.

IVY. 'Tis like about Orpheus, that yü told us.

STRANGWAY. Ah! But St. Francis was a Christian, and Orpheus was a Pagan.

A BIT O' LOVE

Ivy. Oh!

Strangway. Orpheus drew everything after him with music; St. Francis by love.

Ivy. Perhaps it was the same, really.

Strangway. [*Looking at his flute.*] Perhaps it was, Ivy.

Gladys. Did 'e 'ave a flute like yü?

Ivy. The flowers smell sweeter when they 'ear music; they dü. [*She holds up the glass of flowers.*

Strangway. [*Touching one of the orchis.*] What's the name of this one?

   [*The girls cluster, save* Mercy, *who is taking a stealthy interest in what she has behind her.*]

Connie. We call it a cuckoo, Mr. Strangway.

Gladys. 'Tis awful common down by the streams. We've got one medder where 'tis so thick almost as the goldie cups.

Strangway. Odd! I've never noticed it.

Ivy. Please, Mr. Strangway, yü don't notice when yü're walkin'; yü go along like this.

   [*She holds up her face as one looking at the sky.*

Strangway. Bad as that, Ivy?

Ivy. Mrs. Strangway often used to pick it last spring.

Strangway. Did she? Did she?

   [*He has gone off again into a kind of dream.*

Mercy. I like being confirmed.

Strangway. Ah! Yes. Now—— What's that behind you, Mercy?

Mercy. [*Engagingly producing a cage a little bigger than a mouse-trap, containing a skylark.*] My skylark.

Strangway. What!

Mercy. It can fly; but we're goin' to clip its wings. Bobbie caught it.

Strangway. How long ago?

Mercy. [*Conscious of impending disaster.*] Yesterday.

STRANGWAY. [*White hot.*] Give me the cage!

MERCY. [*Puckering.*] I want my skylark. [*As he steps up to her and takes the cage—thoroughly alarmed.*] I gave Bobbie thrippence for it!

STRANGWAY. [*Producing a sixpence.*] There!

MERCY. [*Turning it down—passionately.*] I want my skylark!

STRANGWAY. God made this poor bird for the sky and the grass. And you put it in *that!* Never cage any wild thing! Never!

MERCY. [*Faint and sullen.*] I want my skylark.

STRANGWAY. [*Taking the cage to the door.*] No! [*He holds up the cage and opens it.*] Off you go, poor thing!

> [*The bird flies out and away.*
> [*The girls watch with round eyes the fling up of his arm, and the freed bird flying away.*]

IVY. I'm glad.

> [MERCY *kicks her viciously and sobs.* STRANGWAY *comes from the door, looks at* MERCY *sobbing, and suddenly clasps his head. The girls watch him with a queer mixture of wonder, alarm, and disapproval.*]

GLADYS. [*Whispering.*] Don't cry, Mercy, Bobbie'll soon catch yü another.

> [STRANGWAY *has dropped his hands, and is looking again at* MERCY. IVY *sits with hands clasped, gazing at* STRANGWAY. MERCY *continues her artificial sobbing.*]

STRANGWAY. [*Quietly.*] The class is over for to-day.

> [*He goes up to* MERCY, *and holds out his hand. She does not take it, and runs out knuckling her eyes.* STRANGWAY *turns on his heel and goes into the house.*]

CONNIE. 'Twasn't his bird.

A BIT O' LOVE

Ivy. Skylarks belong to the sky. Mr. Strangway said so.

Gladys. Not when they'm caught, they don't.

Ivy. They dü.

Connie. 'Twas her bird.

Ivy. He gave her sixpence for it.

Gladys. She didn't take it.

Connie. There it is on the ground.

Ivy. She might have.

Gladys. He'll p'raps take my squirrel, tü.

Ivy. The bird sang—I 'eard it! Right up in the sky. It wouldn't have sanged if it weren't glad.

Gladys. Well, Mercy cried.

Ivy. I don't care.

Gladys. 'Tis a shame! And I know something. Mrs. Strangway's at Durford.

Connie. She's—never!

Gladys. I saw her yesterday. An' if she's there she ought to be here. I told mother, an' she said: "Yü mind yer business." An' when she goes in to market to-morrow she'm goin' to see. An' if she's really there, mother says, 'tis a fine tü-dü an' a praaper scandal. So *I* know a lot more'n yü dü. [Ivy *stares at her*.

Connie. Mrs. Strangway told mother she was goin' to France for the winter because her mother was ill.

Gladys. 'Tisn't winter now—Ascension Day. I saw her comin' out o' Dr. Desart's house. I know 'twas her because she had on a blue dress an' a proud lüke. Mother says the doctor come over tü often before Mrs. Strangway went away, just afore Christmas. They was old sweethearts before she married Mr. Strangway. [*To* Ivy.] 'Twas yüre mother told mother that.

[Ivy *gazes at them more and more wide-eyed*.

Connie. Father says if Mrs. Bradmere an' the old

Rector knew about the doctor, they wouldn't 'ave Mr. Strangway 'ere for curate any longer; because mother says it takes more'n a year for a güde wife to leave her 'usband, an' 'e so fond of her. But 'tisn't no business of ours, fəther says.

GLADYS. Mother says so tü. She's praaper set against gossip. She'll know all about it to-morrow after market.

IVY. [*Stamping her foot.*] I don't want to 'ear nothin' at all; I don't, an' I won't.

[*A rather shame-faced silence falls on the girls.*

GLADYS. [*In a quick whisper.*] 'Ere's Mrs. Burlacombe.

[*There enters from the house a stout motherly woman with a round grey eye and very red cheeks.*]

MRS. BURLACOMBE. Ivy, take Mr. Strangway his ink, or we'll never 'ave no sermon to-night. He'm in his thinkin' box, but 'tis not a bit of yüse 'im thinkin' without 'is ink. [*She hands her daughter an inkpot and blotting-pad. IVY takes them and goes out.*] Whatever's this?

[*She picks up the little bird-cage.*

GLADYS. 'Tis Mercy Jarland's. Mr. Strangway let her skylark go.

MRS. BURLACOMBE. Aw! Did 'e now? Serve 'er right, bringin' an 'eathen bird to confirmation class.

CONNIE. I'll take it to her.

MRS. BURLACOMBE. No. Yü leave it there, an' let Mr. Strangway dü what 'e likes with it. Bringin' a bird like that! Well I never!

[*The girls, perceiving that they have lighted on stony soil, look at each other and slide towards the door.*]

MRS. BURLACOMBE. Yes, yü just be off, an' think on what yü've been told in class, an' be'ave like Christians, that's güde maids. An' don't yü come no more in the avenin's dancin' them 'eathen dances in my barn, naighther, till after yü'm confirmed—'tisn't right. I've told Ivy I won't 'ave it.

CONNIE. Mr. Strangway don't mind—he likes us to; 'twas Mrs. Strangway began teachin' us. He's goin' to give a prize.

MRS. BURLACOMBE. Yü just dü what I tell yü an' never mind Mr. Strangway—he'm tü kind to everyone. D'yü think I don't know how gells oughter be'ave before confirmation? Yü be'ave like I did! Now, goo ahn! Shoo!

[*She hustles them out, rather as she might hustle her chickens, and begins tidying the room. There comes a wandering figure to the open window. It is that of a man of about thirty-five, of feeble gait, leaning the weight of all one side of him on a stick. His dark face, with black hair, one lock of which has gone white, was evidently once that of an ardent man. Now it is slack, weakly smiling, and the brown eyes are lost, and seem always to be asking something to which there is no answer.*]

MRS. BURLACOMBE. [*With that forced cheerfulness always assumed in the face of too great misfortune.*] Well, Jim! Better? [*At the faint brightening of the smile.*] That's right! Yü'm gettin' on bravely. Want Parson?

JIM. [*Nodding and smiling, and speaking slowly.*] I want to tell 'un about my cat.

[*His face loses its smile.*

MRS. BURLACOMBE. Why! what's she been düin' then? Mr. Strangway's busy. Won't I dü?

JIM. [*Shaking his head.*] No. I want to tell *him*.

MRS. BURLACOMBE. Whatever she been düin'? Havin' kittens?

JIM. No. She'm lost.

MRS. BURLACOMBE. Dearie me! Aw! she'm not lost. Cats be like maids; they must get out a bit.

JIM. She'm lost. Maybe he'll know where she'll be.

MRS. BURLACOMBE. Well, well. I'll go an' find 'im.

JIM. He's a güde man. He's very güde.

MRS. BURLACOMBE. That's certain zure.

STRANGWAY. [*Entering from the house.*] Mrs. Burlacombe, I can't think where I've put my book on St. Francis—the large, squarish pale-blue one?

MRS. BURLACOMBE. Aw! there now! I knü there was somethin' on me mind. Miss Willis she came in yesterday afternüne when yü was out, to borrow it. Oh! yes—I said—I'm zure Mr. Strangway'll lend it 'ee. Now think o' that!

STRANGWAY. Of course, Mrs. Burlacombe; very glad she's got it.

MRS. BURLACOMBE. Aw! but that's not all. When I tuk it up there come out a whole flutter o' little bits o' paper wi' little rhymes on 'em, same as I see yü writin.' Aw! my güdeness! I says to meself, Mr. Strangway widn' want no one seein' them.

STRANGWAY. Dear me! No; certainly not!

MRS. BURLACOMBE. An' so I putt 'em in your secretary.

STRANGWAY. My—ah! Yes. Thank you; yes.

MRS. BUBLACOMBE. But I'll goo over an' get the büke for yü. 'T won't take me 'alf a minit.

[*She goes out on to the green.* JIM BERE *has come in.*]

STRANGWAY. [*Gently.*] Well, Jim?

JIM. My cat's lost.

STRANGWAY. Lost?

JIM. Day before yesterday. She'm not come back.

A BIT O' LOVE

They've shot 'er, I think; or she'm caught in one o' they rabbit-traps.

STRANGWAY. Oh! no; my dear fellow, she'll come back. I'll speak to Sir Herbert's keepers.

JIM. Yes, zurr. I feel lonesome without 'er.

STRANGWAY. [*With a faint smile—more to himself than to* JIM.] Lonesome! Yes! That's bad, Jim! That's bad!

JIM. I miss 'er when I sits thar in the avenin'.

STRANGWAY. The evenings—— They're the worst—— and when the blackbirds sing in the morning.

JIM. She used to lie on my bed, ye know, zurr. [STRANGWAY *turns his face away, contracted with pain.*] She'm like a Christian.

STRANGWAY. The beasts are.

JIM. There's plenty folk ain't 'alf as Christian as 'er be.

STRANGWAY. Well, dear Jim, I'll do my very best. And any time you're lonely, come up, and I'll play the flute to you.

JIM. [*Wriggling slightly.*] No, zurr. Thank 'ee, zurr.

STRANGWAY. What—don't you like music?

JIM. *Ye-es,* zurr. [*A figure passes the window. Seeing it he says with his slow smile:*] 'Ere's Mrs. Bradmere, comin' from the Rectory. [*With queer malice.*] She don't like cats. But she'm a cat 'erself, I think.

STRANGWAY. [*With his smile.*] Jim!

JIM. She'm always tellin' me I'm lükin' better. I'm not better, zurr.

STRANGWAY. That's her kindness.

JIM. I don't think it is. 'Tis laziness, an' 'avin 'er own way. She'm very fond of 'er own way.

> [*A knock on the door cuts off his speech. Following closely on the knock, as though no doors were licensed to be closed against her, a grey-haired lady enters; a capable, brown-*

faced woman of seventy, whose every tone and movement exhales authority. With a nod and a "good morning" to STRANGWAY *she turns at once to* JIM BERE.]

MRS. BRADMERE. Ah! Jim; you're looking better.

[JIM BERE *shakes his head.*

MRS. BRADMERE. Oh! yes, you are. Getting on splendidly. And now, I just want to speak to Mr. Strangway.

[JIM BERE *touches his forelock, and slowly, leaning on his stick, goes out.*]

MRS. BRADMERE. [*Waiting for the door to close.*] You know how that came on him? Caught the girl he was engaged to, one night, with another man, the rage broke something there. [*She touches her forehead.*] Four years ago.

STRANGWAY. Poor fellow!

MRS. BRADMERE. [*Looking at him sharply.*] Is your wife back?

STRANGWAY. [*Starting.*] No.

MRS. BRADMERE. By the way, poor Mrs. Cremer—is she any better?

STRANGWAY. No; going fast. Wonderful—so patient.

MRS. BRADMERE. [*With gruff sympathy.*] Um! Yes. They know how to die! [*With another sharp look at him.*] D'you expect your wife soon?

STRANGWAY. I—I—hope so.

MRS. BRADMERE. So do I. The sooner the better.

STRANGWAY. [*Shrinking.*] I trust the Rector's not suffering so much this morning?

MRS. BRADMERE. Thank you! His foot's very bad.

[*As she speaks* MRS. BURLACOMBE *returns with a large pale-blue book in her hand.*]

MRS. BURLACOMBE. Good day, M'm! [*Taking the book*

across to STRANGWAY.] Miss Willis, she says she'm very sorry, zurr.

STRANGWAY. She was very welcome, Mrs. Burlacombe. [*To* MRS. BRADMERE.] Forgive me—my sermon.

[*He goes into the house.*
[*The two women gaze after him. Then, at once, as it were, draw into themselves, as if preparing for an encounter, and yet seem to expand as if losing the need for restraint.*]

MRS. BRADMERE. [*Abruptly.*] He misses his wife very much, I'm afraid.

MRS. BURLACOMBE. Ah! Don't he? Poor dear man; he keeps a terrible tight 'and over 'imself, but 'tis suthin' cruel the way he walks about at night. He'm just like a cow when it's calf's weaned. 'T 'as gone to me 'eart truly to see 'im these months past. T'other day when I went up to dü his rüme, I yeard a noise like this [*she sniffs*]; an' ther' 'e was at the wardrobe, snuffin' at 'er things. I did never think a man cud care for a woman so much as that.

MRS. BRADMERE. H'm!

MRS. BURLACOMBE. 'Tis funny rest—an' 'e comin' 'ere for quiet after tearin' great London parish! 'E'm terrible absent-minded tü—don't take no interest in 'is füde. Yesterday, goin' on for one o'clock, 'e says to me, "I expect 'tis nearly breakfast-time, Mrs. Burlacombe!" 'E'd 'ad it twice already!

MRS. BRADMERE. Twice! Nonsense!

MRS. BURLACOMBE. Zurely! I give 'im a nummit afore 'e gets up; an' 'e 'as 'is brekjus reg'lar at nine. Must feed un up. He'm on 'is feet all day, goin' to zee folk that widden want to zee an angel, they'm that busy; an' when 'e comes in 'e'll play 'is flüte there. He'm wastin' away for want of 'is wife. That's what 'tis. An' 'im so sweet-spoken, tü, 'tes a pleasure to year 'im—— Never says a word!

MRS. BRADMERE. Yes, that's the kind of man who gets treated badly. I'm afraid she's not worthy of him, Mrs. Burlacombe.

MRS. BURLACOMBE. [*Plaiting her apron.*] 'Tesn't for me to zay that. She'm a very pleasant lady.

MRS. BRADMERE. Too pleasant. What's this story about her being seen in Durford?

MRS. BURLACOMBE. Aw! I dü never year no gossip, m'm.

MRS. BRADMERE. [*Drily.*] Of course not! But you see the Rector wishes to know.

MRS. BURLACOMBE. [*Flustered.*] Well—folk will talk! But, as I says to Burlacombe—" 'Tes paltry," I says; and they only married eighteen months, and Mr. Strangway so devoted-like. 'Tes nothing but love, with 'im.

MRS. BRADMERE. Come!

MRS. BURLACOMBE. There's puzzivantin' folk as'll set an' gossip the feathers off an angel. But I dü never listen.

MRS. BRADMERE. Now, then, Mrs. Burlacombe?

MRS. BURLACOMBE. Well, they dü say as how Dr. Desart over to Durford and Mrs. Strangway was sweethearts afore she wer' married.

MRS. BRADMERE. I knew that. Who was it saw her coming out of Dr. Desart's house yesterday?

MRS. BURLACOMBE. In a manner of spakin' 'tes Mrs. Freman that says 'er Gladys seen her.

MRS. BRADMERE. That child's got an eye like a hawk.

MRS. BURLACOMBE. 'Tes wonderful how things dü spread. 'Tesn't as if us gossiped. Dü seem to grow-like in the naight.

MRS. BRADMERE. [*To herself.*] I never liked her. That Riviera excuse, Mrs. Burlacombe— Very convenient things, sick mothers. Mr. Strangway doesn't know?

A BIT O' LOVE

MRS. BURLACOMBE. The Lord forbid! 'Twid send un crazy, I think. For all he'm so moony an' gentle-like, I think he'm a terrible passionate man inside. He've a-got a saint in 'im, for zure; but 'tes only 'alf-baked, in a manner of spakin'.

MRS. BRADMERE. I shall go and see Mrs. Freman. There's been too much of this gossip all the winter.

MRS. BURLACOMBE. 'Tes unfortunate-like 'tes the Fremans. Freman he'm a gipsy sort of a feller; and he've never forgiven Mr. Strangway for spakin' to 'im about the way he trates 'is 'orses.

MRS. BRADMERE. Ah! I'm afraid Mr. Strangway's not too discreet when his feelings are touched.

MRS. BURLACOMBE. 'E've a-got an 'eart so big as the full müne. But 'tes no yüse expectin' tü much o' this world. 'Tes a funny place, after that.

MRS. BRADMERE. Yes, Mrs. Burlacombe; and I shall give some of these good people a rare rap over the knuckles for their want of charity. For all they look as if butter wouldn't melt in their mouths, they're an un-Christian lot. [*Looking very directly at* MRS. BURLACOMBE.] It's lucky we've some hold over the village. I'm not going to have scandal. I shall speak to Sir Herbert, and he and the Rector will take steps.

MRS. BURLACOMBE. [*With covert malice.*] Aw! I dü hope 'twon't upset the Rector, an' 'is füte so poptious!

MRS. BRADMERE. [*Grimly.*] His foot'll be sound enough to come down sharp. By the way, will you send me a duck up to the Rectory?

MRS. BURLACOMBE. [*Glad to get away.*] Zurely, m'm; at once. I've some luv'ly fat birds.

[*She goes into the house.*

MRS. BRADMERE. Old puss-cat!

[*She turns to go, and in the doorway encounters*

a very little, red-cheeked girl in a peacock-blue cap, and pink frock, who curtsies stolidly.]

MRS. BRADMERE. Well, Tibby Jarland, what do you want here? Always sucking something, aren't you?

[*Getting no reply from* TIBBY JARLAND, *she passes out.* TIBBY *comes in, looks round, takes a large sweet out of her mouth, contemplates it, and puts it back again. Then, in a perfunctory and very stolid fashion, she looks about the floor, as if she had been told to find something. While she is finding nothing and sucking her sweet, her sister* MERCY *comes in furtively, still frowning and vindictive.*]

MERCY. What! Haven't you found it, Tibby? Get along with 'ee, then!

[*She accelerates the stolid* TIBBY'S *departure with a smack, searches under the seat, finds and picks up the deserted sixpence. Then very quickly she goes to the door. But it is opened before she reaches it, and, finding herself caught, she slips behind the chintz window-curtain. A woman has entered, who is clearly the original of the large photograph. She is not strictly pretty, but there is charm in her pale, resolute face, with its mocking lips, flexible brows, and greenish eyes, whose lids, square above them, have short, dark lashes. She is dressed in blue, and her fair hair is coiled up under a cap and motor-veil. She comes in swiftly, and closes the door behind her; becomes irresolute; then, suddenly deciding, moves towards the door into the house.* MERCY *slips from behind her curtain to make off, but at that moment the door into the house is opened, and she has at*

A BIT O' LOVE

once to slip back again into covert. It is IVY *who has appeared.*]

IVY. [*Amazed.*] Oh! Mrs. Strangway!

[*Evidently disconcerted by this appearance,* BEATRICE STRANGWAY *pulls herself together and confronts the child with a smile.*]

BEATRICE. Well, Ivy—you've grown! You didn't expect me, did you?

IVY. No, Mrs. Strangway; but I hoped yü'd be comin' soon.

BEATRICE. Ah! Yes. Is Mr. Strangway in?

IVY. [*Hypnotized by those faintly smiling lips.*] Yes—oh, yes! He's writin' his sermon in the little room. He *will* be glad!

BEATRICE. [*Going a little closer, and never taking her eyes off the child.*] Yes. Now, Ivy, will you do something for me?

IVY. [*Fluttering.*] Oh, yes, Mrs. Strangway.

BEATRICE. Quite sure?

IVY. Oh, yes!

BEATRICE. Are you old enough to keep a secret?

IVY. [*Nodding.*] I'm fourteen now.

BEATRICE. Well, then—I don't want anybody but Mr. Strangway to know I've been here; nobody, not even your mother. D'you understand?

IVY. [*Troubled.*] No. Only, I *can* keep a secret.

BEATRICE. Mind, if anybody hears, it will hurt—Mr. Strangway.

IVY. Oh! I wouldn't—hurt—him. *Must* yü go away again? [*Trembling towards her.*] I wish yü were goin' to stay. And perhaps some one *has* seen yü— They——

BEATRICE. [*Hastily.*] No, no one. I came motoring; like this. [*She moves her veil to show how it can conceal her face.*] And I came straight down the little lane, and through the barn, across the yard.

IVY. [*Timidly.*] People dü see a lot.

BEATRICE. [*Still with that hovering smile.*] I know, but— Now go and tell him quickly and quietly.

IVY. [*Stopping at the door.*] Mother's pluckin' a duck. Only, please, Mrs. Strangway, if she comes in even after yü've gone, she'll know, because—because yü always have that particular nice scent.

BEATRICE. Thank you, my child. I'll see to that.

> [IVY *looks at her as if she would speak again, then turns suddenly, and goes out.* BEATRICE'S *face darkens; she shivers. Taking out a little cigarette case, she lights a cigarette and watches the puffs of smoke wreathe about her and die away. The frightened* MERCY *peers out, spying for a chance to escape. Then from the house* STRANGWAY *comes in. All his dreaminess is gone.*]

STRANGWAY. Thank God! [*He stops at the look on her face.*] I don't understand, though. I thought you were still out there.

BEATRICE. [*Letting her cigarette fall, and putting her foot on it.*] No.

STRANGWAY. You're staying? Oh! Beatrice; come! We'll get away from here at once—as far, as far—anywhere you like. Oh! my darling—only come! If you knew——

BEATRICE. It's no good, Michael. I've tried and tried.

STRANGWAY. Not! Then why—? Beatrice! You said, when you were right away—I've waited——

BEATRICE. I know. It's cruel—it's horrible. But I told you not to hope, Michael. I've done my best. All these months at Mentone, I've been wondering why I ever let you marry me—when that feeling wasn't dead!

A BIT O' LOVE

STRANGWAY. You can't have come back just to leave me again?

BEATRICE. When you let me go out there with mother I thought—I *did* think I would be able; and I *had* begun—and then—spring came!

STRANGWAY. Spring came here too! Never so—aching! Beatrice, can't you?

BEATRICE. I've something to say.

STRANGWAY. No! No! No!

BEATRICE. You see—I've—fallen.

STRANGWAY. Ah! [*In a voice sharpened by pain.*] Why, in the name of mercy, come here to tell me that? Was *he* out there, then? [*She shakes her head.*

BEATRICE. I came straight back to him.

STRANGWAY. To Durford?

BEATRICE. To the Crossway Hotel, miles out—in my own name. They don't know me there. I told you not to hope, Michael. I've done my best; I swear it.

STRANGWAY. My God!

BEATRICE. It was your God that brought us to live near *him!*

STRANGWAY. Why have you come to me like this?

BEATRICE. To know what you're going to do. Are you going to divorce me? We're in your power. Don't divorce me— Doctor and patient—you must know—it ruins him. He'll lose everything. He'd be disqualified, and he hasn't a penny without his work.

STRANGWAY. Why should I spare him?

BEATRICE. Michael, I came to beg. It's hard.

STRANGWAY. No; don't beg! I can't stand it.

BEATRICE. [*Recovering her pride.*] What are you going to do, then? Keep us apart by the threat of a divorce? Starve us and prison us? Cage me up here with you? I'm not brute enough to ruin him.

STRANGWAY. Heaven!

BEATRICE. I never really stopped loving him. I never loved you, Michael.

STRANGWAY. [*Stunned.*] Is that true? [*Beatrice bends her head.*] Never loved me? Not—that night—on the river—not——?

BEATRICE. [*Under her breath.*] No.

STRANGWAY. Were you lying to me, then? Kissing me, and—hating me?

BEATRICE. One doesn't hate men like you; but it wasn't love.

STRANGWAY. Why did you tell me it was?

BEATRICE. Yes. That was the worst thing I've ever done.

STRANGWAY. Do you think I would have married you? I would have burned first! I never dreamed you didn't. I swear it!

BEATRICE. [*Very low.*] Forget it!

STRANGWAY. Did *he* try to get you away from me? [BEATRICE *gives him a swift look.*] Tell me the truth!

BEATRICE. No. It was—I—alone. But—he loves me.

STRANGWAY. One does not easily know love, it seems.

[*But her smile, faint, mysterious, pitying, is enough, and he turns away from her.*]

BEATRICE. It was cruel to come, I know. For me, too. But I couldn't write. I had to know.

STRANGWAY. Never loved me? *Never* loved me? That night at Tregaron? [*At the look on her face.*] You might have told me before you went away! Why keep me all these——

BEATRICE. I meant to forget him again. I did mean to. I thought I could get back to what I was, when I married you; but, you see, what a girl can do, a woman that's been married—can't.

STRANGWAY. Then it was I—my kisses that—! [*He*

A BIT O' LOVE

laughs.] How did you stand them? [*His eyes dart at her face.*] Imagination helped you, perhaps!

BEATRICE. Michael, don't, don't! And—oh! don't make a public thing of it! You needn't be afraid I shall have too good a time! [*He stays quite still and silent, and that which is writhing in him makes his face so strange that* BEATRICE *stands aghast. At last she goes stumbling on in speech.*] If ever you want to marry some one else—then, of course—that's only fair, ruin or not. But till then—till then— He's leaving Durford, going to Brighton. No one need know. And you—this isn't the only parish in the world.

STRANGWAY. [*Quietly.*] You ask me to help you live in secret with another man?

BEATRICE. I ask for mercy.

STRANGWAY. [*As to himself.*] What am I to do?

BEATRICE. What you feel in the bottom of your heart.

STRANGWAY. You ask me to help you live in sin?

BEATRICE. To let me go out of your life. You've only to do—nothing. [*He goes, slowly, close to her.*

STRANGWAY. I want you. Come back to me! Beatrice, come back!

BEATRICE. It would be torture, now.

STRANGWAY. [*Writhing.*] Oh!

BEATRICE. Whatever's in your heart—do!

STRANGWAY. You'd come back to me sooner than ruin *him*? Would you?

BEATRICE. I can't bring him harm.

STRANGWAY. [*Turning away.*] God!—if there be one—help me! [*He stands leaning his forehead against the window. Suddenly his glance falls on the little bird-cage, still lying on the window-seat.*] Never cage any wild thing! [*He gives a laugh that is half a sob; then, turning to the door, says in a low voice.*] Go! Go please, quickly! Do what you will. I won't hurt you—can't— But—go!

[*He opens the door.*

BEATRICE. [*Greatly moved.*] Thank you!

> [*She passes him with her head down, and goes out quickly.* STRANGWAY *stands unconsciously tearing at the little bird-cage. And while he tears at it he mutters a moaning sound. The terrified* MERCY, *peering from behind the curtain, and watching her chance, slips to the still open door; but in her haste and fright she knocks against it, and* STRANGWAY *sees her. Before he can stop her she has fled out on to the green and away.*]

> [*While he stands there, paralysed, the door from the house is opened, and* MRS. BURLACOMBE *approaches him in a queer, hushed way.*]

MRS. BURLACOMBE. [*Her eyes mechanically fixed on the twisted bird-cage in his hands.*] 'Tis poor Sue Cremer, zurr, I didn't 'ardly think she'd last thrü the mornin'. An' zure enough she'm passed away! [*Seeing that he has not taken in her words.*] Mr. Strangway—yü'm feelin' giddy?

STRANGWAY. No, no! What was it? You said——

MRS. BURLACOMBE. 'Tes Jack Cremer. His wife's gone. 'E'm in a terrible way. 'Tes only yü, 'e ses, can dü 'im any güde. He'm in the kitchen.

STRANGWAY. Cremer? Yes! Of course. Let him——

MRS. BURLACOMBE. [*Still staring at the twisted cage.*] Yü ain't wantin' that—'tes all twizzled. [*She takes it from him.*] Sure yü'm not feelin' yer 'ead?

STRANGWAY. [*With a resolute effort.*] No!

MRS. BURLACOMBE. [*Doubtfully.*] I'll send 'im in, then.

[*She goes.*

A BIT O' LOVE

[*When she is gone,* STRANGWAY *passes his handkerchief across his forehead, and his lips move fast. He is standing motionless when* CREMER, *a big man in labourer's clothes, with a thick, broad face, and tragic, faithful eyes, comes in, and stands a little in from the closed door, quite dumb.*]

STRANGWAY. [*After a moment's silence—going up to him and laying a hand on his shoulder.*] Jack! Don't give way. If we give way—we're done.

CREMER. Yes, zurr. [*A quiver passes over his face.*]

STRANGWAY. She didn't. Your wife was a brave woman. A dear woman.

CREMER. I never thought to lüse her. She never told me 'ow bad she was, afore she tuk to 'er bed. 'Tis a dreadful thing to lüse a wife, zurr.

STRANGWAY. [*Tightening his lips, that tremble.*] Yes. But don't give way! Bear up, Jack!

CREMER. Seems funny 'er goin' blue-bell time, an' the sun shinin' so warm. I picked up an 'orse-shü yesterday. I can't never 'ave 'er back, zurr.

[*His face quivers again.*

STRANGWAY. Some day you'll join her. Think! Some lose their wives for ever.

CREMER. I don't believe as there's a future life, zurr. I think we goo to sleep like the beasts.

STRANGWAY. We're told otherwise. But come here! [*Drawing him to the window.*] Look! Listen! To sleep in that! Even if we do, it won't be so bad, Jack, will it?

CREMER. She wer' a güde wife to me—no man cüdn't 'ave no better wife.

STRANGWAY. [*Putting his hand out.*] Take hold—hard—harder! I want yours as much as you want mine. Pray for me, Jack, and I'll pray for you. And we won't give way, will we?

CREMER. [*To whom the strangeness of these words has given some relief.*] No, zurr; thank 'ee, zurr. 'Tes no güde, I expect. Only, I'll miss 'er. Thank 'ee, zurr; kindly.

> [*He lifts his hand to his head, turns, and uncertainly goes out to the kitchen. And* STRANGWAY *stays where he is, not knowing what to do. Then blindly he takes up his flute, and hatless, hurries out into the air.*]

The curtain falls.

ACT II

SCENE I

About seven o'clock in the taproom of the village inn. The bar, with the appurtenances thereof, stretches across one end, and opposite is the porch door on to the green. The wall between is nearly all window, with leaded panes, one wide-open casement whereof lets in the last of the sunlight. A narrow bench runs under this broad window. And this is all the furniture, save three spittoons.

GODLEIGH, *the innkeeper, a smallish man with thick ruffled hair, a loquacious nose, and apple-red cheeks above a reddish-brown moustache, is reading the paper. To him enters* TIBBY JARLAND *with a shilling in her mouth.*

GODLEIGH. Well, Tibby Jarland, what've yü come for, then? Glass o' beer?

A BIT O' LOVE

[TIBBY *takes the shilling from her mouth and smiles stolidly.*]

GODLEIGH. [*Twinkling.*] I shid zay glass o' 'arf an' 'arf's about yüre form. [TIBBY *smiles more broadly.*] Yü'm a praaper masterpiece. Well! 'Ave sister Mercy borrowed yüre tongue? [TIBBY *shakes her head.*] Aw, she 'aven't. Well, maid?

TIBBY. Father wants six clay pipes, please.

GODLEIGH. 'E dü, dü 'ee? Yü tell yüre father 'e can't 'ave more'n one, not this avenin'. And 'ere 'tis. Hand up yüre shillin'.

[TIBBY *reaches up her hand, parts with the shilling, and receives a long clay pipe and eleven pennies. In order to secure the coins in her pinafore she places the clay pipe in her mouth. While she is still thus engaged,* MRS. BRADMERE *enters the porch and comes in.* TIBBY *curtsies stolidly.*]

MRS. BRADMERE. Gracious, child! What are you doing here? And what have you got in your mouth? Who is it? Tibby Jarland? [TIBBY *curtsies again.*] Take that thing out. And tell your father from me that if I ever see you at the inn again I shall tread on his toes hard. Godleigh, you know the law about children?

GODLEIGH. [*Cocking his eye, and not at all abashed.*] Surely, m'm. But she will come. Go away, my dear.

[TIBBY, *never taking her eyes off* MRS. BRADMERE, *or the pipe from her mouth, has backed stolidly to the door, and vanished.*]

MRS. BRADMERE. [*Eyeing* GODLEIGH.] No, Godleigh, I've come to talk to you. Half the scandal that goes about the village begins here. [*She holds up her finger to check expostulation.*] No, no—it's no good. You know the value of scandal to your business far too well.

GODLEIGH. Wi' all respect, m'm, I knows the vally of it to yourn, tü.

MRS. BRADMERE. What do you mean by that?

GODLEIGH. If there weren't no Rector's lady there widden' be no notice taken o' scandal; an' if there weren't no notice taken, twidden be scandal, to my thinkin'.

MRS. BRADMERE. [*Winking out a grim little smile.*] Very well! You've given me your views. Now for mine. There's a piece of scandal going about that's got to be stopped, Godleigh. You turn the tap of it off here, or we'll turn your tap off. You know me. See?

GODLEIGH. I shouldn' never presume, m'm, to know a lady.

MRS. BRADMERE. The Rector's quite determined, so is Sir Herbert. Ordinary scandal's bad enough, but this touches the Church. While Mr. Strangway remains curate here, there must be no talk about him and his affairs.

GODLEIGH. [*Cocking his eye.*] I was just thinkin' how to dü it, m'm. 'Twid be a brave notion to putt the men in chokey, and slit the women's tongues-like, same as they dü in outlandish places, as I'm told.

MRS. BRADMERE. Don't talk nonsense, Godleigh; and mind what I say, because I mean it.

GODLEIGH. Make yüre mind aisy, m'm—there'll be no scandal-monkeyin' here wi' my permission.

> [MRS. BRADMERE *gives him a keen stare, but seeing him perfectly grave, nods her head with approval.*]

MRS. BRADMERE. Good! You know what's being said, of course?

GODLEIGH. [*With respectful gravity.*] You'll pardon me, m'm, but ef an' in case yü was goin' to tell me, there's a rüle in this 'ouse: "No scandal 'ere!"

A BIT O' LOVE

Mrs. Bradmere. [*Twinkling grimly.*] You're too smart by half, my man.

Godleigh. Aw fegs, no, m'm—child in yüre 'ands.

Mrs. Bradmere. I wouldn't trust you a yard. Once more, Godleigh! This is a Christian village, and we mean it to remain so. You look out for yourself.

> [*The door opens to admit the farmers* Trustaford *and* Burlacombe. *They doff their hats to* Mrs. Bradmere, *who, after one more sharp look at* Godleigh, *moves towards the door.*]

Mrs. Bradmere. Evening, Mr. Trustaford. [*To* Burlacombe.] Burlacombe, tell your wife that duck she sent up was in hard training.

> [*With one of her grim winks, and a nod, she goes.*]

Trustaford. [*Replacing a hat which is black, hard, and not very new, on his long head, above a long face, clean-shaved but for little whiskers.*] What's the old grey mare want, then? [*With a horse-laugh.*] 'Er's lükin' awful wise!

Godleigh. [*Enigmatically.*] Ah!

Trustaford. [*Sitting on the bench close to the bar.*] Drop o' whisky, an' potash.

Burlacombe. [*A taciturn, slim, yellowish man, in a worn soft hat.*] What's nüse, Godleigh? Drop o' cider.

Godleigh. Nüse? There's never no nüse in this 'ouse. Aw, no! Not wi' my permission. [*In imitation.*] This is a Christian village.

Trustaford. Thought the old grey mare seemed mighty busy. [*To* Burlacombe.] 'Tes rather quare about the curate's wife a-comin motorin' this mornin.' Passed me wi' her face all smothered up in a veil, goggles an' all. Haw, haw!

Burlacombe. Aye!

Trustaford. Off again she was in 'alf an hour. 'Er

didn't give poor old curate much of a chance, after six months.

GODLEIGH. Havin' an engagement elsewhere—— No scandal, please, gentlemen.

BURLACOMBE. [*Acidly.*] Never asked to see my missis. Passed me in the yard like a stone.

TRUSTAFORD. 'Tes a little bit rümoursome lately about 'er doctor.

GODLEIGH. Ah! he's the favourite. But 'tes a dead secret, Mr. Trustaford. Don't yü never repate it—there's not a cat don't know it already!

> [BURLACOMBE *frowns, and* TRUSTAFORD *utters his laugh. The door is opened and* FREMAN, *a dark gipsyish man in the dress of a farmer, comes in.*]

GODLEIGH. Don't yü never tell Will Freman what 'e told me!

FREMAN. Avenin'!

TRUSTAFORD. Avenin', Will; what's yüre glass o' trouble?

FREMAN. Drop o' cider, clove, an' dash o' gin. There's blood in the sky to-night.

BURLACOMBE. Ah! We'll 'ave fine weather now, with the full o' the müne.

FREMAN. Dust o' wind an' drop or tü, virst, I reckon. 'Eard t' nüse about curate an' 'is wife?

GODLEIGH. No, indeed; an' don't yü tell us. We'm Christians 'ere in this village.

FREMAN. 'Tain't no very Christian nüse, neither. He's sent 'er off to th' doctor. "Go an' live with un," 'e says; "my blessin' on ye." If 'er'd a-been mine, I'd 'a tuk the whip to 'er. Tam Jarland's maid, she yeard it all. Christian, indeed! That's brave Christianity! "Goo an' live with un!" 'e told 'er.

BURLACOMBE. No, no; that's not sense—a man to say that. I'll not 'ear that against a man that bides in my 'ouse.

A BIT O' LOVE 349

FREMAN. 'Tes sure, I tell 'ee. The maid was hid-up, scared-like, behind the curtain. At it they went, and parson 'e says: "Go," 'e says, "I won't kape 'ee from 'im," 'e says, "an' I won't divorce 'ee, as yü don't wish it!" They was 'is words, same as Jarland's maid told my maid, an' my maid told my missis. If that's parson's talk, 'tes funny work goin' to church.

TRUSTAFORD. [*Brooding.*] 'Tis wonderful quare, zurely.

FREMAN. Tam Jarland's fair mad wi' curate for makin' free wi' his maid's skylark. Parson or no parson, 'e've no call to meddle wi' other people's praperty. He cam' pokin' 'is nose into my affairs. I told un I knew a sight more 'bout 'orses than 'e ever would!

TRUSTAFORD. He'm a bit crazy 'bout bastes an' birds.

[*They have been so absorbed that they have not noticed the entrance of* CLYST, *a youth with tousled hair, and a bright, quick, Celtic eye, who stands listening, with a bit of paper in his hand.*]

CLYST. Ah! he'm that zurely, Mr. Trustaford.

[*He chuckles.*

GODLEIGH. Now, Tim Clyst, if an' in case yü've a-got some scandal on yer tongue, don't yü never unship it here. Yü go up to Rectory where 'twill be more relished-like.

CLYST. [*Waving the paper.*] Will y' give me a drink for thic, Mr. Godleigh? 'Tes rale funny. Aw! 'tes somethin' swate. Bütiful readin'. Poetry. Rale spice. Yü've a luv'ly voice for readin', Mr. Godleigh.

GODLEIGH. [*All ears and twinkle.*] Aw, what is it, then?

CLYST. Ah! Yü want t' know tü much.

[*Putting the paper in his pocket.*
[*While he is speaking,* JIM BERE *has entered*

quietly, with his feeble step and smile, and sits down.]

CLYST. [*Kindly.*] Hallo, Jim! Cat come 'ome?

JIM BERE. No.

[*All nod, and speak to him kindly. And* JIM BERE *smiles at them, and his eyes ask of them the question, to which there is no answer. And after that he sits motionless and silent, and they talk as if he were not there.*]

GODLEIGH. What's all this, now—no scandal in my 'ouse!

CLYST. 'Tes awful peculiar—like a drame. Mr. Burlacombe 'e don't like to hear tell about drames. A guess a won't tell 'ee, arter that.

FREMAN. Out wi' it, Tim.

CLYST. 'Tes powerful thirsty to-day, Mr. Godleigh.

GODLEIGH. [*Drawing him some cider.*] Yü're all wild cat's talk, Tim; yü've a-got no tale at all.

CLYST. [*Moving for the cider.*] Aw, indade!

GODLEIGH. No tale, no cider!

CLYST. Did ye ever year tell of Orphus?

TRUSTAFORD. What? The old vet.: up to Drayleigh?

CLYST. Fegs, no; Orphus that lived in th' old time, an' drawed the bastes after un wi' his music, same as curate was tellin' the maids.

FREMAN. I've 'eard as a gipsy over to Yellacott could dü that wi' 'is viddle.

CLYST. 'Twas no gipsy I see'd this arternüne; 'twas Orphus, down to Mr. Burlacombe's long medder; settin' there all dark on a stone among the dimsy-white flowers an' the cowflops, wi' a bird upon 'is 'ead, playin' his whistle to the ponies.

FREMAN. [*Excitedly.*] Yü did never zee a man wi' a bird on 'is 'ead.

CLYST. Didn' I?

A BIT O' LOVE

FREMAN. What sort o' bird, then? Yü tell me that.

TRUSTAFORD. Praaper old barndoor cock. Haw, haw!

GODLEIGH. [*Soothingly.*] 'Tes a vairy-tale; us mustn't be tü partic'lar.

BURLACOMBE. In my long medder? Where were yü, then, Tim Clyst?

CLYST. Passin' down the lane on my bike. Wonderful sorrowful-fine music 'e played. The ponies they did come round 'e—yü cud zee the tears runnin' down their chakes; 'twas powerful sad. 'E 'adn't no 'at on.

FREMAN. [*Jeering.*] No; 'e 'ad a bird on 'is 'ead.

CLYST. [*With a silencing grin.*] He went on playin' an' playin'. The ponies they never müved. An' all the dimsy-white flowers they waved and waved, an' the wind it went over 'em. Gav' me a funny feelin'.

GODLEIGH. Clyst, yü take the cherry bun!

CLYST. Where's that cider, Mr. Godleigh?

GODLEIGH. [*Bending over the cider.*] Yü've a-'ad tü much already, Tim.

> [*The door is opened, and* TAM JARLAND *appears. He walks rather unsteadily; a man with a heavy jowl, and sullen, strange, epileptic-looking eyes.*]

CLYST. [*Pointing to* JARLAND.] 'Tis Tam Jarland there 'as the cargo aboard.

JARLAND. Avenin', all! [*To* GODLEIGH.] Pint o' beer. [*To* JIM BERE.] Avenin', Jim.

> [JIM BERE *looks at him and smiles.*

GODLEIGH. [*Serving him after a moment's hesitation.*] 'Ere y'are, Tam. [*To* CLYST, *who has taken out his paper again.*] Where'd yü get thiccy paper?

CLYST. [*Putting down his cider-mug empty.*] Yü're tongue dü watter, don't it, Mr. Godleigh? [*Holding out his mug.*] No zider, no poetry. 'Tis amazin' sorrowful;

Shakespeare over again. "The boy stüde on the burnin' deck."

FREMAN. Yü and yer yap!

CLYST. Ah! Yü wait a bit. When I come back down t'lane again, Orphus 'e was vanished away; there was naught in the field but the ponies, an' a praaper old magpie, a-top o' the hedge. I zee somethin' white in the beak o' the fowl, so I giv' a "Whisht," an' 'e drops it smart, an' off 'e go. I gets over bank and picks un up, and here't be.

[*He holds out his mug.*

BURLACOMBE. [*Tartly.*] Here, give 'im 'is cider. Rade it yüreself, ye young teasewings.

[CLYST, *having secured his cider, drinks it off. Holding up the paper to the light, he makes as if to begin, then slides his eye round, tantalizing.*]

CLYST. 'Tes a pity I bain't dressed in a white gown, an' flowers in me 'air.

FREMAN. Read it, or we'll 'ave yü out o' this.

CLYST. Aw, don't 'ee shake my nerve, now!

[*He begins reading with mock heroism, in his soft, high, burring voice. Thus, in his rustic accent, go the lines:*

God lighted the zun in 'eaven far,
Lighted the virefly an' the ztar.
My 'eart 'E lighted not!

God lighted the vields fur lambs to play,
Lighted the bright strames, 'an the may.
My 'eart 'E lighted not!

God lighted the müne, the Arab's way,
He lights to-morrer, an' to-day.
My 'eart 'E 'ath vorgot!

A BIT O' LOVE

[*When he has finished, there is silence. Then* TRUSTAFORD, *scratching his head, speaks:*]

TRUSTAFORD. 'Tes amazin' funny stuff.

FREMAN. [*Looking over* CLYST's *shoulder.*] Be danged! 'Tes the curate's 'andwritin.' 'Twas curate wi' the ponies, after that.

CLYST. Fancy, now! Aw, Will Freman, an't yü bright!

FREMAN. But 'e 'adn't no bird on 'is 'ead.

CLYST. Ya-as, 'e 'ad.

JARLAND. [*In a dull, threatening voice.*] 'E 'ad my maid's bird, this arternüne. 'Ead or no, and parson or no, I'll gie 'im one for that.

FREMAN. Ah! And 'e meddled wi' my 'orses.

TRUSTAFORD. I'm thinkin' 'twas an old cuckoo bird 'e 'ad on 'is 'ead. Haw, haw!

GODLEIGH. "His 'eart *she* 'ath vorgot!"

FREMAN. 'E's a fine one to be tachin' our maids convirmation.

GODLEIGH. Would ye 'ave it the old Rector then? Wi' 'is gouty shoe? Rackon the maids wid rather 'twas curate; eh, Mr. Burlacombe?

BURLACOMBE. [*Abruptly.*] Curate's a güde man.

JARLAND. [*With the comatose ferocity of drink.*] I'll be even wi' un.

FREMAN. [*Excitedly.*] Tell 'ee one thing—'tes not a proper man o' God to 'ave about, wi' 'is lüse goin's on. Out vrom 'ere he oughter go.

BURLACOMBE. You med go further an' fare worse.

FREMAN. What's 'e düin', then, lettin' 'is wife run off?

TRUSTAFORD. [*Scratching his head.*] If an 'in case 'e can't kape 'er, 'tes a funny way o' düin' things not to divorce 'er, after that. If a parson's not to dü the Christian thing, whü is, then?

BURLACOMBE. 'Tes a bit immoral-like to pass over a

thing like that. 'Tes funny if women's goin's on's to be encouraged.

Freman. Act of a coward, I zay.

Burlacombe. The curate ain't no coward.

Freman. He bides in yüre house; 'tes natural for yü to stand up for un; I'll wager *Mrs.* Burlacombe don't, though. My missis was fair shocked. "Will," she says, "if yü ever make vur to let me go like that, I widden never stay wi' yü," she says.

Trustaford. 'Tes settin' a bad example, for zure.

Burlacombe. 'Tes all very aisy talkin'; what shüde 'e dü, then?

Freman. [*Excitedly.*] Go over to Durford and say to that doctor: "Yü come about my missis, an' zee what I'll dü to 'ee." An' take 'er 'ome an' zee she don't misbe'ave again.

Clyst. 'E can't take 'er ef 'er don' want t' come— I've 'eard lawyer, that lodged wi' us, say that.

Freman. All right then, 'e ought to 'ave the law of 'er and 'er doctor; an' zee 'er goin's on don't prosper; 'e'd get damages, tü. But this way 'tes a nice example he'm settin' folks. Parson indade! My missis an' the maids they won't goo near the church to-night, an' I wager no one else won't, neither.

Jarland. [*Lurching with his pewter up to* Godleigh.] The beggar! I'll be even wi' un.

Godleigh. [*Looking at him in doubt.*] 'Tes the last, then, Tam.

[*Having received his beer,* Jarland *stands, leaning against the bar, drinking.*]

Burlacombe. [*Suddenly.*] I don' goo with what curate's düin'—'tes tü soft 'earted; he'm a müney kind o' man altogether, wi' 'is flute an' 'is poetry; but he've a-lodged in my 'ouse this year an' more, and always 'ad an 'elpin' 'and for every one. I've got a likin' for him an' there's an end of it.

JARLAND. The coward!

TRUSTAFORD. I don' trouble nothin' about that, Tam Jarland. [*Turning to* BURLACOMBE.] What gits me is 'e don't seem to 'ave no zense o' what's his own praperty.

JARLAND. Take other folk's property fast enough! [*He saws the air with his empty pewter. The others have all turned to him, drawn by the fascination that a man in liquor has for his fellow-men. The bell for church has begun to ring, the sun is down, and it is getting dusk.*] He wants one on his crop, an' one in 'is belly; 'e wants a man to take an' gie un a güde hidin'—zame as he oughter give 'is fly-be-night of a wife. [STRANGWAY *in his dark clothes has entered, and stands by the door, his lips compressed to a colourless line, his thin, darkish face grey-white.*] Zame as a man wid ha' gi'en the doctor, for takin' what isn't his'n.

> [*All but* JARLAND *have seen* STRANGWAY. *He steps forward,* JARLAND *sees him now; his jaw drops a little, and he is silent.*]

STRANGWAY. I came for a little brandy, Mr. Godleigh—feeling rather faint. Afraid I mightn't get through the service.

GODLEIGH. [*With professional composure.*] Martell's Three Star, zurr, or 'Ennessy's?

STRANGWAY. [*Looking at* JARLAND.] Thank you; I believe I can do without, now. [*He turns to go.*

> [*In the deadly silence,* GODLEIGH *touches the arm of* JARLAND, *who, leaning against the bar with the pewter in his hand, is staring with his strange lowering eyes straight at* STRANGWAY.]

JARLAND. [*Galvanized by the touch into drunken rage.*] Lave me be—I'll talk to un—parson or no. I'll tache un to meddle wi' my maid's bird. I'll tache un to kape 'is thievin' 'ands to 'imself.

[STRANGWAY *turns again.*

CLYST. Be quiet, Tam.

JARLAND. [*Never loosing* STRANGWAY *with his eyes—like a bull-dog who sees red.*] That's for one chake; zee un turn t'other the white-livered büty! Whü lets another man 'ave 'is wife, an' never the sperit to go vor un!

BURLACOMBE. Shame, Jarland; quiet, man!

[*They are all looking at* STRANGWAY, *who, under* JARLAND'S *drunken insults is standing rigid, with his eyes closed, and his hands hard clenched. The church bell has stopped slow ringing, and begun its five minutes' hurrying note.*]

TRUSTAFORD. [*Rising, and trying to hook his arm into* JARLAND'S.] Come away, Tam; yü've a-'ad tü much, man.

JARLAND. [*Shaking him off.*] Zee, 'e darsen't touch me; I might 'it un in the vace an' 'e darsen't; e's afraid— like 'e was o' the doctor.

[*He raises the pewter as though to fling it, but it is seized by* GODLEIGH *from behind, and falls clattering to the floor.* STRANGWAY *has not moved.*]

JARLAND. [*Shaking his fist almost in his face.*] Lüke at un, lüke at un! A man wi' a slut for a wife——

[*As he utters the word* "wife" STRANGWAY *seizes the outstretched fist, and with a jujitsu movement, draws him into his clutch, helpless. And as they sway and struggle in the open window, with the false strength of fury he forces* JARLAND *through. There is a crash of broken glass from outside. At the sound* STRANGWAY *comes to himself. A look of agony passes over his face.*

A BIT O' LOVE

His eyes light on JIM BERE, *who has suddenly risen, and stands feebly clapping his hands.* STRANGWAY *rushes out.*]

[*Excitedly gathering at the windows, they all speak at once.*]

CLYST. Tam's hatchin' of yüre cucumbers, Mr. Godleigh.

TRUSTAFORD. 'E did crash; haw, haw!

FREMAN. 'Twas a brave throw, zürely. Whü wid a' thought it?

CLYST. Tam's crawlin' out. [*Leaning through window.*] Hallo, Tam—'ow's t' base, old man?

FREMAN. [*Excitedly.*] They'm all comin' up from churchyard to zee.

TRUSTAFORD. Tam dü lüke wonderful aztonished; haw, haw! Poor old Tam!

CLYST. Can yü zee curate? Rackon 'e'm gone into church. Aw, yes; gettin' a bit dimsy—sarvice time.

[*A moment's hush.*

TRUSTAFORD. Well, I'm jiggered. In 'alf an hour he'm got to prache.

GODLEIGH. 'Tes a Christian village, boys.

[*Feebly, quietly,* JIM BERE *laughs. There is silence; but the bell is heard still ringing.*]

The curtain falls.

SCENE II

The same—in daylight dying fast. A lamp is burning on the bar. A chair has been placed in the centre of the room, facing the bench under the window, on which are seated from right to left, GODLEIGH, SOL POTTER, *the village shopman,* TRUSTAFORD, BURLACOMBE, FREMAN, JIM BERE, *and* MORSE, *the blacksmith.* CLYST

*is squatting on a stool by the bar, and at the other end,
JARLAND, sobered and lowering, leans against the lintel
of the porch leading to the door, round which are gathered five or six sturdy fellows, dumb as fishes. No one
sits in the chair. In the unnatural silence that reigns,
the distant sound of the wheezy church organ and
voices singing can be heard.*

TRUSTAFORD. [*After a prolonged clearing of his throat.*]
What I mean to zay is that 'tes no yüse, not a bit o' yüse
in the world, not düin' of things properly. If an' in case
we'm to carry a resolution disapprovin' o' curate, it must
all be done so as no one can't zay nothin'.

SOL POTTER. That's what I zay, Mr. Trustaford; ef so
be as 'tis to be a village meetin', then it must be all done
proper.

FREMAN. That's right, Sol Potter. I purpose Mr. Sol
Potter into the chair. Whü seconds that?

    [*A silence. Voices from among the dumb-as-fishes: "I dü."*]

CLYST. [*Excitedly.*] Yü can't putt that to the meetin'.
Only a chairman can putt it to the meetin'. I purpose that
Mr. Burlacombe—bein' as how he's chairman o' the Parish
Council—take the chair.

FREMAN. Ef so be as I can't putt it, yü can't putt that
neither.

TRUSTAFORD. 'Tes not a bit o' yüse; us can't 'ave no
meetin' without a chairman.

GODLEIGH. Us can't 'ave no chairman without a meetin'
to elect un, that's züre.   [*A silence.*

MORSE. [*Heavily.*] To my way o' thinkin', Mr. Godleigh
speaks zense; us must 'ave a meetin' before us can 'ave a
chairman.

CLYST. Then what we got to dü's to elect a meetin'.

A BIT O' LOVE

BURLACOMBE. [*Sourly.*] Yü'll not find no procedure for that.

> [*Voices from among the dumb-as-fishes:* "Mr. Burlacombe 'e oughter know."]

SOL POTTER. [*Scratching his head—with heavy solemnity.*] 'Tes my belief there's no other way to dü, but to elect a chairman to call a meetin'; an' then for that meetin' to elect a chairman.

CLYST. I purpose Mr. Burlacombe as chairman to call a meetin'.

FREMAN. I purpose Sol Potter.

GODLEIGH. Can't 'ave tü propositions together before a meetin'; that's apple-pie züre vur zurtain.

> [*Voice from among the dumb-as-fishes:* "There ain't no meetin' yet, Sol Potter zays."]

TRUSTAFORD. Us must get the rights of it zettled some'ow. 'Tes like the darned old chicken an' the egg—meetin' or chairman—which comes virst?

SOL POTTER. [*Conciliating.*] To my thinkin' there shid be another way o' düin' it, to get around it like with a circumbendibus. 'T'all comes from takin' different vüse, in a manner o' spakin'.

FREMAN. Yü goo an' zet in that chair.

SOL POTTER. [*With a glance at* BURLACOMBE—*modestly.*] I shid'n never like fur to dü that, with Mr. Burlacombe zettin' there.

BURLACOMBE. [*Rising.*] 'Tes all darned fülishness.

> [*Amidst an uneasy shufflement of feet he moves to the door, and goes out into the darkness.*]

CLYST. [*Seeing his candidate thus depart.*] Rackon curate's pretty well thrü by now, I'm goin' to zee. [*As he passes* JARLAND.] 'Ow's ta base, old man?

> [*He goes out.*
> [*One of the dumb-as-fishes moves from the door*

and fills the space left on the bench by BURLACOMBE's *departure.*]

JARLAND. Darn all this puzzivantin'! [*To* SOL POTTER.] Goo an' zet in that chair.

SOL POTTER. [*Rising and going to the chair; there he stands, changing from one to the other of his short broad feet and sweating from modesty and worth.*] 'Tes my düty now, gentlemen, to call a meetin' of the parishioners of this parish. I beg therefore to declare that this is a meetin' in accordance with my düty as chairman of this meetin' which elected me chairman to call this meetin.' And I purceed to vacate the chair so that this meetin' may now purceed to elect a chairman.

[*He gets up from the chair, and wiping the sweat from his brow, goes back to his seat.*]

FREMAN. Mr. Chairman, I rise on a point of order.

GODLEIGH. There ain't no chairman.

FREMAN. I don't give a darn for that. I rise on a point of order.

GODLEIGH. 'Tes a chairman that decides points of order. 'Tes certain yü can't rise on no points whatever till there's a chairman.

TRUSTAFORD. 'Tes no yüse yüre risin', not the least bit in the world, till there's some one to zet yü down again. Haw, haw!

[*Voice from the dumb-as-fishes:* "Mr. Trustaford 'e's right."]

FREMAN. What I zay is the chairman ought never to 'ave vacated the chair till I'd risen on my point of order. I purpose that he goo and zet down again.

GODLEIGH. Yü can't purpose that to this meetin'; yü can only purpose that to the old meetin' that's not zettin' any longer.

FREMAN. [*Excidedly.*] I don' care what old meetin' 'tis

A BIT O' LOVE

that's zettin'. I purpose that Sol Potter goo an' zet in that chair again, while I rise on my point of order.

TRUSTAFORD. [*Scratching his head.*] 'Tesn't regular—but I guess yü've got to goo, Sol, or us shan't 'ave no peace.

[SOL POTTER, *still wiping his brow, goes back to the chair.*]

MORSE. [*Stolidly—to* FREMAN.] Zet down, Will Freman. [*He pulls at him with a blacksmith's arm.*

FREMAN. [*Remaining erect with an effort.*] I'm not a-goin' to zet down till I've arisen.

JARLAND. Now then, there 'e is in the chair. What's yüre point of order?

FREMAN. [*Darting his eyes here and there, and flinging his hand up to his gipsy-like head.*] 'Twas—'twas—Darned ef y' 'aven't putt it clean out o' my 'ead.

JARLAND. We can't wait for yüre points of order. Come out o' that chair, Sol Potter.

[SOL POTTER *rises and is about to vacate the chair.*]

FREMAN. I know! There ought to 'a been minutes taken. Yü can't 'ave no meetin' without minutes. When us comes to electin' a chairman o' the next meetin', 'e won't 'ave no minutes to read.

SOL POTTER. 'Twas only to putt down that I was elected chairman to elect a meetin' to elect a chairman to preside over a meetin' to pass a resolution dalin' wi' the curate. That's aisy set down, that is.

FREMAN. [*Mollified.*] We'll 'ave that zet down, then, while we're electin' the chairman o' the next meetin.'

[*A silence.*

TRUSTAFORD. Well then, seein' this is the praaper old meetin' for carryin' the resolution about the curate, I purpose Mr. Sol Potter take the chair.

FREMAN. I purpose Mr. Trustaford. I 'aven't a-got

nothin' against Sol Potter, but seein' that he elected the meetin' that's to elect 'im, it might be said that 'e was electin' of himzelf in a manner of spakin'. Us don't want that said.

MORSE. [*Amid meditative grunts from the dumb-as-fishes.*] There's some-at in that. One o' they tü purposals must be putt to the meetin'.

FREMAN. Second must be putt virst, fur züre.

TRUSTAFORD. I dunno as I wants to zet in that chair. To hiss the curate, 'tis a ticklish sort of a job after that. Vurst comes afore second, Will Freeman.

FREMAN. Second is amendment to virst. 'Tes the amendments is putt virst.

TRUSTAFORD. 'Ow's that, Mr. Godleigh? I'm not particular eggzac'ly to a dilly zort of a point like that.

SOL POTTER. [*Scratching his head.*] 'Tes a very nice point, for züre.

GODLEIGH. 'Tes undoubtedly for the chairman to decide.

> [*Voice from the dumb-as-fishes:* "But there ain't no chairman yet."]

JARLAND. Sol Potter's chairman.

FREMAN. No, 'e aint.

MORSE. Yes, 'e is—'e's chairman till this second old meetin' gets on the go.

FREMAN. I deny that. What dü yü say, Mr. Trustaford?

TRUSTAFORD. I can't 'ardly tell. It dü zeem a darned long-sufferin' sort of a business altogether.

[*A silence.*

MORSE. [*Slowly.*] Tell 'ee what 'tis, us shan't dü no güde like this.

GODLEIGH. 'Tes for Mr. Freman or Mr. Trustaford, one or t'other to withdraw their motions.

TRUSTAFORD. [*After a pause, with cautious generosity.*]

A BIT O' LOVE

I've no objections to withdrawin' mine, if Will Freman'll withdraw his'n.

FREMAN. I won't never be be'indhand. If Mr. Trustaford withdraws, I withdraws mine.

MORSE. [*With relief.*] That's zensible. Putt the motion to the meetin'.

SOL POTTER. There ain't no motion left to putt.

> [*Silence of consternation.*
> [*In the confusion* JIM BERE *is seen to stand up.*]

GODLEIGH. Jim Bere to spake. Silence for Jim!

VOICES. Aye! Silence for Jim!

JIM. [*Smiling and slow.*] Nothin' düin'.

TRUSTAFORD. Bravo, Jim! Yü'm right. Best zense yet!

> [*Applause from the dumb-as-fishes.*
> [*With his smile brightening,* JIM *resumes his seat.*

SOL POTTER. [*Wiping his brow.*] Dü seem to me, gentlemen, seein' as we'm got into a bit of a tangle in a manner of spakin', 'twid be the most zimplest and vairest way to begin all over vrom the beginnin', so's t'ave it all vair an' square for every one.

> [*In the uproar of "Aye" and "No," it is noticed that* TIBBY JARLAND *is standing in front of her father with her finger, for want of something better, in her mouth.*]

TIBBY. [*In her stolid voice.*] Please, sister Mercy says, curate 'ave got to "Lastly." [JARLAND *picks her up, and there is silence.*] An' please to come quick.

JARLAND. Come on, mates; quietly now!

> [*He goes out, and all begin to follow him.*

MORSE. [*Slowest, save for* SOL POTTER.] 'Tes rare lucky us was all agreed to hiss the curate afore us began the botherin' old meetin', or us widn' 'ardly 'ave 'ad time to settle what to dü.

Sol Potter. [*Scratching his head.*] Aye, 'tes rare lucky, but I dunno if 'tes altogether reg'lar.

The curtain falls.

SCENE III

The village green before the churchyard and the yew-trees at the gate. Into the pitch dark under the yews, light comes out through the half-open church door. Figures are lurking, or moving stealthily—people waiting and listening to the sound of a voice speaking in the church words that are inaudible. Excited whispering and faint giggles come from the deepest yew-tree shade, made ghostly by the white faces and the frocks of young girls continually flitting up and back in the blackness. A girl's figure comes flying out from the porch, down the path of light, and joins the stealthy group.

Whispering Voice of Mercy. Where's 'e got to now, Gladys?

Whispering Voice of Gladys. 'E've just finished.

Voice of Connie. Whü pushed t'door open?

Voice of Gladys. Tim Clyst—I giv' it a little push, meself.

Voice of Connie. Oh!

Voice of Gladys. Tim Clyst's gone in!

Another Voice. O-o-o-h!

Voice of Mercy. Whü else is there, tü?

Voice of Gladys. Ivy's there, an' old Mrs. Potter, an' tü o' the maids from th' Hall; that's all as ever.

Voice of Connie. Not the old grey mare?

Voice of Gladys. No. She ain't ther'. 'Twill just be th'ymn now, an' the Blessin'. Tibby gone for 'em?

A BIT O' LOVE

Voice of Mercy. Yes.

Voice of Connie. Mr. Burlacombe's gone in home. I saw 'im pass by just now—'e don' like it. Father don't like it neither.

Voice of Mercy. Mr. Strangway shouldn' 'ave taken my skylark, an' thrown father out o' winder. 'Tis goin' to be awful fun! Oh!

> [*She jumps up and down in the darkness. And a voice from far in the shadow says: "Hsssh! Quiet, yü maids!" The voice has ceased speaking in the church. There is a moment's dead silence. The voice speaks again; then from the wheezy little organ come the first faint chords of a hymn.*]

Gladys. "Nearer, my God, to Thee!"

Voice of Mercy. 'Twill be funny, with no one 'ardly singin'.

> [*The sound of the old hymn sung by just six voices comes out to them rather sweet and clear.*]

Gladys. [*Softly.*] 'Tis pretty, tü. Why! They're only singin' one verse!

> [*A moment's silence, and the voice speaks, uplifted, pronouncing the Blessing: "The peace of God———" As the last words die away, dark figures from the inn approach over the grass, till quite a crowd seems standing there without a word spoken. Then from out the church porch come the congregation. Tim Clyst first, hastily lost among the waiting figures in the dark; old Mrs. Potter, a half-blind old lady groping her way and perceiving nothing out of the ordinary; the two maids from the Hall, self-conscious and*]

scared, scuttling along. Last, IVY BURLA-
COMBE *quickly, and starting back at the dim,
half-hidden crowd.*]

VOICE OF GLADYS. [*Whispering.*] Ivy! Here, quick!
[IVY *sways, darts off towards the voice, and is
lost in the shadow.*]

VOICE OF FREMAN. [*Low.*] Wait, boys, till I give signal.
[*Two or three squirks and giggles;* TIM CLYST'S
voice: "Ya-as! Don't 'ee tread on my toe!"
A soft, frightened "O-o-h!" *from a girl. Some
quick, excited whisperings:* "Lüke!" "Zee
there!" "He's comin'!" *And then a perfectly
dead silence. The figure of* STRANGWAY *is seen
in his dark clothes, passing from the vestry to
the church porch. He stands plainly visible in
the lighted porch, locking the door, then steps
forward. Just as he reaches the edge of the
porch, a low hiss breaks the silence. It swells
very gradually into a long, hissing groan.*
STRANGWAY *stands motionless, his hand over
his eyes, staring into the darkness. A girl's
figure can be seen to break out of the darkness
and rush away. When at last the groaning has
died into sheer expectancy,* STRANGWAY *drops
his hand.*]

STRANGWAY. [*In a low voice.*] Yes! I'm glad. Is Jarland there?

FREMAN. He's 'ere—no thanks to yü! Hsss!

[*The hiss breaks out again, then dies away.*
JARLAND'S VOICE. [*Threatening.*] Try if yü can dü it again.

STRANGWAY. No, Jarland, no! I ask you to forgive me. Humbly!

[*A hesitating silence, broken by muttering.*

CLYST'S VOICE. Bravo!

A VOICE. That's vair!

A VOICE. 'E's afraid o' the sack—that's what 'tis.

A VOICE. [*Groaning.*] 'E's a praaper coward.

A VOICE. Whü funked the doctor?

CLYST'S VOICE. Shame on 'ee, therr!

STRANGWAY. You're right—all of you! I'm not fit!

[*An uneasy and excited muttering and whispering dies away into renewed silence.*]

STRANGWAY. What I did to Tam Jarland is not the real cause of what you're doing, is it? I understand. But don't be troubled. It's all over. I'm going—you'll get some one better. Forgive me, Jarland. I can't see your face—it's very dark.

FREMAN'S VOICE. [*Mocking.*] Wait fer the full müne.

GOLDLEIGH. [*Very low.*] "My 'eart 'E lighted not!"

STRANGWAY. [*Staring at the sound of his own words thus mysteriously given him out of the darkness.*] Whoever found that, please tear it up! [*After a moment's silence.*] Many of you have been very kind to me. You won't see me again— Good-bye, all!

[*He stands for a second motionless, then moves resolutely down into the darkness so peopled with shadows.*]

UNCERTAIN VOICES AS HE PASSES. Good-bye, zurr! Good luck, zurr! [*He has gone.*

CLYST'S VOICE. Three cheers for Mr. Strangway!

[*And a queer, strangled cheer, with groans still threading it, arises.*]

The curtain falls.

ACT III

SCENE I

In the BURLACOMBES' *hall sitting-room, the curtains are drawn, a lamp burns, and the door stands open.* BURLACOMBE *and his wife are hovering there, listening to the sound of mingled cheers and groaning.*

MRS. BURLACOMBE. Aw! my güdeness—what a thing t'appen! I'd süner 'a lost all me ducks. [*She makes towards the inner door.*] I can't never face 'im.

BURLACOMBE. 'E can't expect nothin' else, if 'e act like that.

MRS. BURLACOMBE. 'Tes only düin' as 'e'd be done by.

BURLACOMBE. Aw! Yü can't go on forgivin' 'ere, an' forgivin' there. 'Tesn't nat'ral.

MRS. BURLACOMBE. 'Tes the mischief 'e'm a parson. 'Tes 'im bein' a lamb o' God—or 'twidden be so quare for 'im to be forgivin'.

BURLACOMBE. Yü goo an' make un a güde 'ot drink.

MRS. BURLACOMBE. Poor soul! What'll 'e dü now, I wonder? [*Under her breath.*] 'E's comin'!

> [*She goes hurriedly.* BURLACOMBE, *with a startled look back, wavers and makes to follow her, but stops undecided in the inner doorway.* STRANGWAY *comes in from the darkness. He turns to the window and drops overcoat and hat and the church key on the window-seat, looking about him as men do when too hard driven, and never fixing his eyes long enough on anything to see it.* BURLACOMBE, *closing the door into the house, advances a step. At the sound* STRANGWAY *faces round.*]

A BIT O' LOVE

BURLACOMBE. I wanted for yü to know, zurr, that me an' mine 'adn't nothin' to dü wi' that darned fülishness, just now.

STRANGWAY. [*With a ghost of a smile.*] Thank you, Burlacombe. It doesn't matter. It doesn't matter a bit.

BURLACOMBE. I 'ope yü won't take no notice of it. Like a lot o' silly bees they get. [*After an uneasy pause.*] Yü'll excuse me spakin' of this mornin', an' what 'appened. 'Tes a brave pity it cam' on yü so sudden-like before yü 'ad time to think. 'Tes a sort o' thing a man shüde zet an' chew upon. Certainly 'tes not a bit o' yüse goin' against human nature. Ef yü don't stand up for yüreself there's no one else not goin' to. 'Tes yüre not 'avin' done that 'as made 'em so rampageous. [*Stealing another look at* STRANGWAY.] Yü'll excuse me, zurr, spakin' of it, but 'tes amazin' sad to zee a man let go his own, without a word o' darin'. 'Tes as ef 'e 'ad no passions-like.

STRANGWAY. Look at me, Burlacombe.

[BURLACOMBE *looks up, trying hard to keep his eyes on* STRANGWAY'S, *that seem to burn in his thin face.*]

STRANGWAY. Do I look like that? Please, please! [*He touches his breast.*] I've too much here. Please!

BURLACOMBE. [*With a sort of startled respect.*] Well, zurr, 'tes not for me to zay nothin', certainly.

[*He turns and after a slow look back at* STRANGWAY *goes out.*]

STRANGWAY. [*To himself.*] Passions! No passions! Ha!

[*The outer door is opened and* IVY BURLACOMBE *appears, and, seeing him, stops. Then, coming softly towards him, she speaks timidly.*]

IVY. Oh! Mr. Strangway, Mrs. Bradmere's comin' from the Rectory. I ran an' told 'em. Oh! 'twas awful.

[STRANGWAY *starts, stares at her, and turning*

on his heel, goes into the house. Ivy's face is all puckered, as if she were on the point of tears. There is a gentle scratching at the door, which has not been quite closed.]

VOICE OF GLADYS. [*Whispering.*] Ivy! Come on!

IVY. I won't.

VOICE OF MERCY. Yü must. Us can't dü without yü.

IVY. [*Going to the door.*] I don't want to.

VOICE OF GLADYS. "Naughty maid, she won't come out," Ah! dü 'ee!

VOICE OF CONNIE. Tim Clyst an' Bobbie's comin'; us'll only be six anyway. Us can't dance "figure of eight" without yü.

IVY. [*Stamping her foot.*] I don't want to dance at all! I don't.

MERCY. Aw! She's temper. Yü can bang on tambourine, then!

GLADYS. [*Running in.*] Quick, Ivy! Here's the old grey mare comin' down the green. Quick.

[*With whispering and scuffling, gurgling and speaking, the reluctant Ivy's hand is caught and she is jerked away. In their haste they have left the door open behind them.*]

VOICE OF MRS. BRADMERE. [*Outside.*] Who's that?

[*She knocks loudly, and rings a bell; then, without waiting, comes in through the open door.*]

[*Noting the overcoat and hat on the window-sill she moves across to ring the bell. But as she does so, MRS. BURLACOMBE, followed by BURLACOMBE, comes in from the house.*]

MRS. BRADMERE. This disgraceful business! Where's Mr. Strangway? I see he's in.

MRS. BURLACOMBE. Yes, m'm, he'm in—but—but Burlacombe dü zay he'm terrible upzet.

A BIT O' LOVE

MRS. BRADMERE. I should think so. I must see him—at once.

MRS. BURLACOMBE. I doubt bed's the best place for un, an' a güde 'ot drink. Burlacombe zays he'm like a man standin' on the edge of a cliff, and the laste tipsy o' wind might throw un over.

MRS. BRADMERE. [*To* BURLACOMBE.] You've seen him, then?

BURLACOMBE. Yeas; an' I don't like the lüke of un—not a little bit, I don't.

MRS. BURLACOMBE. [*Almost to herself.*] Poor soul; 'e've a-'ad tü much to try un this yer long time past. I've a-seen 'tis sperrit comin' thrü 'is body, as yü might say. He's torn to bits, that's what 'tis.

BURLACOMBE. 'Twas a praaper cowardly thing to hiss a man when he's down. But 'twas natural tü, in a manner of spakin'. But 'tesn't that troublin' 'im. 'Tes in here [*touching his forehead*], along of his wife, to my thinkin'. They zay 'e've a-known about 'er afore she went away. Think of what 'e've 'ad to kape in all this time. 'Tes enough to drive a man silly after that. I've a-locked my gun up. I see a man lüke like that once before—an' sure enough 'e was dead in the mornin'!

MRS. BRADMERE. Nonsense, Burlacombe! [*To* MRS. BURLACOMBE.] Go and tell him I want to see him—must see him. [MRS. BURLACOMBE *goes into the house.*] And look here, Burlacombe; if we catch any one, man or woman, talking of this outside the village, it'll be the end of their tenancy, whoever they may be. Let them all know that. I'm glad he threw that drunken fellow out of the window though it was a little——

BURLACOMBE. Aye! The nüspapers would be praaper glad of that, for a tiddy bit o' nüse.

MRS. BRADMERE. My goodness! Yes! The men are all

up at the inn. Go and tell them what I said—*it's not to get about.* Go at once, Burlacombe.

BURLACOMBE. Must be a turrable job for 'im, every one's knowin' about 'is wife like this. He'm a proud man, tü, I think. 'Tes a funny business altogether!

MRS. BRADMERE. Horrible! Poor fellow! Now, come! Do your best, Burlacombe!

> [BURLACOMBE *touches his forelock and goes.* MRS. BRADMERE *stands quite still, thinking. Then going to the photograph, she stares up at it.*]

MRS. BRADMERE. You baggage!

> [STRANGWAY *has come in noiselessly, and is standing just behind her. She turns, and sees him. There is something so still, so startlingly still in his figure and white face, that she cannot for the moment find her voice.*]

MRS. BRADMERE. [*At last.*] This is most distressing. I'm deeply sorry. [*Then as he does not answer, she goes a step closer.*] I'm an old woman, and old women must take liberties, you know, or they couldn't get on at all. Come now! Let's try and talk it over calmly and see if we can't put things right.

STRANGWAY. You were very good to come; but I would rather not.

MRS. BRADMERE. I know you're in as grievous trouble as a man can be.

STRANGWAY. Yes.

MRS. BRADMERE. [*With a little sound of sympathy.*] What are you—thirty-five? I'm sixty-eight if I'm a day —old enough to be your mother. I can feel what you must have been through all these months, I can indeed. But you know you've gone the wrong way to work. We aren't angels down here below! And a son of the Church can't

A BIT O' LOVE

act as if for himself alone. The eyes of every one are on him.

STRANGWAY. [*Taking the church key from the window-sill.*] Take this, please.

MRS. BRADMERE. No, no, no! Jarland deserved all he got. You had great provocation——

STRANGWAY. It's not Jarland. [*Holding out the key.*] Please take it to the Rector. I beg his forgiveness. [*Touching his breast.*] There's too much I can't speak of—can't make plain. Take it to him, please.

MRS. BRADMERE. Mr. Strangway—I don't accept this. I am sure my husband—the Church—will never accept——

STRANGWAY. Take it!

MRS. BRADMERE. [*Almost unconsciously taking it.*] Mind! We don't accept it. You must come and talk to the Rector to-morrow. You're overwrought. You'll see it all in another light, then.

STRANGWAY. [*With a strange smile.*] Perhaps. [*Lifting the blind.*] Beautiful night! Couldn't be more beautiful!

MRS. BRADMERE. [*Startled—softly.*] Don't turn away from those who want to help you! I'm a grumpy old woman, but I can feel for you. Don't try and keep it all back, like this! A woman would cry, and it would all seem clearer at once. Now won't you let me——?

STRANGWAY. No one can help, thank you.

MRS. BRADMERE. Come! Things haven't gone beyond mending, really, if you'll face them. [*Pointing to the photograph.*] You know what I mean. We dare not foster immorality.

STRANGWAY. [*Quivering as at a jabbed nerve.*] Don't speak of that!

MRS. BRADMERE. But think what you've done, Mr. Strangway! If you can't take your wife back, surely you must divorce her. You can never help her to go on like this in secret sin.

STRANGWAY. Torture her—one way or the other?

MRS. BRADMERE. No, no; I want you to do as the Church—as all Christian society would wish. Come! You can't let this go on. My dear man, do your duty at all costs!

STRANGWAY. Break her heart?

MRS. BRADMERE. Then you love that woman—more than God!

STRANGWAY. [*His face quivering.*] Love!

MRS. BRADMERE. They told me— Yes, and I can see you're in a bad way. Come, pull yourself together! You can't defend what you're doing.

STRANGWAY. I do not try.

MRS. BRADMERE. I *must* get you to see! My father was a clergyman; I'm married to one; I've two sons in the Church. I know what I'm talking about. It's a priest's business to guide the people's lives.

STRANGWAY. [*Very low.*] But not mine! No more!

MRS. BRADMERE. [*Looking at him shrewdly.*] There's something very queer about you to-night. You ought to see a doctor.

STRANGWAY. [*A smile coming and going on his lips.*] If I am not better soon——

MRS. BRADMERE. I know it must be terrible to feel that everybody— [*A convulsive shiver passes over* STRANGWAY, *and he shrinks against the door.*] But come! Live it down! [*With anger growing at his silence.*] Live it down, man! You can't desert your post—and let these villagers do what they like with us? Do you realize that you're letting a woman, who has treated you abominably—yes, abominably—go scot-free, to live comfortably with another man? What an example!

STRANGWAY. Will you, please, not speak of that!

A BIT O' LOVE

Mrs. Bradmere. I must! This great Church of ours is based on the rightful condemnation of wrong-doing. There are times when forgiveness is a sin, Michael Strangway. You must keep the whip hand. You must fight!

Strangway. Fight! [*Touching his heart.*] My fight is *here*. Have *you* ever been in hell? For months and months —burned and longed; hoped against hope; killed a man in thought day by day? Never rested, for love and hate? I—condemn! I—judge! No! It's rest I have to find— somewhere—somehow—rest! And how—how can I find rest?

Mrs. Bradmere. [*Who has listened to his outburst in a sort of coma.*] You are a strange man! One of these days you'll go off your head if you don't take care.

Strangway. [*Smiling.*] One of these days the flowers will grow out of me; and I shall sleep.

> [Mrs. Bradmere *stares at his smiling face a long moment in silence, then with a little sound, half sniff, half snort, she goes to the door. There she halts.*]

Mrs. Bradmere. And you mean to let all this go on— Your wife——

Strangway. Go! Please go!

Mrs. Bradmere. Men like you have been buried at cross-roads before now! Take care! God punishes!

Strangway. Is there a God?

Mrs. Bradmere. Ah! [*With finality.*] You must see a doctor.

> [*Seeing that the look on his face does not change, she opens the doors and hurries away into the moonlight.*]
>
> [Strangway *crosses the room to where his wife's picture hangs, and stands before it, his hands grasping the frame. Then he takes it from*

A BIT O' LOVE

the wall, and lays it face upwards on the window-seat.]

STRANGWAY. [*To himself.*] Gone! What is there, now?

[*The sound of an owl's hooting is floating in, and of voices from the green outside the inn.*]

STRANGWAY. [*To himself.*] Gone! Taken faith—hope—life!

[JIM BERE *comes wandering into the open doorway.*]

JIM BERE. Güde avenin', zurr.

[*At his slow gait, with his feeble smile, he comes in, and standing by the window-seat beside the long dark coat that still lies there, he looks down at* STRANGWAY *with his lost eyes.*]

JIM. Yü threw un out of winder. I cud 'ave, once, I cud. [STRANGWAY *neither moves nor speaks; and* JIM BERE *goes on with his unimaginably slow speech.*] They'm laughin' at yü, zurr. An' so I come to tell 'ee how to dü. 'Twas full müne—when I caught 'em, him an' my girl. I caught 'em. [*With a strange and awful flash of fire.*] I did; an' I tuk un [*He takes up* STRANGWAY'S *coat and grips it with his trembling hands, as a man grips another's neck*] like that—I tuk un.

[*As the coat falls, like a body out of which the breath has been squeezed,* STRANGWAY, *rising, catches it.*]

STRANGWAY. [*Gripping the coat.*] And he fell!

[*He lets the coat fall on the floor, and puts his foot on it. Then, staggering back, he leans against the window.*]

JIM. Yü see, I loved 'er—I did. [*The lost look comes back to his eyes.*] Then somethin'—I dunno—and—and— [*He lifts his hand and passes it up and down his side.*] 'Twas like this for ever.

[They gaze at each other in silence.

JIM. [*At last.*] I come to tell yü. They'm all laughin' at yü. But yü'm strong—yü go over to Durford to that doctor man, an' take un like I did. [*He tries again to make the sign of squeezing a man's neck.*] They can't laugh at yü no more, then. Tha's what I come to tell yü. Tha's the way for a Christian man to dü. Güde naight, zurr. I come to tell yee.

> [STRANGWAY *motions to him in silence. And, very slowly,* JIM BERE *passes out.*]
> [*The voices of men coming down the green are heard.*]

VOICES. Güde naight, Tam. Güde naight, old Jim!

VOICES. Güde naight, Mr. Trustaford. 'Tes a wonderful fine müne.

VOICE OF TRUSTAFORD. Ah! 'Tes a brave müne for th' poor old curate!

VOICE. "My 'eart 'E lighted not!"

> [TRUSTAFORD'S *laugh, and the rattling, fainter and fainter, of wheels. A spasm seizes on* STRANGWAY'S *face, as he stands there by the open door, his hand grips his throat; he looks from side to side, as if seeking a way of escape.*]

The curtain falls.

SCENE II

The BURLACOMBES' *high and nearly empty barn. A lantern is hung by a rope that lifts the bales of straw, to a long ladder leaning against a rafter. This gives all the light there is save for a slender track of moonlight, slanting in from the end, where the two great doors are not quite closed. On a rude bench in front of a few remaining*

*stacked, square-cut bundles of last year's hay, sits
TIBBY JARLAND, a bit of apple in her mouth, sleepily
beating on a tambourine. With stockinged feet GLADYS,
IVY, CONNIE, and MERCY, TIM CLYST, and BOBBIE
JARLAND, a boy of fifteen, are dancing a truncated
"Figure of Eight"; and their shadows are dancing
alongside on the walls. Shoes and some apples have
been thrown down close to the side door through which
they have come in. Now and then IVY, the smallest
and best of the dancers, ejaculates words of direction, and one of the youths grunts or breathes loudly
out of the confusion of his mind. Save for this and
the dumb beat and jingle of the sleepy tambourine,
there is no sound. The dance comes to its end, but
the drowsy TIBBY goes on beating.*

MERCY. That'll dü, Tibby; we're finished. Ate yüre apple.   [*The stolid TIBBY eats her apple.*

CLYST. [*In his teasing, excitable voice.*] Yü maids don't dance 'alf's well as us dü. Bobbie 'e's a great dancer. 'E dance vine. I'm a güde dancer, meself.

GLADYS. A'n't yü conceited just?

CLYST. Aw! Ah! Yü'll give me kiss for that. [*He chases, but cannot catch that slippery white figure.*] Can't she glimmer!

MERCY. Gladys! Up ladder!

CLYST. Yü go up ladder; I'll catch 'ee then. Naw, yü maids, don't yü give her succour. That's not vair.

[*Catching hold of MERCY, who gives a little squeal.*

CONNIE. Mercy, don't! Mrs. Burlacombe'll hear. Ivy, go an' peek.

[*IVY goes to the side door and peers through.*

CLYST. [*Abandoning the chase and picking up an apple —they all have the joyous irresponsibility that attends forbidden doings.*] Ya'as, this is a güde apple. Lüke at Tibby!

> [TIBBY, *overcome by drowsiness, has fallen back into the hay, asleep.* GLADYS, *leaning against the hay breaks into humming:*]

"There cam' three dükes a-ridin', a-ridin', a-ridin',
There cam' three dükes a-ridin'
With a ransy-tansy tay!"

CLYST. Us 'as got on vine; us'll get prize for our dancin'.

CONNIE. There won't be no prize if Mr. Strangway goes away. 'Tes funny 'twas Mrs. Strangway started us.

IVY. [*From the door.*] 'Twas wicked to hiss him.

[*A moment's hush.*

CLYST. 'Twasn't I.

BOBBIE. I never did.

GLADYS. Oh! Bobbie, yü did! Yü blew in my ear.

CLYST. 'Twas the praaper old wind in the trees. Did make a brave noise, zürely.

MERCY. 'E shouldn' 'a let my skylark go.

CLYST. [*Out of sheer contradictoriness.*] Ya'as, 'e shüde, then. What dü yü want with th' birds of the air? They'm no güde to yü.

IVY. [*Mournfully.*] And now he's goin' away.

CLYST. Ya'as; 'tes a pity. He's the best man I ever seen since I was comin' from my mother. He's a güde man. He'm got a zad face, sure enough, though.

IVY. Güde folks always 'ave zad faces.

CLYST. I knü a güde man—'e sold pigs—very güde man: 'e 'ad a büdiful bright vace like the müne. [*Touching his stomach.*] I was sad, meself, once. 'Twas a funny scrabblin'-like feelin'.

GLADYS. If 'e go away, whü's goin' to finish us for confirmation?

CONNIE. The Rector and the old grey mare.

MERCY. I don' want no more finishin'; I'm confirmed enough.

CLYST. Ya'as; yü'm a büty.

GLADYS. Suppose we all went an' asked 'im not to go?

IVY. 'Twouldn't be no güde.

CONNIE. Where's 'e goin'?

MERCY. He'll go to London, of course.

IVY. He's so gentle; I think 'e'll go to an island, where there's nothin' but birds and beasts and flowers.

CLYST. Aye! He'm awful fond o' the dumb things.

IVY. They're kind and peaceful; that's why.

CLYST. Aw! Yü see tü praaper old tom cats; they'm not tü peaceful, after that, nor kind naighther.

BOBBIE. [*Surprisingly.*] If 'e's sad, per'aps 'e'll go to 'Eaven.

IVY. Oh! not yet, Bobbie. He's tü young.

CLYST. [*Following his own thoughts.*] Ya'as. 'Tes a funny place, tü, nowadays, judgin' from the papers.

GLADYS. Wonder if there's dancin' in 'Eaven?

IVY. There's beasts, and flowers, and waters, and trees—'e told us.

CLYST. Naw! There's no dumb things in 'Eaven. Jim Bere 'e says there is! 'E thinks 'is old cat's there.

IVY. Yes. [*Dreamily.*] There's stars, an' owls, an' a man playin' on the flute. Where 'tes güde, there must be müsic.

CLYST. Old brass band, shouldn' wonder, like th' Salvation Army.

IVY. [*Putting up her hands to an imaginary pipe.*] No; 'tis a boy that goes so; an' all the dumb things an' all the people goo after 'im—like this.

[*She marches slowly, playing her imaginary pipe, and one by one they all fall in behind her, padding round the barn in their stockinged feet. Passing the big doors,* IVY *throws them open.*]

An' 'tes all like that in 'Eaven.

[*She stands there gazing out, still playing on her imaginary pipe. And they all stand a moment silent, staring into the moonlight.*]

CLYST. 'Tes a glory-be full müne to-night!

IVY. A goldie-cup—a big one. An' millions o' little goldie-cups on the floor of 'Eaven.

MERCY. Oh! Bother 'Eaven! Let's dance "Clapperclaws"! Wake up, Tibby!

GLADYS. Clapperclaws, clapperclaws! Come on, Bobbie—make circle!

CLYST. Clapperclaws! I dance that one fine.

IVY. [*Taking the tambourine.*] See, Tibby; like this.

[*She hums and beats gently, then restores the tambourine to the sleepy* TIBBY, *who, waking, has placed a piece of apple in her mouth.*]

CONNIE. 'Tes awful difficult, this one.

IVY. [*Illustrating.*] No; yü just jump, an' clap yüre 'ands. Lovely, lovely!

CLYST. Like ringin' bells! Come ahn!

[TIBBY *begins her drowsy beating,* IVY *hums the tune; they dance, and their shadows dance again upon the walls. When she has beaten but a few moments on the tambourine,* TIBBY *is overcome once more by sleep and falls back again into her nest of hay, with her little shoed feet just visible over the edge of the bench.* IVY *catches up the tambourine, and to her beating and humming the dancers dance on.*]

[*Suddenly* GLADYS *stops like a wild animal sur-*

prised, and cranes her neck towards the side door.]

CONNIE. [*Whispering.*] What is it?

GLADYS. [*Whispering.*] I hear—some one—comin' across the yard.

[*She leads a noiseless scamper towards the shoes. BOBBIE JARLAND shins up the ladder and seizes the lantern. IVY drops the tambourine. They all fly to the big doors, and vanish into the moonlight, pulling the doors nearly to again after them.*]

[*There is the sound of scrabbling at the latch of the side door, and STRANGWAY comes into the nearly dark barn. Out in the night the owl is still hooting. He closes the door, and that sound is lost. Like a man walking in his sleep, he goes up to the ladder, takes the rope in his hand, and makes a noose. He can be heard breathing, and in the darkness the motions of his hands are dimly seen, freeing his throat and putting the noose around his neck. He stands swaying to and fro at the foot of the ladder; then, with a sigh, sets his foot on it to mount. One of the big doors creaks and opens in the wind, letting in a broad path of moonlight.*]

STRANGWAY *stops; freeing his neck from the noose, he walks quickly up the track of moonlight, whitened from head to foot, to close the doors.*]

[*The sound of his boots on the bare floor has awakened TIBBY JARLAND. Struggling out of her hay nest she stands staring at his whitened figure, and bursts suddenly into a wail.*]

A BIT O' LOVE

TIBBY. O-oh! Mercy! Where are yü? I'm frightened! I'm frightened! O-oooo!

STRANGWAY. [*Turning—startled.*] Who's that? Who is it?

TIBBY. O-oh! A ghosty! Oo-ooo!

STRANGWAY. [*Going to her quickly.*] It's me, Tibby— Tib—only me!

TIBBY. I see'd a ghosty.

STRANGWAY. [*Taking her up.*] No, no, my bird, you didn't! It was me.

TIBBY. [*Burying her face against him.*] I'm frightened. It was a big one. [*She gives tongue again.*] O-o-oh!

STRANGWAY. There, there! It's nothing but me. Look!

TIBBY. No. [*She peeps out all the same.*]

STRANGWAY. See! It's the moonlight made me all white. See! You're a brave girl now?

TIBBY. [*Cautiously.*] I want my apple.

> [*She points towards her nest.* STRANGWAY *carries her there, picks up an apple, and gives it her.* TIBBY *takes a bite.*]

TIBBY. I want my tambouline.

STRANGWAY. [*Giving her the tambourine, and carrying her back into the track of moonlight.*] Now we're both ghosties! Isn't it funny?

TIBBY. [*Doubtfully.*] Yes.

STRANGWAY. See! The moon's laughing at us! See? Laugh then!

> [TIBBY, *tambourine in one hand and apple in the other, smiles stolidly. He sets her down on the ladder, and stands, holding her level with him.*]

TIBBY. [*Solemnly.*] I'se still frighted.

STRANGWAY No! Full moon, Tibby! Shall we wish for it?

TIBBY. Full müne.

STRANGWAY. Moon! We're wishing for you. Moon, Moon! TIBBY. Müne, we're wishin' for yü!

STRANGWAY. What do you wish it to be?

TIBBY. Full müne.

STRANGWAY. Moon! We're wishing for you. Moon, Moon!

TIBBY. Müne, we're wishin' for yü!

STRANGWAY. [*Taking out a shilling and spinning it so that it falls into her pinafore.*] See! *Your* wish comes true.

TIBBY. Oh! [*Putting the shilling in her mouth.*] Müne's still there!

STRANGWAY. Wish for *me*, Tibby!

TIBBY. Müne, I'm wishin' for yü!

STRANGWAY. Not yet!

TIBBY. Shall I shake my tambouline?

STRANGWAY. Yes, shake your tambouline.

TIBBY. [*Shaking her tambourine.*] Müne, I'm shakin' at yü.

[STRANGWAY *lays his hand suddenly on the rope, and swings it up on to the beam.*]

TIBBY. What d'yü dü that for?

STRANGWAY. To put it out of reach. It's better——

TIBBY. Why is it better? [*She stares up at him.*]

STRANGWAY. Come along, Tibby! [*He carries her to the big doors, and sets her down.*] See! All asleep! The birds, and the fields, and the moon!

TIBBY. Müne, müne, we're wishing for yü!

STRANGWAY. Send her your love, and say good-night.

TIBBY. [*Blowing a kiss.*] Good-night, müne!

[*From the barn roof a little white dove's feather comes floating down in the wind.* TIBBY *follows it with her hand, catches it, and holds it up to him.*]

A BIT O' LOVE

TIBBY. [*Chuckling.*] Lüke. The müne's sent a bit o' love!

STRANGWAY. [*Taking the feather.*] Thank you, Tibby! I want that bit o' love. [*Very faint, comes the sound of music.*] Listen!

TIBBY. It's Miss Willis, playin' on the pianny!

STRANGWAY. No; it's Love; walking and talking in the world.

TIBBY. [*Dubiously.*] Is it?

STRANGWAY. [*Pointing.*] See! Everything coming out to listen! See them, Tibby! All the little things with pointed ears, children, and birds, and flowers, and bunnies; and the bright rocks, and—men! Hear their hearts beating! And the wind listening!

TIBBY. I can't hear—nor I can't see!

STRANGWAY. Beyond—— [*To himself.*] They are—they must be; I swear they are! [*Then, catching sight of* TIBBY's *amazed eyes.*] And now say good-bye to me.

TIBBY. Where yü goin'?

STRANGWAY. I don't know, Tibby.

VOICE OF MERCY. [*Distant and cautious.*] Tibby! Tibby! Where are yü?

STRANGWAY. Mercy calling; run to her!

> [TIBBY *starts off, turns back and lifts her face. He bends to kiss her, and flinging her arms round his neck, she gives him a good hug. Then, knuckling the sleep out of her eyes, she runs.*]

> [STRANGWAY *stands, uncertain. There is a sound of heavy footsteps; a man clears his throat, close by.*]

STRANGWAY. Who's that?

CREMER. Jack Cremer. [*The big man's figure appears out of the shadow of the barn.*] That yü, zurr?

STRANGWAY. Yes, Jack. How goes it?

CREMER. 'Tes empty, zurr. But I'll get on some'ow.

STRANGWAY. You put me to shame.

CREMER. No, zurr. I'd be killin' meself, if I didn' feel I must stick it, like yü zaid.

> [*They stand gazing at each other in the moonlight.*]

STRANGWAY. [*Very low.*] I honour you.

CREMER. What's that? [*Then, as* SRANGWAY *does not answer.*] I'll just be walkin'—I won' be goin' 'ome to-night. 'Tes the full müne—lucky.

STRANGWAY. [*Suddenly.*] Wait for me at the cross-roads, Jack. I'll come with you. Will you have me, brother?

CREMER. Sure!

STRANGWAY. Wait, then.

CREMER. Aye, zurr.

> [*With his heavy tread* CREMER *passes on. And* STRANGWAY *leans against the lintel of the door, looking at the moon, that, quite full and golden, hangs not far above the straight horizon, where the trees stand small, in a row.*]

STRANGWAY. [*Lifting his hand in the gesture of prayer.*] God, of the moon and the sun; of joy and beauty, of loneliness and sorrow—give me strength to go on, till I love every living thing!

> [*He moves away, following* JACK CREMER. *The full moon shines; the owl hoots; and some one is shaking* TIBBY's *tambourine.*]

The curtain falls.

LOYALTIES

PERSONS OF THE PLAY

In the Order of Appearance

CHARLES WINSOR, *owner of Meldon Court, near Newmarket*
LADY ADELA, *his wife*
FERDINAND DE LEVIS, *young, rich, and new*
TREISURE, *Winsor's butler*
GENERAL CANYNGE, *a racing oracle*
MARGARET ORME, *a society girl*
CAPTAIN RONALD DANCY, D. S. O., *retired*
MABEL, *his wife*
INSPECTOR DEDE, *of the County Constabulary*
ROBERT, *Winsor's footman*
A CONSTABLE, *Attendant on Dede*
AUGUSTUS BORRING, *a clubman*
LORD ST ERTH, *a peer of the realm*
A FOOTMAN, *of the club*
MAJOR COLFORD, *a brother officer of Dancy's*
EDWARD GRAVITER, *a solicitor*
A YOUNG CLERK, *of Twisden & Graviter's*
GILMAN, *a large grocer*
JACOB TWISDEN, *senior partner of Twisden & Graviter's*
RICARDOS, *an Italian, in wine*

ACT I.
    SCENE   I. CHARLES WINSOR's *dressing-room at Meldon Court, near Newmarket, of a night in early October.*
    SCENE II. DE LEVIS's *bedroom at Meldon Court, a few minutes later.*

ACT II.
    SCENE   I. *The card room of a London Club between four and five in the afternoon, three weeks later.*
    SCENE II. *The sitting-room of the* DANCY's *flat, the following morning.*

ACT III.
    SCENE   I. *Old* MR. JACOB TWISDEN's *room at* TWISDEN & GRAVITER's *in Lincoln's Inn Fields at four in the afternoon, three months later.*
    SCENE II. *The same, next morning at half-past ten.*
    SCENE III. *The sitting-room of the* DANCY's *flat, an hour later.*

ACT I

SCENE I

The dressing-room of CHARLES WINSOR, *owner of Meldon Court, near Newmarket; about eleven-thirty at night. The room has pale grey walls, unadorned; the curtains are drawn over a window Back Left Centre. A bed lies along the wall, Left. An open door, Right Back, leads into* LADY ADELA'S *bedroom; a door, Right Forward, into a long corridor, on to which abut rooms in a row, the whole length of the house's left wing.* WINSOR'S *dressing-table, with a light over it, is Stage Right of the curtained window. Pyjamas are laid out on the bed, which is turned back. Slippers are handy, and all the usual gear of a well-appointed bed-dressing-room.* CHARLES WINSOR, *a tall, fair, good-looking man about thirty-eight, is taking off a smoking-jacket.*

WINSOR. Hallo! Adela!

V. OF LADY A. [*From her bedroom.*] Hallo!

WINSOR. In bed?

V. OF LADY A. No.

> [*She appears in the doorway in under-garment and a wrapper. She, too, is fair, about thirty-five, rather delicious, and suggestive of porcelain.*]

WINSOR. Win at Bridge?

LADY A. No fear.

WINSOR. Who did?

LADY A. Lord St Erth and Ferdy De Levis.

WINSOR. That young man has too much luck—the young bounder won two races to-day; and he's as rich as Crœsus.

LADY A. Oh! Charlie, he did look so exactly as if he'd sold me a carpet when I was paying him.

WINSOR. [*Changing into slippers.*] His father did sell carpets, wholesale, in the City.

LADY A. Really? And you say I haven't intuition! [*With a finger on her lips.*] Morison's in there.

WINSOR. [*Motioning towards the door, which she shuts.*] Ronny Dancy took a tenner off him, anyway, before dinner.

LADY A. No! How?

WINSOR. Standing jump on to a book-case four feet high. De Levis had to pay up, and sneered at him for making money by parlour tricks. That young Jew gets himself disliked.

LADY A. Aren't you rather prejudiced?

WINSOR. Not a bit. I like Jews. That's not against him—rather the contrary these days. But he pushes himself. The General tells me he's deathly keen to get into the Jockey Club. [*Taking off his tie.*] It's amusing to see him trying to get round old St Erth.

LADY A. If Lord St Erth and General Canynge backed him he'd get in if he *did* sell carpets!

WINSOR. He's got some pretty good horses. [*Taking off his waistcoat.*] Ronny Dancy's on his bones again, I'm afraid. He had a bad day. When a chap takes to doing parlour stunts for a bet—it's a sure sign. What made him chuck the Army?

LADY A. He says it's too dull, now there's no fighting.

WINSOR. Well, he can't exist on backing losers.

LADY A. Isn't it just like him to get married now? He really is the most reckless person.

WINSOR. Yes. He's a queer chap. I've always liked

LOYALTIES

him, but I've never quite made him out. What do you think of his wife?

LADY A. Nice child; awfully gone on him.

WINSOR. Is *he?*

LADY A. Quite indecently—both of them. [*Nodding towards the wall, Left.*] They're next door.

WINSOR. Who's beyond them?

LADY A. De Levis; and Margaret Orme at the end. Charlie, do you realise that the bathroom out there has to wash those four?

WINSOR. I know.

LADY A. Your grandfather was crazy when he built this wing; six rooms in a row with balconies like an hotel, and only one bath—if we hadn't put ours in.

WINSOR. [*Looking at his watch.*] Half-past eleven. [*Yawns.*] Newmarket always makes me sleepy. You're keeping Morison up.

> [LADY ADELA *goes to the door, blowing a kiss.*]
> [CHARLES *goes up to his dressing-table and begins to brush his hair, sprinkling on essence. There is a knock on the corridor door.*]

Come in.

> [DE LEVIS *enters, clad in pyjamas and flowered dressing-gown. He is a dark, good-looking, rather Eastern young man. His face is long and disturbed.*]

Hallo! De Levis! Anything I can do for you?

DE LEVIS. [*In a voice whose faint exoticism is broken by a vexed excitement.*] I say, I'm awfully sorry, Winsor, but I thought I'd better tell you at once. I've just had—er—rather a lot of money stolen.

WINSOR. What! [*There is something of outrage in his tone and glance, as who should say: "In my house?"*] How do you mean *stolen?*

DE LEVIS. I put it under my pillow and went to have a bath; when I came back it was gone.

WINSOR. Good Lord! How much?

DE LEVIS. Nearly a thousand—nine hundred and seventy, I think.

WINSOR. Phew! [*Again the faint tone of outrage, that a man should have so much money about him.*]

DE LEVIS. I sold my Rosemary filly to-day on the course to Kentman the bookie, and he paid me in notes.

WINSOR. What? That weed Dancy gave you in the Spring?

DE LEVIS. Yes. But I tried her pretty high the other day; and she's in the Cambridgeshire. I was only out of my room a quarter of an hour, and I locked my door.

WINSOR. [*Again outraged.*] You *locked*——

DE LEVIS. [*Not seeing the fine shade.*] Yes, and had the key here. [*He taps his pocket.*] Look here! [*He holds out a pocket-book.*] It's been stuffed with my shaving papers.

WINSOR. [*Between feeling that such things don't happen, and a sense that he will have to clear it up.*] This is damned awkward, De Levis.

DE LEVIS. [*With steel in his voice.*] Yes, I should like it back.

WINSOR. Have you got the numbers of the notes?

DE LEVIS. No.

WINSOR. What were they?

DE LEVIS. One hundred, three fifties, and the rest tens and fives.

WINSOR. What d'you want me to do?

DE LEVIS. Unless there's anybody you think——

WINSOR. [*Eyeing him.*] Is it likely?

DE LEVIS. Then I think the police ought to see my room. It's a lot of money.

LOYALTIES

WINSOR. Good Lord! We're not in Town; there'll be nobody nearer than Newmarket at this time of night—four miles.

[*The door from the bedroom is suddenly opened and* LADY ADELA *appears. She has on a lace cap over her finished hair, and the wrapper.*]

LADY A. [*Closing the door.*] What is it? Are you ill, Mr. De Levis?

WINSOR. Worse; he's had a lot of money stolen. Nearly a thousand pounds.

LADY A. Gracious! Where?

DE LEVIS. From under my pillow, Lady Adela—my door was locked—I was in the bathroom.

LADY A. But how fearfully thrilling!

WINSOR. Thrilling! What's to be done? He wants it back.

LADY A. Of course! [*With sudden realisation.*] Oh! But—— Oh! it's quite too unpleasant!

WINSOR. Yes! What am I to do? Fetch the servants out of their rooms? Search the grounds? It'll make the devil of a scandal.

DE LEVIS. Who's next to me?

LADY A. [*Coldly.*] Oh! Mr. De Levis!

WINSOR. Next to you? The Dancys on this side, and Miss Orme on the other. What's that to do with it?

DE LEVIS. They may have heard something.

WINSOR. Let's get them. But Dancy was downstairs when I came up. Get Morison, Adela! No, look here! When *was* this exactly? Let's have as many alibis as we can.

DE LEVIS. Within the last twenty minutes, certainly.

WINSOR. How long has Morison been up with you?

LADY A. I came up at eleven, and rang for her at once.

WINSOR. [*Looking at his watch.*] Half an hour. Then

she's all right. Send her for Margaret and the Dancys—there's nobody else in this wing. No; send her to bed. We don't want gossip. D'you mind going yourself, Adela?

LADY A. Consult General Canynge, Charlie.

WINSOR. Right. Could you get him too? D'you really want the police, De Levis?

DE LEVIS. [*Stung by the faint contempt in his tone of voice.*] Yes, I do.

WINSOR. Then, look here, dear! Slip into my study and telephone to the police at Newmarket. There'll be somebody there; they're sure to have drunks. I'll have Treisure up, and speak to him. [*He rings the bell.*]

[LADY ADELA *goes out into her room and closes the door.*]

WINSOR. Look here, De Levis! This isn't an hotel. It's the sort of thing that doesn't happen in a decent house. Are you sure you're not mistaken, and didn't have them stolen on the course?

DE LEVIS. Absolutely. I counted them just before putting them under my pillow; then I locked the door and had the key here. There's only one door, you know.

WINSOR. How was your window?

DE LEVIS. Open.

WINSOR. [*Drawing back the curtains of his own window.*] You've got a balcony like this. Any sign of a ladder or anything?

DE LEVIS. No.

WINSOR. It must have been done from the window, unless someone had a skeleton key. Who knew you'd got that money? Where did Kentman pay you?

DE LEVIS. Just round the corner in the further paddock.

WINSOR. Anybody about?

DE LEVIS. Oh, yes!

WINSOR. Suspicious?

LOYALTIES

DE LEVIS. I didn't notice anything.

WINSOR. You must have been marked down and followed here.

DE LEVIS. How would they know my room?

WINSOR. Might have got it somehow. [*A knock from the corridor.*] Come in.

> [TREISURE, *the Butler, appears, a silent, grave man of almost supernatural conformity.* DE LEVIS *gives him a quick, hard look, noted and resented by* WINSOR.]

TREISURE. [*To* WINSOR.] Yes, sir?

WINSOR. Who valets Mr. De Levis?

TREISURE. Robert, sir.

WINSOR. When was he up last?

TREISURE. In the ordinary course of things, about ten o'clock, sir.

WINSOR. When did he go to bed?

TREISURE. I dismissed at eleven.

WINSOR. But did he go?

TREISURE. To the best of my knowledge. Is there anything *I* can do, sir?

WINSOR. [*Disregarding a sign from* DE LEVIS.] Look here, Treisure, Mr. De Levis has had a large sum of money taken from his bedroom within the last half hour.

TREISURE. Indeed, sir!

WINSOR. Robert's quite all right, isn't he?

TREISURE. He is, sir.

DE LEVIS. How do you know?

> [TREISURE'S *eyes rest on* DE LEVIS.

TREISURE. I am a pretty good judge of character, sir, if you'll excuse me.

WINSOR. Look here, De Levis, eighty or ninety notes must have been pretty bulky. You didn't have them on you at dinner?

De Levis. No.

Winsor. Where did you put them?

De Levis. In a boot, and the boot in my suitcase, and locked it.

[Treisure *smiles faintly.*

Winsor. [*Again slightly outraged by such precautions in his house.*] And you found it locked—and took them from there to put under your pillow?

De Levis. Yes.

Winsor. Run your mind over things, Treisure—has any stranger been about?

Treisure. No, sir.

Winsor. This seems to have happened between 11.15 and 11.30. Is that right? [De Levis *nods.*] Any noise—anything outside—anything suspicious anywhere?

Treisure. [*Running his mind—very still.*] No, sir.

Winsor. What time did you shut up?

Treisure. I should say about eleven-fifteen, sir. As soon as Major Colford and Captain Dancy had finished billiards. What was Mr. De Levis doing out of his room, if I may ask, sir.

Winsor. Having a bath; with his room locked and the key in his pocket.

Treisure. Thank you, sir.

De Levis. [*Conscious of indefinable suspicion.*] Damn it! What do you mean? I *was*.

Treisure. I beg your pardon, sir.

Winsor. [*Concealing a smile.*] Look here, Treisure, it's infernally awkward for everybody.

Treisure. It is, sir.

Winsor. What do you suggest?

Treisure. The proper thing, sir, I suppose, would be a cordon and a complete search—in our interests.

Winsor. I entirely refuse to suspect anybody.

TREISURE. But if Mr. De Levis feels otherwise, sir?

DE LEVIS. [*Stammering.*] All I know is—the money was there, and it's gone.

WINSOR. [*Compunctious.*] Quite! It's pretty sickening for you. But so it is for anybody else. However, we must do our best to get it back for you.

[*A knock on the door.*

WINSOR. Hallo!

[TREISURE *opens the door, and* GENERAL CANYNGE *enters.*]

Oh! It's you, General. Come in. Adela's told you?

[GENERAL CANYNGE *nods. He is a slim man of about sixty, very well preserved, intensely neat and self-contained, and still in evening dress. His eyelids droop slightly, but his eyes are keen and his expression astute.*]

WINSOR. Well, General, what's the first move?

CANYNGE. [*Lifting his eyebrows.*] Mr. De Levis presses the matter?

DE LEVIS. [*Flicked again.*] Unless you think it's too plebeian of me, General Canynge—a thousand pounds.

CANYNGE. [*Drily.*] Just so! Then we must wait for the police, Winsor. Lady Adela has got through to them. What height are these rooms from the ground, Treisure?

TREISURE. Twenty three feet from the terrace, sir.

CANYNGE. Any ladders near?

TREISURE. One in the stables, sir, very heavy. No others within three hundred yards.

CANYNGE. Just slip down, and see whether that's been moved.

TREISURE. Very good, General. [*He goes out.*

DE LEVIS. [*Uneasily.*] Of course, he—I suppose you——

WINSOR. We do.

CANYNGE. You had better leave this in our hands, De Levis.

DE LEVIS. Certainly; only, the way he——

WINSOR. [*Curtly.*] Treisure has been here since he was a boy. I should as soon suspect myself.

DE LEVIS. [*Looking from one to the other—with sudden anger.*] You seem to think——! What was I to do? Take it lying down and let whoever it is get clear off? I suppose it's natural to want my money back?

> [CANYNGE *looks at his nails;* WINSOR *out of the window.*]

WINSOR. [*Turning.*] Of course, De Levis!

DE LEVIS. [*Sullenly.*] Well, I'll go to my room. When the police come, perhaps you'll let me know.

[*He goes out.*

WINSOR. Phew! Did you ever see such a dressing-gown?

> [*The door is opened.* LADY ADELA *and* MARGARET ORME *come in. The latter is a vivid young lady of about twenty-five in a vivid wrapper; she is smoking a cigarette.*]

LADY A. I've told the Dancys—she was in bed. And I got through to Newmarket, Charles, and Inspector Dede is coming like the wind on a motor cycle.

MARGARET. Did he say "like the wind," Adela? He must have imagination. Isn't this gorgeous? Poor little Ferdy!

WINSOR. [*Vexed.*] You might take it seriously, Margaret; it's pretty beastly for us all. What time did *you* come up?

MARGARET. I came up with Adela. Am I suspected, Charles? How thrilling!

WINSOR. Did you hear anything?

MARGARET. Only little Ferdy splashing.

WINSOR. And saw nothing?

LOYALTIES

MARGARET. Not even that, alas!

LADY A. [*With a finger held out.*] *Leste! Un peu leste!* Oh! Here are the Dancys. Come in, you two!

> [MABEL *and* RONALD DANCY *enter. She is a pretty young woman with bobbed hair, fortunately, for she has just got out of bed, and is in her nightgown and a wrapper.* DANCY *is in his smoking-jacket. He has a pale, determined face with high cheek-bones, small, deep-set dark eyes, reddish crisp hair, and looks like a horseman.*]

WINSOR. Awully sorry to disturb you, Mrs. Dancy; but I suppose you and Ronny haven't heard anything. De Levis's room is just beyond Ronny's dressing-room, you know.

MABEL. I've been asleep nearly half an hour, and Ronny's only just come up.

CANYNGE. Did you happen to look out of your window, Mrs. Dancy?

MABEL. Yes. I stood there quite five minutes.

CANYNGE. When?

MABEL. Just about eleven, I should think. It was raining hard then.

CANYNGE. Yes, it's just stopped. You saw nothing?

MABEL. No.

DANCY. What time does he say the money was taken?

WINSOR. Between the quarter and half past. He'd locked his door and had the key with him.

MARGARET. How quaint! Just like an hotel. Does he put his boots out?

LADY A. Don't be so naughty, Meg.

CANYNGE. When exactly did *you* come up, Dancy?

DANCY. About ten minutes ago. I'd only just got into my dressing-room before Lady Adela came. I've been writing letters in the hall since Colford and I finished billiards.

CANYNGE. You weren't up or anything in between?

DANCY. No.

MARGARET. The mystery of the grey room.

DANCY. Oughtn't the grounds to be searched for footmarks?

CANYNGE. That's for the police.

DANCY. The deuce! Are they coming?

CANYNGE. Directly. [*A knock.*] Yes?

[TREISURE *enters.*

Well?

TREISURE. The ladder has not been moved, General. There isn't a sign.

WINSOR. All right. Get Robert up, but don't say anything to him. By the way, we're expecting the police.

TREISURE. I trust they will not find a mare's nest, sir, if I may say so. [*He goes.*

WINSOR. De Levis has got wrong with Treisure. [*Suddenly.*] But, I say, what would any of us have done if *we'd* been in his shoes?

MARGARET. A thousand pounds? I can't even conceive having it.

DANCY. We probably shouldn't have found it out.

LADY A. No—but if we had.

DANCY. Come to you—as he did.

WINSOR. Yes; but there's a way of doing things.

CANYNGE. We shouldn't have wanted the police.

MARGARET. No. That's it. The hotel touch.

LADY A. Poor young man; I think we're rather hard on him.

WINSOR. He sold that weed you gave him, Dancy, to Kentman, the bookie, and these were the proceeds.

DANCY. Oh!

WINSOR. He'd tried her high, he said.

DANCY. [*Grimly.*] He would.

MABEL. Oh! Ronny, what bad luck!

WINSOR. He must have been followed here. [*At the window.*] After rain like that, there ought to be footmarks.

[*The splutter of a motor cycle is heard.*

MARGARET. Here's the wind!

WINSOR. What's the move now, General?

CANYNGE. You and I had better see the Inspector in De Levis's room, Winsor. [*To the others.*] If you'll all be handy, in case he wants to put questions for himself.

MARGARET. I hope he'll want me; it's just too thrilling.

DANCY. I hope he won't want me; I'm dog-tired. Come on, Mabel. [*He puts his arm in his wife's.*]

CANYNGE. Just a minute, Charles.

[*He draws close to* WINSOR *as the others are departing to their rooms.*]

WINSOR. Yes, General?

CANYNGE. We must be careful with this Inspector fellow. If he pitches hastily on somebody in the house it'll be very disagreeable.

WINSOR. By Jove! It *will*.

CANYNGE. We don't want to rouse any ridiculous suspicion.

WINSOR. Quite. [*A knock.*] Come in!

[TREISURE *enters.*

TREISURE. Inspector Dede, sir.

WINSOR. Show him in.

TREISURE. Robert is in readiness, sir; but I could swear he knows nothing about it.

WINSOR. All right.

[TREISURE *reopens the door, and says:* "Come in, please." *The* INSPECTOR *enters, blue, formal, moustachioed, with a peaked cap in his hand.*]

WINSOR. Good-evening, Inspector. Sorry to have brought you out at this time of night.

INSPECTOR. Good evenin', sir. Mr. Winsor? You're the owner here, I think?

WINSOR. Yes. General Canynge.

INSPECTOR. Good evenin', General. I understand, a large sum of money?

WINSOR. Yes. Shall we go straight to the room it was taken from? One of my guests, Mr. De Levis. It's the third room on the left.

CANYNGE. We've not been in there yet, Inspector; in fact, we've done nothing, except to find out that the stable ladder has not been moved. We haven't even searched the grounds.

INSPECTOR. Right, sir; I've brought a man with me.

[*They go out.*

The curtain falls.

Interval of a minute.

SCENE II *

The bedroom of DE LEVIS *is the same in shape as* WINSOR'S *dressing-room, except that there is only one door— to the corridor. The furniture, however, is differently arranged; a small four-poster bedstead stands against the wall, Right Back, jutting into the room. A chair, on which* DE LEVIS'S *clothes are thrown, stands at its foot. There is a dressing-table against the wall to the left of the open windows, where the curtains are drawn back and a stone balcony is seen. Against the*

* The same set is used for this Scene, with the different arrangement of furniture, as specified.

wall to the right of the window is a chest of drawers, and a washstand is against the wall, Left. On a small table to the right of the bed an electric reading lamp is turned up, and there is a light over the dressing-table. The INSPECTOR *is standing plumb centre looking at the bed, and* DE LEVIS *by the back of the chair at the foot of the bed.* WINSOR *and* CANYNGE *are close to the door, Right Forward.*

INSPECTOR. [*Finishing a note.*] Now, sir, if this is the room as you left it for your bath, just show us exactly what you did after takin' the pocket-book from the suitcase. Where was that, by the way?

DE LEVIS. [*Pointing.*] Where it is now—under the dressing-table.

> [*He comes forward to the front of the chair, opens the pocket-book, goes through the pretence of counting his shaving papers, closes the pocket-book, takes it to the head of the bed and slips it under the pillow. Makes the motion of taking up his pyjamas, crosses below the* INSPECTOR *to the washstand, takes up a bath sponge, crosses to the door, takes out the key, opens the door.*]

INSPECTOR. [*Writing.*] We now have the room as it was when the theft was committed. Reconstruct accordin' to 'uman nature, gentlemen—assumin' the thief to be in the room, what would he try first?—the clothes, the dressin' table, the suitcase, the chest of drawers and last, the bed.

> [*He moves accordingly, examining the glass on the dressing-table, the surface of the suitcases, and the handles of the drawers, with a spy-glass, for finger-marks.*]

CANYNGE. [*Sotto voce to* WINSOR.] The order would have been just the other way.

[*The* INSPECTOR *goes on hands and knees and examines the carpet between the window and the bed.*]

DE LEVIS. Can I come in again?

INSPECTOR. [*Standing up.*] Did you open the window, sir, or was it open when you first came in?

DE LEVIS. I opened it.

INSPECTOR. Drawin' the curtains back first?

DE LEVIS. Yes.

INSPECTOR. [*Sharply.*] Are you sure there was nobody in the room already?

DE LEVIS. [*Taken aback.*] I don't know. I never thought. I didn't look under the bed, if you mean that.

INSPECTOR. [*Jotting.*] Did not look under bed. Did you look under it after the theft?

DE LEVIS. No. I didn't.

INSPECTOR. Ah! Now, what *did* you do after you came back from your bath? Just give us that precisely.

DE LEVIS. Locked the door and left the key in. Put back my sponge, and took off my dressing-gown and put it there. [*He points to the footrails of the bed.*] Then I drew the curtains again.

INSPECTOR. Shutting the window?

DE LEVIS. No. I got into bed, felt for my watch to see the time. My hand struck the pocket-book, and somehow it felt thinner. I took it out, looked into it, and found the notes gone, and these shaving papers instead.

INSPECTOR. Let me have a look at those, sir. [*He applies the spy-glasses.*] And then?

DE LEVIS. I think I just sat on the bed.

INSPECTOR. Thinkin' and cursin' a bit, I suppose. Ye'es?

DE LEVIS. Then I put on my dressing-gown and went straight to Mr. Winsor.

INSPECTOR. Not lockin' the door?

LOYALTIES

DE LEVIS. No.

INSPECTOR. Exactly. [*With a certain finality.*] Now, sir, what time did you come up?

DE LEVIS. About eleven.

INSPECTOR. Precise, if you can give it me.

DE LEVIS. Well, I *know* it was eleven-fifteen when I put my watch under my pillow, before I went to the bath, and I suppose I'd been about a quarter of an hour undressing. I should say after eleven, if anything.

INSPECTOR. Just undressin'? Didn't look over your bettin' book?

DE LEVIS. No.

INSPECTOR. No prayers or anything?

DE LEVIS. No.

INSPECTOR. Pretty slippy with your undressin' as a rule?

DE LEVIS. Yes. Say five past eleven.

INSPECTOR. Mr. Winsor, what time did the gentleman come to you?

WINSOR. Half-past eleven.

INSPECTOR. How do you fix that, sir?

WINSOR. I'd just looked at the time, and told my wife to send her maid off.

INSPECTOR. Then we've got it fixed between 11.15 and 11.30. [*Jots.*] Now, sir, before we go further I'd like to see your butler and the footman that valets this gentleman.

WINSOR. [*With distaste.*] Very well, Inspector; only —my butler has been with us from a boy.

INSPECTOR. Quite so. This is just clearing the ground, sir.

WINSOR. General, d'you mind touching that bell?

[CANYNGE *rings a bell by the bed.*

INSPECTOR. Well, gentlemen, there are four possibilities. Either the thief was here all the time, waiting under the bed, and slipped out after this gentleman had gone to Mr. Winsor. Or he came in with a key that fits the lock; and I'll want to see all the keys in the house. Or he came in with a skeleton key and out by the window, probably droppin' from the balcony. Or he came in by the window with a rope or ladder and out the same way. [*Pointing.*] There's a footmark here from a big foot which has been out of doors since it rained.

CANYNGE. Inspector—you er—walked up to the window when you first came into the room.

INSPECTOR. [*Stiffly.*] I had not overlooked that, General.

CANYNGE. Of course.

[*A knock on the door relieves a certain tension.*]

WINSOR. Come in.

[*The footman* ROBERT, *a fresh-faced young man, enters, followed by* TREISURE.]

INSPECTOR. You valet Mr.—Mr. De Levis, I think?

ROBERT. Yes, sir.

INSPECTOR. At what time did you take his clothes and boots?

ROBERT. Ten o'clock, sir.

INSPECTOR. [*With a pounce.*] Did you happen to look under his bed?

ROBERT. No, sir.

INSPECTOR. Did you come up again, to bring the clothes back?

ROBERT. No, sir; they're downstairs.

INSPECTOR. Did you come up again for anything?

ROBERT. No, sir.

INSPECTOR. What time did you go to bed?

ROBERT. Just after eleven, sir.

INSPECTOR. [*Scrutinising him.*] Now, be careful. Did you go to bed at all?

ROBERT. No, sir.

INSPECTOR. Then why did you say you did? There's

LOYALTIES

been a theft here, and anything you say may be used against you.

ROBERT. Yes, sir. I meant, I went to my room.

INSPECTOR. Where is your room?

ROBERT. On the ground floor, at the other end of the right wing, sir.

WINSOR. It's the extreme end of the house from this, Inspector. He's with the other two footmen.

INSPECTOR. Were you there alone?

ROBERT. No, sir. Thomas and Frederick was there too.

TREISURE. That's right; I've seen them.

INSPECTOR. [*Holding up his hand for silence.*] Were you out of the room again after you went in?

ROBERT. No, sir.

INSPECTOR. What were you doing, if you didn't go to bed?

ROBERT. [*To* WINSOR.] Beggin' your pardon, sir, we were playin' Bridge.

INSPECTOR. Very good. You can go. I'll see *them* later on.

ROBERT. Yes, sir. They'll say the same as me.

[*He goes out, leaving a smile on the face of all except the* INSPECTOR *and* DE LEVIS.]

INSPECTOR. [*Sharply.*] Call him back.

[TREISURE *calls* "Robert," *and the* FOOTMAN *re-enters.*]

ROBERT. Yes, sir?

INSPECTOR. Did you notice anything particular about Mr. De Levis's clothes?

ROBERT. Only that they were very good, sir.

INSPECTOR. I mean—anything peculiar?

ROBERT. [*After reflection.*] Yes, sir.

INSPECTOR. Well?

ROBERT. A pair of his boots this evenin' was reduced to one, sir.

INSPECTOR. What did you make of that?

ROBERT. I thought he might have thrown the other at a cat or something.

INSPECTOR. Did you look for it?

ROBERT. No, sir; I meant to draw his attention to it in the morning.

INSPECTOR. Very good.

ROBERT. Yes, sir. [*He goes again.*]

INSPECTOR. [*Looking at* DE LEVIS.] Well, sir, there's *your* story corroborated.

DE LEVIS. [*Stiffly.*] I don't know why it should need corroboration, Inspector.

INSPECTOR. In my experience, you can never have too much of that. [*To* WINSOR.] I understand there's a lady in the room on this side [*pointing Left*] and a gentleman on this [*pointing Right*]. Were they in their rooms?

WINSOR. Miss Orme was; Captain Dancy not.

INSPECTOR. Do they know of the affair?

WINSOR. Yes.

INSPECTOR. Well, I'd just like the keys of their doors for a minute. My man will get them.

[*He goes to the door, opens it, and speaks to a constable in the corridor.*]

[*To* TREISURE.] You can go with him.

[TREISURE *goes out.*

In the meantime I'll just examine the balcony.

[*He goes out on the balcony, followed by* DE LEVIS.]

WINSOR. [*To* CANYNGE.] Damn De Levis and his money! It's deuced invidious, all this, General.

CANYGNE. The Inspector's no earthly.

[*There is a simultaneous re-entry of the* IN-

LOYALTIES

spector *from the balcony and of* Treisure *and the* Constable *from the corridor.*]

Constable. [*Handing key.*] Room on the left, sir. [*Handing key.*] Room on the right, sir.

[*The* Inspector *tries the keys in the door, watched with tension by the others. The keys fail.*]

Inspector. Put them back.

[*Hands keys to* Constable, *who goes out, followed by* Treisure.]

I'll have to try every key in the house, sir.

Winsor. Inspector, do you really think it necessary to disturb the whole house and knock up all my guests? It's most disagreeable, all this, you know. The loss of the money is not such a great matter. Mr. De Levis has a very large income.

Canynge. You could get the numbers of the notes from Kentman, the bookmaker, Inspector; he'll probably have the big ones, anyway.

Inspector. [*Shaking his head.*] A bookie. I don't suppose he will, sir. It's come and go with them, all the time.

Winsor. We don't want a Meldon Court scandal, Inspector.

Inspector. Well, Mr. Winsor, I've formed my theory.

[*As he speaks,* De Levis *comes in from the balcony.*]

And I don't say to try the keys is necessary to it; but strictly, I ought to exhaust the possibilities.

Winsor. What do you say, De Levis? D'you want everybody in the house knocked up so that their keys can be tried?

De Levis. [*Whose face, since his return, expresses a curious excitement.*] No, I don't.

INSPECTOR. Very well, gentlemen. In my opinion the thief walked in before the door was locked, probably during dinner; and was under the bed. He escaped by dropping from the balcony—the creeper at that corner [*he points stage Left*] has been violently wrenched. I'll go down now, and examine the grounds, and I'll see you again, sir. [*He makes another entry in his note-book.*] Good-night, then, gentlemen!

CANYNGE. Good-night!

WINSOR. [*With relief.*] I'll come with you, Inspector.
[*He escorts him to the door, and they go out.*

DE LEVIS. [*Suddenly.*] General, I know who took them.

CANYNGE. The deuce you do! Are you following the Inspector's theory?

DE LEVIS. [*Contemptuously.*] That ass! [*Pulling the shaving papers out of the case.*] No! The man who put those there was clever and cool enough to wrench that creeper off the balcony, as a blind. Come and look here, General. [*He goes to the window; the* GENERAL *follows.* DE LEVIS *points stage Right.*] See the rail of my balcony, and the rail of the next? [*He holds up the cord of his dressing-gown, stretching his arms out.*] I've measured it with this. Just over seven feet, that's all! If a man can take a standing jump on to a narrow book-case four feet high and balance there, he'd make nothing of that. And, look here! [*He goes out on the balcony and returns with a bit of broken creeper in his hand, and holds it out into the light.*] Someone's stood on that—the stalk's crushed— the inner corner too, where he'd naturally stand when he took his jump back.

CANYNGE. [*After examining it—stiffly.*] That other balcony is young Dancy's, Mr. De Levis; a soldier and a gentleman. This is an extraordinary insinuation.

DE LEVIS. Accusation.

CANYNGE. What!

DE LEVIS. I have intuitions, General; it's in my blood. I see the whole thing. Dancy came up, watched me into the bathroom, tried my door, slipped back into his dressing-room, saw my window was open, took that jump, sneaked the notes, filled the case up with these, wrenched the creeper there [*He points stage Left*] for a blind, jumped back, and slipped downstairs again. It didn't take him four minutes altogether.

CANYNGE. [*Very gravely.*] This is outrageous, De Levis. Dancy says he was downstairs all the time. You must either withdraw unreservedly, or I must confront you with him.

DE LEVIS. If he'll return the notes and apologise, I'll do nothing—except cut him in future. He gave me that filly, you know, as a hopeless weed, and he's been pretty sick ever since, that he was such a flat as not to see how good she was. Besides, he's hard up, I know.

CANYNGE. [*After a vexed turn up and down the room.*] It's mad, sir, to jump to conclusions like this.

DE LEVIS. Not so mad as the conclusion Dancy jumped to when he lighted on my balcony.

CANYNGE. Nobody could have taken this money who did not know you had it.

DE LEVIS. How do you know that he didn't?

CANYNGE. Do you know that he did?

DE LEVIS. I haven't the least doubt of it.

CANYNGE. Without any proof. This is very ugly, De Levis. I must tell Winsor.

DE LEVIS. [*Angrily.*] Tell the whole blooming lot. You think I've no feelers, but I've felt the atmosphere here, I can tell you, General. If I were in Dancy's shoes and he in mine, your tone to me would be very different.

CANYNGE. [*Suavely frigid.*] I'm not aware of using any

tone, as you call it. But this is a private house, Mr. De Levis, and something is due to our host and to the *esprit de corps* that exists among gentlemen.

DE LEVIS. Since when is a thief a gentleman? Thick as thieves—a good motto, isn't it?

CANYNGE. That's enough! [*He goes to the door, but stops before opening it.*] Now, look here! I have some knowledge of the world. Once an accusation like this passes beyond these walls no one can foresee the consequences. Captain Dancy is a gallant fellow, with a fine record as a soldier; and only just married. If he's as innocent as—Christ—mud will stick to him, unless the real thief is found. In the old days of swords, either you or he would not have gone out of this room alive. If you persist in this absurd accusation, you will *both* of you go out of this room dead in the eyes of Society: you for bringing it, he for being the object of it.

DE LEVIS. Society! Do you think I don't know that I'm only tolerated for my money? Society can't add injury to insult and have my money as well, that's all. If the notes are restored I'll keep my mouth shut; if they're not, I shan't. I'm certain I'm right. I ask nothing better than to be confronted with Dancy; but, if you prefer it, deal with him in your own way—for the sake of your *esprit de corps*.

CANYNGE. 'Pon my soul, Mr. Levis, you go too far.

DE LEVIS. Not so far as I shall go, General Canynge, if those notes aren't given back.

[WINSOR *comes in*.

WINSOR. Well, De Levis, I'm afraid that's all we can do for the present. So very sorry this should have happened in my house.

CANYNGE. [*After a silence.*] There's a development, Winsor. Mr. De Levis accuses one of your guests.

WINSOR. What?

CANYNGE. Of jumping from his balcony to this, taking the notes, and jumping back. I've done my best to dissuade him from indulging the fancy—without success. Dancy must be told.

DE LEVIS. You can deal with Dancy in your own way. All I want is the money back.

CANYNGE. [*Drily.*] Mr. De Levis feels that he is only valued for his money, so that it is essential for him to have it back.

WINSOR. Damn it! This is monstrous, De Levis. I've known Ronald Dancy since he was a boy.

CANYNGE. You talk about adding injury to insult, De Levis. What do you call such treatment of a man who gave you the mare out of which you made this thousand pounds?

DE LEVIS. I didn't want the mare; I took her as a favour.

CANYNGE. With an eye to possibilities, I venture to think —the principle guides a good many transactions.

DE LEVIS. [*As if flicked on a raw spot.*] In my race, do you mean?

CANYNGE. [*Coldly.*] I said nothing of the sort.

DE LEVIS. No; you don't *say* these things, any of you.

CANYNGE. Nor did I think it.

DE LEVIS. Dancy does.

WINSOR. Really; De Levis, if this is the way you repay hospitality——

DE LEVIS. Hospitality that skins my feelings and costs me a thousand pounds!

CANYNGE. Go and get Dancy, Winsor; but don't say anything to him.

[WINSOR *goes out.*

CANYNGE. Perhaps you will kindly control yourself, and leave this to me.

[DE LEVIS *turns to the window and lights a cigarette.* WINSOR *comes back, followed by* DANCY.]

CANYNGE. For Winsor's sake, Dancy, we don't want any scandal or fuss about this affair. We've tried to make the police understand that. To my mind the whole thing turns on our finding who knew that De Levis had this money. It's about that we want to consult you.

WINSOR. Kentman paid De Levis round the corner in the further paddock, he says.

[DE LEVIS *turns round from the window, so that he and* DANCY *are staring at each other.*]

CANYNGE. Did you hear anything that throws light, Dancy? As it was your filly originally, we thought perhaps you might.

DANCY. I? No.

CANYNGE. Didn't hear of the sale on the course at all?

DANCY. No.

CANYNGE. Then you can't suggest anyone who could have known? Nothing else was taken, you see.

DANCY. De Levis is known to be rolling, as I am known to be stony.

CANYNGE. There are a good many people still rolling, besides Mr. De Levis, but not many people with so large a sum in their pocket-books.

DANCY. He won two races.

DE LEVIS. Do you suggest that I bet in ready money?

DANCY. I don't know how you bet, and I don't care.

CANYNGE. You can't help us, then?

DANCY. No, I can't. Anything else? [*He looks fixedly at* DE LEVIS.]

CANYNGE. [*Putting his hand on* DANCY'S *arm.*] Nothing else, thank you, Dancy.

[DANCY *goes.* CANYNGE *puts his hand up to his face. A moment's silence.*]

WINSOR. You see, De Levis? He didn't even know you'd got the money.

DE LEVIS. Very conclusive.

WINSOR. Well! You *are*——!

[*There is a knock on the door, and the* INSPECTOR *enters.*]

INSPECTOR. I'm just going, gentlemen. The grounds, I'm sorry to say, have yielded nothing. It's a bit of a puzzle.

CANYNGE. You've searched thoroughly?

INSPECTOR. We have, General. I can pick up nothing near the terrace.

WINSOR. [*After a look at* DE LEVIS, *whose face expresses too much.*] H'm! You'll take it up from the other end, then, Inspector?

INSPECTOR. Well, we'll see what we can do with the bookmakers about the numbers, sir. Before I go, gentlemen—you've had time to think it over—there's no one you suspect in the house, I suppose?

[DE LEVIS'S *face is alive and uncertain.* CANYNGE *is staring at him very fixedly.*]

WINSOR. [*Emphatically.*] No.

[DE LEVIS *turns and goes out on to the balcony.*

INSPECTOR. If you're coming in to the racing to-morrow, sir, you might give us a call. I'll have seen Kentman by then.

WINSOR. Right you are, Inspector. Good-night, and many thanks.

INSPECTOR. You're welcome, sir. [*He goes out.*

WINSOR. Gosh! I thought that chap [*With a nod towards the balcony*] was going to ——! Look here, General, we *must* stop his tongue. Imagine it going the rounds. They may never find the real thief, you know. It's the very devil for Dancy.

CANYNGE. Winsor! Dancy's sleeve was damp.

WINSOR. How d'you mean?

CANYNGE. Quite damp. It's been raining.

[*The two look at each other.*

WINSOR. I—I don't follow—[*His voice is hesitative and lower, showing that he does.*]

CANYNGE. It was coming down hard; a minute out in it would have been enough—— [*He motions with his chin towards the balcony.*]

WINSOR. [*Hastily.*] He must have been out on his balcony since.

CANYNGE. It stopped before I came up, half an hour ago.

WINSOR. He's been leaning on the wet stone, then.

CANYNGE. With the outside of the *upper* part of the arm?

WINSOR. Against the wall, perhaps. There may be a dozen explanations. [*Very low and with great concentration.*] I entirely and absolutely refuse to believe anything of the sort against Ronald Dancy—in my house. Dash it, General, we must do as we'd be done by. It hits us all—it hits us all. The thing's intolerable.

CANYNGE. I agree. Intolerable. [*Raising his voice.*] Mr. De Levis.

[DE LEVIS *returns into view, in the centre of the open window.*]

CANYNGE. [*With cold decision.*] Young Dancy was an officer and is a gentleman; this insinuation is pure supposition, and you must not make it. Do you understand me?

DE LEVIS. My tongue is still mine, General, if my money isn't!

CANYNGE. [*Unmoved.*] Must not. You're a member of three Clubs, you want to be a member of a fourth. No one who makes such an insinuation against a fellow-guest in a country house, except on absolute proof, can do so without complete ostracism. Have we your word to say nothing?

DE LEVIS. Social blackmail? H'm!

CANYNGE. Not at all—simply warning. If you consider it necessary in your interests to start this scandal—no matter how, we shall consider it necessary in ours to dissociate ourselves completely from one who so recklessly disregards the unwritten code.

DE LEVIS. Do you think your code applies to me? Do you, General?

CANYNGE. To anyone who aspires to be a gentleman, sir.

DE LEVIS. Ah! But you haven't known *me* since I was a boy.

CANYNGE. Make up your mind.

[*A pause.*

DE LEVIS. I'm not a fool, General. I know perfectly well that you can get me ousted.

CANYNGE. [*Icily.*] Well?

DE LEVIS. [*Sullenly.*] I'll say nothing about it, unless I get more proof.

CANYNGE. Good. We have implicit faith in Dancy.

[*There is a moment's encounter of eyes; the* GENERAL'S *steady, shrewd, impassive;* WINSOR'S *angry and defiant;* DE LEVIS'S *mocking, a little triumphant, malicious. Then* CANYNGE *and* WINSOR *go to the door, and pass out.*]

DE LEVIS. [*To himself.*] Rats!

The curtain falls.

ACT II

SCENE I

Afternoon, three weeks later, in the card room of a London Club. A fire is burning, Left. A door, Right, leads to

*the billiard-room. Rather Left of Centre, at a card
table,* LORD ST ERTH, *an old John Bull, sits facing the
audience; to his right is* GENERAL CANYNGE, *to his left*
AUGUSTUS BORRING, *an essential Clubman, about thirty-
five years old, with a very slight and rather becoming
stammer or click in his speech. The fourth Bridge
player,* CHARLES WINSOR, *stands with his back to the
fire.*

BORRING. And the r-rub.

WINSOR. By George! You do hold cards, Borring.

ST ERTH. [*Who has lost.*] Not a patch on the old whist
—this game. Don't know why I play it—never did.

CANYNGE. St Erth, shall we raise the flag for whist
again?

WINSOR. No go, General. You can't go back on pace.
No getting a man to walk when he knows he can fly. The
young men won't look at it.

BORRING. Better develop it so that t-two can sit out,
General.

ST ERTH. We ought to have stuck to the old game. Wish
I'd gone to Newmarket, Canynge, in spite of the weather.

CANYNGE. [*Looking at his watch.*] Let's hear what's
won the Cambridgeshire. Ring, won't you, Winsor?

[WINSOR *rings.*

ST ERTH. By the way, Canynge, young De Levis was
blackballed.

CANYNGE. What!

ST ERTH. I looked in on my way down.

[CANYNGE *sits very still and* WINSOR *utters a disturbed sound.*]

BORRING. But of c-course he was, General. What did
you expect?

[*A* FOOTMAN *enters.*

LOYALTIES

FOOTMAN. Yes, my lord?

ST ERTH. What won the Cambridgeshire?

FOOTMAN. Rosemary, my lord. Sherbet second; Barbizon third. Nine to one the winner.

WINSOR. Thank you. That's all.

[FOOTMAN *goes*.

BORRING. Rosemary! And De Levis sold her! But he got a good p-price, I suppose.

[*The other three look at him.*

ST ERTH. Many a slip between price and pocket, young man.

CANYNGE. Cut! [*They cut.*]

BORRING. I say, is that the yarn that's going round about his having a lot of m-money stolen in a country house? By Jove! He'll be pretty s-sick.

WINSOR. You and I, Borring.

[*He sits down in* CANYNGE'*s chair, and the* GENERAL *takes his place by the fire.*]

BORRING. Phew! Won't Dancy be mad! He gave that filly away to save her keep. He was rather pleased to find somebody who'd take her. Kentman must have won a p-pot. She was at thirty-threes a fortnight ago.

ST ERTH. All the money goes to fellows who don't know a horse from a haystack.

CANYNGE. [*Profoundly.*] And care less. Yes! We want men racing to whom a horse means something.

BORRING. I thought the horse m-meant the same to everyone, General—chance to get the b-better of one's neighbour.

CANYNGE. [*With feeling.*] The horse is a noble animal, sir, as you'd know if you'd owed your life to them as often as I have.

BORRING. They always try to *take* mine, General. I shall never belong to the noble f-fellowship of the horse.

ST ERTH. [*Drily.*] Evidently. Deal!

[*As* Borring *begins to deal the door is opened and* Major Colford *appears—a lean and moustached cavalryman.*]

Borring. Hallo, C-Colford.

Colford. General!

[*Something in the tone of his voice brings them all to a standstill.*]

Colford. I want your advice. Young De Levis in there [*He points to the billiard-room from which he has just come*] has started a blasphemous story——

Canynge. One moment. Mr. Borring, d'you mind——

Colford. It makes no odds, General. Four of us in there heard him. He's saying it was Ronald Dancy robbed him down at Winsor's. The fellow's mad over losing the price of that filly now she's won the Cambridgeshire.

Borring. [*All ears.*] Dancy! Great S-Scott!

Colford. Dancy's in the Club. If he hadn't been I'd have taken it on myself to wring the bounder's neck.

[Winsor *and* Borring *have risen.* St Erth *alone remains seated.*]

Canynge. [*After consulting* St Erth *with a look.*] Ask De Levis to be good enough to come in here. Borring, you might see that Dancy doesn't leave the Club. We shall want him. Don't say anything to him, and use your tact to keep people off.

[Borring *goes out, followed by* Colford.

Winsor. Result of hearing he was blackballed—pretty slippy.

Canynge. St Erth, I told you there was good reason when I asked you to back young De Levis. Winsor and I knew of this insinuation; I wanted to keep his tongue quiet. It's just wild assertion; to have it bandied about was unfair to Dancy. The duel used to keep people's tongues in order.

LOYALTIES

St Erth. H'm! It never settled anything, except who could shoot straightest.

Colford. [*Reappearing.*] De Levis says he's nothing to add to what he said to you before, on the subject.

Canynge. Kindly tell him that if he wishes to remain a member of this Club he must account to the Committee for such a charge against a fellow-member. Four of us are here, and form a quorum.

[Colford *goes out again.*

St Erth. Did Kentman ever give the police the numbers of those notes, Winsor?

Winsor. He only had the numbers of two—the hundred, and one of the fifties.

St Erth. And they haven't traced 'em?

Winsor. Not yet.

[*As he speaks,* De Levis *comes in. He is in a highly-coloured, not to say excited state.* Colford *follows him.*]

De Levis. Well, General Canynge! It's a little too strong all this—a little too strong. [*Under emotion his voice is slightly more exotic.*]

Canynge. [*Calmly.*] It is obvious, Mr. De Levis, that you and Captain Dancy can't both remain members of this Club. We ask you for an explanation before requesting one resignation or the other.

De Levis. You've let me down.

Canynge. What!

De Levis. Well, I shall tell people that you and Lord St Erth backed me up for one Club, and asked me to resign from another.

Canynge. It's a matter of indifference to me, sir, what you tell people.

St Erth. [*Drily.*] You seem a venomous young man.

De Levis. I'll tell you what seems to me venomous, my

lord—chasing a man like a pack of hounds because he isn't your breed.

CANYNGE. You appear to have your breed on the brain, sir. Nobody else does, so far as I know.

DE LEVIS. Suppose I had robbed Dancy, would you chase him out for complaining of it?

COLFORD. My God! If you repeat that——

CANYNGE. Steady, Colford!

WINSOR. You make this accusation that Dancy stole your money in my house on no proof—no proof; and you expect Dancy's friends to treat you as if you were a gentleman! That's too strong, if you like!

DE LEVIS. No proof? Kentman told me at Newmarket yesterday that Dancy *did* know of the sale. He told Goole, and Goole says that he himself spoke of it to Dancy.

WINSOR. Well—if he did?

DE LEVIS. Dancy told you he *didn't* know of it in General Canynge's presence, and mine. [*To* CANYNGE.] You can't deny that, if you want to.

CANYNGE. Choose your expressions more nicely, please!

DE LEVIS. Proof! Did they find any footmarks in the grounds below that torn creeper? Not a sign! You saw how he can jump; he won ten pounds from me that same evening betting on what he knew was a certainty. That's your Dancy—a common sharper!

CANYNGE. [*Nodding towards the billiard-room.*] Are those fellows still in there, Colford?

COLFORD. Yes.

CANYNGE. Then bring Dancy up, will you? But don't say anything to him.

COLFORD. [*To* DE LEVIS.] You may think yourself damned lucky if he doesn't break your neck.

[*He goes out. The three who are left with* DE LEVIS *avert their eyes from him.*]

De Levis. [*Smouldering.*] I have a memory, and a sting too. Yes, my lord—since you are good enough to call me venomous. [*To* Canynge.] I quite understand—I'm marked for Coventry now, whatever happens. Well, I'll take Dancy with me.

St Erth. [*To himself.*] This Club has always had a decent, quiet name.

Winsor. Are you going to retract, and apologise in front of Dancy and the members who heard you?

De Levis. No fear!

St Erth. You must be a very rich man, sir. A jury is likely to take the view that money can hardly compensate for an accusation of that sort.

[De Levis *stands silent.*

Canynge. Courts of law require proof.

St Erth. He can make it a criminal action.

Winsor. Unless you stop this at once, you may find yourself in prison. *If* you can stop it, that is.

St Erth. If I were young Dancy, nothing should induce me.

De Levis. But you didn't steal my money, Lord St Erth.

St Erth. You're deuced positive, sir. So far as I could understand it, there were a dozen ways you could have been robbed. It seems to me you value other men's reputations very lightly.

De Levis. Confront me with Dancy and give me fair play.

Winsor. [*Aside to* Canynge.] Is it fair to Dancy not to let him know?

Canynge. Our duty is to the Club now, Winsor. We must have this cleared up.

[Colford *comes in, followed by* Borring *and* Dancy.]

St Erth. Captain Dancy, a serious accusation has been

made against you by this gentleman in the presence of several members of the Club.

DANCY. What is it?

ST ERTH. That you robbed him of that money at Winsor's.

DANCY. [*Hard and tense.*] Indeed! On what grounds is he good enough to say that?

DE LEVIS. [*Tense too.*] You gave me that filly to save yourself her keep, and you've been mad about it ever since; you knew from Goole that I had sold her to Kentman and been paid in cash, yet I heard you myself deny that you knew it. You had the next room to me, and you can jump like a cat, as we saw that evening; I found some creepers crushed by a weight on my balcony on that side. When I went to the bath your door was open, and when I came back it was shut.

CANYNGE. That's the first we have heard about the door.

DE LEVIS. I remembered it afterwards.

ST ERTH. Well, Dancy?

DANCY. [*With intense deliberation.*] I'll settle this matter with any weapons, when and where he likes.

ST ERTH. [*Drily.*] It can't be settled that way— you know very well. You must take it to the Courts, unless he retracts.

DANCY. Will you retract?

DE LEVIS. Why did you tell General Canynge you didn't know Kentman had paid me in cash?

DANCY. Because I didn't.

DE LEVIS. Then Kentman and Goole lied—for no reason?

DANCY. That's nothing to do with me.

DE LEVIS. If you were downstairs all the time, as you say, why was your door first open and then shut?

LOYALTIES

DANCY. Being downstairs, how should I know? The wind, probably.

DE LEVIS. I should like to hear what your wife says about it.

DANCY. Leave my wife alone, you damned Jew!

ST ERTH. Captain Dancy!

DE LEVIS. [*White with rage.*] Thief!

DANCY. Will you fight?

DE LEVIS. You're very smart—dead men tell no tales. No! Bring your action, and we shall see.

[DANCY *takes a step towards him, but* CANYNGE *and* WINSOR *interpose.*

ST ERTH. That'll do, Mr. De Levis; we wont keep you. [*He looks round.*] Kindly consider your membership suspended till this matter has been threshed out.

DE LEVIS. [*Tremulous with anger.*] Don't trouble yourselves about my membership. I resign it. [*To* DANCY.] You called me a damned Jew. My race was old when you were all savages. I am proud to be a Jew. *Au revoir,* in the Courts.

[*He goes out, and silence follows his departure.*

ST ERTH. Well, Captain Dancy?

DANCY. If the brute won't fight, what am I to do, sir?

ST ERTH. We've told you—take action, to clear your name.

DANCY. Colford, you saw me in the hall writing letters after our game.

COLFORD. Certainly I did; you were there when I went to the smoking-room.

CANYNGE. How long after you left the billiard-room?

COLFORD. About five minutes.

DANCY. It's impossible for me to prove that I was there all the time.

CANYNGE. It's for De Levis to prove what he asserts. You heard what he said about Goole?

DANCY. If he told me, I didn't take it in.

ST ERTH. This concerns the honour of the Club. Are you going to take action?

DANCY. [*Slowly.*] That is a very expensive business, Lord St Erth, and I'm hard up. I must think it over. [*He looks round from face to face.*] Am I to take it that there is a doubt in your minds, gentlemen?

COLFORD. [*Emphatically.*] No.

CANYNGE. That's not the question, Dancy. This accusation was overheard by various members, and we represent the Club. If you don't take action, judgment will naturally go by default.

DANCY. I might prefer to look on the whole thing as beneath contempt.

> [*He turns and goes out. When he is gone there is an even longer silence than after* DE LEVIS's *departure.*]

ST ERTH. [*Abruptly.*] I don't like it.

WINSOR. I've known him all his life.

COLFORD. You may have my head if he did it, Lord St Erth. He and I have been in too many hotels together. By Gad! My toe itches for that fellow's butt end.

BORRING. I'm sorry; but has he t-taken it in quite the right way? I should have thought—hearing it s-suddenly——

COLFORD. Bosh!

WINSOR. It's perfectly damnable for him.

ST ERTH. More damnable if he did it, Winsor.

BORRING. The Courts are b-beastly distrustful, don't you know.

COLFORD. His word's good enough for me.

LOYALTIES 427

CANYNGE. We're as anxious to believe Dancy as you, Colford, for the honour of the Army and the Club.

WINSOR. Of course, he'll bring a case, when he's thought it over.

ST ERTH. What are we to do in the meantime?

COLFORD. If Dancy's asked to resign, you may take my resignation too.

BORRING. I thought his wanting to f-fight him a bit screeny.

COLFORD. Wouldn't you have wanted a shot at the brute? A law court? Pah!

WINSOR. Yes. What'll be his position even if he wins?

BORRING. Damages, and a stain on his c-character.

WINSOR. Quite so, unless they find the real thief. People always believe the worst.

COLFORD. [*Glaring at* BORRING.] They do.

CANYNGE. There *is* no decent way out of a thing of this sort.

ST ERTH. No. [*Rising.*] It leaves a bad taste. I'm sorry for young Mrs. Dancy—poor woman!

BORRING. Are you going to play any more?

ST ERTH. [*Abruptly.*] No, sir. Good night to you. Canynge, can I give you a lift?

[*He goes out, followed by* CANYNGE.

BORRING. [*After a slight pause.*] Well, I shall go and take the t-temperature of the Club.

[*He goes out.*

COLFORD. Damn that effeminate stammering chap. What can we do for Dancy, Winsor?

WINSOR. Colford! [*A slight pause.*] The General felt his coat sleeve that night, and it was wet.

COLFORD. Well! What proof's that? No, by George! An old school-fellow, a brother officer, and a pal.

WINSOR. If he did it——

COLFORD. He didn't. But if he did. I'd stick to him, and see him through it, if I could.

[WINSOR *walks over to the fire, stares into it, turns round and stares at* COLFORD, *who is standing motionless.*]

COLFORD. Yes, by God!

The curtain falls.

SCENE II*

Morning of the following day. The DANCYS' *flat. In the sitting-room of this small abode* MABEL DANCY *and* MARGARET ORME *are sitting full face to the audience, on a couch in the centre of the room, in front of the imaginary window. There is a fireplace, Left, with fire burning; a door below it, Left, and a door on the Right, facing the audience, leads to a corridor and the outer door of the flat, which is visible. Their voices are heard in rapid exchange; then as the curtain rises, so does* MABEL.

MABEL. But it's monstrous!

MARGARET. Of course! [*She lights a cigarette and hands the case to* MABEL, *who, however, sees nothing but her own thoughts.*] De Levis might just as well have pitched on me, except that I can't jump more than six inches in these skirts.

MABEL. It's wicked! Yesterday afternoon at the Club, did you say? Ronny hasn't said a word to me. Why?

MARGARET. [*With a long puff of smoke.*] Doesn't want you bothered.

* NOTE—This should be a small set capable of being set quickly within that of the previous scene.

LOYALTIES

MABEL. But—— Good heavens!—— Me!

MARGARET. Haven't you found out, Mabel, that he isn't exactly communicative? No desperate character is.

MABEL. Ronny?

MARGARET. Gracious! Wives *are* at a disadvantage, especially early on. You've never hunted with him, my dear. I have. He takes more sudden decisions than any man I ever knew. He's taking one now, I'll bet.

MABEL. That beast, De Levis! I was in our room next door all the time.

MARGARET. Was the door into Ronny's dressing-room open?

MABEL. I don't know; I—I think it was.

MARGARET. Well, you can say so in Court anyway. Not that it matters. Wives are liars by law.

MABEL. [*Staring down at her.*] What do you mean—Court?

MARGARET. My dear, he'll have to bring an action for defamation of character, or whatever they call it.

MABEL. Were they talking of this last night at the Winsors'?

MARGARET. Well, you know a dinner-table, Mabel—Scandal is heaven-sent at this time of year.

MABEL. It's terrible, such a thing—terrible!

MARGARET. [*Gloomily.*] If only Ronny weren't known to be so broke.

MABEL. [*With her hands to her forehead.*] I can't realise—I simply can't. If there's a case would it be all right afterwards?

MARGARET. Do you remember St Offert—cards? No, you wouldn't—you were in high frocks. Well, St Offert got damages, but he also got the hoof, underneath. He lives in Ireland. There isn't the slightest connection, so far as

I can see, Mabel, between innocence and reputation. Look at me!

MABEL. We'll fight it tooth and nail!

MARGARET. Mabel, you're pure wool, right through; everybody's sorry for you.

MABEL. It's for *him* they ought——

MARGARET. [*Again handing the cigarette-case.*] Do smoke, old thing.

> [MABEL *takes a cigarette this time, but does not light it.*]

It isn't altogether simple. General Canynge was there last night. You don't mind my being beastly frank, do you?

MABEL. No. I want it.

MARGARET. Well, he's all for *esprit de corps* and that. But he was awfully silent.

MABEL. I hate half-hearted friends. Loyalty comes before everything.

MARGARET. Ye-es; but loyalties cut up against each other sometimes, you know.

MABEL. I *must* see Ronny. D'you mind if I go and try to get him on the telephone?

MARGARET. Rather not.

> [MABEL *goes out by the door, Left.*

Poor kid!

> [*She curls herself into a corner of the sofa, as if trying to get away from life. The bell rings.* MARGARET *stirs, gets up, and goes out into the corridor, where she opens the door to* LADY ADELA WINSOR, *whom she precedes into the sitting-room.*]

Enter the second murderer! D'you know that child knew nothing?

LADY A. Where is she?

MARGARET. Telephoning. Adela, if there's going to be

an action, we shall be witnesses. I shall wear black georgette with an écru hat. Have you ever given evidence?

LADY A. Never.

MARGARET. It must be too frightfully thrilling.

LADY A. Oh! Why did I ever ask that wretch De Levis? I used to think him pathetic. Meg—did you know—— Ronald Dancy's coat was wet? The General happened to feel it.

MARGARET. So that's why he was so silent.

LADY A. Yes; and after the scene in the Club yesterday he went to see those bookmakers, and Goole—what a name! —is sure he told Dancy about the sale.

MARGARET. [*Suddenly.*] I don't care. He's my third cousin. Don't you feel you *couldn't,* Adela?

LADY A. Couldn't—what?

MARGARET. Stand for De Levis against one of ourselves?

LADY A. That's very narrow, Meg.

MARGARET. Oh! I know lots of splendid Jews, and I rather liked Ferdy; but when it comes to the point——! *They* all stick together; why shouldn't we? It's in the blood. Open your jugular, and see if you haven't got it.

LADY A. My dear, my great grandmother was a Jewess. I'm very proud of her.

MARGARET. Inoculated. [*Stretching herself.*] Prejudices, Adela—or are they loyalties—I don't know— criss-cross—we all cut each other's throats from the best of motives.

LADY A. Oh! I shall remember that. Delightful! [*Holding up a finger.*] You got it from Bergson, Meg. Isn't he wonderful?

MARGARET. Yes; have you ever read him?

LADY A. Well—No. [*Looking at the bedroom door.*]

That poor child! I quite agree. I shall tell everybody it's ridiculous. You don't really think Ronald Dancy——?

MARGARET. I don't know, Adela. There are people who simply can't live without danger. I'm rather like that myself. They're all right when they're getting the D.S.O. or shooting man-eaters; but if there's no excitement going, they'll make it—out of sheer craving. I've seen Ronny Dancy do the maddest things for no mortal reason except the risk. He's had a past, you know.

LADY A. Oh! Do tell!

MARGARET. He did splendidly in the war, of course, because it suited him; but—just before—don't you remember—a very queer bit of riding?

LADY A. No.

MARGARET. Most dare-devil thing—but not quite. You must remember—it was awfully talked about. And then, of course, right up to his marriage——[*She lights a cigarette.*]

LADY A. Meg, you're very tantalising!

MARGARET. A foreign-looking girl—most plummy. Oh! Ronny's got charm—this Mabel child doesn't know in the least what she's got hold of!

LADY A. But they're so fond of each other!

MARGARET. That's the mistake. The General isn't mentioning the coat, is he?

LADY A. Oh, no! It was only to Charles.

[MABEL *returns.*

MARGARET. Did you get him?

MABEL. No; he's not at Tattersall's, nor at the Club.

[LADY ADELA *rises and greets her with an air which suggests bereavement.*]

LADY A. Nobody's going to believe this, my dear.

MABEL. [*Looking straight at her.*] Nobody who does need come here, or trouble to speak to *us* again.

LOYALTIES

LADY A. That's what I was afraid of; you're going to be defiant. Now don't! Just be perfectly natural.

MABEL. So easy, isn't it? I could kill anybody who believes such a thing.

MARGARET. You'll want a solicitor, Mabel. Go to old Mr. Jacob Twisden.

LADY A. Yes; he's so comforting.

MARGARET. He got my pearls back once—without loss of life. A frightfully good fireside manner. Do get him here, Mabel, and have a heart-to-heart talk, all three of you!

MABEL. [*Suddenly.*] Listen! There's Ronny!

[DANCY *comes in.*

DANCY. [*With a smile.*] Very good of you to have come.

MARGARET. Yes. We're just going. Oh! Ronny, this is quite too—— [*But his face dries her up; and sidling past, she goes.*]

LADY A. Charles sent his—love—— [*Her voice dwindles on the word, and she, too, goes.*]

DANCY. [*Crossing to his wife.*] What have they been saying?

MABEL. Ronny! Why didn't you tell me?

DANCY. I wanted to see De Levis again first.

MABEL. That wretch! How dare he? Darling! [*She suddenly clasps and kisses him. He does not return the kiss, but remains rigid in her arms, so that she draws away and looks at him.*] It's hurt you awfully, I know.

DANCY. Look here, Mabel! Apart from that muck—this is a ghastly tame-cat sort of life. Let's cut it and get out to Nairobi. I can scare up the money for that.

MABEL. [*Aghast.*] But how can we? Everybody would say——

DANCY. Let them! We shan't be here.

MABEL. I couldn't bear people to think——

DANCY. I don't care a damn what people think—monkeys and cats. I never could stand their rotten menagerie. Besides, what does it matter how I act; if I bring an action and get damages—if I pound him to a jelly—it's all no good! I can't *prove* it. There'll be plenty of people unconvinced.

MABEL. But they'll find the real thief.

DANCY. [*With a queer little smile.*] Will staying here help them to do that?

MABEL. [*In a sort of agony.*] Oh! I couldn't—it looks like running away. We *must* stay and fight it!

DANCY. Suppose I didn't get a verdict—you never can tell.

MABEL. But you must—I was there all the time, with the door open.

DANCY. Was it?

MABEL. I'm almost sure.

DANCY. Yes. But you're my wife.

MABEL. [*Bewildered.*] Ronny, I don't understand—suppose I'd been accused of stealing pearls!

DANCY. [*Wincing.*] I can't.

MABEL. But I might—just as easily. What would you think of me if I ran away from it?

DANCY. I see. [*A pause.*] All right! You shall have a run for your money. I'll go and see old Twisden.

MABEL. Let me come! [DANCY *shakes his head.*] Why not? I can't be happy a moment unless I'm fighting this.

[DANCY *puts out his hand suddenly and grips hers.*]

DANCY. You are a little brick!

MABEL. [*Pressing his hand to her breast and looking into his face.*] Do you know what Margaret called you?

RONNY. No.

LOYALTIES

MABEL. A desperate character.

DANCY. Ha! I'm not a tame cat, any more than she.

[*The bell rings.* MABEL *goes out to the door and her voice is heard saying coldly:*]

MABEL. Will you wait a minute, please?

[*Returning.* It's De Levis—to see you. [*In a low voice.*] Let me see him alone first. Just for a minute! Do!

DANCY. [*After a moment's silence.*] Go ahead!

[*He goes out into the bedroom.*

MABEL. [*Going to the door, Right.*] Come in.

[*De Levis comes in, and stands embarrassed.* Yes?

DE LEVIS. [*With a slight bow.*] Your husband, Mrs. Dancy?

MABEL. He is in. Why do you want to see him?

DE LEVIS. He came round to my rooms just now, when I was out. He threatened me yesterday. I don't choose him to suppose I'm afraid of him.

MABEL. [*With a great and manifest effort at self-control.*] Mr. De Levis, you are robbing my husband of his good name.

DE LEVIS. [*Sincerely.*] I admire your trustfulness, Mrs. Dancy.

MABEL. [*Staring at him.*] How can you do it? What do you want? What's your motive? You can't possibly believe that my husband is a *thief!*

DE LEVIS. Unfortunately.

MABEL. How dare you? How dare you? Don't you know that I was in our bedroom all the time with the door open? Do you accuse me too?

DE LEVIS. No, Mrs. Dancy.

MABEL. But you do. I must have seen, I must have heard.

DE LEVIS. A wife's memory is not very good when her husband is in danger.

MABEL. In other words, I'm lying.

DE LEVIS. No. Your wish is mother to your thought, that's all.

MABEL. [*After staring again with a sort of horror, turns to get control of herself. Then turning back to him.*] Mr. De Levis, I appeal to you as a gentleman to behave to us as you would we should behave to you. Withdraw this wicked charge, and write an apology that Ronald can show.

DE LEVIS. Mrs. Dancy, I am not a gentleman, I am only a—damned Jew. Yesterday I might possibly have withdrawn to spare you. But when my race is insulted I have nothing to say to your husband, but as he wishes to see me, I've come. Please let him know.

MABEL. [*Regarding him again with that look of horror—slowly.*] I think what you are doing is too horrible for words.

> [DE LEVIS *gives her a slight bow, and as he does so* DANCY *comes quickly in, Left. The two men stand with the length of the sofa between them.* MABEL, *behind the sofa, turns her eyes on her husband, who has a paper in his right hand.*]

DE LEVIS. You came to see me.

DANCY. Yes. I want you to sign this.

DE LEVIS. I will sign nothing.

DANCY. Let me read it: "I apologise to Captain Dancy for the reckless and monstrous charge I made against him, and I retract every word of it."

DE LEVIS. Not much!

DANCY. You will sign.

DE LEVIS. I tell you this is useless. I will sign nothing.

LOYALTIES

The charge is true; you wouldn't be playing this game if it weren't. I'm going. You'll hardly try violence in the presence of your wife; and if you try it anywhere else—— look out for yourself.

DANCY. Mabel, I want to speak to him alone.

MABEL. No, no!

DE LEVIS. Quite right, Mrs. Dancy. Black and tan swashbuckling will only make things worse for him.

DANCY. So you shelter behind a woman, do you, you skulking cur!

[DE LEVIS *takes a step, with fists clenched and eyes blazing.* DANCY, *too, stands ready to spring—the moment is cut short by* MABEL *going quickly to her husband.*]

MABEL. Don't, Ronny. It's undignified! He isn't worth it.

[DANCY *suddenly tears the paper in two, and flings it into the fire.*]

DANCY. Get out of here, you swine!

[DE LEVIS *stands a moment irresolute, then, turning to the door, he opens it, stands again for a moment with a smile on his face, then goes.* MABEL *crosses swiftly to the door, and shuts it as the outer door closes. Then she stands quite still, looking at her husband—her face expressing a sort of startled suspense.*]

DANCY. [*Turning and looking at her.*] Well! Do you agree with him?

MABEL. What do you mean?

DANCY. That I wouldn't be playing this game unless——

MABEL. Don't! You hurt me!

DANCY. Yes. You don't know much of me, Mabel.

MABEL. Ronny!

DANCY. What did you say to that swine?

MABEL. [*Her face averted.*] That he was robbing *us*. [*Turning to him suddenly.*] Ronny—you—didn't? I'd rather know.

DANCY. Ha! I thought that was coming.

MABEL. [*Covering her face.*] Oh! How horrible of me —how horrible!

DANCY. Not at all. The thing looks bad.

MABEL. [*Dropping her hands.*] If *I* can't believe in you, who can? [*Going to him, throwing her arms round him, and looking up into his face.*] Ronny! If all the world—*I'd* believe in you. You know I would.

DANCY. That's all right, Mabs! That's all right! [*His face, above her head, is contorted for a moment, then hardens into a mask.*] Well, what shall we do?

MABEL. Oh! Let's go to that lawyer—let's go at once!

DANCY. All right. Get your hat on.

> [MABEL *passes him, and goes into the bedroom, Left.* DANCY, *left alone, stands quite still, staring before him. With a sudden shrug of his shoulders he moves quickly to his hat and takes it up just as* MABEL *returns, ready to go out. He opens the door; and crossing him, she stops in the doorway, looking up with a clear and trustful gaze as*
>
> *The curtain falls.*

ACT III

SCENE I

Three months later. Old MR. JACOB TWISDEN'S *Room, at the offices of Twisden & Graviter, in Lincoln's Inn Fields, is spacious, with two large windows at back,*

LOYALTIES

a fine old fireplace, Right, a door below it, and two doors, Left. Between the windows is a large table sideways to the window wall, with a chair in the middle on the right-hand side, a chair against the wall, and a client's chair on the left-hand side.

> [GRAVITER, TWISDEN'S *much younger partner, is standing in front of the right-hand window, looking out on to the Fields, where the lamps are being lighted, and a taxi's engine is running down below. He turns his sanguine, shrewd face from the window towards a grandfather clock, between the doors, Left, which is striking "four." The door, Left Forward, is opened.*]

YOUNG CLERK. [*Entering.*] A Mr. Gilman, sir, to see Mr. Twisden.

GRAVITER. By appointment?

YOUNG CLERK. No, sir. But important, he says.

GRAVITER. I'll see him.   [*The* CLERK *goes.*

> [GRAVITER *sits right of table. The* CLERK *returns, ushering in an oldish man, who looks what he is, the proprietor of a large modern grocery store. He wears a dark overcoat and carries a pot hat. His gingery-grey moustache and mutton-chop whiskers give him the expression of a cat.*]

GRAVITER. [*Sizing up his social standing.*] Mr. Gilman? Yes.

GILMAN. [*Doubtfully.*] Mr. Jacob Twisden?

GRAVITER. [*Smiling.*] His partner. Graviter my name is.

GILMAN. Mr. Twisden's not in, then?

GRAVITER. No. He's at the Courts. They're just up; he should be in directly. But he'll be busy.

GILMAN. Old Mr. Jacob Twisden—I've heard of him.

GRAVITER. Most people have. [*A pause.*

GILMAN. It's this Dancy-De Levis case that's keepin' him at the Courts, I suppose?

[GRAVITER *nods.*

Won't be finished for a day or two?

[GRAVITER *shakes his head.*

No. Astonishin' the interest taken in it.

GRAVITER. As you say.

GILMAN. The Smart Set, eh? This Captain Dancy got the D. S. O., didn't he?

[GRAVITER *nods.*

Sad to have a thing like that said about you. I thought he gave his evidence well; and his wife too. Looks as if this De Levis had got some private spite. *Searchy la femme,* I said to Mrs. Gilman only this morning, before I——

GRAVITER. By the way, sir, what is your business?

GILMAN. Well, my business here—— No, if you'll excuse me, I'd rather wait and see old Mr. Jacob Twisden. It's delicate, and I'd like his experience.

GRAVITER. [*With a shrug.*] Very well; then, perhaps you'll go in there. [*He moves towards the door, Left Back.*]

GILMAN. Thank you. [*Following.*] You see, I've never been mixed up with the law——

GRAVITER. [*Opening the door.*] No?

GILMAN. And I don't want to begin. When you do, you don't know where you'll stop, do you? You see, I've only come from a sense of duty; and—other reasons.

GRAVITER. Not uncommon.

GILMAN. [*Producing card.*] This is my card. Gilman's —several branches, but this is the 'ead.

GRAVITER. [*Scrutinising card.*] Exactly.

GILMAN. Grocery—I daresay you know me; or your

LOYALTIES

wife does. They say old Mr. Jacob Twisden refused a knighthood. If it's not a rude question, why was that?

GRAVITER. Ask him, sir; ask him.

GILMAN. I said to my wife at the time, "He's holdin' out for a baronetcy."

> [*Graviter closes the door with an exasperated smile.*]

YOUNG CLERK. [*Opening the door, Left Forward.*] Mr. Winsor, sir, and Miss Orme.

> [*They enter, and the* CLERK *withdraws.*

GRAVITER. How d'you do, Miss Orme? How do you do, Winsor?

WINSOR. Twisden not back, Graviter?

GRAVITER. Not yet.

WINSOR. Well, they've got through De Levis's witnesses. Sir Frederic was at the very top of his form. It's looking quite well. But I hear they've just subpœnaed Canynge after all. His evidence is to be taken to-morrow.

GRAVITER. Oho!

WINSOR. I said Dancy ought to have called him.

GRAVITER. We considered it. Sir Frederic decided that he could use him better in cross-examination.

WINSOR. Well! I don't know that. Can I go and see him before he gives evidence to-morrow?

GRAVITER. I should like to hear Mr. Jacob on that, Winsor. He'll be in directly.

WINSOR. They had Kentman, and Goole, the Inspector, the other bobby, my footman, Dancy's banker, and his tailor.

GRAVITER. Did we shake Kentman or Goole?

WINSOR. Very little. Oh! by the way, the numbers of those two notes were given, and I see they're published in the evening papers. I suppose the police wanted that.

I tell you what I find, Graviter—a general feeling that there's something behind it all that doesn't come out.

GRAVITER. The public wants its money's worth—always does in these Society cases; they brew so long beforehand, you see.

WINSOR. They're looking for something lurid.

MARGARET. When I was in the box, I thought they were looking for me. [*Taking out her cigarette-case.*] I suppose I mustn't smoke, Mr. Graviter?

GRAVITER. Do!

MARGARET. Won't Mr. Jacob have a fit?

GRAVITER. Yes, but not till you've gone.

MARGARET. Just a whiff. [*She lights a cigarette.*]

WINSOR. [*Suddenly.*] It's becoming a sort of Dreyfus case—people taking sides quite outside the evidence.

MARGARET. There are more of the chosen in Court every day. Mr. Graviter, have you noticed the two on the jury?

GRAVITER. [*With a smile.*] No; I can't say——

MARGARET. Oh! but quite distinctly. Don't you think they ought to have been challenged?

GRAVITER. De Levis might have challenged the other ten, Miss Orme.

MARGARET. Dear me, now! I never thought of that.

> [*As she speaks, the door Left Forward is opened and old* MR. JACOB TWISDEN *comes in. He is tallish and narrow, sixty-eight years old, grey, with narrow little whiskers curling round his narrow ears, and a narrow bow ribbon curling round his collar. He wears a long, narrow-tailed coat, and strapped trousers on his narrow legs. His nose and face are narrow, shrewd, and kindly. He has a way of narrowing his shrewd and kindly eyes. His nose is seen to twitch and sniff.*]

TWISDEN. Ah! How are you, Charles? How do you do, my dear?

MARGARET. Dear Mr. Jacob, I'm smoking. Isn't it disgusting? But they don't allow it in Court, you know. Such a pity! The Judge might have a hookah. Oh! wouldn't he look sweet—the darling!

TWISDEN. [*With a little, old-fashioned bow.*] It does not become everybody as it becomes you, Margaret.

MARGARET. Mr. Jacob, how charming! [*With a slight grimace she puts out her cigarette.*]

GRAVITER. Man called Gilman waiting in there to see you specially.

TWISDEN. Directly. Turn up the light, would you, Graviter?

GRAVITER. [*Turning up the light.*] Excuse me.

[*He goes.*

WINSOR. Look here, Mr. Twisden——

TWISDEN. Sit down; sit down, my dear.

[*And he himself sits behind the table, as a cup of tea is brought in to him by the* YOUNG CLERK, *with two Marie biscuits in the saucer.*]

Will you have some, Margaret?

MARGARET. No, dear Mr. Jacob.

TWISDEN. Charles?

WINSOR. No, thanks.

[*The door is closed.*

TWISDEN. [*Dipping a biscuit in the tea.*] Now, then?

WINSOR. The General knows something which on the face of it looks rather queer. Now that he's going to be called, oughtn't Dancy to be told of it, so that he may be ready with his explanation, in case it comes out?

TWISDEN. [*Pouring some tea into the saucer.*] Without knowing, I can't tell you.

[Winsor *and* Margaret *exchange looks, and* Twisden *drinks from the saucer.*]

Margaret. Tell him, Charles.

Winsor. Well! It rained that evening at Meldon. The General happened to put his hand on Dancy's shoulder, and it was damp.

[Twisden *puts the saucer down and replaces the cup in it. They both look intently at him.*]

Twisden. I take it that General Canynge won't say anything he's not compelled to say.

Margaret. No, of course; but, Mr. Jacob, they might ask; they know it rained. And he is such a George Washington.

Twisden. [*Toying with a pair of tortoise-shell glasses.*] They didn't ask either of *you*. Still—no harm in your telling Dancy.

Winsor. I'd rather *you* did it, Margaret.

Margaret. I daresay. [*She mechanically takes out her cigarette-case, catches the lift of* Twisden's *eyebrows, and puts it back.*]

Winsor. Well, we'll go together. I don't want Mrs. Dancy to hear.

Margaret. Do tell me, Mr. Jacob; is he going to win?

Twisden. I think so, Margaret; I think so.

Margaret. It'll be too frightful if he doesn't get a verdict, after all this. But I don't know what we shall do when it's over. I've been sitting in that Court all these three days, watching, and it's made me feel there's nothing we like better than seeing people skinned. Well, bye-bye, bless you!

[Twisden *rises and pats her hand.*

Winsor. Half a second, Margaret. Wait for me.

[*She nods and goes out.*

Mr. Twisden, what do you really think?

LOYALTIES 445

TWISDEN. I am Dancy's lawyer, my dear Charles, as well as yours.

WINSOR. Well, can I go and see Canynge?

TWISDEN. Better not.

WINSOR. If they get that out of him, and recall me, am I to say he told me of it at the time?

TWISDEN. You didn't feel the coat yourself? And Dancy wasn't present? Then what Canynge told you is not evidence. *We'll* stop your being asked.

WINSOR. Thank goodness. Good-bye!

[WINSOR *goes out.*

[TWISDEN, *behind his table, motionless, taps his teeth with the eyeglasses in his narrow, well-kept hand. After a long shake of his head and a shrug of his rather high shoulders he sniffs, goes to the window and opens it. Then crossing to the door, Left Back, he throws it open and says:*]

TWISDEN. At your service, sir.

[GILMAN *comes forth, nursing his pot hat.*] Be seated.

[TWISDEN *closes the window behind him, and takes his seat.*]

GILMAN. [*Taking the client's chair, to the left of the table.*] Mr. Twisden, I believe? My name's Gilman, head of Gilman's Department Stores. You have my card.

TWISDEN. [*Looking at the card.*] Yes. What can we do for you?

GILMAN. Well, I've come to you from a sense of duty, sir, and also a feelin' of embarrassment. [*He takes from his breast pocket an evening paper.*] You see, I've been followin' this Dancy case—it's a good deal talked of in Putney—and I read this at half-past two this afternoon. To be precise, at 2.25. [*He rises and hands the paper to*

TWISDEN, *and with a thick gloved forefinger indicates a passage.*] When I read these numbers, I 'appened to remember givin' change for a fifty-pound note—don't often 'ave one in, you know—so I went to the cash-box out of curiosity, to see that I 'adn't got it. Well, I 'ad; and here it is. [*He draws out from his breast pocket and lays before* TWISDEN *a fifty-pound banknote.*] It was brought in to change by a customer of mine three days ago, and he got value for it. Now, that's a stolen note, it seems, and you'd like to know what I did. Mind you, that customer of mine I've known 'im—well—eight or nine years; an Italian he is —wine salesman, and so far's I know, a respectable man —foreign-lookin', but nothin' more. Now, this was at 'alf-past two, and I was at my head branch at Putney, where I live. I want you to mark the time, so as you'll see I 'aven't wasted a minute. I took a cab and I drove straight to my customer's private residence in Putney, where he lives with his daughter—Ricardos his name is, Paolio Ricardos. They tell me there that he's at his business shop in the City. So off I go in the cab again, and there I find him. Well, sir, I showed this paper to him and I produced the note. "Here," I said, "you brought this to me and you got value for it." Well, that man was taken aback. If I'm a judge, Mr. Twisden, he was taken aback, not to speak in a guilty way, but he was, as you might say, flummoxed. "Now," I said to him, "where did you get it—that's the point?" He took his time to answer, and then he said: "Well, Mr. Gilman," he said, "you know me; I am an honourable man. I can't tell you offhand, but I am above the board." He's foreign, you know, in his expressions. "Yes," I said, "that's all very well," I said, "but here I've got a stolen note and you've got the value for it. Now I tell you," I said, "what I'm going to do; I'm going straight with this note to Mr. Jacob Twisden,

LOYALTIES

who's got this Dancy-De Levis case in 'and. He's a well-known Society lawyer," I said, "of great experience." "Oh!" he said, "that is what you do?"—funny the way he speaks! "Then I come with you!"—And I've got him in the cab below. I want to tell you everything before he comes up. On the way I tried to get something out of him, but I couldn't—I could *not*. "This is very awkward," I said at last. "It is, Mr. Gilman," was the reply; and he began to talk about his Sicilian claret—a very good wine, mind you; but under the circumstances it seemed to me uncalled for. Have I made it clear to you?

TWISDEN. [*Who has listened with extreme attention.*] Perfectly, Mr. Gilman. I'll send down for him. [*He touches a hand-bell.*]

  [*The* YOUNG CLERK *appears at the door, Left Forward.*]

A gentleman in a taxi—waiting. Ask him to be so good as to step up. Oh! and send Mr. Graviter here again.

  [*The* YOUNG CLERK *goes out.*

GILMAN. As I told you, sir, I've been followin' this case. It's what you might call piquant. And I should be very glad if it came about that this helped Captain Dancy. I take an interest, because, to tell you the truth [*Confidentially*] I don't like—well, not to put too fine a point upon it—'Ebrews. They work harder; they're more sober; they're honest; and they're everywhere. I've nothing against them, but the fact is—they get *on* so.

TWISDEN. [*Cocking an eye.*] A thorn in the flesh, Mr. Gilman.

GILMAN. Well, I prefer my own countrymen, and that's the truth of it.

  [*As he speaks,* GRAVITER *comes in by the door, Left Forward.*]

TWISDEN. [*Pointing to the newspaper and the note.*] Mr.

Gilman has brought this, of which he is holder for value. His customer, who changed it three days ago, is coming up.

GRAVITER. The fifty-pounder. I see. [*His face is long and reflective.*]

YOUNG CLERK. [*Entering.*] Mr. Ricardos, sir.

[*He goes out.*

[RICARDOS *is a personable, Italian-looking man in a frock coat, with a dark moustachioed face and dark hair a little grizzled. He looks anxious, and bows.*]

TWISDEN. Mr. Ricardos? My name is Jacob Twisden. My partner. [*Holding up a finger, as* RICARDOS *would speak.*] Mr. Gilman has told us about this note. You took it to him, he says, three days ago; that is, on Monday, and received cash for it?

RICARDOS. Yes, sare.

TWISDEN. You were *not* aware that it was stolen?

RICARDOS. [*With his hand to his breast.*] Oh! no, sare.

TWISDEN. You received it from——?

RICARDOS. A minute, sare; I would weesh to explain—— [*With an expressive shrug*] in private.

TWISDEN. [*Nodding.*] Mr. Gilman, your conduct has been most prompt. You may safely leave the matter in our hands, now. Kindly let us retain this note; and ask for my cashier as you go out and give him [*He writes*] this. He will reimburse you. We will take any necessary steps ourselves.

GILMAN. [*In slight surprise, with modest pride.*] Well, sir, I'm in your 'ands. I must be guided by you, with your experience. I'm glad you think I acted rightly.

TWISDEN. Very rightly, Mr. Gilman—very rightly. [*Rising.*] Good-afternoon!

GILMAN. Good-afternoon, sir. Good-afternoon, gentle-

LOYALTIES

men! [*To* Twisden.] I'm sure I'm very 'appy to have made your acquaintance, sir. It's a well-known name.

Twisden. Thank you.

> [Gilman *retreats, glances at* Ricardos, *and turns again.*]

Gilman. I suppose there's nothing else I ought to do, in the interests of the law? I'm a careful man.

Twisden. If there is, Mr. Gilman, we will let you know. We have your address. You may make your mind easy; but don't speak of this. It might interfere with Justice.

Gilman. Oh! I shouldn't dream of it. I've no wish to be mixed up in anything conspicuous. That's not my principle at all. Good-day, gentlemen.

> [*He goes.*

Twisden. [*Seating himself.*] Now, sir, will you sit down.

> *But* Ricardos *does not sit; he stands looking uneasily across the table at* Graviter.]

You may speak out.

Ricardos. Well, Mr. Tweesden and sare, this matter is very serious for me, and very delicate—it concairns my honour. I am in a great difficulty.

Twisden. When in difficulty—complete frankness, sir.

Ricardos. It is a family matter, sare, I——

Twisden. Let me be frank with you. [*Telling his points off on his fingers.*] We have your admission that you changed this stopped note for value. It will be our duty to inform the Bank of England that it has been traced to you. You will have to account to them for your possession of it. I suggest to you that it will be far better to account frankly to us.

Ricardos. [*Taking out a handkerchief and quite openly wiping his hands and forehead.*] I received this note, sare, with others, from a gentleman, sare, in settlement of a debt of honour, and I know nothing of where he got them.

TWISDEN. H'm! that is very vague. If that is all you can tell us, I'm afraid——

RICARDOS. Gentlemen, this is very painful for me. It is my daughter's good name—— [*He again wipes his brow.*]

TWISDEN. Come, sir, speak out!

RICARDOS. [*Desperately.*] The notes were a settlement to her from this gentleman, of whom she was a great friend.

TWISDEN. [*Suddenly.*] I am afraid we must press you for the name of the gentleman.

RICARDOS. Sare, if I give it to you, and it does 'im 'arm, what will my daughter say? This is a bad matter for me. He behaved well to her; and she is attached to him still; sometimes she is crying yet because she lost him. And now we betray him, perhaps, who knows? This is very unpleasant for me. [*Taking up the paper.*] Here it gives the number of another note—a 'undred-pound note. I 'ave that too. [*He takes a note from his breast pocket.*]

GRAVITER. How much did he give you in all?

RICARDOS. For my daughter's settlement one thousand pounds. I understand he did not wish to give a cheque because of his marriage. So I did not think anything about it being in notes, you see.

TWISDEN. When did he give you this money?

RICARDOS. The middle of Octobare last.

TWISDEN. [*Suddenly looking up.*] Mr. Richardos, was it. Captain Dancy?

RICARDOS. [*Again wiping his forehead.*] Gentlemen, I am so fond of my daughter. I have only the one, and no wife.

TWISDEN. [*With an effort.*] Yes, yes; but I must know.

RICARDOS. Sare, if I tell you, will you give me your good word that my daughter shall not hear of it?

LOYALTIES 451

TWISDEN. So far as we are able to prevent it—certainly.

RICARDOS. Sare, I trust you. It was Captain Dancy.

[*A long pause.*

GRAVITER. [*Suddenly.*] Were you blackmailing him?

TWISDEN. [*Holding up his hand.*] My partner means, did you press him for this settlement?

RICARDOS. I did think it my duty to my daughter to ask that he make compensation to her.

TWISDEN. With threats that you would tell his wife?

RICARDOS. [*With a shrug.*] Captain Dancy was a man of honour. He said: "Of course I will do this." I trusted him. And a month later I did remind him, and he gave me this money for her.. I do not know where he got it—I do not know. Gentlemen, I have invested it all on her— every penny—except this note, for which I had the purpose to buy her a necklace. That is the sweared truth.

TWISDEN. I must keep this note. [*He touches the hundred-pound note.*] You will not speak of this to anyone. I may recognise that you were a holder for value received— others might take a different view. Good-day, sir. Graviter, see Mr. Ricardos out, and take his address.

RICARDOS. [*Pressing his hands over the breast of his frock coat—with a sigh.*] Gentlemen, I beg you—remember what I said. [*With a roll of his eyes.*] My daughter— I am not happee. Good-day.

[*He turns and goes out slowly, Left Forward, followed by* GRAVITER.]

TWISDEN. [*To himself.*] Young Dancy! [*He pins the two notes together and places them in an envelope, then stands motionless except for his eyes and hands, which restlessly express the disturbance within him.*]

[GRAVITER *returns, carefully shuts the door, and going up to him, hands him* RICARDOS' *card.*]

[*Looking at the card.*] Villa Benvenuto. This will have

to be verified, but I'm afraid it's true. That man was not acting.

GRAVITER. What's to be done about Dancy?

TWISDEN. Can you understand a gentleman——?

GRAVITER. I don't know, sir. The war loosened "form" all over the place. I saw plenty of that myself. And some men have no moral sense. From the first I've had doubts.

TWISDEN. We can't go on with the case.

GRAVITER. Phew! . . . [*A moment's silence.*] Gosh! It's an awful thing for his wife.

TWISDEN. Yes.

GRAVITER. [*Touching the envelope.*] Chance brought this here, sir. That man won't talk. He's too scared.

TWISDEN. Gilman.

GRAVITER. Too respectable. If De Levis got those notes back, and the rest of the money, anonymously?

TWISDEN. But the case, Graviter; the case.

GRAVITER. I don't believe this alters what I've been thinking.

TWISDEN. Thought is one thing—knowledge another. There's duty to our profession. Ours is a fine calling. On the good faith of solicitors a very great deal hangs. [*He crosses to the hearth as if warmth would help him.*]

GRAVITER. It'll let him in for a prosecution. He came to us in confidence.

TWISDEN. Not as against the law.

GRAVITER. No. I suppose not. [*A pause.*] By Jove, I don't like losing this case. I don't like the admission we backed such a wrong 'un.

TWISDEN. Impossible to go on. Apart from ourselves, there's Sir Frederic. We must disclose to him—can't let him go on in the dark. Complete confidence between solicitor and counsel is the essence of professional honour.

LOYALTIES

GRAVITER. What are you going to do then, sir?

TWISDEN. See Dancy at once. Get him on the 'phone.

GRAVITER. [*Taking up the telephone.*] Get me Captain Dancy's flat. . . . What? . . . [*To* TWISDEN.] Mrs. Dancy is here. That's *à propos* with a vengeance. Are you going to see her, sir?

TWISDEN. [*After a moment's painful hesitation.*] I must.

GRAVITER. [*Telephoning.*] Bring Mrs. Dancy up. [*He turns to the window.*]

> [MABEL DANCY *is shown in, looking very pale.* TWISDEN *advances from the fire, and takes her hand.*]

MABEL. Major Colford's taken Ronny off in his car for the night. I thought it would do him good. I said I'd come round in case there was anything you wanted to say before to-morrow.

TWISDEN. [*Taken aback.*] Where have they gone?

MABEL. I don't know, but he'll be home before ten o'clock to-morrow. Is there anything?

TWISDEN. Well, I'd like to see him before the Court sits. Send him on here as soon as he comes.

MABEL. [*With her hand to her forehead.*] Oh! Mr. Twisden, when will it be over? My head's getting awful sitting in that Court.

TWISDEN. My dear Mrs. Dancy; there's no need at all for you to come down to-morrow; take a rest and nurse your head.

MABEL. Really and truly?

TWISDEN. Yes; it's the very best thing you can do.

> [GRAVITER *turns his head, and looks at them unobserved.*]

MABEL. How do you think it's going?

TWISDEN. It went very well to-day; very well indeed.

MABEL. You must be awfully fed up with us.

TWISDEN. My dear young lady, that's our business. [*He takes her hand.*]

> [MABEL's *face suddenly quivers. She draws her hand away, and covers her lips with it.*]

There, there! You want a day off badly.

MABEL. I'm tired of——! Thank you so much for all you're doing. Good-night! Good-night, Mr. Graviter!

GRAVITER. Good-night, Mrs. Dancy.

> [MABEL *goes.*

GRAVITER. D'you know, I believe she knows.

TWISDEN. No, no! She believes in him implicitly. A staunch little woman. Poor thing!

GRAVITER. Hasn't that shaken you, sir? It has me.

TWISDEN. No, no! I—I can't go on with the case. It's breaking faith. Get Sir Frederic's chambers.

GRAVITER. [*Telephoning, and getting a reply, looks round at* TWISDEN.] Yes?

TWISDEN. Ask if I can come round and see him.

GRAVITER. [*Telephoning.*] Can Sir Frederic spare Mr. Twisden a few minutes now if he comes round? [*Receiving reply.*] He's gone down to Brighton for the night.

TWISDEN. H'm! What hotel?

GRAVITER. [*Telephoning.*] What's his address? What . . .? [*To* TWISDEN.] The Bedford.

TWISDEN. I'll go down.

GRAVITER. [*Telephoning.*] Thank you. All right. [*He rings off.*]

TWISDEN. Just look out the trains down and up early to-morrow.

> [GRAVITER *takes up an A B C, and* TWISDEN *takes up the Ricardos card.*]

TWISDEN. Send to this address in Putney, verify the fact that Ricardos has a daughter, and give me a trunk call to Brighton. Better go yourself, Graviter. If you see

her, don't say anything, of course—invent some excuse.
[GRAVITER *nods*.] I'll be up in time to see Dancy.

GRAVITER. By George! I feel bad about this.

TWISDEN. Yes. But professional honour comes first. What time is that train? [*He bends over the A B C.*]

The curtain falls.

SCENE II

The same room on the following morning at ten-twenty-five, by the Grandfather clock.

> [*The* YOUNG CLERK *is ushering in* DANCY, *whose face is perceptibly harder than it was three months ago, like that of a man who has lived under great restraint.*]

DANCY. He wanted to see me before the Court sat.

YOUNG CLERK. Yes, sir. Mr. Twisden will see you in one minute. He had to go out of town last night. [*He prepares to open the waiting-room door.*]

DANCY. Were *you* in the war?

YOUNG CLERK. Yes.

DANCY. How can you stick this?

YOUNG CLERK. [*With a smile.*] My trouble was to stick that, sir.

DANCY. But you get no excitement from year's end to year's end. It'd drive me mad.

YOUNG CLERK. [*Shyly.*] A case like this is pretty exciting. I'd give a lot to see us win it.

DANCY. [*Staring at him.*] Why? What is it to you?

YOUNG CLERK. I don't know, sir. It's—it's like football—you want your side to win. [*He opens the waiting-room door. Expanding.*] You see some rum starts, too, in a lawyer's office in a quiet way.

[DANCY *enters the waiting-room, and the* YOUNG CLERK, *shutting the door, meets* TWISDEN *as he comes in, Left Forward, and takes from him overcoat, top hat, and a small bag.*]

YOUNG CLERK. Captain Dancy's waiting, sir. [*He indicates the waiting-room.*]

TWISDEN. [*Narrowing his lips.*] Very well. Mr. Graviter gone to the Courts?

YOUNG CLERK. Yes, sir.

TWISDEN. Did he leave anything for me?

YOUNG CLERK. On the table, sir.

TWISDEN. [*Taking up an envelope.*] Thank you.

[*The* CLERK *goes.*

TWISDEN. [*Opening the envelope and reading.*] "All corroborates." H'm! [*He puts it in his pocket and takes out of an envelope the two notes, lays them on the table, and covers them with a sheet of blotting-paper; stands a moment preparing himself, then goes to the door of the waiting-room, opens it, and says:*] Now, Captain Dancy. Sorry to have kept you waiting.

DANCY. [*Entering.*] Winsor came to me yesterday about General Canynge's evidence. Is that what you wanted to speak to me about?

TWISDEN. No. It isn't that.

DANCY. [*Looking at his wrist watch.*] By me it's just on the half-hour, sir.

TWISDEN. Yes. I don't want you to go to the Court.

DANCY. Not?

TWISDEN. I have very serious news for you.

DANCY. [*Wincing and collecting himself.*] Oh!

TWISDEN. These two notes. [*He uncovers the notes.*] After the Court rose yesterday we had a man called Ricardos here. [*A pause.*] Is there any need for me to say more?

LOYALTIES

DANCY. [*Unflinching.*] No. What now?

TWISDEN. Our duty was plain; we could not go on with the case. I have consulted Sir Frederic. He felt—he felt that he must throw up his brief, and he will do that the moment the Court sits. Now I want to talk to you about what you're going to do.

DANCY. That's very good of you, considering.

TWISDEN. I don't pretend to understand, but I imagine you may have done this in a moment of reckless bravado, feeling, perhaps, that as you gave the mare to De Levis, the money was by rights as much yours as his.

[*Stopping* DANCY, *who is about to speak, with a gesture.*]

To satisfy a debt of honour to this—lady; and, no doubt, to save your wife from hearing of it from the man Ricardos. Is that so?

DANCY. To the life.

TWISDEN. It was mad, Captain Dancy, mad!—— But the question now is: What do you owe to your wife? She doesn't dream—I suppose?

DANCY. [*With a twitching face.*] No.

TWISDEN. We can't tell what the result of this collapse will be. The police have the theft in hand. They may issue a warrant. The money could be refunded, and the costs paid—somehow that can all be managed. But it may not help. In any case, what end is served by your staying in the country. You can't save your honour—that's gone. You can't save your wife's peace of mind. If she sticks to you—do you think she will?

DANCY. Not if she's wise.

TWISDEN. Better go! There's a war in Morocco.

DANCY. [*With a bitter smile.*] Good old Morocco!

TWISDEN. Will you go, then, at once, and leave me to break it to your wife?

DANCY. I don't know yet.

TWISDEN. You must decide quickly, to catch a boat train. Many a man has made good. You're a fine soldier.

DANCY. There are alternatives.

TWISDEN. Now, go straight from this office. You've a passport, I suppose; you won't need a *visa* for France, and from there you can find means to slip over. Have you got money on you? [DANCY *nods*.] We will see what we can do to stop or delay proceedings.

DANCY. It's all damned kind of you. [*With difficulty*.] But I must think of my wife. Give me a few minutes.

TWISDEN. Yes, yes; go in there and think it out.

> [*He goes to the door, Right, and opens it.* DANCY *passes him and goes out.* TWISDEN *rings a bell and stands waiting.*]

CLERK. [*Entering.*] Yes, sir?

TWISDEN. Tell them to call a taxi.

CLERK. [*Who has a startled look.*] Yes, sir. Mr. Graviter has come in, sir, with General Canynge. Are you disengaged?

TWISDEN. Yes.

> [*The* CLERK *goes out, and almost immediately* GRAVITER *and* CANYNGE *enter.*]

Good-morning, General. [*To* GRAVITER.] Well?

GRAVITER. Sir Frederic got up at once and said that since the publication of the numbers of those notes, information had reached him which forced him to withdraw from the case. Great sensation, of course. I left Bromley in charge. There'll be a formal verdict for the defendant, with costs. Have you told Dancy?

TWISDEN. Yes. He's in there deciding what he'll do.

CANYNGE. [*Grave and vexed.*] This is a dreadful thing, Twisden. I've been afraid of it all along. A soldier! A gallant fellow, too. What on earth got into him?

LOYALTIES

TWISDEN. There's no end to human nature, General.

GRAVITER. You can see queerer things in the papers, any day.

CANYNGE. That poor young wife of his! Winsor gave me a message for you, Twisden. If money's wanted quickly to save proceedings, draw on him. Is there anything *I* can do?

TWISDEN. I've advised him to go straight off to Morocco.

CANYNGE. I don't know that an asylum isn't the place for him. He must be off his head at moments. That jump —crazy! He'd have got a verdict on that alone—if they'd seen those balconies. I was looking at them when I was down there last Sunday. Daring thing, Twisden. Very few men, on a dark night—— He risked his life twice. That's a shrewd fellow—young De Levis. He spotted Dancy's nature.

[*The* YOUNG CLERK *enters.*

CLERK. The taxi's here, sir. Will you see Major Colford and Miss Orme?

TWISDEN. Graviter—— No; show them in.

[*The* YOUNG CLERK *goes.*

CANYNGE. Colford's badly cut up.

[MARGARET ORME *and* COLFORD *enter.*

COLFORD. [*Striding forward.*] There must be some mistake about this, Mr. Twisden.

TWISDEN. Hssh! Dancy's in there. He's admitted it.

[*Voices are subdued at once.*

COLFORD. What? [*With emotion.*] If it were my own brother, I couldn't feel it more. But—damn it! What right had that fellow to chuck up the case—without letting him know, too. I came down with Dancy this morning, and he knew nothing about it.

TWISDEN. [*Coldly.*] That was unfortunately unavoidable.

COLFORD. Guilty or not, you ought to have stuck to him—it's not playing the game, Mr. Twisden.

TWISDEN. You must allow me to judge where my duty lay, in a very hard case.

COLFORD. I thought a man was safe with his solicitor.

CANYNGE. Colford, you don't understand professional etiquette.

COLFORD. No, thank God!

TWISDEN. When you have been as long in your profession as I have been in mine, Major Colford, you will know that duty to your calling outweighs duty to friend or client.

COLFORD. But I serve the Country.

TWISDEN. And I serve the Law, sir.

CANYNGE. Graviter, give me a sheet of paper. I'll write a letter for him.

MARGARET. [*Going up to* TWISDEN.] Dear Mr. Jacob—pay De Levis. You know my pearls—put them up the the spout again. Don't let Ronny be——

TWISDEN. Money isn't the point, Margaret.

MARGARET. It's ghastly! It really is.

COLFORD. I'm going in to shake hands with him. [*He starts to cross the room.*]

TWISDEN. Wait! We want him to go straight off to Morocco. Don't upset him. [*To* COLFORD *and* MARGARET.] I think you had better go. If, a little later, Margaret, you could go round to Mrs. Dancy——

COLFORD. Poor little Mabel Dancy! It's perfect hell for her.

> [*They have not seen that* DANCY *has opened the door behind them.*]

DANCY. It is!

> [*They all turn round in consternation.*

COLFORD. [*With a convulsive movement.*] Old boy!

DANCY. No good, Colford. [*Gazing round at them.*]

LOYALTIES

Oh! clear out. I can't stand commiseration—and let me have some air.

> [TWISDEN *motions to* COLFORD *and* MARGARET *to go; and as he turns to* DANCY, *they go out.* GRAVITER *also moves towards the door. The* GENERAL *sits motionless.* GRAVITER *goes out.*]

TWISDEN. Well?

DANCY. I'm going home, to clear up things with my wife. General Canynge, I don't quite know why I did the damned thing. But I did, and there's an end of it.

CANYNGE. Dancy, for the honour of the Army, avoid further scandal if you can. I've written a letter to a friend of mine in the Spanish War Office. It will get you a job in their war. [CANYGNE *closes the envelope.*]

DANCY. Very good of you. I don't know if I can make use of it.

> [CANYNGE *stretches out the letter, which* TWISDEN *hands to* DANCY, *who takes it.* GRAVITER *reopens the door.*]

TWISDEN. What is it?

GRAVITER. De Levis is here.

TWISDEN. De Levis? Can't see him.

DANCY. Let him in!

> [*After a moment's hesitation* TWISDEN *nods, and* GRAVITER *goes out. The three wait in silence with their eyes fixed on the door, the* GENERAL *sitting at the table,* TWISDEN *by his chair,* DANCY *between him and the door Right.* DE LEVIS *comes in and shuts the door. He is advancing towards* TWISDEN *when his eyes fall on* DANCY, *and he stops.*]

TWISDEN. You wanted to see me?

DE LEVIS. [*Moistening his lips.*] Yes. I came to say that—that I overheard—I am afraid a warrant is to issued.

I wanted you to realise—it's not *my* doing. I'll give it no support. I'm content. I don't want my money. I don't even want costs. Dancy, do you understand?

> [DANCY *does not answer, but looks at him with nothing alive in his face but his eyes.*]

TWISDEN. We are obliged to you, sir. It was good of you to come.

DE LEVIS. [*With a sort of darting pride.*] Don't mistake me. I didn't come because I feel Christian. I am a Jew. I will take no money—not even that which was stolen. Give it to a charity. I'm proved right. And now I'm done with the damned thing. Good-morning!

> [*He makes a little bow to* CANYNGE *and* TWISDEN, *and turns to face* DANCY, *who has never moved. The two stand motionless, looking at each other, then* DE LEVIS *shrugs his shoulders and walks out. When he is gone there is a silence.*]

CANYNGE. [*Suddenly.*] You heard what he said, Dancy. You have no time to lose.

> [*But* DANCY *does not stir.*

TWISDEN. Captain Dancy?

> [*Slowly, without turning his head, rather like a man in a dream,* DANCY *walks across the room, and goes out.*]

The curtain falls.

SCENE III

The DANCYS' *sitting-room, a few minutes later.*

> [MABEL DANCY *is sitting alone on the sofa with a newspaper on her lap; she is only just up, and has a bottle of smelling-salts in her hand.*

LOYALTIES

Two or three other newspapers are dumped on the arm of the sofa. She topples the one off her lap and takes up another as if she couldn't keep away from them; drops it in turn, and sits staring before her, sniffing at the salts. The door, Right, is opened and DANCY *comes in.*]

MABEL. [*Utterly surprised.*] Ronny! Do they want me in Court?

DANCY. No.

MABEL. What is it, then? Why are you back?

DANCY. Spun.

MABEL. [*Blank.*] Spun? What do you mean? What's spun?

DANCY. The case. They've found out through those notes.

MABEL. Oh! [*Staring at his face.*] Who?

DANCY. Me!

MABEL. [*After a moment of horrified stillness.*] Don't Ronny! Oh! No! Don't! [*She buries her face in the pillows of the sofa.*]

[DANCY *stands looking down at her.*

DANCY. Pity you wouldn't come to Africa three months ago.

MABEL. Why didn't you tell me then? I would have gone.

DANCY. You wanted this case. Well, it's fallen down.

MABEL. Oh! Why didn't I face it? But I couldn't— I *had* to believe.

DANCY. And now you can't. It's the end, Mabel.

MABEL. [*Looking up at him.*] No.

[DANCY *goes suddenly on his knees and seizes her hand.*]

DANCY. Forgive me!

MABEL. [*Putting her hand on his head.*] Yes; oh, yes!

I think I've known a long time, really. Only—why? What made you?

DANCY. [*Getting up and speaking in jerks.*] It was a crazy thing to do; but, damn it, I was only looting a looter. The money was as much mine as his. A decent chap would have offered me half. You didn't see the brute look at me that night at dinner as much as to say: "You blasted fool!" It made me mad. That wasn't a bad jump—twice over. Nothing in the war took quite such nerve. [*Grimly.*] I rather enjoyed that evening.

MABEL. But—money! To keep it!

DANCY. [*Sullenly.*] Yes, but I had a debt to pay.

MABEL. To a woman?

DANCY. A debt of honour—it wouldn't wait.

MABEL. It was—it was to a woman. Ronny, don't lie any more.

DANCY. [*Grimly.*] Well! I wanted to save your knowing. I'd promised a thousand. I had a letter from her father that morning, threatening to tell you. All the same, if that tyke hadn't jeered at me for parlour tricks!—But what's the good of all this now? [*Sullenly.*] Well—it may cure you of loving me. Get over that, Mab; I never was worth it—and I'm done for!

MABEL. The woman—have you—since——?

DANCY. [*Energetically.*] No! You supplanted her. But if you'd known I was leaving a woman for you, you'd never have married me. [*He walks over to the hearth.*]

> [MABEL *too gets up. She presses her hands to her forehead, then walks blindly round to behind the sofa and stands looking straight in front of her.*]

MABEL. [*Coldly.*] What has happened, exactly?

DANCY. Sir Frederic chucked up the case. I've seen Twisden; they want me to run for it to Morocco.

LOYALTIES

MABEL. To the war there?

DANCY. Yes. There's to be a warrant out.

MABEL. A prosecution? Prison? Oh, go! Don't wait a minute! Go!

DANCY. Blast them!

MABEL. Oh, Ronny! Please! Please! Think what you'll want. I'll pack. Quick! No! Don't wait to take things. Have you got money?

DANCY. [*Nodding.*] This'll be good-bye, then!

MABEL. [*After a moment's struggle.*] Oh! No! No, no! I'll follow—I'll come out to you there.

DANCY. D'you mean you'll stick to me?

MABEL. Of course I'll stick to you.

[DANCY *seizes her hand and puts it to his lips. The bell rings.*]

MABEL. [*In terror.*] Who's that?

[*The bell rings again.* DANCY *moves towards the door.*]

No! Let *me!*

[*She passes him and steals out to the outer door of the flat, where she stands listening. The bell rings again. She looks through the slit of the letter-box. While she is gone* DANCY *stands quite still, till she comes back.*]

MABEL. Through the letter-box—I can see—— It's—it's police. Oh! God . . . Ronny! I can't bear it.

DANCY. Heads up, Mab! Don't show the brutes!

MABEL. Whatever happens. I'll go on loving you. If it's prison—*I'll wait.* Do you understand? I don't care what you did—I don't *care!* I'm just the same. I will be just the same when you come back to me.

DANCY. [*Slowly.*] That's not in human nature.

MABEL. It is. It's in *me.*

DANCY. I've crocked up your life.

MABEL. No, no! Kiss me!

[*A long kiss, till the bell again startles them apart, and there is a loud knock.*]

DANCY. They'll break the door in. It's no good—we must open. Hold them in check a little. I want a minute or two.

MABEL. [*Clasping him.*] Ronny! Oh, Ronny! It won't be for long—I'll be waiting! I'll be waiting—I swear it.

DANCY. Steady, Mab! [*Putting her back from him.*] Now!

[*He opens the bedroom door, Left, and stands waiting for her to go. Summoning up her courage, she goes to open the outer door. A sudden change comes over* DANCY'S *face; from being stony it grows almost maniacal.*]

DANCY. [*Under his breath.*] No! No! By God! No!

[*He goes out into the bedroom, closing the door behind him.*]

[MABEL *has now opened the outer door, and disclosed* INSPECTOR DEDE *and the* YOUNG CONSTABLE *who were summoned to Meldon Court on the night of the theft, and have been witnesses in the case. Their voices are heard.*]

MABEL. Yes?

INSPECTOR. Captain Dancy in, madam?

MABEL. I am not quite sure—I don't think so.

INSPECTOR. I wish to speak to him a minute. Stay here, Grover. Now, madam!

MABEL. Will you come in while I see?

[*She comes in, followed by the* INSPECTOR.

INSPECTOR. I should think you must be sure, madam. This is not a big place.

MABEL. He was changing his clothes to go out. I think he has gone.

INSPECTOR. What's that door?

MABEL. To our bedroom.

INSPECTOR. [*Moving towards it.*] He'll be in there, then.

MABEL. What do you want, Inspector?

INSPECTOR. [*Melting.*] Well, madam, it's no use disguising it. I'm exceedingly sorry, but I've a warrant for his arrest.

MABEL. Inspector!

INSPECTOR. I'm sure I've every sympathy for you, madam; but I must carry out my instructions.

MABEL. And break my heart?

INSPECTOR. Well, madam, we're—we're not allowed to take that into consideration. The Law's the Law.

MABEL. Are you married?

INSPECTOR. I am.

MABEL. If you—your wife——

[*The* INSPECTOR *raises his hand, deprecating.* [*Speaking low.*] Just half an hour! Couldn't you! It's two lives—two whole lives! We've only been married four months. Come back in half an hour. It's such a little thing—nobody will know. Nobody. Won't you?

INSPECTOR. Now, madam—you must know my duty.

MABEL. Inspector, I beseech you—just half an hour.

INSPECTOR. No, no—don't you try to undermine me—I'm sorry for you; but don't you try it! [*He tries the handle, then knocks at the door.*]

DANCY'S VOICE. One minute!

INSPECTOR. It's locked. [*Sharply.*] Is there another door to that room? Come, now! [*The bell rings.* [*Moving towards the door, Left; to the* CONSTABLE.] Who's that out there?

CONSTABLE. A lady and gentleman, sir.

INSPECTOR. What lady and—— Stand by, Grover!

DANCY'S VOICE. All right! You can come in *now*.
> [*There is the noise of a lock being turned. And almost immediately the sound of a pistol shot in the bedroom.* MABEL *rushes to the door, tears it open, and disappears within, followed by the* INSPECTOR, *just as* MARGARET ORME *and* COLFORD *come in from the passage, pursued by the* CONSTABLE. *They, too, all hurry to the bedroom door and disappear for a moment; then* COLFORD *and* MARGARET *reappear, supporting* MABEL, *who faints as they lay her on the sofa.* COLFORD *takes from her hand an envelope, and tears it open.*]

COLFORD. It's addressed to *me*. [*He reads it aloud to* MARGARET *in a low voice.*]

"DEAR COLFORD,—This is the only decent thing I can do. It's too damned unfair to her. It's only another jump. A pistol keeps faith. Look after her. Colford—my love to her, and you."

> [MARGARET *gives a sort of choking sob, then, seeing the smelling bottle, she snatches it up, and turns to revive* MABEL.]

COLFORD. Leave her! The longer she's unconscious, the better.

INSPECTOR. [*Re-entering.*] This is a very serious business, sir.

COLFORD. [*Sternly.*] Yes, Inspector; you've done for my best friend.

INSPECTOR. I, sir? He shot himself.

COLFORD. Hari-kari.

INSPECTOR. Beg pardon?

COLFORD. [*He points with the letter to* MABEL.] For her sake, and his own.

INSPECTOR. [*Putting out his hand.*] I'll want that, sir.

COLFORD. [*Grimly.*] You shall have it read at the inquest. Till then—it's addressed to me, and I stick to it.

INSPECTOR. Very well, sir. Do you want to have a look at him?

> [COLFORD *passes quickly into the bedroom, followed by the* INSPECTOR. MARGARET *remains kneeling beside* MABEL.]
> COLFORD *comes quickly back.* MARGARET *looks up at him. He stands very still.*]

COLFORD. Neatly—through the heart.

MARGARET [*wildly.*] Keeps faith! We've all done that. It's not enough.

COLFORD. [*Looking down at* MABEL.] All right, old boy!

The curtain falls.

FEB 21
MAR 4
FEB 9 '40
FEB 24 '40
MAY 1 8 '40
DEC 1 5 '40
FEB 1 8 '41
MAR 3 '41

SAINT JOSEPH'S COLLEGE, INDIANA
PR6013.A5 R4 1924   c.2   ISJA
Galsworthy / Representative plays

3 2302 00060 7129